W9-BWD-905

2-

Ship Modeling from Stem to Stern

Milton Roth

TAB Books

Division of McGraw-Hill

New York San Francisco Washington, D.C. Auckland Bogotá
Caracas Lisbon London Madrid Mexico City Milan
Montreal New Delhi San Juan Singapore
Sydney Tokyo Toronto

LIST OF TRADEMARKS

Floquil® and Polly S	Floquil-Polly S Color Corp.
Humbrol	Monogram Models Inc.
Dremel®	Dremel Mfg., a division of Emerson Electric Co.
Tamiya®	Tamiya, Inc.
Pactra®	Pactra Coatings Inc., a Plasti-Kote Co.
Elmer's®	Borden
Krazy Glue®	Krazy Glue Inc.
Titebond	Franklin
3M®	Minnesota Mining and Mfg.
Depen and Duro®	Duro
GOO	Hosco
ZAP and Z-7 Debonder	Zip Kicker
Hot Stuff, Super 'T', and Special 'T'	Satellite City
Jet	Carl Goldberg Models Inc.
Ultra	Golden West Fuels
PanaVise®	Pana Vise Products Inc.
MicroLux and Micro-Mark	Micro Mark
Unimat 3	Emco Maier and Co.

© 1988 by **Milton Roth**.
Published by TAB Books.
TAB Books is a division of McGraw-Hill, Inc.

Printed in the United States of America. All rights reserved. The publisher takes no responsibility for the use of any of the materials or methods described in this book nor for the products thereof.

pbk   17 DOC/DOC   0 9 8 7 6 5 4

Library of Congress Cataloging-in-Publication Data

Roth, Milton.
   Ship modeling from stem to stern / by Milton Roth.
      p.   cm.
   Includes index.
   ISBN 0-8306-2844-4 (pbk.)
   1. Ship models.   I. Title.
   VM298.R58   1987
   623.8′201—dc19   87-24609
                                              CIP
Cover photographs courtesy of Vanguard Group of Investment Companies.

Edited by Suzanne L. Cheatle   HT3
Designed by Jaclyn J. Boone   2844

CONTENTS

ACKNOWLEDGMENTS

YEAR AFTER YEAR I WATCH AWARD SHOWS ON TELEVI-sion. Year after year I say to myself, "I hope the ac-ceptance speech and the acknowledgments are short." Year after year I am wrong. This book has won no awards. It is in your possession, however, and that in itself should be considered an award of some sort.

No book could have reached this state without the help of many and the direct assistance of a few. It would be impossible to name the many. To the ship modelers of the world, at all stages of development, at all levels of experience, I would have a word. To you who have corresponded with me, talked end-lessly on the telephone, exchanged ideas, given en-couragement, and in general answered my questions; your time is appreciated. I trust you received as much information from me as I did from you. To you who wanted to share with me your pride and accomplish-ments, your cooperation has made this work possi-ble. I acknowledge you all. Allow those who are named to represent you.

Those who are named as direct contributors will be known to some of you. Many are already well known for their skills. Some have asked not to be ac-knowledged. Their wishes have been respected.

John Shedd and his able crew at Model Shipways have been more than generous. The accuracy that this organization has instituted in the producing of materials to build ship models is legend. The fine texts and plans, as well as the assistance to this hum-ble writer, are acknowledged.

The team of Dee Roberts and A. Richard Mansir of Moonraker Publications must be recognized. To the former for her encouragement and her support, to the latter for his talent and ability, my heartfelt ap-preciation. The many hours at the drawing board that you, good friend Dick, have already spent were not wasted. I trust that I gave your talents a rebirth. They deserve constant exposure.

Jack Coggins, a talented artist, noted historian, and ship enthusiast, has expanded this work from dullness to a high polish.

Words of praise and compliments are not enough to tell the accomplishments of Portia Takakjian. No one can deny her ability as a ship-model builder or for warmth and understanding. I am proud to call her friend. The strength of her friendship can be seen on these pages. Anyone who knows contemporary ship models will recognize Portia's contributions. Her contributions to the world of ship modeling is heart-warming. She blushes.

Maybe not a blush, but I trust a warm glow will be felt by Lawrence Hubbell, *admiral*, and Norman P. Wexler, *captain*, of The North Shore Deadeyes, Ltd. (an Illinois Corporation). Their unselfish sharing of the contents of past issues of the *Northshore Deadeyes, Ltd. Quarterly* has more than enhanced my work. The members of NSD both past, present, and worldwide will recognize the work that has been reproduced. It is an outstanding club publication, and I am sorry for its hiatus.

A picture is worth a thousand words. Permit me to thank my friend of many years, Morton Tenner. His knowledge of photography has earned him his own collection of ribbons and show awards. His dark-room and talents have assisted in making the illus-trations you see on these pages acceptable for the printing process. Not many take pictures of their models in black and white anymore. He converted a lot of you, in a pictorial sense.

The many publications, periodicals, club news-papers, etc., which have over the years stimu-lated the subconscience of many a ship modeler have literally exploded on these pages as a collected work.

Ship Modeler's Associates of Fullerton, California, their publication, their members' contributions and the talents of their resident hints-and-tips artist Richard Roos cannot go unmentioned.

I would also like to acknowledge those organizations, publishers, and individuals who did not give permission to use any of their material. By their refusal they forced me to seek other sources. In many cases, the other sources were better than the originals for which I had sought permission and intended to use. Your overprotection of what you felt was information that should be known only to your selected patrons is understood—not condoned but understood. What you represent by your thinking and your actions is exactly what I wish to acknowledge.

Certainly the publisher of this book must be acknowledged. Writing a book is hard work. Finding a publisher is even harder. Books are seldom published out of love. Books have been published without expected monetary rewards when the message or the vanity was strong enough. I trust that this gamble has paid off for TAB BOOKS of Blue Ridge Summit, PA. I acknowledge that I am the heavy die that you had to roll.

To my father, Eugene Roth (1900-1959), who once said to me,
''God gave us books so one man could tell others what he had learned.''
I respectfully dedicate this book to his philosophy and memory.

INTRODUCTION

When you steal from one author, it's plagiarism;
if you steal from many, it's research.
—WILSON MIZNER
1876-1933

THIS IS A BOOK ABOUT HOW TO BUILD SHIP MODELS. moreover, it is a book on where to look for the information that will assist you to build ship models easier, faster, and better, as well as a book on who has accomplished methods you can use in your work.

Hopefully this work will be a learning experience for many, a reference for most, and a review for others. I could say that I have written this book to please those friends who requested my assistance over the years. I prefer to say that I assembled, cataloged, and clarified the works of myself and others. I did it for all of my friends.

Tons of silt must be sifted to find a few ounces of gold. Herein are the offerings of those few ounces gleaned from the diggings of my own mine. My wealth is selected from the dusty shelves of assorted volumes on the subject and coupled with the uncounted years of a challenging, creative, art experience. The value of my treasure is like gold. It is subject to the fluctuations of market demand, both for the decorative form into which it has been worked, and for its value as a whole.

What is presented and perhaps claimed as original can no longer be determined. Material and methods that have been stolen, borrowed, or learned from others are presented without shame as perhaps my own. The subject of building ship models, like so many art forms, is a continuous addition of subliminal stimulation. I consider these pages as a gathering of useful information interspersed with flashes of originality.

If I have, after you read these pages, stimulated you, so much the better. If you feel that I am speaking about you personally, good. If you see yourself here, fine. It will be for you to decide what you have learned as distinguished from what you have not already known.

The thought that there ever was an original thought eludes me. Richard Bach said it best, ''Learning is finding out what you already know. Doing is demonstrating that you know it. Teaching is reminding others that they know just as well as you.'' I consider myself a teacher.

The details of how to build any specific ship and the instructions in building the complete ship model are avoided. This is best left to the undisputed masters of the craft, many still among us, who through their works and writings perpetuate ''our'' skills.

Even the greatest master is subject to challenge now and again. Latter-day self-appointed experts are still among us who will constantly attempt to homogenize skill and classify talent. Controversy, criticism, and comment attract attention. Self-styled experts in every field wear rust-spotted armor and fight with dull-edged weapons. The greatest idols of yesteryear have been found with feet of clay. However, quality, like cream, will always rise to the top.

Thomas Edison said, ''There's a way to do it better—find it!'' Your search for a better way makes you the personal architect of the structure, which is the building of your knowledge. Will your completed structure be a chicken coop or a skyscraper? The outcome will be determined by your efforts alone. Knowledge is the foundation of your building, and learning is the steel of the supporting skeletal frame. Thousands of bricks—each a thought, each an idea— will be needed to create the walls.

The strength of the building is held together with as much acquired know-how as could be compared to the material that binds the parts together. There must be nails for the boards, mortar between the bricks, and rivets and welding for the steel beams to complete the tallest building or the smallest shack.

If this offering, in any small way, assists you in your career, I am happy. If in reading these pages, you are stimulated to go further and do better, I am pleased. If you become a good modeler through my humble efforts, I will be satisfied. If, however, you knew everything that is presented here, I shall be surprised.

Although Mr. Edison did promote the idea of discovery, he made no mention of speed. Speed comes with confidence. Every experience is a training session. You are the only judge of the success of your education. Knowledge is the light along the path to perfection. Should this path lead to the most perfect ship model ever built—yours—I will be content.

The ultimate experience is in accomplishing what might seem impossible. Doing so while expending as little effort as possible is the intended purpose of this work. The more you know about a subject, the simpler the task becomes.

There is no such thing as a bad ship model. The perfect one is yet to be built. You can only strive to build the world's most perfect ship model. That perfect ship model is not the end. The next one you will build will be even greater.

I would like to think that in some small way I helped. I wish you success in every undertaking, whether building ship models or just plain living. May I now number you among my new friends.

ONE

Why We Build Ship Models

Now sails are past, and still the sail ship
grips the carpenter with wood dust on his hair,
and down below he fashions from slim strips
the rakish models of the ships that were.
—CHARLES NORMAN

MAN IS THE ONLY CREATURE ON EARTH THAT BUILDS models. If he is unable to display the full-sized version, then a scaled miniaturized representation will have to do. He uses models to explain what he intends to build. He uses models to explain his prowess in having achieved his goal. Bragging, in a sense, he is showing what he has built. He exhibits his models to others in life, and they speak for him after his death. Models are a testimony. Models are a three-dimensional demonstration of man's ability (FIG. 1-1).

The contents of the tomb of Tutankhamen stirred the imagination of millions. The world tour was a huge success. Crowds came to see what the boy king, brought back from the dawn of civilization, had taken with him for his voyage to the afterlife. Many were as impressed by the ship models as the masks of gold.

The evacuations at Ur in the valley of the Euphrates near Chaldea yielded a model that predated the life of King Tut. It was a vessel of nine oars: four on each side and one for steering (FIG. 1-2). Beautifully executed, it revealed what ships were like 3,500 years before the Christian era. Far from crude, it was smooth of surface, crafted in silver.

The tombs of Thebes yielded models of the type of ship used by traders of the Eleventh Dynasty (around 2,500 B.C.), the type of ship that sailed to the land of Punt, and ship models from the time of Sanhka-Ka-Ra (who founded the trade with far-away

lands). They are identical to the vessels that still ply their trade on the Red Sea.

These models of ancient vessels are testimony to man's unchanging ways. They reinforce the statement that the more things change, the more they remain the same.

Underwater archaeology, excavations beneath the waves, is stirring the public interest. People want to know about the past. Full-sized ships, buried by man's design or nature's accident on land or under the waves, are being found. These historical relics offer conclusive proof that this was in truth how man journeyed upon the waters. A Roman grain ship, a Greek trader, the Viking long ships, the *Wasa, Mary Rose, Hamilton,* and *Scourge*—all types from all ages have been located. Several have been raised and restored. Sailing ships, which have not fallen to decay and destruction beneath the waves, are being raised and restored.

Dedicated individuals are researching, restoring, and raising ships in an effort to preserve our sea heritage. This stimulating full-sized ship salvation is causing great interest. We are all sea and ship buffs. We know more when we can see the real thing. We have to see the real thing. If we are unable to view the original, however, we are often content with a model. Models of these ships are being made in ever increasing numbers. Historians build them to study.

Fig. 1-1. Model of the *Bear*, Rear Admiral Richard E. Byrd's flagship during his 1932-1935 expedition to Antarctica. Built in 1874, purchased by the United States Government in 1885, with continuous service in the Arctic and Antarctic until sold to a Canadian in 1948 (Photo courtesy of Naval Memorial Museum, Washington, DC).

Fig. 1-2. Cheop's tomb was opened 4400 years after interment. Cedar planks within formed a vessel 147 feet long. The lines were similar to the Viking ships 4000 years later. The ship lacked a keel and the structural strength to withstand the sea (Courtesy of Moonraker Publishing).

Modelers build them, perhaps for study, but more for pleasure and profit.

Ship models were built as a direct result of a religious experience. In the early days of sail, it was customary for a crew, grateful for their safe return, to present a model of their ship to the church. It was a sincere expression of thanks to God for their safe deliverance from the perils of the deep. Often, by choice and more often because of the manner of display, the model was large. Six to ten feet or more in length, the models were suspended from the ceiling of the cathedral high above the congregation. Several are still there in the old churches by the sea in Europe.

A recently constructed ship model is of a ship that played a part in the history of a church. The ship model of the *Enoch Train*, almost 4 years in the making, tells the story of the immigration of a people to the shores of the United States to form a religious colony. (See the Color Section).

The model is 1:32 scale (3/8 inch = 1 foot) so it will not overwhelm the other exhibits in the museum. The openings in the sides enable the viewer to see life as it was in 1856. It is a frozen moment in time, the afternoon of April 6. Incidentally, this was the date of the 26th anniversary of the Church of Jesus Christ of Latter-day Saints.

The builder of the model was James Raines, working under the supervision of Steven Olsen, curator of the Museum of Church History and Art. The project began with an idea and a painting now on display at the Mariner's Museum in Newport News, Virginia. The internal structures were determined from extensive research and the diaries and journals of the passengers.

The openings in the sides were placed to allow the viewer to see the activities of the passengers and crew aboard. Enhanced by the figures carved by Curt Grinaker, the model seems to be alive. You can almost visualize what life was like, both below decks with the traveling families and above decks with the crew at their chores.

BUILDING MODELS

The building of a ship model is a challenge to the skills of an enterprising craftsman. There is something in the actual building that appeals to the latent talent hiding within most creative individuals. Is the making of a ship model just another form of relaxa-

tion? Can you find escape from the cares of the day in the act of physical creation? Has it become a form of psychotherapy? Is it just, as most individuals believe, a hobby? Building a ship model can be, and probably is, any or all of these things.

Models of ships have decorative appeal. Ship models were planned for in the construction of one restaurant (serving seafood, understandably). Interior decorators have also used models of ships of the past successfully in the design of a bank, a board room, a private home, and in many other decorative ideas. There will always be someone looking for a ship model, for its beauty as well as its historical significance.

Modelers are made, not born. Perhaps they were given a model to build. Perhaps they were presented with a kit as a child or upon retiring. If the new builder was patient, persistent, followed directions, and perhaps worked methodically, the model turned out well. If the model was finished with some degree of satisfaction, there is the beginning of a modeler. Continuation as a modeler depends on a person's motivation. Dedicated modelers are not quitters.

THE APPEAL OF MODELS

Ship models create mental images. Thoughts form in the mind of the person looking at a ship model. Thoughts creating, in some cases, a fantasy. Senses are stimulated. The smell of salt air fills the nostrils, spray dampens the face, the deck moves beneath the feet. The mind's eye sees people on the deck. Are they fighting men, men in national uniforms, or gentlemen in silks and laces? Are they ruffians, pirates, or princes?

The sounds of battle come to the ears. Cannons roar, guns fire, aircraft fly close by overhead. Participation in selected combat at sea begins. You can be with Nelson at Trafalgar or Nimitz at Midway.

See once again the tall ships with white sails spread on the yards. Become one of the crew making a trip on a vessel of bygone days. Moby Dick is out there. Wooden ships and iron men—those were the days of bravado, the true test of a man.

Is it the steamships that you visualize, belching black smoke from the stacks, moving slowly but steadily across the waters? Visions are called up from the past, induced memories of books read or movies seen. This is the excitement of your youth revisited. All this and more comes from building or looking at a ship model.

Ships have been around for a long time, bringing people from far-away lands and taking people to places yet unseen. Ships are a vital, inexpensive form of transportation. Cargos and people still move cheaper by water—not faster, but cheaper. There is a wide variety of ships that can be modeled. A strong personal and geographical appeal is indicated in their building. A ship model can be a tribute to the transportation of a family, part of its historical roots.

Were your relatives, or perhaps you personally, ever involved with the sea? Those who have can always name, describe, and recall "their" ship. The nostalgia evoked by the sight of that craft stirs memories of better days.

Was your particular vessel associated with service days, employment, or a vacation? Your cruise ship, sleek and white with clean lines took you and your companion(s) to some place far away. Perhaps, your "love boat" had a shipboard romance, real or imagined. A model of her might bring back pleasant memories. A ship model nearby, all your own—a model of your ship, built, bought, and displayed—can reestablish the broken connection of a fond memory.

SHIP MODELERS

Ship modeling is truly democratic. People from all walks of life can and do build ship models. Most modelers will, if given the slightest encouragement, talk about their hobby to anyone.

The people who engage in the many forms of miniature construction—car, railroad, airplane, or dollhouse—seek only personal achievement. Achieving and developing greater skills is something that is common to all modelers. It can be a spiritual uplift beyond description. Modelers know this sensation. Ask one.

Ship modeling is essentially a lone worker's avocation, a task of personal effort. The builder is solely responsible for the final outcome. He is completely involved, from the planning stage to the final display. The vast majority of ship modelers are solitary, studious, and in most cases, successful people.

Modelers spend a lot of time in research. They will contact authorities at institutions of higher learning or museums, fellow modelers, and naval authorities. It is not a waste of time. This is time spent to ensure accurate renditions of ship models. Research sometimes ends in argument and debate. This, too, is healthy. Modelers pore over moot points, abstract items, and details in search of the truth. Countless letters are written, telephone calls made, and meetings attended. This is the way it is done.

All this energy in the search for the facts is not wasted. More historical research and data is uncovered and reported by dedicated ship modelers than all museums, universities, or institutions put together. Modelers draw and redraw plans and drafts, make and remake parts. Is it all worth it? To them, yes.

The builder of ship models, if he is able or in the vicinity, also visits a maritime museum. The reason for a visit varies. It might be to do research or to view other ship models. Advancement is enhanced by research, as well as admiration.

Preparation is all important. Even if you never intend to become a professional, you should prepare. Doing your best is all that anyone can ask. The change comes gradually. Your best is not good enough. As your skills improve, there will be a greater demand for your products. The demand for your talents will force you to spend more time building ship models. Your time will be paid for in ever-increasing amounts. The modeler does not decide at what point he will become a professional. When the time comes to make the change, he will know.

Financial reward is not always the compelling reason. The constant desire for perfection will earn you a reputation and a living. You will be considered a professional, not because that's all you do for a living, but because that's the way you conduct your life. You are a professional in every sense of the word.

If you are a professional modeler, you could be employed. Working in a company organization as a modeler is your career (FIG. 1-3). You could, on the other hand, be self-employed. You accept commissions (contracts) to build models for others. You build and maintain a portfolio for sale, no different than any other full-time artist. Your skills earn you a living.

No mention was made of wealth. This is not, nor should it ever be considered, a rich man's "hobby." What you spend building a ship model has no bearing on the final product. Museum-quality ship models

Fig. 1-3. Building a museum model of the luxury liner H.M.S. *Titanic* at the studios of Bassett Lowke, England (Photo courtesy of Bassett Lowke).

have been built from what some might consider scraps.

You should be most concerned with the investment of time. Modelers don't bother with the often-asked, and foolish, question, "Where do you find the time?" A smile is all that should be given in reply. I do.

Ship modelers have taught themselves and those around them how to use the same 24 hours given to us all. There is no way of ever "finding" the time. What is important is a method of using time—budgeting. The busiest person always has the time. There is never enough time unless you know how to find it.

Each of a modeler's lovingly created products bears his unmistakable stamp. The touch of the individual modeler's hand is hidden within the small details of the finished ship model. The results of the labor of the creator leave an indelible mark on the workmanship. Contemporaries within the "craft" know the creator of the work. They know the style of the artist. Those who care to look—be they casual friend, observer, or show judge—need but to view the model once again to identify the builder.

Sooner or later each ship modeler settles into a selected pattern. He chooses what he believes is the most comfortable media, the most satisfying type of ship, the most "fun," the best scale.

Then for no apparent reason he will experience a sudden and unexplainable need to explore other methods of building, styles, types, or media. Was it just for a change of pace? The sudden switch may be for reasons beyond the modeler's control. A commission to build a specific model, at a stated scale, using a selected media forces the decision, the change. The modeler complies.

TYPES OF MODELS

A ship model constructed from a kit might be one of thousands off an assembly line. When complete, the result of hours of labor is evident. No two ship models will ever be identical. Not even the pressure-molded plastic models, manufactured to be identical in every detail, are built exactly the same. Somehow, somewhere, every kit model has been altered by the touch of a modeler's hand. Understandably, the same plastic model is assembled, painted with care, and displayed with pride by thousands. Each one is slightly, ever so slightly, different. The difference is noticeable because the desire to achieve perfection altered the result expected.

The greatest problem confronting the modeler is the question, ''What ship model shall I make?'' Among sailors or people of the sea, love of ship and sentiment play the largest part in the selection of a model to build. For others, the memory of a favorite book, a ship seen on vacation, might play a part.

RESTORED SHIPS

We are still awed at the sight of a sailing ship. Most of the ships of this type are gone, victims of progress. The sailing ship as a commercial enterprise has all but disappeared from the Western civilized nations. All we have left are the tourist ships, the barefoot cruises. The remainders, working ships under sail, are simple, quaint coastal vessels plying their trade (FIG. 1-4). They can be seen still engaged in the commerce of poorer nations.

Ships from the hey-day of sail can still be seen today, however. They are preserved in their berths, on exhibition. Sailing ships, warships, submarines, tugs, steamships, and many prototypes have become floating museums.

Wooden hulls were constructed of such magnitude that they defy the concept of construction. How could a ship of such a size have been controlled by sheer manpower (FIG. 1-5)? An excellent example is the great naval ship of the line, a floating home to over 400 souls still alive today, the beloved and often modeled *Victory*.

All of these ships are seen daily by thousands. People flock to the berths in England to see the *Cutty Sark* and the H.M.S. *Victory. The Wavertree, Star of India,* U.S.S. *Texas,* U.S.S. *Olympia, Constitution,* and *Balcutha* in San Francisco are just a few in the United States. The list grows. More will be joining them as they, too, are restored in near perfect condition. Once you have seen such a ship, stood on her decks, wouldn't you like to build a model of her?

A visit to the restored ship could verify all your collected data. Examination can end all questions of what she is like now. Historical data is preserved for the modeler to study.

A whole city has been recreated to become a living museum (FIG. 1-6). Mystic Seaport, Connecticut, a 17-acre maritime museum, is a reconstructed whal-

Fig. 1-4. Model of an 80-foot-long Scottish ''fifie'' fishing boat of 1890. The model by Colin Shephard of Vanda Cottage, Taynuilt, Argyll, Scotland, is an example of models he builds for his clients. The scale is 1:60 (Photo courtesy of Colin Shephard).

ing village. Gathered from far places, artifacts and real ships have been restored. The Mallory Building, a tribute to the family whose sailmaking business was established in 1816, houses the shipping and ship-building activities. Seafaring endeavors of the family are shown up to 1941. They continue to tell the story of man's conflict and conquest of the sea—full-sized models, as it were.

The nation's 200th birthday was celebrated in 1976. The tall ships entered New York Harbor, sailing up the Hudson. There was an unpredicted stirring of interest. The sight seen by the millions lining the Hudson was shown to millions more through the media's coverage. Pictures of the ships that took part

Fig. 1-5. *Le Protecteur*, a model of exceptional detail, is in the city of Paris, France. Exact in every detail even to the sails, the model of the French ship of the line is an example of a vessel of the French navy c. 1760 (Photo courtesy of Association des Amis des Musees de la Marine, Paris).

were on the covers and in the articles of uncounted magazines. Books were written, paintings commissioned. They returned again on July 4, 1986, for the 100th birthday of the Statue of Liberty.

The ships were not forgotten by those who saw them. They are active ships under sail even to this day—tall ships that are training navy personnel and representing many seafaring nations. They continue to make their calls at ports throughout the world. These ships are often requested to call. Tall ships are gathered together whenever possible. Every anniversary, each and any city-on-the-sea with something to celebrate or commemorate, any exhibition or World's Fair—all are looking for a reason to have the tall ships come. The number of these ships still in existence that have been rendered as ship models is un-

Fig. 1-6. America's maritime heritage is preserved at Mystic Seaport, Connecticut. The sails of the whaleship *Charles W. Morgan* tower along the waterfront as the 1908 steamboat *Sabino* cruises down river. To the right is the ship *Joseph Conrad*, built in 1882 (Photo by Claire White Peterson, Mystic Seaport).

countable. Once you have stood on the deck, or thrilled at the sight of one of them under sail, you will have reason enough to make a model of her.

HISTORY OF MODELS

The work of building ship models was done by professionals from 3,500 B.C. to the sixteenth century—a long time by any measurement. These professionals were people working for pay or upkeep. We cannot consider the amateur modeler, usually a sailor, whose works were considered a toy. Then, even as today, these professional modelers were commissioned by others, paid to ply their craft. Building ship models was a task for men who were under the protection and pay of the affluent. Kings and nobles commissioned ship models to be made. They didn't make them.

Over 200 years ago, Louis XVI ordered five such ship models. They were built to enable the shipwrights to study, contemplate, and correct the original idea of a ship before it became a reality. The famous 300-year-old model of *Ville de Paris*, a 120-gun ship of the line, is in the United States Naval Academy Museum.

The dawn of using ship models for explanatory purposes—the dockside models of France and later England—began with Samuel Pepys. Pepys, an Englishman, was the Secretary of the Admiralty under Charles II in the late 1600s. Prior to that time, ships were built by shipwrights without a formal plan or prestated design. The ships were ornate and covered with gilded carvings, or *gingerbread*. They were highly decorated warships—display things built by the rulers of one country trying to outdo a rival. Designers of the ships of great fleets were directed to produce a platform for as many guns as could be carried. The ships also were as ornate as possible and better gilded than any other previously built. The peak of decorative foolishness was the *Sovereign of the Seas* in 1627.

It was Samuel Pepys who constructed his own models to enable the Board of Admirals to view the proposed vessel. The name, *Admiralty Model*, is used to this day in describing this type of model building. For the most part, the members of the board could not read or understand the drafts. So they studied the models.

This method of "show and tell and hope to sell" is still used today. Professional modelers make ship models for the naval architect and shipyard companies to show clients, backers, the public (stockholders), and lawmakers what their money will be spent for. Not much has changed in 300 years.

Some of the ship models built by these professionals of the past have survived. They represent a style, a workmanship, that even the modeler of today seeks to achieve. Many, but not all, modelers hope someday to construct a scratch-built "Admiralty" or dockside-type model. If you wish to become a master model shipwright, you can acquire skill by copying the masters as a learning experience. Copying the masters is accepted in any art form. It helps you develop your own style.

TYPES OF MODELS

Half models are those carved to scale and line. The vessel is the same on both sides of the centerline. A complete hull is not needed. Half models are made to "take off the lines." Simple ships, catboats, racing yachts, and even the complicated clippers of the past were all built from half models. Ocean liners, oil tankers, commercial fishing boats, speedboats, and pleasure craft are all modeled, many as a half model. Any shipyard or boatyard of today, worth its salt at making boats or ships uses half models.

Ship models are built with their shape and lines reproduced accurately from the proposed ship's plans. They are constructed in scale before the actual ship is on the ways. These are the *test tank models*, built by master modelers to study the ship's move-

ments through the water. These ship models indicate wave patterns, handling characteristics, waterline calculation, etc. They allow all ideas to be studied in model form, enabling improvements in design to be made. These models are masterpieces and are rendered in true scale. For the most part, there is no construction above the deckline showing any of the structural details. They are termed *hull models*.

An undertaking that is a true test of modeling skills is making a model for movies or television (FIG. 1-7). Every working detail must be in perfect scale. The camera reveals every flaw. It is a model-building experience for anyone bent on achievement. It is difficult, however. Getting into this industry is hard. This is professional ship modeling.

Models can be huge in construction. Consider the model of a ship in half size, as distinguished from 1/2 scale. Models of such proportions are made for educational purposes. These are the models to train cadets and teach sailing to "land lubbers." Models of this size are constructed for naval, merchant marine, and sail training academies, and maritime museums.

A *working model*, as the name implies, should work. This is a ship model of visible performance. If it is a sailing ship, then all the blocks that work the yards, booms, and sails, and raise and lower anything aboard should work. It is a complete vessel with everything rendered in miniature.

The power source that is placed aboard can make this a working ship model that is a tribute in motion to the builder. It must be scaled even to the speed. Representation should be as accurate and as true to scale as skill allows, not only in the ship, but also in its power plant. Electric, steam, or gas power can be used to propel the ship across the water.

If it moves, it must be controlled. Response to command can be accomplished by a tethering line or some other form of remote control. Radio control is the answer. The remote control, which will steer and work the ship, is relayed to the model through the use of radio impulses.

Inside the miniature scale model, small servo (electric) motors will move the parts through an intricate system of pulleys and blocks. Radio signals will fire guns and torpedos, and control noises and sounds to be heard through small speakers. A ship model that not only moves but sounds like a real ship is a joy to behold.

Fig. 1-7. A fantasy warship created for fun and built with skill in Austria-Hungary. The intricate carvings are of wood (Photo courtesy of Navy Memorial Museum, Washington, DC).

Not only powered models but sailing ship models can be built and controlled by radio. Models need not be motionless, static.

WHY BUILD SHIP MODELS?

What, then, are the true reasons that an individual would want to build a ship model? Why would anyone subject himself to untold hours of eye-strain, cramped fingers, or frustration in the pursuit of scale-modeled perfection? How can anyone take this in stride, suffering in silence? You need but look at the ship model to find the answer.

There it is, finished at last! A thing of beauty, a joy forever. This creation is a modeler's child. It was conceived in his mind, born of his skill, delivered by his own hand. It is a ship model for all to see, for all to admire. He built this ship model. It is, in his eyes, sheer perfection—that is, until the next one is completed.

A modeler, a good modeler, is constantly planning while he builds. As he works, he can see what

needs to be improved. The mistakes, corrected or covered over, need to be eliminated. The next model will be even better than this one. It must be. Believe me, I know.

Only the builder has a need to know where the flaws lie. He is under no obligation to confess their existence. Confession, if it can be called such, will be in the interest of increasing shipbuilding skills. Flaws and minor building mistakes are to be shown only to understanding fellows. They, who have made the same mistakes, will assist in eliminating his.

Mistakes will always be made. It is the process of learning. *Advancement* can be defined as not making the same mistakes again. *Wisdom* is seeing the mistakes made by others, based on your own education, and pointing it out—tactfully. A modeler is a mover. Standing still is stagnation of creative talent. A constant, never-ending process of improvement should be going on at all times.

A good modeler will continue this dedication to the end of his days. Modeling might not be continuous, but the dedication is there, implanted forever. He will dream his dreams. He will gather his materials, storing supplies for the future like a squirrel. He will maintain that hidden desire for constant self-improvement. The bits and pieces that make up his model are not mere inanimate objects, nor is his creation. Ship models will always be in preparation, to be built and completed in the future. Ship models he will build will be those that will carry him to his greatest reward, his own personal adventure.

He will build, create, and display the fruits of his labor without shame, proudly telling all who will listen the history of the ship, the struggle of construction. Then the day will come, as it must to us all, when he will lay his tools aside for the last time. He will close his eyes to dream of that perfect model yet to come. Remaining behind will be his models. They are and will always be the tangible tribute to his everlasting memory—a legacy to his descendants and to the world. His life was dedicated to his craft, devoid of despair, yet filled with failures. The failures that were overcome are the tribute in the making of a memory of a man. What finer tribute can be said of a person than ''...and he built ship models.''

TWO

Working Areas

Things are only worth what you make them worth.
—MOLIERE

NO AMOUNT OF SPACE OR AREA IS REQUIRED FOR modeling ships. Masterpieces have been built in the strangest places and under the most bizarre circumstances. Most ship models are created on card or kitchen tables. No area is so small as to be confining, nor so vast as to be sufficient.

Modelers, independent souls that they are, select the area and the time to work. One individual I know builds ship models in the cab of his eighteen-wheeler. His work takes him between two cities with several hours between unloading and loading for the return trip. Unusual loads require an overnight stay. While he is waiting, he can be found in the cab of his truck building his treasures.

Another ship modeler is a sailor in the U.S. Navy, who works out of a portable hinged box that he made on shore leave. He keeps it stored under his bunk in a submarine.

A suburban commuter, escaping the boredom of travel, saves a small area of his briefcase for a particular project during the 2-hour ride from home to city and back each working day.

The methods that modelers will devise to accomplish their task are ingenious. The places that they do and store their work are often unbelievable. Their designs and ideas could fill volumes. Some belong in Robert Ripley's writings.

Most of us, probably as kids, began our careers working out of a cigar or shoe box. This treasure chest contained our valuable tools and solutions to assemble our models. The parts and pieces were kept in another box, often the carton from the model.

The tools and parts came out of the box when the time was right. The model grew, was assembled, progressed, and soon it was stored on top of the box in a corner or on a closet shelf. More models were built, acquired, displayed. There were two, three boxes, a crowded shelf in the closet, and finally a table. It was set up in the corner of the bedroom or wherever the deciding adult said. Mother usually made the decision. Brothers and sisters had their instructions. You shared or they kept away. Hands off.

Mom knew how to handle that room and space rule. She laid it down. She knew where you were spending your spare time. Your models gained you approval and an area all your own. At least you weren't "running with that bunch."

You're grown up now, and you have a choice on how to use your time and what space you're going to need to accomplish your goals. If you are single, you have no problem. You can make your own decision should you have your own quarters. If you are married, tell your wife (or husband) what your mom said about modeling and add the fact that at least she will know where you are every spare moment, every evening.

The size of the area is not always the end consideration. A neat freak has a place for everything and everything in its place. He might need less area, or he might need more. Tools must be kept in neat little rows, laid out in boxes, stored in drawers, or hung on a rack. Waste receptacles, cutting boards, and a place to hang plans need room. The tabletop area must be abundant. Serious things must be considered. He needs rooms for parts layout before assemblage. Time and space are part of personality.

At the other end of the human scale is the "slob." How he can produce such quality work amidst the chaos and clutter of his working area is beyond belief. Sawdust and chips are everywhere; plastic and wood parts are in various stages of assembly; tools, bags, boxes, bottles, and spills of glues and paint are all mixed in. It is a mess! Yet it all gets done.

Your work area can be predetermined by your pocketbook. Your expenditures can be within a balanced budget or completely out of hand. Few of us are the "starving artist" variety who go without food to buy something to complete a ship model. Don't laugh, I know one.

Designing a perfect work area is impossible. Just when you have it all on paper or in your mind's eye, something happens. It could be a new power tool you just acquired after long self-searching sessions of planning. You decided you couldn't afford it, but must have it.

Individual desires vary. Some must have a studio, a larger room, a whole floor, or even a building devoted to their space considerations. It is the talent, not the area, however, that determines the results.

Chapter 3 of the publication *Ship Modeler's Shop Notes* (Nautical Research Guild, Bethesda, MD) has some suggestions and details of work space. This volume, compiled from the many contributions of the members of the Nautical Research Guild from 1958 to 1979 and edited by Merritt Edson, should be in your library. You can buy a copy by writing the N.R.G. See Chapter 3, "Plans & Planning" for the address.

EXAMPLES OF WORK AREAS

It should not come as a surprise that space problems for modelers, builders, everyone in general exist all over the world. I ran across this plan for a work storage bench (FIG. 2-1) in *Model Shipwright*. The drawing and the idea come from Russia. Putting the bench together should pose no problem. Plywood is, it seems, universal.

The dimensions are in the metric system. TABLE 2-1 is included to save you a few hours in conversion should you elect to go with the American "foot" measurements.

The "average" modeler, the guy or gal like yourself who has a workspace is not, nor should he ever be, satisfied. Openly perhaps, but secretly, never. Admit it.

The tabletop builder, fearful of anyone disturbing his sacred territory, has undoubtedly created some hard feelings in his time. He insists on a zone of nonintervention. He uses a rule or threat to safeguard the project.

Many modelers, for reasons other than storage, have built and worked out of cases (cabinets) such as just mentioned. Most, myself included, would like

Table 2-1. Conversion from Metric to English Measurements for Building the Russian Workbench. (Courtesy of *Model Shipwright*).

| METRIC | LINEAR INCHES | |
Millimetres	Decimal	Fractions
10	0.39	13/32
20	0.79	25/32
22	0.87	7/8
50	1.97	1 31/32
60	2.36	2 11/32
80	3.15	3 5/32
110	4.33	4 11/32
120	4.72	4 23/32
170	6.69	6 11/16
175	6.89	6 7/8
330	12.99	13
400	15.75	15 3/4
440	17.32	17 5/16
470	18.50	17½
480	19.20	19 3/16
500	19.68	19 11/16
522	20.55	20 9/16
526	20.71	20 23/32
540	21.26	21¼
720	28.35	28 11/32
730	28.74	28¾
780	30.71	30 23/32
20 × 30	0.79 × 1.18	25/32 × 13/16

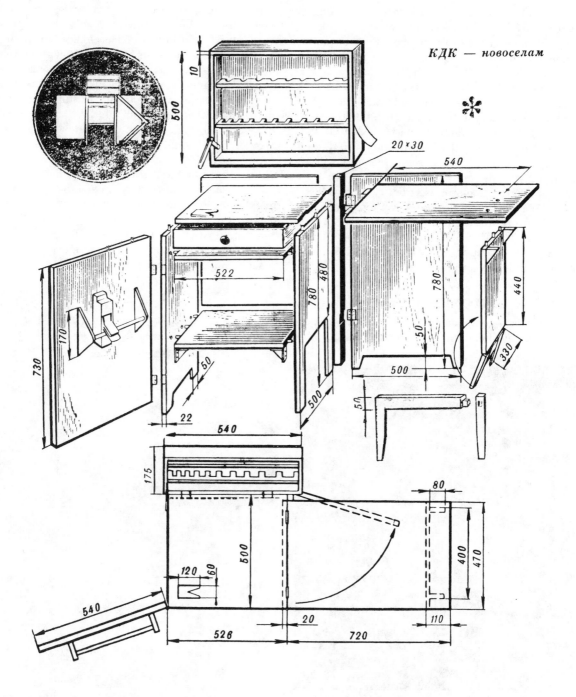

КДК — новоселам

Fig. 2-1. Exploded drawing of a work cabinet designed and built in Russia. Fold-away components allow ideal storage and ample workspace (Courtesy of *Model Shipwright*).

to have an area where we could leave everything as it was, lock it up, and just walk away.

Workshops have that reputation. Proper communication with those who share your living space might even eliminate the need for a lock and key.

When the children were smaller, my work area was protected by a look that could melt stone. The look was backed by a sharp, loud, threatening voice. Only once was physical contact needed. If you thought that is all past when the kids were grown and gone, forget it! The same scenario will be replayed with the grandchildren.

Dick Roos of California is a true ''closet modeler.'' With the exception of the few power tools in the garage, his work area is literally a closet (FIG. 2-2). Don't think it can't be done. I call your attention to his prize-winning ribbons hung on the back wall of his closet. They were justly earned.

ANTONIO MENDEZ

There is a gentleman of my acquaintance, perhaps you have heard of him, who has an outstanding workspace. Antonio Mendez is quite a well-renowned ship modeler. He is also a great ''gadgeteer'' and inventor. His dedication to ship modeling and all its facets has become an obsession. A trip to his ''shop'' is an experience you will never forget. I promise you will dream about it as your cherished goal of what a complete ship modeler's shop—make that studio —should be.

A quick tour, in photographs and words, is now in order. Step into the area through the main entrance and take a look (FIG. 2-3). The model under completion is a radio-controlled topsail schooner.

Antonio's studio includes one of the things that might come in handy to you. It is a plans display area (FIG. 2-4).

Antonio is, contrary to what the photograph shows, very organized. He has designed and uses what he has termed his ''movable tool organizers.''

Fig. 2-2. A real ''closet modeler'' and his closet. Dick Roos of Tustin, California, displays his workspace and awards (Photo courtesy of Dick Roos).

Fig. 2-3. Atop the main workbench of Antonio Mendez C. is the almost finished radio-controlled topsail schooner. Construction is entirely of wood (Photo by Jose Luis Mendez).

Fig. 2-4. Two styles of movable tool organizers in the studio of Antonio Mendez. Movability allows the tools to come to the work area (Photo by Jose Luis Mendez).

They are equipped with wheels to move about the shop (FIG. 2-4). The tools are held in position on the organizers by hooks and pegs. The electrical items are run off the main power boxes on the side. Power is fed to the plugs through a foot rheostat. Swung out of the way, just under the open drawer is Antonio's Unimat. I intend to make my roll-around workbench with pegboard fronts.

The movable tool organizer in the far end of (FIG. 2-4) has a swivel top, as well as drawers and a pull-out work board. The possibilities are endless in the design of each. They were, I was told, the outgrowth of several designs.

The sketches Antonio made back in 1979 are shown in FIG. 2-5. He didn't draw any plans or make blueprints. The idea, like Topsy, just grew. The dimensions are in metric, which is what they use in Mexico.

If you have any questions about the items you see, you can contact Antonio at:

ANTONIO MENDEZ C.
APDO, Postal Num. 441
Xalapa - Veracruz, Mexico

Our host owns and operates a coffee plantation. Not surprisingly, many of his models are made of coffee wood. There are days on end when the work on the plantation allows time for modeling. He loves the rainy and growing seasons. During these days of relaxation he almost lives in the three rooms he has allotted to his avocation.

The largest room is 6 × 4 meters. The second room, which he calls his room for "painting and messy jobs," is 2 × 3 meters. The smallest, which contains wood for building and seasoning, is 2 × 1.2 meters.

Areas are allotted for each of the progressive stages of ship modeling. There are even drafting and correspondence desks and areas for this work along the walls, as well as a plans storage area, a battery charging corner, and overhead, a traveling light.

A fluorescent lamp fixture is mounted and hung by pulleys from a rail atop a track. The power cord is strung through loops along the track. The loops also roll along when the lamp is moved. Moving the light and adjusting the cord, Antonio has ample illumination no matter where he is working in the shop.

Each area has its function and each is organized well. One feature that struck me was the "rigging area." The lines, in all sizes, are suspended on spools over long pegs or wire racks (FIG. 2-6). Below, also in their proper places, is the disassembled rope walk and an expanded version of a STRING-ALONG. Antonio is demonstrating the tilt-out fluorescent lamp he has mounted on an old venetian blind top.

This is an improvement over his portable "spool table" of earlier years, which was not unlike the portable tool bench in FIG. 2-5. The spools were mounted on pegs on the reverse side of a pull-out drawer. The unit was hinged and slanted like the side of a pyramid. The line was fed through a hole in the slanted drawer.

Note also that the shelves above the work areas, which are display spaces for his models and storage for his "stuffs," are supported by chains. The shelves are hung, rather than installed on wall-mounted racks

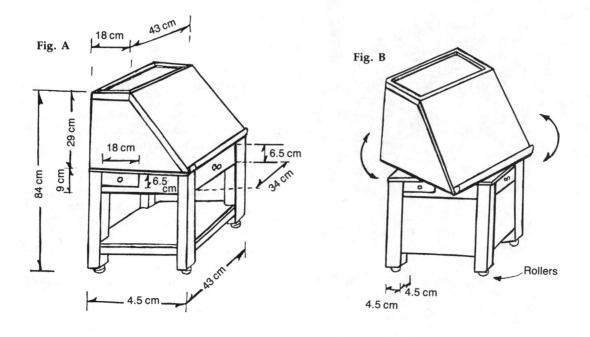

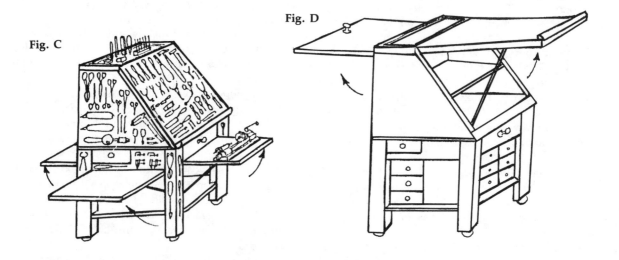

Fig. 2-5. Sketches of the movable tool organizers created by Antonio Mendez. Dimensions are in metric units. (Drawing by Antonio Mendez).

Fig. 2-6. Antonio demonstrates the tilt-down fluorescent lamp at the area designated for rigging. The ropewalk and "customized" String-Along are mounted below (Photo by Jose Luis Mendez).

or brackets. Antonio says, "I keep shifting things around as my work needs change, so I move the shelves too."

A vast array of tools and the abundance of items in the "collection" give the place a cluttered appearance. Antonio hates to waste time looking for something. Perhaps it is even his fascination of the world of tools and their uses that makes him constantly add to his purchases. He insists that there be a tool to fit the job—all sizes, all jobs.

There is much more to show you in this dream shop; unfortunately space and photographs lack something in the telling. There are gadgets you wouldn't believe unless you saw them—useful things made from discards; materials and tools stored and ready in the most unusual places.

All of the illustrations and ideas alluded to in this chapter came from ship modelers like you. Like you they have had their goals. In their minds, they have reached them. Have you reached yours?

THREE

Tools

It is better to wear out than to rust out.
—RICHARD CUMBERLAND

RECOMMENDED LISTS OF TOOLS ARE OFFERED IN publications, books, catalogs, and periodicals. Many a modeler has been trapped by the recommended tool lists of the ''expert.'' I don't believe in tool lists. Assembling a collection of tools is the act of an individual, based on his needs and tempered by his desire. Each addition to your tool chest should be thought out with great care. Each addition should be based on intended or actual use. Your collection will be held together by the prolonged familiar use of the tools contained within your shop. Through a well-planned collection and orderly storage, you will know which tool will do the proper job.

How much impulse can you control? Buying tools for the sake of possession is simply collecting. Keeping tools in your tool chest is a waste. Keeping the tool handy is storage. Keeping the tool in your hand getting the work done is accomplishment.

What will become your final collection, if there ever is a final gathering, will cover the world of tools from cutting edges to bending, clamping, holding, prying, fastening, and driving tools, and will run the gamut of all the other assorted devices created by man over the centuries. Hand-held or powered, the tools will be your servants. Your task is to think of what has been produced that can make your work easier. These tools you will include in your ''personal'' collection.

In order to build something as precise as a ship model, you must remove selected, measured, and predetermined segments of material so that the parts fit together properly. Preshaped parts will require attention to assemble. Nothing goes together by itself. Not even the so-called ''snap-together'' plastic kits are perfect. It takes a few tools and a degree of skill on the part of the builder to put something together.

How refined the tool and how skillful the builder need to be are matters for conjecture. A powered cutting edge or a simple razor blade will not make one iota of difference to the dedicated modeler. It will be the cutting that counts. Masterpieces have been built with a single cutting edge. Does it matter if the tool was as simple as a razor blade, a pocket knife, or a piece of broken glass?

Fancy files and rasps remove material in segments. The trick is to remember to push off the material. Files and rasps don't cut on the return trip. Bear down on the push and lift up on the pull. Scraping was discovered long before sandpaper.

Choose your tools carefully, individually. Do not be drawn into the false impression that a ''set'' of tools is a savings. More often it is a loss. Add your tools as the need arises. It is better to have only a few of your selected favorites to work with than a drawer full of tools. Start with the basics. As your experience grows, so will your tool chest.

CUTTING TOOLS

The final outcome, the result, of the work you are doing depends on the edge. That is all that comes in contact with the material you are shaping. Your first tool will be a cutting edge.

Will the edge be one that must be kept sharpened or a modern disposable blade? Which is the best tool for your future working habits? What is the difference in each of the cutting tools? Constant problems in building, the need for a different approach, and impulse buying will soon add more cutting blades to your tool collection.

Hand-held or powered, cutting edges must be sharp to accomplish the task you assign to them. Sharp tools make the work go faster and with less fatigue. There is no perfect tool for the perfect job. The only perfection is the hand that guides the tool. The craftsman makes the tool a perfection. Power tools don't make better modelers, only shorter working hours.

If it doesn't feel right, you will want to sharpen it or change the blade. A good cutting edge makes the work faster and easier, agreed. The harder the material, the sharper the blade should be, right! There is no difference between a scalpel and a saw in their respective cutting abilities as long as they are sharp. There is no difference in their cutting action either.

Microscopically, a scalpel blade is a saw. It cuts smoothly and *slices* because the saw-toothed edge is very sharp (FIG 3-1). It is very sharp because the saw teeth are very small and very close together. Now if you can remember that when you are working with hand tools (blades), you will slice your work and not attempt to ''push'' the edge through.

Crushing the material ahead of the blade is not cutting. Not only does this practice slow down the accurate work, it dulls the blade faster. You are breaking off the teeth. You wouldn't try to push a saw through the wood. Then get into the habit of drawing your blade across the work and cut through (FIG 3-2). Pushing is for chisels and gouges.

There are few hand tools (knives) left that are not available with replaceable cutting edges. Gouges, knife blades, and even saws are available with disposable blades. Every catalog, hobby shop, and hardware and craft store sells a wide variety of sizes and shapes. Several of the brand names will use the same handle to fit most of their blades.

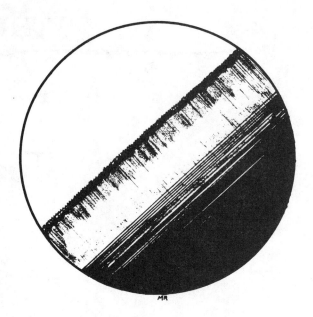

Fig. 3-1. The edge of a knife blade viewed under the microscope. Note the saw-tooth appearance.

Blades from various companies not only bear the same shapes and numbers, but will fit handles not made by other companies. The trade name is the only thing that is different in the blades' design.

Saws

Saws are cutting tools, and a selection of saws is a most important consideration for the modeler. There are two types of hand-held saws in the world of (carpentry) wood crafting. The crosscut saw and ripsaw are different in use because of the set of the teeth and the resistance of the material being cut. Their names describe their actions and intended uses. Craftsmen who work wood are familiar with these types of saws. They are the full-sized brothers to the much smaller saws used by miniaturists, hobbyists, and ship modelers.

There is not much need for a ripsaw in a modeler's toolbox. Most of the cuts in the modeler's world are crosscuts.

Use power saws to do ripping, if you have such a need. The majority of the long strips of wood used

22

RIGHT	TYPE OF CUTTING	WRONG
	Parting off cuts—use really sharp knife or razor saw for all larger sections	 Knife will crush
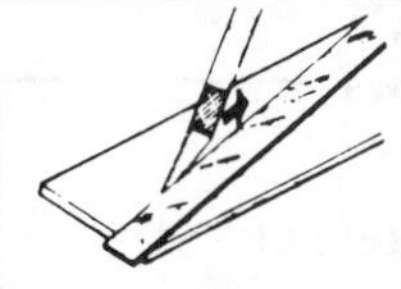	Straight cuts with the grain—use metal rule as guide—cut in direction that grain pulls blade against straightedge	 Blade will run off line
	Straight cuts in thick sheet—use saw where possible and always for edge to edge cuts across grain	 Will tear or split
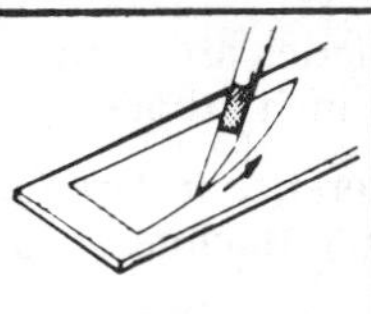	Freehand curves—cut in direction where grain will pull blade away from shape. clean up later as necessary	 Blade runs inside outline
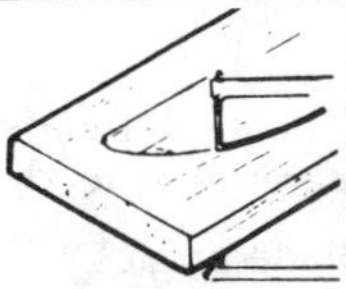	For curve cuts in thicker sheet use fretsaw or coping saw and finish to final true outline with sandpaper	 Difficult and cut not square
	Cross grain knife cuts—always cut from edge to centre never outwards to an edge	 Edge will tear
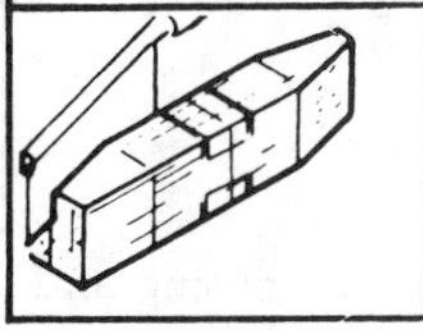	For cutting blands—use a stiff back saw as far as possible	 Fretsaw etc. will not cut square

Fig. 3-2. Proper use of woodworking tools (Courtesy of Northshore Deadeyes, Ltd.).

by ship modelers are available ready cut. The commercial strips of wood, in the most common sizes and most often used woods, are used by all types of model builders. You can either purchase exotic woods in bulk and render them with your power saw or purchase them from a professional source.

The most popular crosscut saws are those with disposable blades. It costs more to sharpen a saw than to replace it. Several grades and sizes are offered. Select them by the number of teeth per inch. The greater the number, the finer the cut. It is a good policy to have both a coarser blade for faster work and a finer blade for more careful work. The closer the fit, the tighter the glued joint. The width of the saw blade is important. The use of a miter box (by all means get or make a miter box) and the thickness of the material to be cut might determine the number of saws you use.

Power saws are a subject unto themselves. The models offered by the manufacturers can range from the tiny, portable, hand-held to the powerful, shop-sized, floor-mounted band and circular saws.

What type of power saws will you need? Make your choice after consideration. Think over what uses you will have for it and if you are ready for such a saw. Where will you use it? Where will you put it? Who cleans up afterwards?

Your first consideration should be a "good" versatile circular saw (TABLE 3-1). Will you need one with a tilt-top table? If you will be making fancy angle cuts and fit various shapes together, fine. If you are not sure, get one with the tilt feature anyway. Nobody says you need to use the feature at all, and it will always be there if you want to experiment later.

Table 3-1. Comparison Chart of the Abilities of Small Radial Saws.

DATA Characteristics	DREMEL 580	JARMAX Tilting 1002	JARMAX Deluxe 1010	JARMAX Non-Tilt 1001	TINY TOOLS	UNIMAT 3 150380	REMARKS
Weight / UNIT	15 lbs.	9 lbs.	12 lbs.	7 lbs	900 Grm	6 lbs.	Shipping Weight
Table top size	10×12	6½×9	9×12	5½×7½	4½×5¾	200× 173mm	
Diameter of Blade	4″	4″	4″	4″	60mm 50mm	80mm 60mm	4″ blades are with ½ inch arbors
Thickness of blade	.035	.032 .016	.032 .016	.032 .016	.4, .5, .8 mm	.9mm .0354	No difference in Dremel blade thickness
Teeth per inch	30 100	66 232	66 232	66 232	50 72/.8mm	54/80mm 90/.60mm	
Maximum depth of cut	1″/90°	5/8th	5/8th	5/8th	1/4 (?)	23mm	Tiny Tools—depends on material & feed
Angle of cuts degrees to work	45/90	45/90	45/90	45/90	90	90	Blade angles
R.P.M. (rated) of blade	9800	5000	5000	5000	16000 Adjust.	Variable	Unimat/Basic unit Tiny Tools, w/var. Therm.
Blade drive	belt	shaft	shaft	shaft	shaft	unit shaft	
Blade guard	yes	yes	yes	yes	yes	yes	
Rip fence guide	yes	yes	yes	yes	yes	yes	
Miter guide Adjustable angles	yes	yes	yes	yes	no	yes	
Adjustable blade height	yes	yes	yes	no	no	yes	Adjusted by raising and lowering blade & motor
Special features	yes (1)				yes (2)	yes (3)	see footnotes below

(1) Dust bag or vacuum attachment
Special on-off switch
(2) Rheostat controlled transformer available
Direct current as source of power—transformer required
w/110V Pressure regulated control switch (motor)
(3) Used as an accessory to basic lathe motor drive unit
All parts, saws, etc., sold separately
Complete woodworking unit included

For cross cuts on a power saw, an accurate miter gauge is essential. The cross bar should hold the set angle securely and not vary during use. You will do most of the work at either 90 or 45 degrees. To be sure that the angle is correct, check it occasionally during work with a fixed square.

The rip (stop) fence is the guide to cutting strips. If at all possible, it should be fixed at both ends to prevent any drift. At all times, it must be perfectly parallel with the saw blade.

Power saws in the lower price ranges, as well as some of the expensive but poorly designed models, have a set screw arrangement at one end of the stop fence and a grip or floating end at the back of the saw's tabletop. No matter how tightly you force the set screw, it seems to drift during use. Full-sized carpenter's models all feature a double end fastener. Why not the modeler's version? If you can't find one with this feature, make one.

If the stop fence runs the length of the cutting table and does not have a good, reliable set feature at both ends, use C-clamps. A small C-clamp at the far end of the fence, affixed to the top and facing outward, does not get in the way of the work.

If you don't have confidence that a saw you bought has a secure double end-fastening feature, there is no need to buy a new stop fence. If you have a Dremel tool, you can customize the saw fence with a simple adapter. Richard Roos, disgusted with the

drifting on his fence, made it stable (FIG. 3-3).

If you wish, lay aside the fence that came with the saw and ask your local glass installer for a piece of 90-degree extruded aluminum the length of your table-saw top. He might even give you a scrap piece. If there is no plate-glass dealer in your town, then get some 90-degree iron with a sharp bend. The flatter the bend, the closer to the tabletop it will fit. The narrower the "slice," the firmer the stop fence should fit. Place two small C-clamps at the inner side of the homemade stop fence, and you are ready to make "ripped" strips.

Check to see that the saw is equipped with a standard *arbor*. This is the side of the shaft that turns the mounted blade. There might come a time when you will wish to make thinner cuts using a thinner blade, a slitting blade, or one with a greater number of teeth. A slitting blade is excellent for making parts and pieces for grates (combing).

Your saw will be doing more of your tedious work as you learn its capabilities. You need to have an arbor that accepts standard blades. Imported saws have arbors with metric sizes, and the sizes of blades are limited to those that fit the arbors. American-built saws tend to stick to the 1/2-inch arbor.

When you are sawing (ripping) thin or very narrow strips, they will sometimes be drawn into the saw by the rotation and teeth of the blade. When this happens, you are not cutting strips, you are making

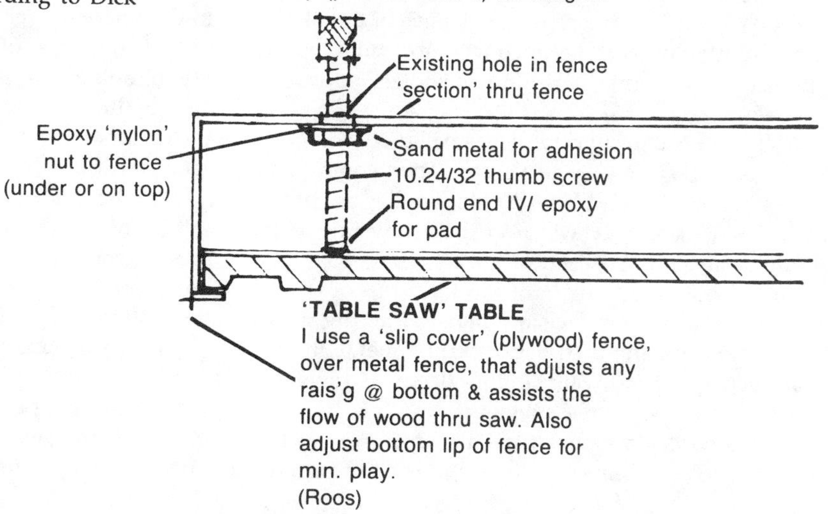

Fig. 3-3. Customizing the stop fence on a Dremel radial table saw according to Dick Roos (Courtesy of Dick Roos).

DREMEL SAW
Make 'nut' from pc. of nylon & self-tap (prior to instal'n) for snug fit.

Existing hole in fence
'section' thru fence

Epoxy 'nylon'
nut to fence
(under or on top)

Sand metal for adhesion
10.24/32 thumb screw
Round end IV/ epoxy
for pad

'TABLE SAW' TABLE
I use a 'slip cover' (plywood) fence, over metal fence, that adjusts any rais'g @ bottom & assists the flow of wood thru saw. Also adjust bottom lip of fence for min. play.
(Roos)

splinters. The solution is to make a "false" top with a narrower saw opening.

Cut a piece of material (the thinner the better) the same size as your saw's tabletop. Design a slot that allows the blade to protrude sufficiently to slice your wood without it constantly being sucked down alongside the blade. Use a piece of brass, sheet metal, or aluminum. Measure the place where the saw blade will come through and cut a slit in the metal the width of the blade's teeth and long enough to accommodate the blade when it is run up to its fullest height. This process is called *narrowing in*.

You can use a thin piece of wood, hardboard, or presswood for your "ripping" top. Clamp the wood on the saw's tabletop with the saw blade turned below the level of the surface. Turn on the saw and run the blade up slowly until it cuts through the wood.

You can make several of these false tops to use with different sizes of thicknesses of blades. The width should be just enough to allow clearance for the set of the teeth on the narrowest blade you are using in the saw. Hold the false top in place with C-clamps.

Only one power saw to my knowledge has a removable plate at the blade slit: the Dremel. If you do not have a Dremel, you can simply remake the part. Trace the outline and cut a new part from the material of choice. It should be as thick as the original plate. Customize the slit as needed.

You can also cut softer metals, such as aluminum and brass, with a saw. You can saw plastics of all types.

A good hand-held hacksaw will be a welcome addition to your toolbox. The size, length of the blade, and number of teeth per inch used for rougher and finer cuts is another of the many choices you need to make.

If you need to cut extremely small pieces of metal or plastic, you need to use snips. They come in all sizes, from 1/2-inch blades to the familiar tin snips. Sooner or later they will find their way into your "must-have" tool collection. Until then, get a heavy pair of scissors for the light work.

Now carry your decision-making into the realm of power saws and their use in cutting metal. Blades for such work are available for all power saws designed to cut workable metals.

When does a modeler need a scroll saw (often referred to as a *jigsaw* or a *fretsaw*)? The time arrives

in a modeler's career when it becomes a long, tedious, and distasteful job to cut curves and angled parts by hand. The replacement of the hand-held unit is the dream of many a modeler when the time factor becomes critical.

Some modelers have never done jigsawing by hand. They bought a power saw when they started their modeling. Speed is their desire. However, much accuracy is sacrificed by haste and inexperience with power tools.

When you are ready, do not base your choice on price. Consider the electrical power sources. How are the blades driven—by direct drive, belt drive, electromagnetic vibratory impulse, or power take off from an addition to an established unit? Consider all the variables. Should you be able to tilt the tabletop? Should you be able to raise and lower the blade? Your personal desires and possible future needs are the only expert opinions on which you can rely. Don't be afraid to ask questions of anyone who owns one.

What features should you look for in a power-operated jigsaw (TABLE 3-2)? The most important feature to some modelers is the ability to change the cutting line of the blade. There might come a time when you will want to cut from left to right, front to back, or vice versa. Check out the way a blade is mounted before you buy it.

The second most important feature is the "depth" of the throat. Too shallow a throat limits the size of the piece of material you can cut, as well as the angle of a cut.

Thickness of cut is another consideration. Although you shouldn't expect this type of power saw to do heroic chores, it should be able to cut a comfortable thickness of wood. Feed it slowly and it will. If you can't get the guard open far enough, you can't cut the thicker woods at all. Was it designed to take the thickness you want to cut? If it doesn't or won't, then don't use this saw for that job.

All the fancy power takeoffs on some models of scroll saws might be window dressing. Power cable attachments and sanding disks with no table or guard are offered without extra cost. You might never use the options.

The problems you encounter using your scroll saw might mean you are ready for a band saw. Not many band saws are made for small work. If you are looking for a band saw, however, you will soon find one to suit your needs.

Table 3-2. Comparing Characteristics of Scroll, Fret, and Jigsaws.

Characteristics	DREMEL	VIBRO	UNIMAT	UNIMAT	REMARKS
	571	Fret	Fret	Jig	
Depth of throat	15"	11½"	300mm	N/A	
Weight of saw	12 lbs. 7 oz.	4 kgms	N/A	N/A	Shipping Weight
Blade drive	Cam	Elect. Magnetic	Unit Cam	Unit Cam	Unimat—as attached to power source
Strokes of blade	3450	N/A	4000	5000	Strokes per minute
Table top size	9½×9½	230mm Dia.	6×5½	6×5½	
Maximum thickness of cut	2"	60mm	17mm	13mm	Depending on material
Volts/Amps rating	110-115 60A	110/150W (2.2A)	110 60A	110 60A	Vibro Saw—Special Export Motor
Adjustable table height	yes	yes	no	no	
Adjustable blade tension	yes	yes	yes	no	
Blade guard	yes	no	no	no	
Changeable blade positions	yes	no	no	no	4 positions allow 4 cutting directions
Table tilting	yes	no	no	no	Angle cut imparted
Sawing guide (rip/cross-cut)	no	yes	no	no	
Type of male plug	3-way Grnd	3-way* Grnd	3-way Grnd	same same	*Continental Horizontal

While you are thinking about a powered band saw, have you worked with a hand-powered version? Get your hands on a violin saw, sometimes called a *guitar-maker's saw*. My grandfather used one instead of either a scroll or band saw, to do cutouts for inlay work. That is accurate cutting, believe me.

Sharpening Blades

Traditional hand tools made of fine-tooled steel will hold a cutting edge longer when properly sharpened. These are the tools that are preferred by craftsmen, scoffed at by the uninformed, and sold by better grade tool suppliers.

By today's standards, they are expensive. How much should you spend on something that is expected to last a lifetime? Is the lifetime of service, even with the need to sharpen once in a while, worth the price?

I'm still using my grandfather's woodworking tools, and they still hold an edge. There is no way of telling where grandpa acquired them or how long he had them before leaving them to me. His drawknife bears the date 1885. He taught me how to sharpen them "proper like." "Set your angle and hold it," he told me. Experience soon taught me that it takes a long time to sharpen a tool when you're rocking the angle.

The thought of a session at a grinding wheel, goggles on for safety and sparks flying, is enough to deter many from remaking an edge. Even a hand-turned grinding wheel is a frightening experience. If a nick or chip in the cutting edge appears because of careless handling or an accidental "bumping," it must be removed by grinding. A new edge is created by grinding off the damage. Then comes the task of sharpening it properly. If you can't or won't grind a new edge yourself, have it done professionally.

Most of a modeler's sharpening is done on a stone. He seldom must use a grinding wheel to sharpen tools. A sharpening stone belongs in your toolbox. Buy a good one and use it often.

The debate on how to sharpen with a stone still goes on. Should the cutting edge be pushed against the stone or drawn across? Should the metal particles be pushed off into the blade or pulled off away from the edge?

Makers of fine hunting knives recommend the pushing method—*slicing* they call it. My grandfather used the pulling method. "Gets rid of the trash," he used to say. Perhaps the term *wire edge* might make a difference in your thinking.

The wire edge forms as the cutting edge of the tool gets sharper and the edge narrower. This is the rough material left from grinding or filing a cutting edge on a metal blade. Until the wire edge is literally rolled off, no real sharpening can be accomplished. The microscopic saw teeth have got to form and be sharpened. You can, at times, actually see the wire edge roll off.

A "reverse lick" on a stone or a leather strop takes off the wire edge. That is why a barber stroked a blade in reverse directions. Microscopic particles of metal are removed by the abrasive leather. Enough is taken off to make it a sharp blade again.

Some modelers make it a practice to strop their disposable blades. To them it is an established habit to sharpen every new blade upon purchase or just before use. Some strop the blade during use. I do both.

The tool steel used in disposable blades is not the best. The disposable blades dull rapidly. The stainless steel blades will be the first to become dull. Although the material won't rust, it won't keep an edge either.

CARVING TOOLS

The carver prefers the curved blade. Remember the shape of your first pocket knife? The cutting action of whittling is recalled to many by the mere mention of the knife. The curved tip was for carving. The straight edge of the blade was for cutting.

Chip carving, an art in itself, uses a straight chisel-like blade. The cutting is done in flat planes and the material is chipped away, hence the name. In truth, the material is sliced (sawed) away.

The chisel blade is also the favorite cutting edge of the modeler who is cutting small pieces of material away to secure a tight fit with other parts. The amount of the material that is removed by this cut-

ting (or slicing) action is determined by the angle of the slice. The sharper (more acute) the angle, the deeper the cut. For smaller working areas, the blade should have a long and narrow angle.

The length of the cutting edge is a matter of choice. The slice is up to the craftsman. I leave it to you to determine how many different styles, blades, and handles you will need to get the job done.

If you are into disposable blades, get a package of each type and settle in with what you will use the most. A few seconds is all it takes to fit one blade or another to your handle. In a few years, you will find yourself down to one or two favorites.

At the other end of the blade controversy are the *fixed-blade* tools, which are available in most art stores that sell wood carver's tools. Wood-carving tools are also made for modelers and are available in hobby stores and from mail-order houses (FIG. 3-4).

Consider the assorted sizes, shapes, angles, and edges available for carving tools. Approach the purchase of such tools as you did your blade selection: one at a time and as their need becomes apparent. Avoid sets of carving tools as initial purchases.

The so-called *microsized* carving sets might be the exception. A selection of microsized wood-carving chisels and gouges with fine-tooled steel blades should be a part of every ship modeler's tool collection. They are most useful for carving figures, figureheads, ship's decorations, and small details. They are not as expensive as they seem.

Get a good slipstone for the gouges. The curved surfaces of the cutting edge need a good "back lick" for the inner edge once in a while during the sharpening phase. Sharpening this type of tool is a challenge you can accept and a fear you can quickly overcome. Every library, public or private, should contain a text on how to sharpen tools. If your fear continues to overshadow your learning, you can always take the tools to a professional tool sharpener.

SANDING TOOLS

Sanding to the line or smoothing a surface is faster with power equipment. The offerings of power sanders can vary, from a rotating disk mounted as an option on another tool to a special fancy and accurately designed thickness sander. Sanding to fit always should be done by hand. One lick by hand is all you might need. A touch of the power wheel, however, might be the destruction of the whole unit.

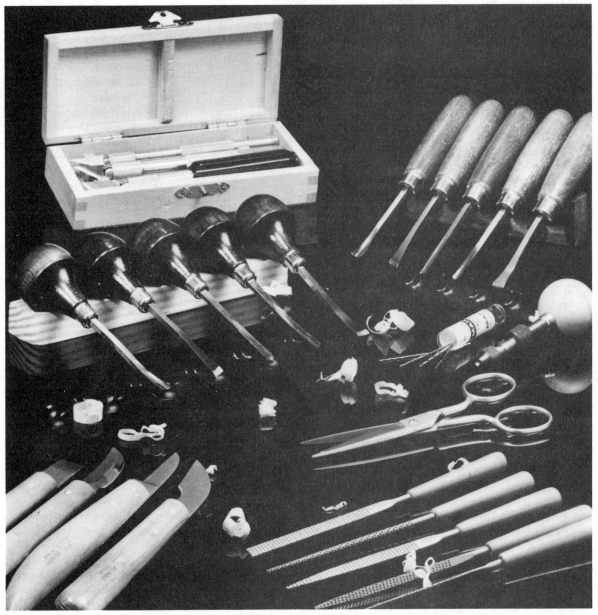

Fig. 3-4. A collection of carving tools, gouges, and rasps. A pin vise and drill bits are shown center right (Photo courtesy of Mascot Tools).

Power devices to accomplish the boring and time-consuming job of sanding are varied in price as well as application. The big boys of the carpenter's trade are easy to find. Securing just what you need in your shop list of tools is another matter.

A vast array of state-of-the-art sanders, imported miniatures which are palm-sized versions of the power tools of industry, are available in hobby shops and through mail-order houses. Some are quite good to do a little sanding after the work is ''on the model.'' Others, improperly used, are engines of destruction.

PLANING TOOLS

Planes, from palm-sized to carpenter's door planes measuring over a foot long, should be considered. You will need a plane, but the size is up to you.

Power planes are now sold in hand-held models in sizes designed for use by modelers. They are small, and they need to be if you are going to use them on a model or for a small job. Use them as they were intended to be used. Don't ask them to do a yeoman's job.

DRILLING TOOLS

To drill a hole, you will need a drill bit. The power source that turns the drill bit can be human or electrical.

The delicate holes made with a drill bit in sizes no larger than a human hair require a delicate touch, pressure, and control. For this work use a (drill) pin vise. Modelers are not above borrowing ideas from other professions. The pin-vise size came from the watchmaking industry years ago.

Larger holes require larger drill bits and a little more power than the fingers. Hand drills turned by gear wheels vary in overall size from tiny to industrial models. Accommodate your needs and secure several sizes, from a few inches all the way up to a carpenter's brace and bit. There is always a need to ''bore'' larger holes once in a while.

If you want to work a little faster and still make small holes, a hand-held power drill might be your next purchase. Like the hand-powered drills, sizes and quality vary. There is a wide selection of power-driven tips. Accessories include carving tips, sanding disks, polishing wheels, and routers. Groups of accessories the manufacturer recommends are offered as packages. Like any set of tools, choose your power accessories carefully.

While we are on the subject of drills, classified as equipment unto themselves, browse through a tool catalog or the tool section of your favorite store. Take note of the many sizes, rated powers (rpm), and accessories. You can buy a drill as a separate unit, with accessories, options, take-offs, or whatever your heart desires. You will be making a lot of holes in your modeling lifetime.

Your power drill is also the power source for attachments that can convert the drill motor into a varied group of hand-held power tools. Router attachments, power cables, grinding wheels, and bench-mounted brackets of all kinds are available. Look around and buy what you are comfortable with.

Do a little advance planning and buy one hand drill (powered) that can be fitted into a drill stand. There are several types of drill stands; most are vertical. Think also about all the power bits you can use in a fixed environment. Note that some of the stands are fixed and the work is brought to the drill or cutting head; others move the power unit to the work. Securing one drill stand doesn't prevent you from getting another, however.

VISES

Every type and size of vise is available. The bench vise is by far the most versatile. The sizes and strengths that this item comes in range from tiny to giant-sized.

Selecting one, or perhaps an assortment, of vises is a common problem. How many will you need, what size and strength, and who makes the best, might be your questions.

My favorite is the PanaVise. The base, either the low or high profile, can accommodate several different heads, affording me versatility.

TINY TOOLS

Several makers of what I shall term *tiny tools* have seen the need for power tools for modelers. Smaller versions of the carpenter's and woodworker's shop tools are being built and offered for sale.

Black & Decker, America's well-known tool maker, bought an entire plant in Germany to make such tools. Some of the selections are sold under the trade name of the parent company. The small power tools, many of which are being imported, are sold in America under the trade name Behrendt Minicraft (FIG. 3-5).

Competition being what it is, another German manufacturer has produced a similar offering. The trade names of its products in America are Micro Mark and MicroLux. I have had the chance to evaluate both and would like to introduce you to this new field of working power tools. The choice of Micro-Lux as an example of such tools is a personal selection. Do not constitute this as an endorsement.

These are not toys. Developed in West Germany and built to quality standards, they are ideal for model building and smaller-than-life projects. The power source is 12 volts. Power can come from a battery, or through the 110-volt ac transformer. There is a built-in speed-control knob. The rotation or action of the tool can be reduced without the loss of torque. The quick disconnect three-pronged female plug at the top allows you to change tools rapidly.

The Power Plane. The adjustable thickness of the cut and the spiral cutting blade of the power plane made planing and even some shaping and carving a breeze. It works well on supersoft wood (balsa), as well as the harder varieties.

Belt Sander. The fiber-backed belt on the belt sander proved tough enough to stand up to metal, Plexiglas, as well as all types of wood.

Orbital Sander. If you are tired of time-consuming hand sanding, the orbital sander might be your answer.

Right-Angle Grinder/Sander/Drill. The most versatile tool in the entire offering is the right-angle grinder/sander/drill. A rotating 5-inch sanding disk in one mode allows rapid removal of materials in desired amounts.

Now for a few changes, adjust the removable and reversible side handle and install a keyless three-jawed Jacobs chuck. You now can use a selection of

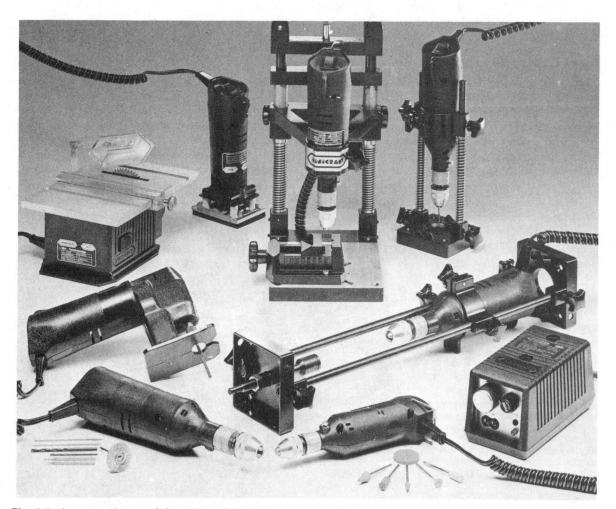

Fig. 3-5. A group picture of the Minicraft Collection (Photo courtesy of Black & Decker Tools).

cutting blades or drills. It can be a small radial saw unit. Mount it in the drill-press stand for controlled vertical movement.

High-Speed Router. The high-speed router's a tool for surface carving. The depth-adjustment wheel, coupled with the lock and edge guide, gave me depths from 0 to 4 1/2 inches. The unit can be mounted in a table. Router bits with 1/8-inch shanks are available everywhere.

1/4″ Dual-Torque Drill. The 1/4-inch dual-torque drill is small, but powerful, and is driven by a set of high torque 8 to 1 gears. The pistol grip gives good control.

The drill mounts in the same drill press unit as the right-angle grinder, turning the unit into a precision drill press. The hand wheel gives you delicate control for precision drilling.

High-Speed Drill. The most exhausting and painful problem (to me) in wood carving has been lessened with this high-speed drill. This unit is not heavy like so many with comparable rpms. Weighing only 5 1/4 ounces and having a length of 6 3/4 inches, this tool is designed with a comfortable flared grip.

Did you notice how many different combinations can be had simply by interchanging work units in the drill press attachment? Micro Mark tools has a full line of other small tools.

A scroll saw is available from the Micro Mark that is a combination of many of the features discussed under the topic of power saws. Many features that should be found on other maker's models have been incorporated into this unit at no extra cost. In particular, a miter guide and stop fence make work accurate and relaxing. The name power saw is appropriate.

Send for the catalog.

MICRO MARK
P.O. Box 5112-159
24 East Main St.
Clinton, NJ 08809

Jarmac also makes a line of tools. The power unit is the same in all the tools. A drill press and a wood-turning lathe are also offered. Saws and sanders are available with or without the tilt-top feature. For detailed information, write:

JARMAC
P.O. Box 2785
Springfield, IL 62708

The Hobby-Lux 450 scroll saw (FIG. 3-6) might be considered Europe's entry with a rating somewhat better than the Dremel, but not as good as some of the scroll saws made in the United States. It, too, has power take-offs and accessories that elevate it above the average. A miter gauge, a stop fence, and other details are available as options.

America's entry in the field of miniature lathes for working metal or wood is the Sheerline. A precision instrument for the machinist-minded modeler, it has no options for conversion into operations other than turning. Horizontal drill and grinding can be

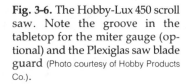

Fig. 3-6. The Hobby-Lux 450 scroll saw. Note the groove in the tabletop for the miter gauge (optional) and the Plexiglas saw blade guard (Photo courtesy of Hobby Products Co.).

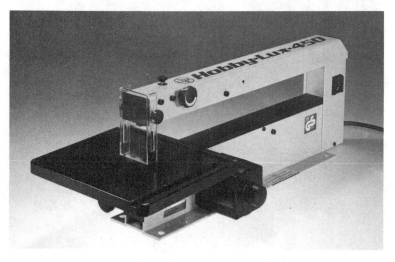

Fig. 3-7. Basic unit of the Unimat 3 from Emco Maier of Austria (Photo courtesy of Hobby Products Co.).

done. Sheerline also offers a miniature vertical milling machine.

UNIMAT 3

Now we come to the dream machine. There is in model building a very versatile tool. With the possible exception of a knife blade, there is nothing that you might need in your modeling career that the Unimat 3 does not offer. I won't discuss any price range. The final cost of the collection of options depends on your ability to control your purse and your self-indulgence.

From its humble beginnings as a watchmaker's or small tool-and-die lathe in Austria, Unimat has grown to become the almost complete tool of the miniaturist and modeler. This precision instrument (FIG. 3-7) works all the materials you will ever need: wood, metal, plastic, and all the exotic items in between.

The Unimat 3 is manufactured in Hallein, Austria, by Emco Maier & Co. This company, world famous for its industrial machinery, has a distributor in the United States. If you are ready for this tool, or think you might be interested, write to:

HOBBY PRODUCTS COMPANY
P.O. Box 218117
Columbus, OH 43221-8117

and ask for a colorful brochure and a price list. From the day of the arrival of the catalog, the stuff dreams are made of, you are on your own.

Using your metric wrench and following instructions, you can avail yourself of all your add-ons. You can convert the basic power unit and milling attachments into every coveted, longed for, and dreamt about power tool known at this time.

Emco & Maier also makes a line of lesser expensive tools for the modeler. The 6-volt battery (4 D cells) or transformer-driven Unimat 1 is available and worthy of consideration. Although it is not designed to handle quite the load and precision of its big brothers, it is a good tool to consider. This unit has a selection of add-on accessories.

PUBLICATIONS

Tool books and catalogs for tools of all types abound throughout the world. There is ample opportunity to browse through these publications for the tools you will dream about, need, eventually buy, and possibly discard. Periodicals for woodworking enthusiasts have a tendency to appear, find favor, and vanish. The better ones remain. Racks in the tool sections of department and hardware specialty stores, bookstores, and magazine stores are full of them. Subscriptions are available.

One such magazine is:

U.S. BOAT & SHIP MODELER
898 W. 16th St.
Newport Beach, CA 92663

FOUR

Sources of Kits

There are two things to aim at in life:
First, to get what you want; and after that, to enjoy it.
Only the wisest of mankind achieve the second.
—LOGAN PEARSALL SMITH

WHERE CAN YOU FIND A KIT TO BUILD A SHIP model? Why must it be an elusive item that must be hunted? Where are the kits that you might buy to get started in ship modeling?

The vast majority of ship modelers in the last 50 years began their careers with a kit. Most first-time purchases are made in a local shop or from a mail-order catalog. Getting one as a gift is always nice. Getting a ship model kit 50 years ago wasn't so difficult. Today, with the changing trends and rapidly changing desires of the buying public, it's a different story.

It is unfortunate that many buyers at department stores, hobby shops, and other retail sales sources consider the offering and stocking of ship-model kits a seasonal business. It is also unfortunate that many buyers consider ship-model kits as toys, gifts, or novelties. Undoubtedly, these are the reasons the models are so plentiful during the gift-giving season.

Hobby shops and mail-order outlets, once the so-called buying season ends, are just as much the culprit as any other. Their crime is that they, like their fellow sales outlets, fail to maintain year-round stock. Several mail-order houses have become merchandise outlets, selling only what they can get at a good price. They then offer the kit at a price no other source can match, dump the load, and flood the market. After that blitz, they do not restock.

The prices are hard to resist. When they are gone, the merchandiser has made his profit and does not restock or backorder for his customer. Those who did not get in on the campaign are unable to locate the kit they wanted to build.

Many first-time ship modelers who come into a hobby shop or browse through catalogs seeking a ship model to build are like kids in a candy store. Their eyes and their appetites are bigger than their capacity. The array of the offering is greater than their ability to perform as model builders. They will have to decide and select a kit within their range until they feel capable of taking on a greater challenge (FIG. 4-1). Having a *Cutty Sark* or a *Victory* as a first kit is not as foolish for some as for others. It is not a crime if you have knowledge, can understand instructions, or have built other models. Experience is a greater teacher. As it is gathered, so knowledge progresses. Discouragement comes easy with confusion.

WOODEN KITS

There are many types of model kits, and definitions are important. When I talk about *ships*, I mean those with sails. Ship-rigged is another term for them. *Boats*, on the other hand, are a separate item altogether. As they say in the Navy, a ship is what you sail on, and a boat goes on a ship.

35

Fig. 4-1. German kit maker Steigraeber offers the Spanish polacre *Isabel*. The scale is 1:90 and produces a model 45 centimeters in length (Photo courtesy of Steingraeber).

There are plenty of terms that can precede the word *boat*. A few are *radio-controlled, power, sail, ship's,* and *pleasure*. My ideas and information concern ship models and ship-model kits.

Geoffrey A. Wheeler, editor of *Model Retailer*, stated in his August 1985 editorial, which was printed along with the results of a survey concerning the average age of the modeler, "There are too many leisure alternatives; too much emphasis on electronics and not enough on the kind of skills that make modelers *modelers*." To which I would like to add: "and not enough knowledgeable hobby-shop owners, mail-order houses, or telephone operators to help make modelers *modelers*."

Not all the ship-model kit builders are retirees. Age has absolutely nothing to do with it. Although many people who are retired build ship models, have you ever met a retired ship modeler? Just as building models transcends all social levels, it also cuts through the age myth. The older modeler who is into radio control, or R/C, might have been a static builder for years. The younger modeler, weary of fast racers and radio-controlled aircraft and ships, wants to build something different than a sleek PT boat—something with a challenge, something that will look nice on his grandfather's mantel or in his own home, something to be left for memories. When any one from an age group wants to build a ship model, a wooden ship model, a static model from a kit, where will he find a selection?

Shops are filled with the quick-construction variety. Plastic snap-together type kits, precut and preassembled units are found in increasing numbers. Hulls are preformed. Nothing must be added except a few quick hours to produce a representative ship model. Catalogs are filled with bargains and combinations of radio gear and fast boats. The emphasis today is on models that go together in a hurry.

The development of hand-crafted skills is looked upon with scorn. The modern concept of what is a ship-model kit is relegated to the materials that can produce a rapid result. Manufacturers are preparing and marketing kits that can be out and moving on land, in the air, or over the water in as short a working time as possible. Designing popular types of ship models that appeal to the insertion of power and control by radio is the newest concept. Skill is not important; results are.

All this is overshadowing what the hobby shop was all about. Trends in sales have made the owners resort to speedy tactics. The rule of thumb is to ride the crest of the wave and to "hang ten" in the foam of profits. The fellow behind the counter should, however, be a fellow modeler willing to help in all ways, as well as an excellent salesman. When you find a shop or a mail-order house that cares how your model will turn out, then that's where you will do your shopping.

Having a place to buy what you need has become secondary to assistance. You should not only secure what you want from a shop owner or mail-order house, but also what you need. That need is information. There must be someone to ask when your question cannot be answered by a fellow modeler or found in a book.

The sellers' motivation seems to be merchandise, rather than service. This is just as much a fault in the shop as it is in the unthinking mail-order houses. Selling the idea that it is easy to build a plank-on-frame ship model by just following the ''easy'' directions is an untrue statement. A full-page ad, a catalog in full color, a promise of a full refund if not satisfied, the words of a slick salesman are the opiates that lead to disaster.

The building instructions in imported kits are usually in the language of another country. The English translation is poor at best. Where does a novice turn when he demands help? How can there be any progress in creating a satisfied modeler if the sale is all that matters? An ever-increasing group needs help. Proper training can make a lifetime modeler.

Foreign Manufacturers

Perhaps a review is in order. Let me offer a list of some of the more popular brand-name wooden ship-model kits. It might be a little difficult to indicate the appropriate American outlet of imported kits. I must warn you that the kit of your desire might not be as readily available as the seller leads you to believe.

Why do the wooden kits cost so much? Not so long ago, imported wooden kits kept rising in price. Then the bottom dropped out and the prices fell. The market is now in a state of constant fluctuation, with a rash of unstable selling prices.

Please understand the plight of the provider of imported ship-model kits. He not only must contend with the fluctuations of currency exchange, and the cost of transportation to his location, but also his home country's import and customs duties.

There is a war going on in the ship-model sales industry. It is being waged for your dollar. Before you buy a kit because of the ''better'' price, make sure

it will be available at that price. Remember the Latin phrase, *caveat emptor* (let the buyer beware).

Aeropicolla, of Torino, Italy; Artesania Latina of Barcelona, Spain; Euro, of Como, Italy; Mantua/Sergal/Panart, of Italy; and Imai, along with Kagkau Co., Ltd., of Japan, to name just a few, are sold by many hobby shops across the land and featured in several mail-order catalogs.

Mail-order houses have a few good wooden kits to offer. Many are being forced to associate themselves with overseas affiliates because the American market is fast coming under the control of the profit-motivated discount houses. Exclusive territorial sales contracts keep the smaller and select mail-order operators from securing wooden ship-model kits at lower prices. If you are patient, they can secure from their sources in other lands, who are not bound by such agreements, any kit that you find in the catalogs of the overseas kit makers.

Billings, of Denmark, is carried by many shops. This line, long established, is now the world's best-known maker of ship-model kits. These kits are found in almost every country in the world. Write to the American distributor for the name and address of the outlet nearest you:

ALTECH MARKETING
P.O. Box 286
Fords, NJ 08817

Constructo, Dikar, and Golden—all manufactured in Spain—can be purchased from the sales sources, mail-order houses, and directly from the American importer.

POLK'S HOBBIES INTL.
346 Bergen Ave.
Jersey City, NJ 07304

Not all the kits shown in catalogs will be available from the importers or distributors. If you desire, you can communicate directly with the manufacturer. The names and addresses of the European makers of wooden ship-model kits follow. You also can request their catalog and the name of their American or home-country sales source.

AEROPICCOLA S.N.C.
Corsoro Monte Cucco 87
10141 Torino, Italy

AERONAUT
Stuttgarter Strabe 18
P.O. Box - Postfach 384
D-7410 Reutlingen 1, Germany

AMATI
118 Vai Madama Cristina
Torino, Italy

ARTESANIA LATINA
Urbanizacion San Jorge
Cabrils (Barcelona), Spain

BILLINGS BOATS A/S
Gejsing
6640 Lunderskov, Denmark

CONSTRUCTO / GOLDEN
San Luis Menorca, Spain

COREL S.r.l.
Via Edolo 6
20125 Milano, Italy

DIKAR S / COOP.
P.O.B. 48
Eibar, Guipuzcoa, Spain

EURO MODEL
Via S. Garovaglio, 19
Como, Italy

C. MAMOLI
Viale Teodorico 2
20149 Milano, Italy

MANTUA (SERGAL) PANART
S. Lucia di Roverbella (Mantova)
Codice Postale 46048, Italy

NEW MAQUETTES
Imprimerie J. Hiver S.A.
92, rue Oberkampf
75011 Paris, France

STEINGRAEBER
Postfach 1208
3570 Stadtallendorf
West Germany

The varieties of historical and contemporary ship models found among these companies are extensive. There seem to be duplications in each line of the more popular and desirable vessels. Whose version is the most accurate is debatable. There are always those who will swear by one product over another.

Recent additions to the largest makers—i.e., Billings, Corel, Artesania Latina, and Mantua-Panart—are made with vacuformed plastic hulls. The demands justify the additions.

American Manufacturers

There are wooden ship kits manufactured in the United States. You are, or should be, familiar with:

BLUEJACKET SHIPCRAFTERS
Castine, ME

DUMAS
909 East 17th St.
Tucson, AZ 85119

A.J. FISHER
1002 Etowah Ave.
Royal Oak, MI 48067

LAUGHING WHALE
174 Front St.
Bath, ME 04530

SCIENTIFIC MODELS
340 Snyder Ave.
Berkley Heights, NJ 07922

MODEL SHIPWAYS
P.O. Box 85
39 West Ft Lee Rd.
Bogata, NJ 07603

MIDWEST PRODUCTS
P.O. Box 564
400 Iniania St.
Hobart, IN 46342

STERLING MODELS
3620 ''G'' St.
Philadelphia, PA 19134

The types and subjects to be modeled and the selections offered by these American kit manufacturers are considerable. They each offer an extended range of products. Vessels range from period ships, such as the *Mayflower,* to contemporary steel-hulled beauties.

Of course, with American manufacturers there is no problem with the language barrier in the written instructions. Replacement of parts (fittings) is much easier. They are here and willing to assist you. If you read the ship-model periodicals and special publications available on the racks of your favorite magazine outlet or hobby shop, or through subscription, you have seen their advertisements. Write and ask for their catalogs.

Most American makers produce *solid-hull kits*. Several are adding built-up hollow-hull construction types. The variations of types becoming popular, such as the pseudo plank-on-frame models (FIG. 4-2), hollow built-up hulls for radio-controlled models, etc. are detailed in Chapter 8.

One of the hull-building methods discussed in Chapter 10 as well as in Chapter 1, is the half hull. There are kits available to build half-hull models.

Plans and complete instructions, woods in several colors and types, a mounting plaque, and a name plate are included. The units are preshaped and, after gluing, can be carved to shape. For a list of half-hull kits available, or to purchase one already completed, contact:

MODEL SHIP MARINA
P.O. Box 15201
Alexandria, VA 22301

PLASTIC KITS

Plastic kits are mass produced and offer a medium that, although not as forgiving of mistakes as wood, is becoming increasingly popular. The period and contemporary vessels in the line are quite

Fig. 4-2. A plank-on-frame kit from Bluejacket Shipcrafters. The frames are preshaped basswood, as are the other wood components. Fittings are of brass and cast Britannia metal (Photo courtesy of Bluejacket Shipcrafters, Inc., Castine, ME).

extensive and variable in scale and price. A well-constructed plastic model is also another established form of ship modeling.

The names of the manufacturers of such kits, because of their widespread distribution, have become household words. Cars, tanks, planes, and ship models of all types are being assembled and painted by the thousands, perhaps millions, even as you read these words.

The better known plastic ship-model kits are Lindberg, Monogram, and Revell. Many who know these names got started on ship models because these companies also manufacture and sell plastic kits of other subjects of modeling interest. Many a devoted ship modeler thought he would like to try a ship model after building a car, a plane, or a tank.

Heller, of France, is a good example of a quality plastic-model manufacturer that can produce outstanding ship models. The fine-cast parts offer a building challenge and result in a proud display. Modern French, German, and American warships, as well as ancient and period ships, are available through American and foreign sales outlets. Distribution of the Heller kits is worldwide.

Sailing ships of today, working ships, and the constant changing military vessels also are shown in Heller's catalog. The models of the *Victory* and *Soliel Royal* are prime examples of complete ship-model kits. Thousands of pieces are included. Produced in plastic, the parts, hulls, and everything except the lines and rigging are included. They are outstandingly accurate reproductions of these famous historic ships.

Hasegawa, Otaki, Imai, Tamyia, and Doyusha are Japanese firms whose offerings are found on the worldwide market. Their ship-model kits range from the small miniseries to full-scale working models of sailing and steel-hulled ships.

Take a quick trip to your local hobby shop or browse through any model magazine, and you can satisfy your interest in this type of building. Catalogs and information are available by simply answering the advertisements. There is always the possibility of discovering new manufacturers.

RADIO-CONTROL KITS

The latest fad is, radio-controlled ship-model kits. Racing boats powered by gas engines roar across the water with rooster tails fanning behind. Graceful sail-boats (FIG. 4-3) part the waves. Workboats, tugs, and fishing trawlers move slowly across the pond. Powered lifeboats and Coast Guard cutters are seen at regattas. Military ships of all types from landing craft and speedy PT boats to full carriers maneuver in formation or fire pellets or powder charges at one another in mock battles.

The ship of your choice is available to build in scale rendition and to power and control. The names of manufacturers are on the pages of every periodical devoted to the subject of modeling under radio control. Not surprisingly, some of the vessels are available from the makers of static models.

Through proper installation, you cannot only make your model move but speak. Input is from a mike on shore; output is from the speaker aboard the model. The component items you must secure, either in a kit or as separate purchases, to install in the model are numerous.

Fig. 4-3. The Dumas kit of the *Hudson* comes with a fiberglass hull and all the items except radio-control equipment (Photo courtesy of International Photographics Associates, Tucson, AZ).

A quick look through the book *The Radio Buyer's Guide* is quite an eye opener. It is published annually by Boynton & Associates and sold by most hobby shops. You can buy direct from the publisher.

BOYNTON & ASSOCIATES
Radio Buyer's Guide
Clifton House
Clifton, VA 22024

The invasion of America by the makers of radio-controlled ship-model kits continues. Germany, France, and even far-off Australia, all have something to offer. Ship models continue to come to our shores. American distributors, always with an eye to profit, introduce names such as New Maquettes of France, Dean's Models of Great Britain, and Sirmar of England. Aeronaut, a well-known manufacturer of planes and ships from West Germany, Hawn from the same nation, and other unfamiliar names will soon be seen on the shelves and in the display windows of the world. All of these companies are be-

Fig. 4-4. Model of the New Bedford whaleboat by Erik A. Ronnberg was produced from a kit by Model Shipways. Copper nails may be used to build this model, which is recommended for modelers with some experience (Photo courtesy of Model Shipways).

coming known to the builder of radio-controlled ship models.

Germany's offerings are topped by the ''blitz'' advertising campaign of Robbe. The offerings include aircraft, as well as ship models. The catalog is available from your local hobby shop dealer or:

ROBBE
180 Township Line Rd.
Belle Mead, NJ 08502

The full-color pages will show you the possibilities of making a radio-controlled model that does everything but think.

FINDING SOURCES OF KITS

The selection and purchase of ship-model kits is endless. Where you find a treasure depends on how hard you look and the route you take. The periodicals listed in this book contain advertisements for the makers of ship-model kits.

Begin with your local public library. Sadly, not enough individuals consider the library as a source of ship-model kits. Disgusting as it sounds, not enough even consider a library as a source of much information to assist in everyday living.

As an example, I offer *The Complete Catalogue of Mail Order Kits*, by Anna Sequoia (Rawson, Wade Publishers, Inc. New York, 1981). Listed in this book are the names and addresses of mail-order sources of kits. This is only one volume of such lists that could aid you in finding ship-model kits.

While you are at the library, ask to see the manufacturers' listings. The librarian might also suggest any of several government and private volumes of sources.

Old, established companies are being bought outright. In the past years, several that were manufacturers of excellent wooden ship-model kits have not been able to stand the rough seas of economic oceans. They went under. Carta Agusta of Italy sank from sight. Some of the debris from others has been salvaged and incorporated into other companies. As an example, I must report that several of Movo's better kits are now being offered by Corel. The same story, with a variation, can be told of Sergal, which is now known as Panart. Art Amb Fusta of Spain has been reformed with the name of Dikar.

Sources of ship-model kits are open-ended. Established manufacturers are adding new models to their lines (Fig. 4-4) that challenge the skills and fire the imaginations of ship modelers. New manufacturers grow from the efforts of the cottage industries. Home-grown assemblies that become, in time, full-grown industrial companies are in their birth pains. What began as an idea, an assemblage of materials, is in time a kit. There will always be someone, who believes he has the right product for the right moment.

FIVE

Size and Scale

*A witty statesman said, you might prove
anything by figures.*
—THOMAS CARLYLE

SHIP MODELS ARE BUILT IN SIZES RANGING FROM microscopic to massive. You might need a magnifying lens to see one of them; you can go aboard another and sail it away. The replicas of the *Golden Hind* and *Mayflower II* are models. The determining factor of the size of the ship model is the scale. What scale to build to and how to select it is the subject of this chapter.

The *scale* is simply the ratio, expressed in comparative measurements, of one size to another. Measurements must be made in the same units. You cannot measure feet against meters. You must convert one of the measurements to the other.

To give you an example, let us expand on the most popular scale used by modelers, railroad modelers being the noted exception. Let us use the scale of 1/4 inch = 1 foot. What does that mean? It means that by actual and comparative measurement, 1 inch will equal 4 feet. Each foot of the subject being modeled can be represented on a drawing as 1/4 inch. How did we arrive at that figure?

There are 4 units to the inch if we divide 1 inch into quarters. Therefore, there would be 48 units (of 1/4 inch) in 1 foot (12 inches × 4 parts = 48). If we express this as a scale, we could then say that 1 unit is equal to 48 units. In this case, it is expressed as a ratio. We could simply say it is 1:48. If you wish, you can call it a fraction: 1/48. It means the same

thing. Reduce it to a decimal equivalent and it becomes .250. Ask a railroad modeler and he will say without hesitation *0 gauge*.

Our ship model built on a 1/4 inch to 1 foot scale will be 1/48 the size of the real-life ship. It is a *quarter-scale* model. The term is *scale*. Do not confuse it with *size*. The model is not 1/4 the size of the original, but 1/48 of that size.

That wasn't so hard. Care to try it again? This time let us use one-eighth scale. One inch divided by 8 equals eight parts to the inch. Multiply by 12 inches and you get 96, the number of units in 1 foot. That gives us a ratio of 1:96. Divide 12 by 96 and we have the decimal equivalent, .1250. That is one-eighth scale, except our railroad modeling friend would call it HO gauge. Not quite, though. There are minute fractions in calculation and/or interpretation to consider.

You don't have to be a mental giant to calculate scale. All you need are a sharp pencil, some paper, a grade-school education, and if necessary, that modern mathematical pacifier, a calculator. It becomes absurdly simple if you can understand a few basic ideas (TABLE 5-1).

It is obvious that *scale* means the ratio of one size to another. For the purposes of illustration, let's consider an object that we can easily identify with: a 6-foot man. Through the magic of mathematics, we

Table 5-1. Comparison Chart of Scales and Equivalents.

Fractional Inch	Decimal Equiv.	% of Size (Scale)	Inch to Foot Equiv.
1/16	.0625	1/192	1″ = 16′
3/32	.0936	1/128	1″ = 10.5′
1/8 (HO Gauge)	.1250	1/96	1″ = 8′
11/64	.1666	1/72	1″ = 6′
3/16 (S Gauge)	.1875	1/64	1″ = 5.2′
1/4 (O Gauge)	.250	1/48	1″ = 4.0′
19/64	.300	1/40	1″ = 3.3′
11/32	.343	1/35	1″ = 3.9′
3/8	.375	1/32	1″ = 2.6′
1/2	.500	1/24	1″ = 2.0′

are going to reduce him in size by using scale. Consider our gentleman at 1:32 scale. He is, for this exercise, 1/32 the size he began. We now have a replica of our six-footer at only 2 1/4 inches. Take him down another peg to the scale of 1:35 scale, and he has become a 2-inch model. At 1:40 scale, he is down to 1 3/4 inches. Using the ever-popular one-quarter scale, or 1:48, he shrinks further to 1 1/2 inches; .996 inch at 1:72 scale. Note that as the bottom number of the ratio gets larger, he gets smaller. Consider his size

as we approach 1:200. We better stop before we lose him altogether in the dust on the workbench (FIG. 5-1).

What did all the fractions mean? If we apply a little of the old-fashioned "times two" idea, it is easily explained. The popular scale, 1/4 inch = 1 foot, which we have established as also being equal to four feet of the size in the original object, is expressed in units. A unit of measurement is the same unit if we measure in parts of the same unit. Let's change inches, the foot unit of measurement, to meters.

Most of the kits that are manufactured in other countries are in the metric scale. The figure at the top of our fraction denotes one complete unit of measurement. Therefore the bottom number is an expression of the number of units it takes, in scale, to make one full-sized unit of measurement. In this case we can say 1 meter.

A word of caution: measurements in the metric system are in tenths. The designations are parts of a meter. As an example, millimeter means 1/1,000 meter. One centimeter, from the Latin *hundred*, gives us a 1/100 meter. Check to see what units you are using in the metric scales when changing from one scale to another. Most popular are the 1:50, 1:70, and 1:98 scales. The number on the bottom of the fraction refers to how many parts of a unit it takes to represent one unit of that particular system of units.

SCALE & SIZE COMPARED
EQUAL TO ONE FOOT

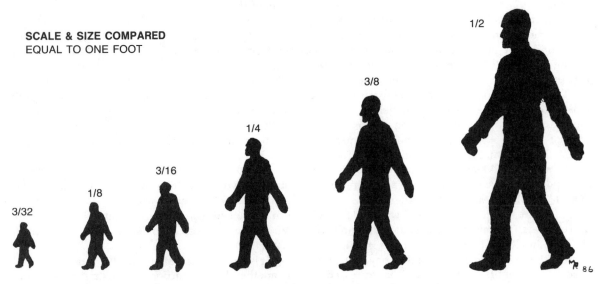

Fig. 5-1. Comparing scale and size as equal to 1-foot dimensions.

Should you find yourself uncomfortable in the metric measurements, you can convert to inches easily. Multiply the millimeters by .039370. To convert inches to millimeters, multiply by 25.4. To convert centimeters, move the decimals one place to the left (.39370 and 2.54). TABLE 5-2 will further simplify the process.

To give a better understanding of how the selection of scale can affect the outcome of your model, let's compare two ships in the same scale. One is a destroyer, a DD four-stacker class, and is 376 feet long in real life. The other is a schooner and is 136 feet long. The scale is 1:48, (1/4 inch to the foot or one-quarter). The model of the destroyer will be, when completed, 76 1/2 inches (6 feet 4 1/2 inches) long, while the schooner model will be 34 inches. If both are going to be rendered in the same scale, you need to consider where you are going to display or store the destroyer.

Following are a few examples of using scale, determining size, etc., that might influence your selection of the scale for building a ship model.

A friend of mine who now resides in Europe sent me a kit of a fishing boat that is quite popular in his region. No scale was indicated on the plan, box, or anywhere.

A little research about the boats of the area quickly established that they were usually 36 to 38 feet long. Measurements of the plans showed that the model would be 12 1/2 inches long and 3.875 inches wide (beam) when completed. Since there were, according to the text, some variances in the boats, I chose an optimum length of 36 feet 3 inches in length and 10 feet 10 inches in the beam. The length was converted to a fraction, reading 36.25. The length of the model was divided into the number: 12.5 ÷ 36.25 = .0344. If we divide 12 (inches to the foot) by .0344, we get a ratio of 1:35. That, as you can see by the table, is rather close to a known scale. I trust you don't mind a little variance at this point. Since 1:34 is so close to 1:35, I am going over to the tables to use it. Actual calculations indicate that the finished model will be 12.4999 inches. That's close enough for me.

The important consideration is the ratio of the sizes. By that I also mean the decimal equivalent. To find the decimal equivalent, divide 12 by the scale you wish to model. For 1:32, we are working in the

inch scale and, 12 ÷ 32 = .375. This is the three-eighth scale decimal equivalent. If you are really into the mathematics of scale, you can carry the decimal to hundredths, thousandths, whatever, parts of an inch, rather than using ratios and percentages.

To find the decimal equivalent, divide the scale by 12. As an example, 12 divided by 40 equals .300.

To find the scale size of the real-life prototype, divide the scale you are using into the life-sized version measured in feet. Then divide by 12 and you have an idea how large your model will be.

Reversing, to find the size of the life-sized prototype as measured from the model, multiply the size by the units of scale. For example, 34 inches × 48 = 1,632 inches. Then divide by 12 to change to feet. The answer is 136.

There are several ways to measure while you are building and after the scale has been established and a plan is at hand: direct measurement from the plan to the work with a pair of dividers or vernier calipers, or use of a measuring device with established graduations (a ruler).

There are also several ways to change the scales if you have all facts available and all plans at hand. Using an architect's scale, flat or triangular, take a measurement in the scale of the plan. Using the same measurement, repeat the dimensions in the scale of your choice.

Assuming a change from one-quarter scale to one-eighth (reducing by half), take a measurement in one-quarter, and set off the equivalent measurement in the one-eighth scale. To enlarge (double) the scale, you would reverse this procedure. You would use the same system with metric.

You also can use a set of proportional dividers to change scales. Proportional dividers are a pair of slotted, equal-length legs that have a groove cut out down their centers or holes drilled at the distances shown in FIG. 5-2. Be sure to drill the scale holes accurately. The ends of the nails are pointed for easy reading.

You can use the complicated mathematical explanations that accompany the set purchased at a good drafting supply or stationery store. I prefer the trial-and-error method in setting the ratio.

This method of changing scale, which I have termed *flip-flopping*, is quite handy in lifting and lofting, will be explained in Chapter 7.

Table 5-2. Conversion of Inches to Metric Equivalents (Courtesy of The Dromedary).

TO CONVERT TO MILLIMETERS: Multiply Inches × 25.4

TO CONVERT TO INCHES: Multiply Millimeters × .039370

INCHES FRACT.	INCHES DECIMALS	MM
	.00004	.001
	.00039	.01
	.00079	.02
	.001	.025
	.00118	.03
	.00157	.04
	.00197	.05
	.002	.051
	.00236	.06
	.00276	.07
	.003	.0762
	.00315	.08
	.00354	.09
	.00394	.1
	.004	.1016
	.005	.1270
	.006	.1524
	.007	.1778
	.00787	.2
	.008	.2032
	.009	.2286
	.00984	.25
	.01	.254
	.01181	.3
1/64	.01563	.3969
	.01575	.4
	.01969	.5
	.02	.508
	.02362	.6
	.025	.635
	.02756	.7
	.0295	.75
	.03	.762
1/32	.03125	.7938
	.0315	.8
	.03543	.9
	.03937	1
	.04	1.016
3/64	.04687	1.191
	.04724	1.2
	.05	1.27
	.05512	1.4
	.05906	1.5
	.06	1.524
1/16	.06250	1.5875
	.06299	1.6
	.06693	1.7
	.07	1.778
	.07087	1.8
	.075	1.905
5/64	.07813	1.9844
	.07874	2
	.08	2.032
	.08661	2.2
	.09	2.286
	.09055	2.3
3/32	.09375	2.3812
	.09843	2.5
	.1	2.54
	.10236	2.6
7/64	.10937	2.7781
	.11811	3
1/8	.1250	3.175

INCHES FRACT.	INCHES DECIMALS	MM
	.13780	3.5
9/64	.14063	3.5719
	.150	3.810
5/32	.15625	3.9688
	.15748	4
11/64	.17188	4.3656
	.1750	4.445
	.17717	4.5
3/16	.18750	4.7625
	.19685	5
	.20	5.08
13/64	.20313	5.1594
	.21654	5.5
7.32	.21875	5.5562
	.2250	5.715
15/64	.23438	5.9531
	.23622	6
1/4	.250	6.35
	.25591	6.5
17/64	.26563	6.7469
	.275	6.985
	.27559	7
9/32	.28125	7.1438
	.29528	7.5
19/64	.29688	7.5406
	.30	7.62
5/16	.3125	7.9375
	.31496	8
21/64	.32813	8.3344
	.33465	8.5
11/32	.34375	8.7312
	.350	8.89
	.35433	9
23/64	.35938	9.1281
	.37402	9.5
3/8	.375	9.525
25/64	.39063	9.9219
	.39370	10
	.400	10.16
13/32	.40625	10.3188
	.41339	10.5
27/64	.42188	10.7156
	.43307	11
7/16	.43750	11.1125
	.450	11.430
	.45276	11.5
29/64	.45313	11.5094
15/32	.46875	11.9062
	.47244	12
31/64	.48438	12.3031
	.49213	12.5
1/2	.50	12.7
	.51181	13
33/64	.51563	13.0969
17/32	.53125	13.4938
	.53150	13.5
35/64	.54688	13.8906
	.550	13.970
	.55118	14
9/16	.56250	14.2875
	.57087	14.5
37/64	.57813	14.6844
	.59055	15

INCHES FRACT.	INCHES DECIMALS	MM
19/32	.59375	15.0812
	.600	15.24
39/64	.60938	15.4781
	.61024	15.5
5/8	.6250	15.875
	.62992	16
41/64	.64063	16.2719
	.64961	16.5
	.650	16.51
21/32	.65625	16.6688
	.66929	17
43/64	.67188	17.0656
11/16	.68750	17.4625
	.68898	17.5
	.700	17.78
45/64	.70313	17.8594
	.70866	18
23/32	.71875	18.2562
	.72835	18.5
47/64	.73438	18.6531
	.74803	19
3/4	.750	19.050
49/64	.76563	19.4469
	.76772	19.5
25/32	.78125	19.8438
	.78740	20
51/64	.79688	20.2406
	.800	20.320
	.80709	20.5
13/16	.81250	20.6375
	.82677	21
53/64	.82813	21.0344
27/32	.84375	21.4312
	.84646	21.5
	.850	21.590
55/64	.85938	21.8281
	.86614	22
7/8	.875	22.225
	.88583	22.5
57/64	.89063	22.6219
	.900	22.860
	.90551	23
29/32	.90625	23.0188
59/64	.92188	23.4156
	.92520	23.5
15/16	.93750	23.8125
	.94488	24
	.950	24.130
61/64	.95313	24.2094
	.96457	24.5
31/32	.96875	24.6062
	.98425	25
63/64	.98438	25.0031
1	1.00000	25.4
	1.06299	27
	1.10240	28
	1.18110	30
1¼	1.250	31.75
	1.29921	33
	1.3780	35
	1.41732	36
1¼	1.500	38.1
	1.53543	39

INCHES FRACT.	INCHES DECIMALS	MM
	1.57480	40
	1.65354	42
1¾	1.750	44.45
	1.77170	45
	1.88976	48
	1.96850	50
2	2.000	50.8
	2.04724	52
	2.16540	55
	2.20472	56
2¼	2.250	57.15
	2.36220	60
2½	2.500	63.5
	2.51968	64
2¾	2.750	69.85
	2.83464	72
	2.95280	75
3	3.000	76.2
	3.14960	80
3½	3.500	88.9
	3.54330	90
	3.9370	100
4	4.000	101.6
	4.33070	110
4½	4.500	114.3
	4.72440	120
5	5.000	127
	5.51180	140
	5.90550	150
6	6.000	152.4
	6.29920	160
	7.08660	180
	7.8740	200
8	8.000	203.2
	8.66140	220
	9.44880	240
	9.84250	250
10	10.000	254
	10.23620	260
	11.02360	280
	11.8110	300
1 Foot	12.000	304.8
	12.59840	320
	13.38580	340
	13.77950	350
	14.17320	360
	14.96060	380
	15.7480	400
16	16.000	406.4
	17.71650	450
	19.6850	500
20	20.000	508
	23.6220	600
2 Feet	24.000	609.6
3 Feet	36.000	914.4
	39.370	1 Meter
4 Feet	48.000	1.219.2
5 Feet	60.000	1.524
6 Feet	72.000	1.828.8
	78.740	2 Meters
8 Feet	96.000	2.438.4
	118.110	3 Meters
	196.850	5 Meters

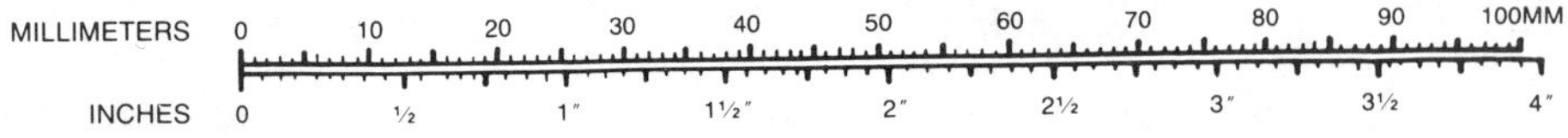
MILLIMETERS
0
10
20
30
40
50
60
70
80
90
100MM
INCHES
0
½
1″
1½″
2″
2½
3″
3½
4″

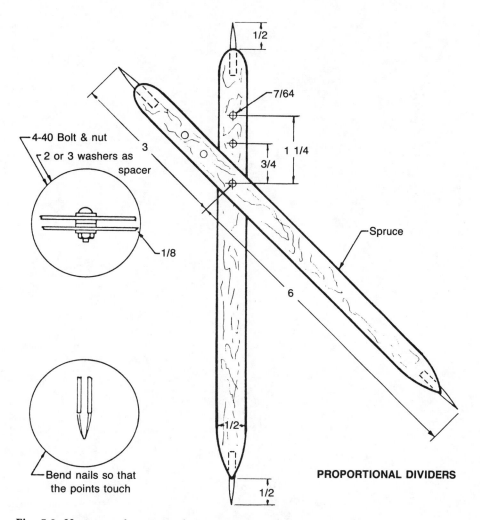

1/2

7/64

1 1/4

3/4

4-40 Bolt & nut
2 or 3 washers as
spacer

3

Spruce

1/8

6

Bend nails so that
the points touch

1/2

1/2

PROPORTIONAL DIVIDERS

Fig. 5-2. How to make a pair of proportional dividers (Courtesy of Northshore Deadeyes, Ltd.).

SIX

Ships in Bottles
and Other Containers

*If you are sure that you understand everything
that is going on, you are hopelessly confused.*
—WALTER MONDALE

SUPPOSE YOU ARE A SAILOR ABOARD A SHIP IN THE 1830s. You are off watch and it is a good sailing day, with fair winds and fair weather. You can't read or write. Since you have time on your hands and all you know is "your" ship, you use your hands. There is plenty of rope around and you know knots. So you fashion decorative items from rope—*macrame*.

A piece of tusk from a walrus or a bone from a whale can be made pretty if decorated by carving. It can be made into something useful before decorating, or even after. If you are so inclined or not too lazy, your creation could be decorated by simply scratching in a design. Rubbing black ink (lampblack and oil were also used) into the cuts to make it stand out and applying a coat of varnish would show it off better—scrimshaw.

Small pieces of wood, bits of twine, some cloth for sails, a sharp knife, and some whittling produced a ship model. What do you do to store and protect the delicate model you have built? Why not put it in an empty bottle (FIG. 6-1)?

When the product of those long hours at sea was viewed by merchants and innkeepers, they saw the commercial possibilities. A new craft was begun. Ships in bottles became items to be made and sold. The idea spread throughout the British and American merchant and naval fleets.

THE MYSTERY

Ships in bottles were not only unique because of the miniature model that was contained within, but even more because of the novelty of how it got in there. These novelties became highly prized. How did a ship model with all the masts and sails, five times the size of the neck of the bottle, get in there? Many suspect that the bottle was opened. Not true.

The mystery of how the ship got in the bottle is the important feature. Didn't you closely examine the (casting) line or check the bottom of the bottle on the first ship in a bottle you saw? These ships are built outside the bottle. Upon completion, the masts, which are built hinged, are folded down. Sales and yards, also hinged (as it were), are turned in line with the hull and the entire model is slipped down the neck and into the bottle. Surprised? So much for how it gets in there.*

How the ship is constructed on the outside and what steps must be taken to prepare the bottle to receive the model, are the subjects of this discussion. Although we will not be getting into the small de-

---

*Editor's Note: Another method of constructing ships, piece by piece, inside bottles is explained in *Bottling Ships and Houses*, by Ronald C. Roush (TAB #1975).

49

Fig. 6-1. A Catalan ship in a bottle by Kiyoshi Shima of Kyoto, Japan (Photo courtesy of *The Bottle Shipwright*).

tails of workmanship or the methods of construction, it is hoped that this presentation will pique your interest in another form of ship-model construction.

There are, without a doubt, names in this field with whom you could become familiar. I refer to the outstanding builders of ships in bottles and other see-through containers. You will recall their names if you have attended any model shows featuring ships in bottles or are a reader of ship-model publications. Some have written books on their methods. All are modelers like you. They were caught up in the intriguing and challenging idea, accepted the task, and excelled at it. This work is no different than the modeling you are doing now. Perhaps it is a little smaller or calls for a few new techniques, but it is ship modeling nonetheless. Try it, just once, and find out for yourself.

Where can you learn about building ships in bottles? Up until a few years ago, you would need to ask around. The sellers of ships in bottles could not help very much. Very often, they didn't know who the maker was. Many producers of ships in bottles were, I am sorry to state, commercial companies in far-off lands who mass-produced the items. Ships in bottles are hot novelty items.

Once in a while you could find an individual builder. A proud possessor of a product of such workmanship would be only too happy to supply the name of the individual from whom he secured his treasure. Modelers can be traced. From such modelers were you then able to learn. Once more, as it has been done over the years, one modeler told another.

If you were unable or unwilling to find such a person, you would either find a book about it or experiment. Your own mental powers often led you to the solution. The art of ships in a bottle had to begin somewhere. Think about that first sailor 150 years ago. Who showed him?

Were you tempted to try a ship in a bottle when you saw one? Maybe it was a kit advertised in one of the publications you read. Some advertisers offer all the parts and the bottle. Others limit their offering to just plans and instructions. Several imported manufacturers of kits furnish only the materials to make the model. The kits to build ships in bottles are also available at your local hobby stores and through mail order. Scratch-building from scaled-down plans seems the best method.

USING A LIGHT BULB

A new and fascinating, rather unusual method of building ships in containers other than bottles is now becoming popular. Building inside a light bulb is challenging (FIG. 6-2). Finding a clear, transparent bulb is not always easy, however, especially finding one that is the right size. Finding a huge bulb, which becomes a conversation piece, is easier.

The large globes are used in industrial plants. The ones that are easy to come by are burned-out bulbs used to illuminate the yard and plant areas. Ask the maintenance supervisor. You can purchase them brand new from lighting supply companies for about $8.00.

For your information, since it is difficult to judge the actual size of an object in a photograph, the measurement of the bulb in Fig. 6-2 is; 12 7/8 inches long and 6 3/8 inches in diameter. The neck, after removal of the screw end, measures 2 1/2 inches in diameter. When you note the size of the model and its tall masts enclosed within, it is apparent that this in itself causes the question "How did it get in there?" The viewer sees a round globe of crystal-clear glass. No line shows.

A special preparation is needed when working with this size globe, or any bulb for that matter. It is best to build a working stand first (FIG. 6-3). This is a simple wooden base with a shaped and tapered hole to steady one side of the bulb. You will also need a cradle to steady the neck, and a fastening device. A rubber band held in place by two protruding wood screws in the neck cradle does the job very well. Use felt or adhesive tape to pad the surfaces that come in contact with the bulb.

Now you are ready to open the bulb and remove the filament. The most important item to consider is the breaking of the vacuum. If the air is admitted too fast, it can shatter the glass of the fragile globe or bulb. Following are two of several methods that you can use. One modeler who reported this method breaks the seal at the end of the screw baseplate. This is the end where the bulb is sealed, and it contains the electrode at the center. Drill a hole in the center of the baseplate. Force a stiff piece of piano wire into the hole to break the glass on the inner side of the globe. The vacuum is released when you hear the hiss of inrushing air. It can occur at either of the two steps described.

Fig. 6-2. The schooner *Go For Broke* by Jack Hinkley of Coraopolis, Pennsylvania, fights rough seas inside a light bulb (Photo courtesy of *The Bottle Shipwright*).

Great care and patience is needed to remove the metal end and the filament. With experience and patience, you can literally twist the end off and not shatter the bulb. Note the replacement of the metal baseplate in FIG. 6-3. The bulb seems never to have been opened.

A method for removing the vacuum and the contents of the light bulb is also described by Peter Thorne in his book *Secrets of Ships in Bottles* (Model and Allied Publications, Ltd. 1975). He cuts the metal base diagonally with a small hacksaw and carefully removes it (FIG. 6-4). The exposed glass around the neck is protected by masking tape. He places the tape prior to making a cut to release the vacuum and remove the end. The air is admitted by cutting a slit slowly through the protective tape and puncturing the glass. After the vacuum is broken, he saws through the entire end of the bulb using turpentine or benzine as a lubricant. You also can saw through the neck of the globe using a Dremel Moto-Tool with a variable-speed motor and a No. 409 cutting wheel. It takes about 2 hours.

Save the metal screw end. You can, after the ship is in the bulb, join the separated neck. After it has been replaced, you can hide the seam under some fancy macrame. Mount the bulb in a cradle stand on its side. The macrame would be part of the decoration around the neck hiding the seam. The viewer's smart remarks won't be of any bother. Everybody knows that the bulb had to be opened anyway. The cut area is hidden in the mounting of the display base. It adds to the mystery.

Peter Thorne turns his model inside the bulb to an upright display position (FIG. 6-5). The manner of turning is described in his book.

PREPARATION

Since you already know that building ships in bottles is done outside the bottle first, the important thing is preparation. Most importantly, take a measurement to ensure you have room to work. You will need to make certain that whatever is built will go through the neck of the bottle. Simple measurement and a tracing of the outline of the globe or the inside dimensions of the bottle will assure you of success. Next you will want to make sure that the model, after it is placed in its full, erect position, will fit inside the bottle or container you have chosen. How is the

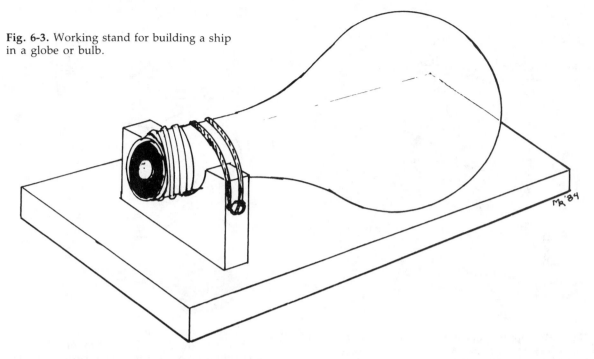

Fig. 6-3. Working stand for building a ship in a globe or bulb.

bottle prepared to receive the model and what about cleaning the inside? What special tools will be needed once the ship is in there?

Those questions that remain unanswered after you read the following text will need to be answered by trail and error. Ask those with more experience in this field.

In addition to the writings of Peter Thorne, the following are a few more selected readings:

✪ *Sailing in Glass*, by Joon Van Schouten. Published by Nautical Books, Macmillan, London, (1981).

✪ *How to Build Historical Bottled Ships*, by Bill Lucas. Published by Bill Lucas, P.O. Box 3623, Green Bay, Wisconsin 54303 (1982).

✪ *Ships in Bottles: A How-to Guide To A Venerable Nautical Craft*, by Don Hubbard. Copies can be secured from the Ships-In-Bottles Association of America.

✪ *Modelling Ships in Bottles*, by Jack Needham. Published by Sterling Publishing Co., Inc. Recently republished.

✪ *Buddelschiff Modellbau*, (German Text). Although now out of print, this could be considered the bible of ships in a bottle builders.

✪ *Ships in Bottles*, by Guy DeMarco. Published by Shiffer Publishing Ltd. (1985). The newest entry into assisting the bottle shipwright.

Several books are devoted to the subject of building ships in bottles. Their titles are not listed. The best source of information is the organization that is devoted to this form of art:

SHIPS-IN-BOTTLES ASSOC. OF AMERICA
P.O. Box 550
Coronado, CA 92118

If you have any questions concerning problems of building ships in bottles or other containers, the membership will be glad to assist you. Don Hubbard, editor of the publication of the organization, *The Bottle Shipwright*, will be most happy to assist you. Becoming a member of the group will more than repay you in time saved and questions answered. The membership fee is not beyond the reach of any modeler who is interested in this art form.

SPECIAL TOOLS

Special tools and instruments have been designed and used by builders of ships in bottles. They have, as you would suspect, become useful in other fields of ship modeling. A piece of doweling with a fitting on the end become a tool. A straightened wire coat hanger with a special twist or a stiff piece of wire of

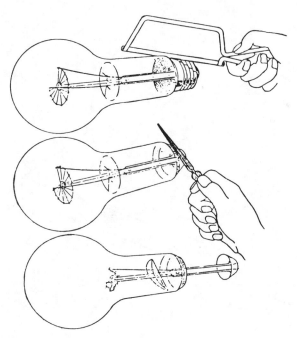

Fig. 6-4. Steps in removing the metal base from a light bulb (Courtesy of Model and Allied Publications, Argus Books).

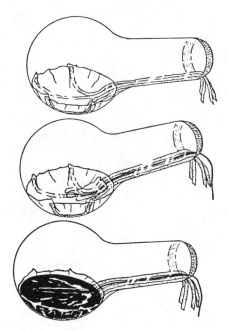

Fig. 6-6. Steps in preparing the base (sea) to receive the model inside a light globe. The tabs to turn the model to an upright position after installation extend through the neck (Courtesy of Model and Allied Publications, Argus Books).

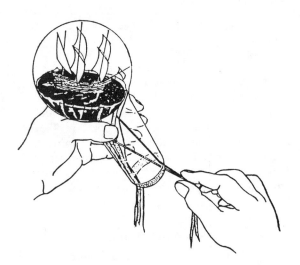

Fig. 6-5. Turning the installed ship model in a light globe using the method of Peter Thorne (Courtesy of Model and Allied Publications, Argus Books).

Fig. 6-7. Working stand used to hold the light globe while removing the turning mechanism and packing the neck (Courtesy of Model and Allied Publications, Argus Books).

54

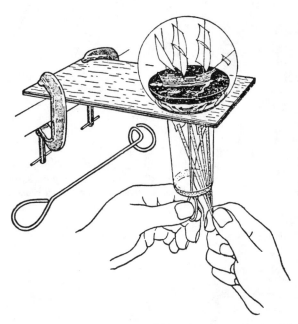

Fig. 6-8. Removing the turning mechanism with the aid of the holding device. The device is made from an old metal coat hanger (Courtesy of Model and Allied Publications, Argus Books).

thinner diameter is the answer to many a problem. Innovation and invention created most of them. The need was the stimulus.

A broken razor blade fitted in the slit of a dowel is the final cutting blade when all the masts are pulled upright and secured in place inside the bottle. A large darning needle, which has been forced point first into a dowel and been altered somewhat, is a fine controllable rigging tool.

You can make your own rigging tools. There is no need to buy a set if you are handy. Simply heat the eye end of a needle red hot and cut the opening with a pair of small wire-cutting pliers. Reheat the area to be worked and shape while hot into any of the hooks, prongs, or twists that you require. Allow it to cool. Force the pointed end into a piece of dowel. You have created a tool.

You can, of course, design and prepare something on an even grander scale. The idea, based on the leverages of tree-pruning tools, can be adapted in miniature. You can use clamps outside the bottle, but how do you pick up or hold something inside the bottle? Most tweezers are not long enough. So invent and create your own.

Surplus medical instruments, some built with long, deep-reaching stems, are excellent. Tonsil snares, obstetrical forceps—all sorts of instruments to reach down and into the body do eventually wear out and are retired from service in time. Look around.

TURNING A MODEL INSIDE A BOTTLE

Ship models are not the only items you can build inside bottles and other containers. I am sure you have seen those miniature scenes and dioramas on display.

The item that took first prize at a local miniature model show was a garden scene, complete with little people walking on the paths. The whole colorful display was inside a five-gallon water bottle. What was so bewildering about the construction was the fact that the bottle was mounted with the neck down. The garden scene filled the upper four-fifths of the space. There were even little birds in the air above the trees. How did they do that?

The answer is simple—simple, that is, when you understand the principle. For the answer let's take a look at the way Peter Thorne turns his ship in a light bulb.

After preparing the bulb, Thorne places a layer of cellophane or plastic in the bulb. The piece is square. Firmly affixed to the corners are lengths of strong cloth or plastic strips of tape. He fits the piece of cellophane on one side of the bulb (FIG. 6-6). Then he fits a piece of wire with a loop formed in the end to the curve of the bulb and lays it down the length of the side of the bulb to the center of the depression, loop side centered. He then carefully places material—colored putty, plasticine, or a pool of tinted glue mixed with a sea-colored filler (Plasticwood)—on top of the plastic. He allows it to cure while he builds the ship (or diorama) outside the bottle.

Thorne places the model in the "sea" of the bulb. Everything, up till now, rested in a side of the bulb, which was secured in a working stand (FIG. 6-7). This is the same stand that was used to build the ship model inside the bulb for a sideways display. Since the area in which the ship model will be placed is round, turning the completed model will present no problem. The diameter is the same. Do not use oblong-shaped bulbs if you plan to turn your model.

You also must make other preparations, including a new stand. A simple piece of plywood with a beveled hole to accommodate the bulb will do (FIG.

Fig. 6-9. An unusual bottle contains the unusual subject, the *Great Harry*. The model contained in a decanter, was made by Kouhei Onoda of Takatsuki, Japan (Photo courtesy of *The Bottle Shipwright*).

6-7). Pad the bevel to avoid scratching or damaging the surface of the globe. Pictures say it better than words.

Turn the model by pulling on the tapes on one side of the enclosed plastic sheet. After the turning comes the filling.

Make a loop-ended holding device to hold the putty sea while drawing away the cellophane sheet. (FIG. 6-8). It is like holding your finger against the clay while peeling off the cover with the four corner tapes. The wire inserted with the sheet remains in place for the filling. Draw out the sheet while using counterpressure with the tool. The wire will now allow you to hold down the sea against the push of adding more material to fill the bottom segment and neck of the bulb. The working stand allows you to use both hands. Believe me, you are going to need them.

When you have completed this phase of the work, you are almost home free. A display stand is next. You can, if you have a wood lathe, make one quite nicely. If you don't have a lathe or cannot find someone to make the round version, then you can use built-up layers of suitable material to make a square base with a hole to accommodate the neck.

UNUSUAL BOTTLES

There are limitless possibilities to make ships models in bulbs, bottles, and other containers. Have you ever thought about using Pyrex laboratory flasks in various sizes? There are many shapes that I can remember from my high-school days.

One individual haunts antique shops and flea markets for his containers. He finds some unusual shapes in which to build ship models. Another has them custom-made at a glass blower's shop in a nearby city. The ultimate example in his collection is a model contained in a perfectly round globe. The only opening was a long, curved neck. The confession, wrung from the modeler under pain of death, was that the neck was straight when he placed the model inside. The long neck was curved by the glass blower after the model was installed.

Bottles come in many sizes and shapes. Square ones are rare. Many modelers of ships in bottles have been able to find odd-shaped bottles (FIG. 6-9). Bottles also come in shades of see-through colors. White sails of a model within a light blue or tinted bottle gives the appearance of a ship sailing in a fog or at twilight. For a dramatic effect, display it with the light source from behind. The triangle-pinched bottle is an unusual version. This pinch bottle is commonly associated with a popular brand of Scotch whiskey. Great conversation pieces can result from odd-shaped containers.

The trick is to find something that can be seen through and has a narrow opening. The smaller the opening, the better, the challenge for the builder and the bewilderment to the viewer. Always find a bottle with a neck that will allow you to admit a hull in the scale you can work in. The neck should be a shade larger than the hull of the model. This alone will be a test for your building skills.

You will need to adjust the scale to fit the bottle. Always, as in any ship-modeling project, keep the model in scale. An added feature is to make a specific ship as your model and so name it. You can place the label inside the glass, for example near the area where the neck joins the body of the bottle, or on the display stand.

SEVEN

Planning and Plans

*In view of the huge quantity of plan material
available it does not seem to me that there
is little excuse other than obstinacy for
reconstructed models.*
—HOWARD I. CHAPELLE

THE CONCEPT OF THE SHAPE OF A SHIP'S HULL BE-
gan in the mind of man when he realized that the
log he was floating on moved more rapidly through
the water if it was pointed on one end. The concept
became a reality when he began to build boats, rather
than carve hulls from a solid log. A pattern for the
basic shape was established by trial and error over
thousands of years.

The boat builder of old directed the shape and
building of the hull. Hulls grew in size as knowledge
accumulated and techniques improved. No longer
was building a one-man job. In order to convey his
ideas, the builder had to have some method of communication with his workers.

A crude drawing in the sand to explain what was
intended gave way to drawings on paper. The drawings in turn were then transferred to the wood. This
was the pattern. Wood was then cut into the shapes,
forming the parts that became the ship. There were
hundreds of parts—thousands for the larger ships.
Since the parts were too big to draw on paper in their
full size, scale renditions were used. Ideas of ship
construction were created by the (boat builder) shipwright. The ideas took the form of a drawing. A scale
model was sometimes built to indicate line, shape of
frames, construction details, or the entire concept of
the vessel. Models and drawings were used in the
construction of naval ships after the fifteenth century.

Actual-sized layout of the ship's timbers was
done in a loft. The shapes and parts were "lifted"
from the plan and "lofted out" full size in chalk on
the floor of the huge building. Hence the term *lifting
and lofting*. Templates were made from the chalk
drawings and transferred in outline to the wood (FIG.
7-1). The cutting and shaping could then proceed.

Thus it was that the boat builder, who in the
course of time became the master shipwright, evolved
to the position of *naval architect*.

There has been some confusion concerning the
title. A person engaged in naval architecture designs
ships, boats, and watercraft. Naval architects do not
work for the Navy exclusively. A *marine architect* on
the other hand, is involved with structures. A *marine engineer* is involved with the power sources that
drive the ships, boats, and watercraft, which were
designed with or by the naval architect. It is not an
unusual practice for any or all three to work together.

Hundreds, even thousands, of plans and drawings are needed to construct a real ship. Today, these
plans are drawn for the shipyard worker (FIG. 7-2).
Much of the drawings concern parts and details of
items that need not concern a modeler, who must cull
plans for the simple information needed to build only
the model. Looking over the plans is not at all unlike shifting through the sand looking for a gold
nugget.

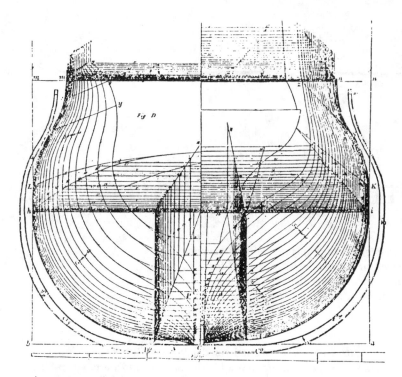

Fig. 7-1. The lines of a ship as drawn for the lofting rooms. The cant frames of the bow are not indicated by the draftsman (Courtesy of the National Maritime Museum, Washington, DC).

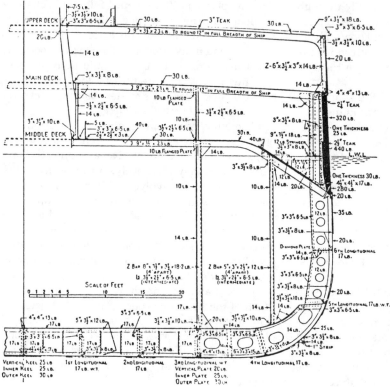

Fig. 7-2. This drawing of the structure of H.M.S. *Dreadnaught*, 1906, shows only one frame station of the ship, indicating part numbers and locations (Courtesy of the National Maritime Museum, Washington, DC).

Some of the plans and drafts secured from museums are incomplete. Perhaps sheets have been lost, destroyed, or never existed in the first place. Don't expect them to be as complete as the set you got from the Navy, a steamship company, or a private shipyard. Museum plans are historical research material.

Ship's lines, external structures, profiles etc. are helpful items of research in producing a model of accurate line and scale. The shape of the hull (ship) is important. The lines drawn on plans will give the shape. There might be only a tracing as an indication of construction. You can, and should, make good use of the information. There is, however, no need to build the model exactly as the real ship.

Although a knowledge of drafting instruments and principles is helpful, it is not mandatory. The ability to read a scale, use a ruler and a pair of dividers, and convert scales is about all that is necessary. With even a limited approach such as this you could build a model from just a set of lines and a photograph, sketch, painting, or description. Many have.

PLAN VIEWS

Ship's plans, or *drafts*, are renditions of three-dimensional objects on a flat plane. Over the years, more by tradition than dictation, a language has

Fig. 7-3. Lines and their designations as used on plans to build a vessel (Drawing by A. Richard Mansir, courtesy of Moon-raker Publications).

evolved. It is not difficult to understand. Each of the views has a specific name. The lines are identified by the same letters or numbers in all views. There is an order to the presentation of the sections (FIG. 7-3). Since the ship is the same on either side of the centerline, sometimes only half of a view is shown.

For purposes of illustration let us assume that the hull is a solid object. It is sliced in both vertical and horizontal planes, as indicated in FIG. 7-4. Each slice is identified by a letter or number. Each view is shown in a logical order. By referring to the same number in each view, you can determine the shape of the hull. This is the ship's draft in its simplest form. If you understand this presentation, you can read a plan.

Quite understandably, the side view is called the *profile*. It is also referred to as the *sheer plan* (FIG. 7-3). The *sheer* is the curve of the ship in a front-to-rear context. In other words, it is the slope of the deck. Most, if not all, ships and boats are higher at the bow and stern than they are in the middle (amidships). This is the side curve of the vessel. Vertical slices, which run parallel to the keel, are referred to as *buttock lines*.

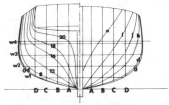

Body Sections in the Body Plan.

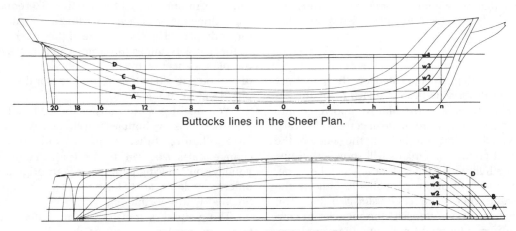

Buttocks lines in the Sheer Plan.

Waterlines in the Half Breadth Plan.

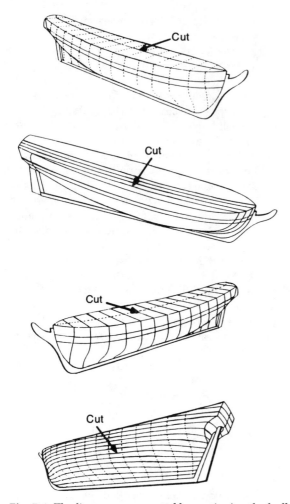

Fig. 7-4. The lines as represented by sectioning the hull as a three-dimensional unit. From the top: centerline, buttocks, body sections, waterlines (Original drawing by E.W. Peterjus).

The lines that are indicated on the plans are termed *waterlines,* as indicated in FIG. 7-3 by the letter W. It would be as if the hull were lowered into the water and stops were made at certain intervals. A line would be drawn to indicate the shape of the hull at that point. Some plans will show either just half of the hull with the lines, or a general outline.

The other half of the plan should indicate the deck layout. This is the *half-breadth plan* (FIG. 7-3). Plans that are drawn to assist the modeler in constructing from a kit might not show the waterlines.

Information might consist of a view of the deck and its layout only.

The most confusing view is the end view, known as the *body plan.* The indication of the slices across the hull at right angles to the keel are called *station lines.* These lines often seem like a jumble. They show the shape of the hull in cross section. Remembering that the ship is the same on both sides of the centerline, the draftsman only indicates one-half of the lines across, ending at the centerline (FIG. 7-3).

The thing to remember is which direction you are facing when you are viewing the lines of the body plan. Let us assume that you are standing inside the ship at the center frame. You are standing amidships and facing the bow. The lines you see drawn on the left-hand side of the centerline are the station (section) lines toward, and ending with, the bow. These lines (FIG. 7-3) are indicated by alphabetical designations. If you turn around and face the stern, the lines represent the cross-station lines toward the stern. These lines are indicated by numerical designations (FIG. 7-3). They appear on the right-hand side of the centerline in the drawing.

TRANSFERRING PLANS

Some body plans will have a grid (squares) drawn over them. This might be the only view that has this feature. Obviously the grid is there for a reason. There is a method for enlarging and reducing scales through the use of a grid and in plotting the curve of a frame. Details are shown in FIG. 7-4. To enlarge the scale with this method, draw the same curve of line shown in one square in a proportionally larger square. Continue for all the squares. To reduce the scale, draw the lines in squares that are smaller than the body plan. The relative size of the squares is the factor that determines the scale. You can place over the plan a sheet of tracing paper with the squares drawn on it to aid in transferring lines if the original plan lacks such a feature.

You might wish to transfer the section lines to the wood as is, without a scale change. You are lifting and lofting. If there is no grid and you wish to change scales, you can draw a grid. I suggest that you lay some tracing paper over your original plan, unless you don't care to keep the plan when you are finished with your model.

The method of transferring the outlines of the frames from plan to wood is described in several

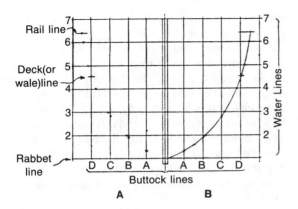

Fig. 7-5. Laying out a frame by the graph method. A good set of dividers or proportional dividers will be mandatory (Original drawing by Harold Underhill).

texts. If you choose to use the plank-on-frame method of building, see *The Colonial Schooner 1763-1775* by Harold Hahn (Naval Institute Press, Annapolis, MD), and *Plank on Frame Models, Volume I*, by Harold A. Underhill (Brown, Son & Ferguson, Ltd. Glasgow).

Other volumes of published works for ship modelers discuss the methods of transferring lines from plans to material. The methods are varied—some simple and many complicated. You will find these chapters in most books concerning the construction of built-up ship models. Each author has developed what he believes to be the perfect style. Try several before you decide on your own style.

Once again, not all kit plans show body lines. Instead, a fairly good kit might indicate full cross sections or bulkheads. They are drawn full-sized. Plans can be purchased separately from the kit. As a rule, the less expensive kits do not contain extensive drawings with bulkhead outlines. Plastic ship-model kits are, for the most part, devoid of plans with hull lines.

Trace the outlines full-sized to the wood. You can trace the outline free hand or with a French curve or ship's curve. You will do your work by reproducing the lines directly on the wood, plywood, or tracing paper. A little carbon paper helps.

There are plans available that were not specifically drawn with the modeler in mind. They are used for information or as illustrations to texts, articles, or books. These plans can be, and often are, used by modelers. I have seen models made with nothing more for a reference than a photocopy of the page of a book.

While we are on the subject, be careful when using photocopiers. For example, when you make copies of the plan, use the section lines as a template. This method, which saves time and drawing, is becoming quite popular. The modeler reproduces as many copies as there are section lines, waterlines, etc. He cuts each copy to the line of the part of the plan that is needed to make a template. Gluing to a stiffer paper or poster board makes a fine template to check carving, construction, or lines of the hull. Grids, as previously described, can be run off on a copy machine. This is a great time-saver when lifting and lofting frame patterns.

The danger is within the copy machine. The copy is usually slightly reduced in size by the photocopying process. Ask someone who knows if the copy machine that you intend to use changes the size of the object copied. You are not building your model according to the plan if there is a change in size.

If you wish to stick to the scale and still use the method just discussed, then take your plan to a blueprint reproduction shop. Having blueprints made, although in some cases a little costly, will ensure you get a faithful reproduction. Computer-operated cameras in some of the advanced shops can enlarge or reduce the plans and photographs any percentage, scale, or size desired. Should you care to have your plan either increased or decreased in scale, they can usually handle the job for you. If there is no such shop in your community, then you should take a course in drafting if you demand accuracy.

DETERMINING THE HULL'S SHAPE

With a basic understanding of the lines of a plan you can build a ship model even though the lines are not complete. You can construct the shape of the hull using a few section lines, a profile view, and determination. You can enlarge the scale to your needs using any of several methods discussed so far.

The techniques of ship-model construction are varied. The need of a good plan is a matter of the modeler's choice, skills, and experience. For example, in plank-on-frame construction, the plan will not indicate each frame, its outline, or its location. However, you can use the *room-and-space rule*.

Simply stated, the space between each frame is usually equal to the thickness of the frame. In shipwright's talk, this would be called the *sided dimension*. The surfaces of a ship's frame are shown in FIG. 7-6.

The rule is different for merchant ships than for men-of-war. Navy ships of the period of wooden walls were made with double-thick frames. The space between was still kept to one thickness as a rule, not made the double thickness. On the other hand, merchant ships didn't need all that protection against enemy cannon balls or the forces created by firing cannon on board. The room-and-space rule was applied: one space for each thickness of the frame. Some ships were designed with 1-1/2 spaces for each frame thickness. It was cheaper to build and strong enough to sail.

If you are planning to build a plank-on-frame model, you need to determine the frame thickness and spacing. Measure the sided dimension, divide it in half to get the centerline, and then apply the room-and-space rule.

FINDING PLANS

If you wish to build a ship model from a plan and do not want to draw the plan completely, or do the research, you can buy a plan. As would be expected, plans can be found for many ships of the past, present, or future. Some are excellent, while others aren't worth the paper they are printed on.

Finding the plan of the ship you wish to build might not be as easy as you think. Plans, like anything else that is published for sale, go out of print. Reprinting depends on popularity. Some, like the more popular vessels of the modeling world, are plentiful. Should your choice be of a ship that either has never been presented in a plan, has gone out of print, or has never existed, you will need to do some looking.

Strange to say, some ship plans that are in demand are for ships that never existed. Also strange is that many models of them have been built by people who swear that they actually existed. Several kits of such fictitious vessels have been produced. The plans would, therefore, also be fictitious. Horatio Hornblower was a popular fictional character and he sailed on ships that never were. A ship model of a ship from his career would be known to be a phony.

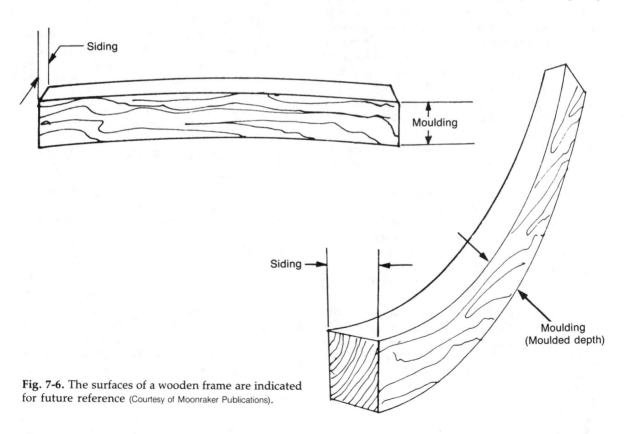

Fig. 7-6. The surfaces of a wooden frame are indicated for future reference (Courtesy of Moonraker Publications).

64

Therefore, it is a good idea to make sure that the ship you are researching to build is not a product of someone's vivid imagination.

Often, as is the case in families, there is a spinner of tales with a memory that nobody would challenge. He will tell of a ship that he, a distant relative, or some local person of importance sailed or served on. It is a name that has been around a long time in your memory. Now, at last you have decided to build her. There is no plan, no record. It happens often. Fake it.

Commercial Sources

When you are looking for a plan, start with commercial sources. They carry a variety of plans of all periods. Several specialize, offering plans of a certain type or class of ship. The older the vessel, the more difficult it is to establish the plan's authenticity. The details of the ship might have been lost or never existed. Modelers have reconstructed ships both as scaled and full-sized models without having full knowledge of the ships. In this case, they should be considered representations, or reconstructions. The controversy over authenticity rages constantly among the experts. As examples, I offer the *Golden Hind* and *Mayflower.*

In addition to the following sources of plans, please add maritime museums, military sources— both navy and army—and national archives in your research. Your local librarian will be of great assistance in securing the addresses of such institutions in other lands.

MODEL & ALLIED PUBLICATIONS.
(Plans Handbook Model Boats & Engineering)
ARGUS SPECIALIST PUBLICATIONS LTD.
P.O. Box 35, Wolsey House
Wolsey Rd. Hemel Hempstead
Hertfordshire HP2 4SS England

STAUBLITZ OF BUFFALO
Dept. C, 105 Hollybrook Dr.
Williamsville, NY 14221

Riverboat ROBERT E. LEE
LOSANTIVILLE BOAT WORKS
P.O. Box 32116
Cincinnati, OH 45232

THE DROMEDARY—SHIP MODELER'S
    CENTER
6324 Belton
El Paso, TX 79912

A.J. FISHER, INC.
1002 Etowah St.
Royal Oak, MI 48067

TAUBMAN PLANS SERVICE
11 College Dr.
Jersey City, NJ 07305

REPLA-TECH INTERNATIONAL
48500 McKenzie Hwy.
Vida, OR 97488

U.S. Fleet Submarine Plans
WORLD WIDE VIDEO PRODUCTIONS
7888 Ostrow St.
San Diego, CA 92111

FLOATING DRYDOCK
General Delivery
Kresgeville, PA 18333

MILITARY RECORDS DIVISION
Natl. Archives & Records Service
Washington, DC 20408

COMMANDANT, U.S. COAST GUARD
(ENE-5)
Washington, DC 20591

NAVY PUBS. & PRINTING SERVICE
Building 157-3
Washington Navy Yard
Washington, DC 20390

DOCUMENTATION & DRAWING SERVICES
Canadian Forces Headquarters
Department of National Defense
Ottawa, Ontario KIA OK2
Canada

THE SMITHSONIAN INSTITUTION
Department of Transportation
Division of Naval History
Room 5010 HTB
Washington, DC 20560

NATIONAL MARITIME MUSEUM
Greenwich SEIO
London, England

Periodicals

Sources of plans that are often overlooked are the periodicals. Every profession, group, or organization with interested people sharing a like interest has publications. Sailing magazines, boat-builders' annuals, and ship modeling magazines are available for those who are interested. Perhaps the plan you are looking for has been printed on their pages.

Articles about specific ships, the models produced, or the plans used might offer the stimulus to build. Currently there are a few periodicals devoted to ship models and the making of ship models. For a listing of these sources, see Chapter 10. They are listed with my critical comments.

Some periodicals are quite scholarly, while others are more dedicated to specializations of various aspects of ship modeling, from beginner to advanced. Secure a sample copy of each periodical. You can then select what best suits you and stick with it.

Organizations

People of a like persuasion congregate together and form organizations to perpetuate their interests. Ship modelers are no different. Many clubs produce their own periodicals. Some are quite good and contain valuable information. Others are devoted to meeting notes and events. Their printed offerings can, and often do, contain plans or sources of plans. Several organizations have plans libraries. It might be in your best interests to seek out the club in your vicinity. Ship modeling periodicals often have the addresses of such clubs or organizations.

If no organization exists nearby, form one. There are ship modelers everywhere who love to get together and exchange ideas. A notice posted in a local hobby shop could call your first meeting. Community centers are most cooperative in forming ship-model clubs.

If you can't find or start a group in your vicinity, you should still join a ship-model club as an associate, nonresident, or similar member classification. You can secure information by mail. A lot can be accomplished in the simple act of belonging. You can exchange plans with the members. If they don't have them, they can help you find them.

Kit Manufacturers

You wish to build a model of the same type as manufactured by a company, except you want to do

it by scratch. Somebody gave or asked you to do a kit, but the plans have been lost, completely or in segments. Plans of the models produced by American and European kit manufacturers are also available. They can be purchased individually. Their low prices might surprise you.

Be prepared for what you will receive. In some plans, there is little detail of ship's lines. On the other hand, the plans might be complete, showing not only the lines of the hull but also construction details of the deck, masts, etc. It all depends on the quality of the original kit (FIG. 7-7).

Not all manufacturers sell the plans separately. Instructions that accompany the kit are also available; however, don't expect those that do not sell the plans separately to sell the instructions.

A word of caution in requesting plans from the European makers of wooden ship-model kits: they are often slow in replying. Should you care to write them their addresses are listed in Chapter 4. After a reasonable length of time without response, try contacting the national distributor of their kits. Ship-model periodicals or local hobby shops will assist you in finding out who imports the products into this country and who sells the kits or plans you want to buy.

PLANS DRAFTSMEN

Who draws the plans that ship modelers use? I assure you, it is not always the modeler. Here are some names that soon will become familiar: Harold A. Underhill, Lambert Lavis, and David MacGregor, of England; Vincenzo Lusci and Franco Gay from Italy; George Parker of the United States; and the most beloved and highly regarded researcher of the Smithsonian, the late Howard I. Chapelle.

Chapelle's drawings of sailing ships are standard reference. You can purchase his plans individually and in full size from the Smithsonian catalog. Write:

SMITHSONIAN INSTITUTION PRESS
955 L'Enfant Plaza, Suite 2100
Washington, DC 20560

You should record the plans and lists of plans that are available, the sources of such plans, as well as information concerning them. The reference list that follows will assist you greatly in your selection of the plans of the ships you will build.

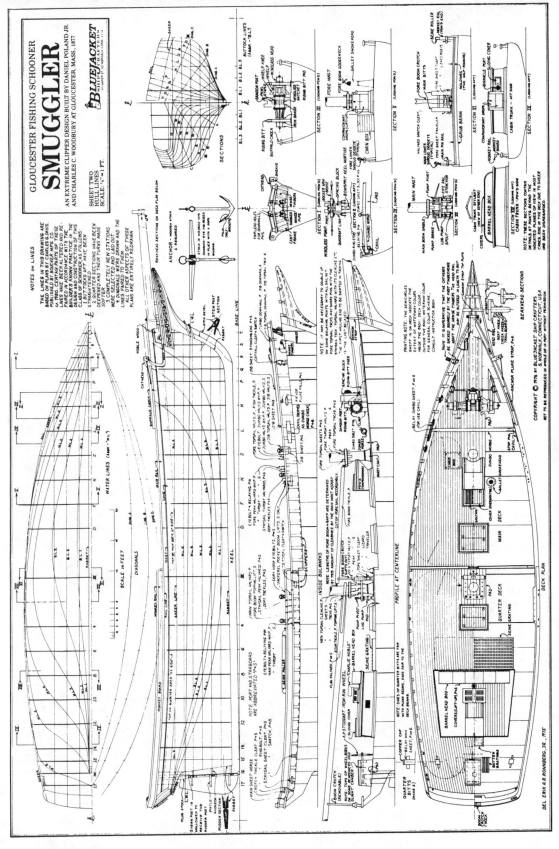

Fig. 7-7. Plans of the Gloucester fishing schooner *Smuggler*, with construction notes, drawn for a kit by Erik A. Ronnberg, Jr. and manufactured by Bluejacket Shipcrafters (Copyright © and courtesy of Bluejacket Shipcrafters, Inc., Castine, ME).

Plans

WALTER E. CHANNING. Barks, brigs, schooners, and whaleboats, details of masts and yards, belaying points, etc. 13 plans, including the famous *Charles W. Morgan.* Authoritative and complete. Covers 1841 to 1910.

WILLIAM CROTHERS. American clippers, steam frigates, destroyer *Farragut* (1937), submarines (1914-1937). Detailed and complete plans, including the history of the ships. Covers period 1814 to 1937.

DR. FRANCO GAY (Italian Language). A portfolio of 28 plans of ships from the fifteenth century to the modern sail training ship *Amerigo Vespucci.* Collection includes American ship *Essex, Cairo,* Civil War Ironclad. Includes a group of Italian warships, patrol vessels, and submarines. Excellent renditions.

FRANK A. LESS'ARD. 17 offerings of American ships, including clippers, Chesapeake Bay and American East Coast types, *Tiki, Coeur de Lion, Sunny South,* and two whalers.

MUSSES DE LA MARINE (French Language). Museum-accurate plans drawn for the modeler. Contains a portfolio of plans drawn from museum models and information from sixteenth century to 1948. 42 offerings of French and world-famous ships. Photographs of the actual models made from the plans, along with a history of the vessel are included.

HAROLD A. UNDERHILL, noted author and authority. Prolific offering of ships, both sail and modern from Elizabethan era to post-World War II. Wood ships, composite hulls, steel-hulled clippers, coastal vessels, the *Queen Mary,* and QE I & II. Plank-on-frame construction indicated. Many are found in his offerings of textbooks concerning classes and types of ships.

DR. ALVARO MATTEUCCI (Italian Language). 40 offerings of ships: sailing, steam, oil, and fishing vessels, mostly of Italian origin. Some American ships. All plans made for plank-on-bulkhead (plywood) construction (FIG. 7-8). Full-sized templates.

DAVID MACGREGOR. Noted English author and draftsman who specialized in the clipper and merchant ships of the world. Barks, multimasted schooners, steel hulls, etc. Offers plans of Basil Lavis, the famous H.M.S. *Victory* of 1805, Lambert, Ogh, and others of his nation.

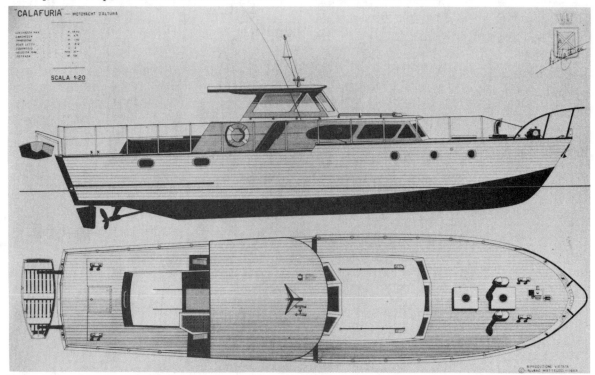

Fig. 7-8. The pleasure craft *Calafuria* of Italy as indicated in the plans by Alvaro Matteucci. The construction sheets contain lofted (plywood) bulkhead templates and building instructions in Italian (Courtesy of A-Model Plans, Italy).

R.K. MCCANDLISS. American destroyers, tugs, submarines, and cargo vessels of here and abroad. 24 plans offered in popular scales.

VINCENZO LUSCI (Italian Language). A wide variety of plans as would be drawn for use in kits. Ample details and illustrations. Full-sized templates for plank-on-bulkhead construction. Covers all periods from prehistoric to late sailing ships.

EDWARD H. WISWESSER. Prolific offerings of warships of all nations taken from pre-Civil War to modern ballistics missile ships drawn in outline scale. Some complete with good lines and details. Surprisingly inexpensive.

ALBERT ROSS. PT boats, classes and types are his offering. The commercial outlets will gladly acquaint you with the offers of the draftsmen referred to here. Most offer illustrated catalogs.

Imported Plans

Plans by the makers mentioned are imported from other countries to the local markets through the sources just listed. Some of the names you might wish to investigate follow:

CHRISTIAN NIELSEN. Denmark. Noted for his drawings of wooden boats of the Scandinavian countries.

VIC SMEED. England. Offers several plans, in addition to his famous sailing yachts and those selected from his books.

THE BORRAS EDICIONES PORTFOLIO. Spain. Includes a wide variety of ships, from sail to modern fishing and pleasure boats, warships of the Spanish Navy, as well as the ships of other nations.

ANKER PLANS, from Denmark, BRIESINGER of Germany, and others too numerous to list are available.

Plank-on-Frame Plans

Plans for plank-on-frame construction of models with full-sized templates of the frames to be constructed are offered by the draftsmen and model ship plan designers of America and the world:

ROBIN REILY. The renditions offered are a limited selection. They include H.M.S. *Triumph* (74 gun), *Prince De Neufchatel* (Baltimore clipper), *Elsie* (an American fishing schooner), and *Lucy M.* (a Chesapeake Bay Skipjack).

PORTIA TAKAKJIAN. American frigate *Essex*, Hudson River Sloop, *Victorine*, fifteenth century *Caravell*, and the American Revolutionary War ship, *Sultana*. This list continues to grow. FIGURE 7-9 will give you an indication of a plan with the frames completely lifted and lofted.

CLYDE M. LEAVITT. American brig *Lexington*, to accompany book, *Built Up Ship Model* by Davis (Conway Maritime Press, London). A 74-gun ship of the line is also offered.

HAROLD HAHN. Author and renowned builder offers the plans from his collection, including full-sized templates. Size and shapes of the frame blanks, as illustrated in FIG. 7-10, are also included. The plans are sold separately by the author. They were featured in his book, *Colonial Schooner 1763 to 1775*. Others in the offering are: the privateer *Oliver Cromwell*, H.M.S. *Bounty, Hannah*, the American schooner *Halifax, Hancock, Confederacy*, and H.M.S. *Druid*, a 16-gun sloop of war of 1776.

Historical American Merchant Marine Survey

During the Great Depression, the Works Progress Administration was creating work for the nation. After a struggle over the objections of Congress, the Historical American Merchant Marine Survey was born. Officially it was the Works Progress Administration, Federal Project No. 6. Work began in 1936.

Draftsmen and workers in the field of ship construction were hired to document, through accurate plans of lines taken from the actual vessels, the vanishing ships of America. Through their efforts, many ships have been preserved. They have been collected under the direction of the Smithsonian Institution into seven large 23-×-18-inch volumes, and include 1,009 scale drawings and foldouts (37-×-18-inches) of 360 ships. The set costs $3,000. Area volumes—the United States was divided into seven coastal and Great Lakes regions—are sold separately.

You can buy the plans individually in costs from $15.00 to $100.00, depending on the ship and the number of sheets. (See FIG. 7-11.) The plans are printed on heavy vellum, and are full sized. They are suitable for framing.

Write to the publisher for a free list with a full description of the available plans. Most are usable by ship modelers.

AYER CO. PUBS. INC.
47 Pelham Rd.
Salem, NH 03079

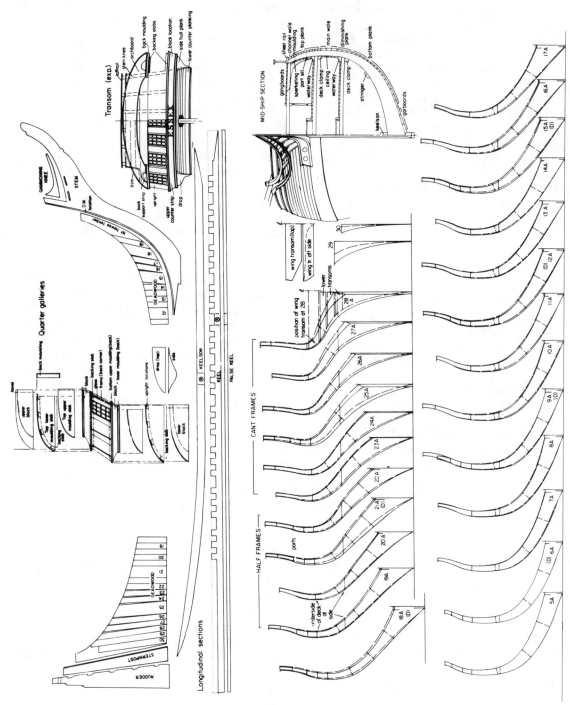

Fig. 7-9. Fully lofted frames are indicated in the plans of the *Essex* (1:64) by Portia Takakjian. Construction details, keel, and keelson are shown (Courtesy of Portia Takakjian).

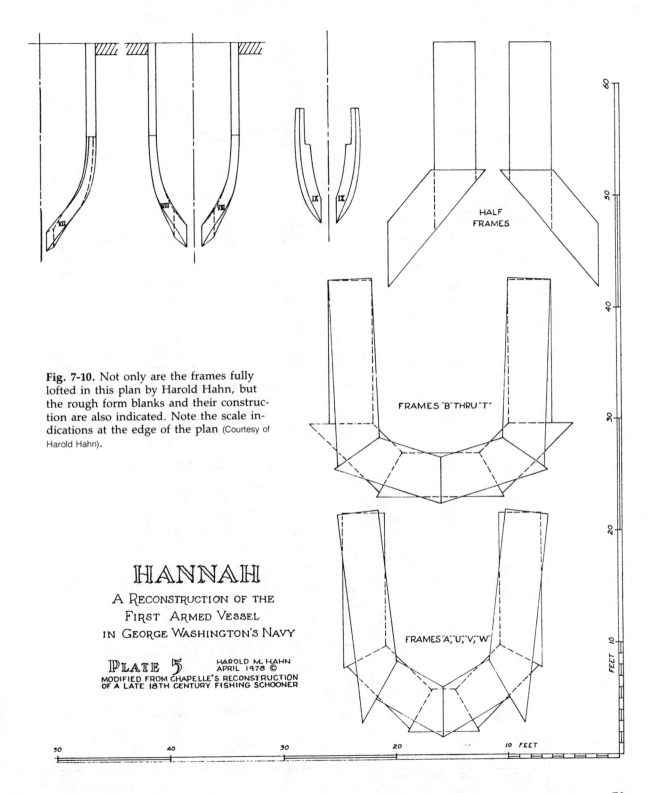

Fig. 7-10. Not only are the frames fully lofted in this plan by Harold Hahn, but the rough form blanks and their construction are also indicated. Note the scale indications at the edge of the plan (Courtesy of Harold Hahn).

HALF FRAMES

FRAMES "B" THRU "T"

FRAMES "A", "U", "V", "W"

HANNAH

A RECONSTRUCTION OF THE
FIRST ARMED VESSEL
IN GEORGE WASHINGTON'S NAVY

PLATE 5   HAROLD M. HAHN
APRIL 1978 ©
MODIFIED FROM CHAPELLE'S RECONSTRUCTION
OF A LATE 18TH CENTURY FISHING SCHOONER

60

50

40

30

20

FEET 10

50   40   30   20   10 FEET

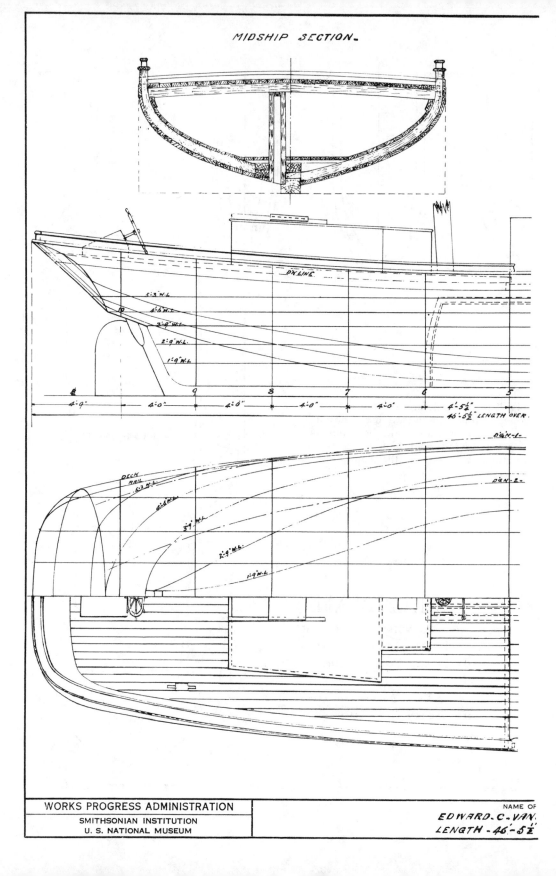

MIDSHIP SECTION.

DK LINE

5:3 W.L

4:6 W.L

3:9 W.L

2:9 W.L

1:9 W.L

10

8   9   8   7   6   5

4:9"   4:0"   4:0"   4:0"   4:0"   4:5½"

46:5½" LENGTH OVER.

D'GN-1-

DECK
RAIL   5:3 W.L

D'GN-2-

4:6 W.L

3:9 W.L

2:9 W.L

1:9 W.L

WORKS PROGRESS ADMINISTRATION

SMITHSONIAN INSTITUTION
U. S. NATIONAL MUSEUM

NAME OF

EDWARD.C.VAN

LENGTH - 46'-5½'

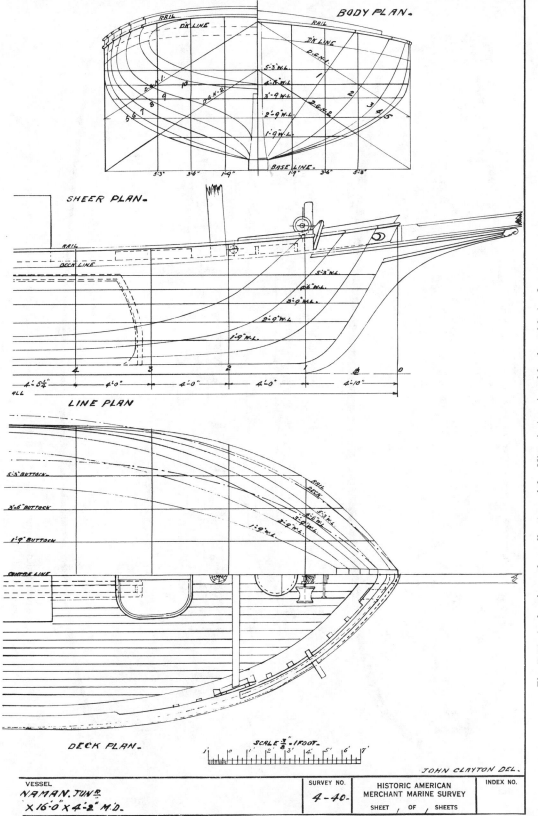

BODY PLAN.

SHEER PLAN.

LINE PLAN

DECK PLAN.

SCALE ⅜" = 1 FOOT

JOHN CLAYTON DEL.

VESSEL	SURVEY NO.	HISTORIC AMERICAN	INDEX NO.
NAMAN. JUNR	4-40-	MERCHANT MARINE SURVEY	
X 16'-0" X 4'-2" M.D.		SHEET OF SHEETS	

Fig. 7-11. A plan from the collection of the *Historic American Merchant Marine Survey* (Courtesy of Ayer Co. Publishers, Inc.).

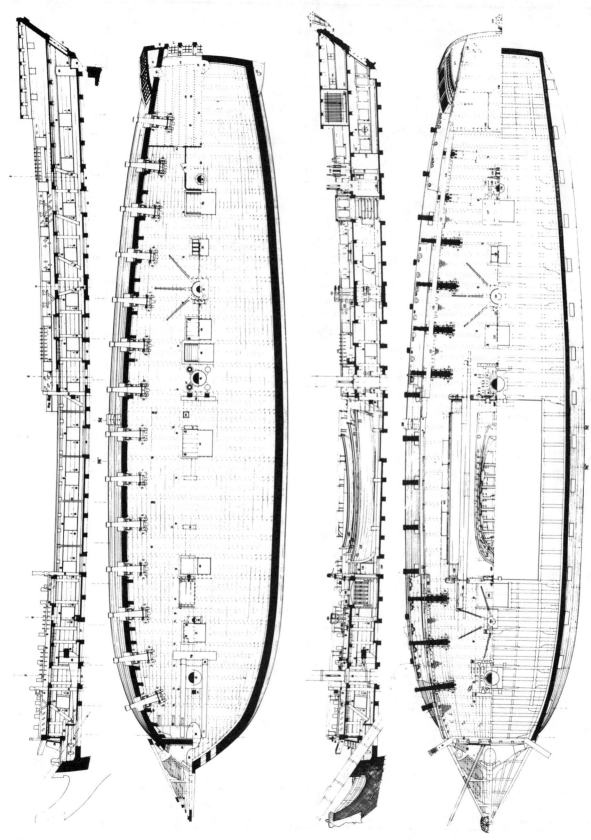

Fig. 7-12. The exceptional drawings of Jean Boudroit indicate every detail of the construction of the ship (Courtesy of A.N.C.R.E. and Jean Boudroit, France).

Plans in Books

I now name the monographs and books of Jean Boudriot and Hubert Berti. Although a limited series, this is the state of the art as far as modelers are concerned. Photographs of the models as produced from the plans and supplemented by accurate research are included. A study is complete when the drawings are accurate, as rendered in the sampling of Mr. Boudriot's works in FIG. 7-12. The text is French. The removable, folded, full-scale plans are rendered in such clarity that you do not need to read French. A color chart of the paint used is included for each ship.

The books, portfolios, monographs, and all information are not without an above-average cost. They are, by most standards, expensive. To all who desire and acquire them, however, they are priceless.

Fig. 7-13. The frigate *Challenge* of Independence, 1776-1815, is on display at Mystic Seaport. The display includes the anatomical hull and the rigging plan of the pattern of a frigate of the war of 1812. A plan can be part of the display of a model (Photo by Claire L. White).

The list of the offerings from the French Naval Archaeology Collection, as they are known, contains:

○ Cutter, *Le Cerf* 1779-1780 (Recently translated into English). Monograph, with 11 plates Scale 1/4″ = 1 foot.

○ Frigate, *LaVenus*, 1782, 18-pounder. Monograph, with 13 plates, Scale 1/6″ = 1 foot.

○ Brig, *Le Cygne*, 1806-1808, 24-pounder. Monograph, with 19 plates, Scale 1/4″ = 1 foot.

○ Bomb Ketch, *La Salamander*. Monograph, with 38 plates, Scale 1/4″ = 1 foot.

○ Frigate, *Le Vaisseau De 74 Canons*, 74 guns. 4 volumes, with 72 plates, 512 illustrations, and plans, 1,000 pages. Plans may be secured separately.

○ Indiaman, *Compagnie Des Indes*. The ship is detailed in 2 volumes, *Book*, with plans, and illustrations.

○ French Slave Trader, *Aurore*.

○ Cutter-Schooner, *Courer*, 1776.

In all of the books and monographs of Boudriot, nothing is left to chance. Every detail of structure and construction is illustrated. These works are not recommended for the individual who cannot create. There are no instructions for modelers. The information is complete, however. The model that can be made from the plans is shown in photographs.

The popularity of the works in French was such that they are being translated into English. *Le Cerf* has been released and others are expected soon. H. Bartlett Wells is translating the works, and they have lost none of the technical aspects in the translation. You can obtain copies of this and all works from American book dealers who specialize in maritime and ship-modeling texts. You also can secure this work directly from:

ANCRE, EDITOR
15, Avenue Paul-Doumer
75016 Paris, France

It is impossible to list all the plans and producers of plans. The list grows and diminishes at too rapid a rate. The best stay, constantly reprinted.

What is the best plan you can buy to build a ship model? Unanswerable question. Plans, like beauty, are in the eye of the beholder. If you know what to look for, it is a great plan. If you can use the information you seek to your advantage, it is a better plan.

Many, seeking accuracy, secure several plans of the same vessel as produced by different draftsmen. They then study the obvious omissions and errors, and use the best of each and the information of all.

If the model made from the simplest of plans or the slightest bits of information, or from a plan you created yourself, turns out to be a good model, who remembers the plan? Who cares? You found it, used it, filed it away, and, above all, turned out a great ship model (FIG. 7-13). Later on, don't forget to share your knowledge.

EIGHT

Paint and Painting
Ship Models

Advice is seldom welcome; And those who want it most
always like it the least.
—EARL OF CHESTERFIELD, in a letter to his son
January 29, 1748

THE CONTROVERSY RAGES. SHOULD A SHIP MODEL be painted? Does the use of color add to the beauty, or is it a matter of necessity? Can a ship model—a scale ship model, a reproduced miniaturized bit of history—be complete without color? Let's take a look at these and the many other questions that arise on the subject of "coloring" the model.

There are those who feel that the beauty of the wood is enough. The contrasting colors of natural, exotic, or stained wood are the finished model. Most assuredly, the use of wood colors can be said to be painting. The palette is created by the color of the wood used in construction. I call your attention to the Color Section of this book.

Admiralty models, dockside models, half models, and models that show the internal construction would be unusual if they were painted. The natural color of the wood is used to express the internal construction.

Clayton A. Feldman said, "Furthermore, I am not of the holly and ebony school of model ship building and I do not like models that have such contrasting treenails that they look like they have maritime measles." He also, quite justifiably, said that ships were not painted with wood; they were painted with paint—tar, tallow, and other disgusting things. I cannot agree with him that such a lack of a painting finish is an unfinished hull. It all depends on the interpretation of the model and what period of time the model represents.

Unless the model is reputed to be of "museum quality," it is an expression of the modeler. Again, what is museum quality, accuracy, or antiquity?

Painting a ship model for purposes of accuracy is a laudable undertaking. It indicates that the modeler is a devotee of accuracy, as well as construction. Undoubtedly, he has researched the ship of his rendition, and the colors are, so far as he is able to establish, correct. His is a model of museum quality.

Suppose the modeler had selected other colors—colors he thought would "look nice" on his model. It is the modeler's choice. He chose the model he wanted to build, and can he not select the colors he feels his model should "wear?" We are not talking accuracy; we are talking achievement.

PAINT

Comment and controversy now having been cleared, let's discuss paints and painting. According to *Webster's New World Dictionary of the American Language*, College Edition (World Publishing Co., New York, 1951), *paint* is "a mixture of colored pigment with oil, water, etc., in liquid or paste form, applied as with a brush, roller, or spray gun, and used for protective covering or coloring of a surface or for making pictures on canvas, paper, etc." This is an all-encompassing definition.

The color in paint comes from the pigment. Over the years, new forms of pigments have been added and several, because of their dangerous characteristics, have been removed. The basic pigments of most paints used by modelers has not changed since the discovery of the pigments themselves. White is still a compound of lead, zinc, or gypsum. White lead has been used for over 2,000 years. Green is copper arsenic (seldom used now) or chrome salts. Blue is lapis lazuli. Yellow comes from other earth sources. Red can range from basic iron oxide to exotic chemical compounds. Basic black is still lampblack or other carbon mixtures.

Today, the modeler does not need to blend pigments with the vehicles. Manufacturers are most precise in doing the job. The selections of color and vehicles are endless. One such is the *thinner*, a volatile liquid blended with the pigments that dissolves or thins the paint. You can choose from the natural thinners such as turpentine or benzine, both of which have been processed and tested for constant purity. Modern thinners are the other alternative. There are blends of chemicals and are not compatible with other thinners.

Varnish has become a modeler's basic coating. It is a resinous solution containing a component that, after the solvent evaporates, imparts a shining surface to wood. It also makes the wood impervious to air and moisture. The resin is usually dissolved in linseed oil, alcohol, liquid hydrocarbons, turpentine, or benzine. Varnish is classed as oil varnish and spirit varnish. The difference is in the solvent. Oil varnish contains linseed oil in addition to the volatile vehicles.

Varnish resins are derived directly or as byproducts of lac, benzoin, copal, amber, asphalt, or mastic. The newer, synthetic varnishes are complex chemical compounds. Their formulas, for the most part, are closely guarded trade secrets and are patented.

Shellac, on the other hand, is a product of the insect world. For centuries, this "paint" has been used to protect and preserve wood and wood products. It was first used in the Orient when it was discovered that the deposits on the banyan tree produced by an insect could be dissolved like any other resin, and made into a fine protective paint. The product is also known as lac. The solvent is alcohol.

USING PAINT

We have established that paint, regardless of purpose, consists of two basic elements: the pigment, and the vehicle. The pigment is the color, and the vehicle is the fluid that flows the color onto the surface. The quality of the pigment and the vehicle not only determines the quality of the color, it also determines the price. The better the paint, however, the less is needed to do the job.

The amount used to cover a surface depends on the opacity of the color. Two reds from two manufacturers, for example, both labeled as the same color, will not have the same opacity. The "thin" color can't cover. Continued applications of paint eventually cut down on the cost effectiveness. The buildup can, in time, cause an aged look to paint. It wrinkles when it is too thick, and cracks when it is too thin.

Using paint is a matter of experience. Manufacturing paint is a matter of quality and adherence to regulations. If it is a good paint, it will conform to The National Bureau of Standards. A manufacturer who meets or exceeds these standards will state this fact on the can or tube.

PAINT BRANDS

How do you know what is a good paint? If you will pardon the paraphrasing, a good paint is only as good as the person who knows how to use it. It is not how much it cost that matters. There are many paints from which to choose. A trip to the local hobby shop, supermarket, or paint store will establish the fact that confusion dominates.

Most modelers, when they find "their" good paint, tend to rely on the brand. The dependability begins with the medium. Plastic models, wood models, fiberglass, etc. all require a specialized paint. Airplane modelers need a paint that is a "dope" and, if the airplane is a flying gas-powered model, is also fuelproof. Automobile modelers need metallic paints for some of the "sleek" models. Railroaders seek special colors and finishes that show aging, wear, etc. The need for special paints has, for the most part, been met by the manufacturers. Each claim it makes the best, most accurate, and longest lasting.

Pactra states that its Model Enamel fast-drying formula can be used on most woods, plastics, paper, cardboards, ceramics, metal, and expanded foam. The true touch of realism is assured, as the company's advertisement expresses it. Formula-U is offered as a polyurethane fuelproof finish. AeroGloss is a hot fuel dope. As would be expected, each company has its own special solvent or thinner.

Testors, a name that is well-known and whose products are seen in almost every model store, features enamels classed as "popular regular" and "professional." The former is touted as the finest hobby and household enamel for the plastic modeler, craft hobbyist, and do-it-yourselfers. The professional, or Master Modeler, line boasts that this is "a professional finishing system for museum-quality models." Master Modeler enamels are compatible with all Testor paints and finishing materials.

Humbrol offers authentic color enamels in a wide and impressive variety. The finishes imparted vary from matte to high gloss. The difference between gloss enamel and authentic enamel is not explained.

As the world advanced, so did the formulation of paints. Today, a whole new line of products is available, based on the magic of chemistry. *Acrylics*, water-based paints that can be painted on plastics, can now be secured. Epoxy and polyester resin-based paints will, if directions are followed, apply to any surface. There are shiny paints, flat finishes, stippled drying paints, wrinklers, metalizers, even paints that glow in the dark. Paints that do not require undercoats or primers for metal surfaces are advertised.

Tamiya has a line of acrylic paints. The company, which advertises itself as the "master of modeling" offers a prize paint for plastic models. The durable, smooth-flowing, fast-drying acrylic finish goes on bubble free with brush or airbrush. This is a water-based paint. It can be used on plastic, wood, glass, and Styrofoam. This company also makes paint markers.

The Floquil-Polly S Color Corporation has multiple offerings. The colors are offered for railroaders under the name Floquil Railroad Colors. The general modeler might prefer the Flopaque Arts and Craft Colors. The Polly-S colors are formulated in a water-based vehicle. They can be used on plastics, as well as other surfaces and are interchangeable. You can choose your colors and the thinner with which you are most comfortable.

I have it on good authority that the pigments are an alkyd resin. The pigments are the main colors that are used throughout the line. Therefore, they are the same no matter what the named color. For example,

Engine Black, Number R-10, for railroad modelers is the same as F-10, Black for Flopaque general-purpose, or P-10 in the specialized Polly-S colors.

Polly-S colors are water soluble. For general painting and cleanup, you use water. These colors can be used on wood or plastic. Thinning for airbrushing is done with ethyl alcohol, not rubbing alcohol. Use one part Polly-S with three parts alcohol. The other colors use a thinner and solvent identified as Dio-Sol.

Dio-Sol is a unique thinner. The active ingredients are listed as Xylene and distilled petroleum products. The formulation, which is an industrial secret, is not compatible with other paints or solvents. This thinner was specially formulated to give the outstanding qualities to this line of paints. It is also used in the wood stains.

Floquil makes a full range of wood stains. The color of the desired and simulated wood can be given to any lighter colored wood. Driftwood is a stain that is particularly used as an all-purpose aging color. The hardwoods and fruit woods are represented. Cherry, walnut, oak and maple are a few that give attractive colors to wood. If you "paint" with wood, consider using these stains. I recommend that you stain the wood before you use it in construction.

Not to be confused with the Floquil stains is the newest formulation known as Swedish Wood Oil. It is a combination of penetrating wood oils and resins. It will, if directions are followed, seal the wood and protect it with a natural oil finish. The product is for use on "new" wood.

Wood can be stained with Floquil wood stains and still be classified as a new wood. To use Swedish Wood Oil, apply liberally with brush or rag and remove after 30 minutes by wiping. In 24 hours a hard surface is assured. By combining stains and Swedish Wood Oil or varnish, you can paint your ship model in natural contrasting wood colors.

The company also offers a "Barrier" for all the colors when painting plastics. This is a crystal-clear, medium-gloss coating that is used to protect unpainted polystyrene surfaces from the solvent action of practically all paints. The "unique" formulation supposedly seals the unpainted plastic surface completely. It is not to be used on metal or previously painted surfaces. This barrier prevents the plastic from cracking, crazing, or softening when paints are applied by brush or spray. It contains acetone and petroleum distillate. The usual caution with a highly flammable and toxic substance applies. The same Barrier solution is used with all the Floquil products for plastic models.

Another product of this company you might consider is called Foundation. It is a base coat (primer) for simulating wood grain on nonwood surfaces. This is valuable for making a plastic hull simulate wood. It looks good on the masts and spars of the plastic models of sailing ships.

APPLICATION OF PAINT

Application of paint has developed from dipping, to brushing, and then to spraying. This is another choice for the modeler to make. Once the paint has been selected, how will he apply it to his model? It could depend on the laziness of the modeler, how careful a worker he is, or the ''selling'' of the paint and its recommended form of application.

All of the makers of paints offer various forms of application. They will sell you their special brushes that promise a better finish. You can have the same paint in a spray can. The gas propellant might be self-contained or from an external source. The identical formula can be thinned and used in your own spray system. Certainly you are going to buy a spray gun or an airbrush someday (FIG. 8-1).

Fig. 8-1. The business end of a spray gun setup (Courtesy of X-ACTO).

Spray painting, no matter if from a can or an expensive airbrush outfit, is a method that is fast and artistic. The ''artist'' must learn his media, however. Distance is the thing in spray painting—too close and you have a running mess; too far and dried sandlike granules of paint coat the surface.

Stripping with tape produces a proper waterline. You can paint a waterline by brush. A brush separates color very nicely, but the line looks even better when sprayed.

Small items are quickly covered by spraying. Small, fine details of small parts are not obliterated, however.

The time to choose which method of painting is before the assembling progresses too far. It is a good idea to paint before assembling, no matter what form of modeling medium you use. The plastic modeler is a devotee of prepainting. It matters not if you use brush or spray. You can paint without worry of slopping on another part if you paint before assembling.

The application of paint is a matter of experience. Each form of paint application has its merits and each one should be known. It then becomes a matter of choice.

The modeler with experience will not yield to the temptation of one quick, thick coat. He knows that several thin coats are best. A perfect finish is achieved by sanding the dried undercoat between coats. A good cabinetmaker knows this method, as well as a good ship's carpenter.

A pause for a word of caution. Each of the products mentioned here are manufactured. Although I am not completely familiar with each one, I do issue this caution: It is not recommended to mix one manufacturer's product with another, including paints. The components, although sometimes compatible, most often will react adversely.

The danger, especially in handling synthetic paints, is the *resin system* vs. the *solvent system*. Remember that each time you apply a coat of paint you are ''rewetting'' the surface with a solvent. If the paint is not completely dry, say 7 to 10 days of air drying, the solvent can and will dissolve the resin (pigment). There is still no guarantee that even this drying time will protect the finish. The longer the drying out, the more stable the color. You can destroy the finish with bleeding, crazing, and other painting disasters.

The ''working'' component in the solvent of one maker might be the disaster maker in another manufacturer's offering. As an example, an opaque color painted over a water-based undercoating might bleed through. Primers can come through water-based overcoats also as a result of action of the solvent. Here you are faced with a compatibility problem. Should you risk painting over or strip down to the base media, then undercoat and start again?

There is another method of protecting one coating of paint from solvent rewetting. You can use a sealing coating. It could be a primer, varnish, undercoating, or shellac. Whatever your choice, allow ample drying time before repainting. It is always the hope that the "overcoating" will seal the two paints from action by their solvents.

It is suggested that you paint a *test strip* before you paint the model. A few hours delay is worth the time saved in stripping and repainting a surface. You can see what will happen before the disaster takes place. After a while, experience will tell you which "store-bought" paints can be mixed with others.

Painting a model is an art in itself. Aging a model with paint is the challenge of the art form of painting. The discussion of "how to" would and does fill volumes. Talk to the seller first. The hobby shop salesman, the friend who uses the product, and anyone with some knowledge will only be too happy to share their experiences.

Each manufacturer will, if you take the time and trouble to ask, send you as much information as you would need to do a commendable job with his product. It behooves you to avail yourself of this information even though most of the information will be slanted toward that paint.

COLORS OF PERIOD SHIPS

Can a modeler make a mistake so obvious as using the wrong color or decorations on period sailing ship models? All too often, one does. Nothing can destroy the goal of a museum-quality ship model than to present your work with the improper finish.

Whose fault is it? Is it the kit manufacturer? Could it be the modeler's? I have seen vessels from the 1700s in the black-and-white checkerboard pattern of the 1840s. These models were built from kits.

Museum-quality ship models not only need to be accurate in scale and rendition, but must be accurate in coloring. In these cases you must use paint. There is no room for artistic license in this field. It behooves you to do your homework and produce a model worthy of your skill and expressive of your talents. I offer a little help.

Tudor ships, in the period between 1500 and 1610, were painted in bright geometrical patterns above the gunwales. Names of the ships of the period include the *Mary Rose* and the *Great Harry*. The colors had, in most cases, a heraldic meaning. There was no universal color scheme. The royal colors of green and white were popular. Shades of strong red, blue, black, and white were mixed in. Shields, or *pavises*, were carried on the fore and after castles.

The majority of the ship was painted in varnish. The colors of the woods were apparent, even under the many layers of protection. Red was the predominant color in the interior coloring. Red lead, an oxide, was suspended in varnish to achieve the color of this paint. It was thinned with turpentine. The blacks were lampblack, Stockholm tars, pitch, or a mixture of unknown colorings of heavy metals suspended in an evaporating vehicle, usually varnish based.

The interior gunwales of warships were painted red in the mistaken idea that it would not show the color of the blood of the crew shed in battle. The idea of such color camouflage was extended even to the gun carriage. This idea prevailed in warship coloring until well into the mid-1800s. It was all wrong, of course, when you consider that the decks were holystoned to a near white color in contrast.

It was around 1610, with the building of the *Prince Royal*, that color and decoration began to change. Carved work became the vogue. Much of this decoration was gilded. The more "gingerbread," the better. The elaborate and expensive decorative fashion continued on and off for the next 200 years. Each ruler tried to outdo his contemporary (FIG. 8-2). The apex of such elaborate decorations can be seen in the *Sovereign of the Seas,* later known as the *Royal Sovereign,* best known to the Dutch from 1627 to 1690 as the "Golden Devil." Decorations cost more than the ship itself. Providing the funds literally cost the king his head. The *Soleil Royal* of France and the *Wasa* of Sweden were all in the same period.

Background paints of black or blue were used along the wales and gun deck lines to enhance the gilding. Interiors continued to be painted red. Below the waterline, the colors were white. This color was the result of an attempt to protect the hull from the wood-boring worms of the sea by using felts, matted horsehair, and other materials with tallows. The color usually became a yellowish-white to even a buff color in time. Coppering did not appear until around 1775.

There was a period of time in England when the Commonwealth banned all carved work. The carv-

Fig. 8-2. Edward Marple's *Royal Katherine*, 1664, has no areas of paint above the waterline (Courtesy of Edward Marple).

ings were removed or painted black. With the Restoration, it was all back and brighter than ever. From 1703 to 1712, it was all gone again by orders of the king. When he left for a more powerful kingdom, the gingerbread was back, stronger than ever.

There was also a short period, from 1690 to 1695, when British naval ships were painted yellow on the exterior sides. Many captains, however, failed to follow orders. They were allowed only one coat of paint per year and had to pay for maintenance out of their own pockets. There was considerable color variance among the king's ships. It depended on the time of the annual paint job, the private capital of the captain, and the length of time before an overhaul. The practice, like the paint, simply faded away.

Masts and spars of ships were treated the same as the hull sides. They were varnished. Some of the merchant ships of the time would protect the structures by darkening them with mixtures of lampblack added to the varnish. The practice of darkening the booms, yards, and topgallant masts continued until the French wars. The Royal Navy whitened the lower masts before a general action. This was a mark of distinction. It allowed the British gunners to distinguish their ships from the black masts of the enemy in the heat of combat. Gunpowder smoke was often so thick that it obscured everything except the shape, outline, and masts.

Some French ships were painted blood red. This feature was noted during the Revolutionary War. The early Spanish ships were black with red trim during the so-called "Black Treasure Ship" era of the 1500s. The *Santissima Trinidad,* fighting with her ally France, was painted red with black trim at Trafalgar.

The color scheme of black and red appealed to the British also. In the late 1790s, navy ships were black with red streaks along the sides of the gunports. Larger ships, ratings above fifth, did not use this color combination. It was never used by any ship larger than a frigate.

During the Napoleonic Wars, there was a great variance of color among ships of the Royal Navy. The most common colorings were a narrow black line along the wales, yellow sides, with black upperworks lined in gold. To show off the gold carvings, blue was used as a background color. Gunports were painted black.

The so-called "Nelson fashion" was first found among the ships that fought along the Nile. The style became the scheme of any ship that would serve under Nelson's command. The wales, which up till then were the separation points of the line of color, were disregarded. The new line followed the line of the gunports from stem to stern, often cutting through the wales. The yellow sides between the lines were offset by the black gunports. This made the fleet a uniform color. Inside, the bulkheads and bulwarks were changed to a stone color.

After Trafalgar, "Nelson fashion" was the accepted style until 1813 when a modification was introduced. A thin, white line appeared on each side of the yellow streaks. By 1820, the yellow had been replaced with white. This color contrast of black and white lasted in the navies of the world until steel hulls replaced the wooden walls.

Merchant vessels copied the colors of naval ships in the early days of sail. The Indiamen, which were in reality warships carrying cargo, followed the Royal Navy colors. Hues of green and blue made their appearance after 1800. The cost of painting a ship was the consideration of the owner. There was no set color scheme as determined by regulation. Companies and ships owned by one individual did have a standard set color pattern, however. Black on the hulls was the main color. Decorative trim was usually white on American ships. Whalers painted fake black gunports in white between the wales as an attempt to fool observers into thinking they were naval vessels.

The French preference ran to the use of deep blues with white trim. The Spanish clung to the black hull offset with red, a carryover from the galleon and pirate days off the Spanish Main of the Caribbean Sea. Gilded carvings were the general rule until the late 1700s. Deck furnishings and other inboard areas were varnished.

Records of the coloring of merchant ships were sketchy at best. Research would be a difficult task, considering the many color changes a vessel incurred in her lifetime. On the other hand, the naval and military records are very reliable. In their zeal to set everything down in writing to avoid misunderstanding, elaborate records were kept by the Royal Navy, as well as the American and French navies.

Establishing the color schemes of a warship is not difficult. That which is not recorded is preserved in the paintings of the period. There are countless sources for study to ensure accuracy in the color of your model.

TABLE 8-1 is a quick reference table of colors of British naval warships. The American navy colors followed the same patterns as the British for the most part (FIG. 8-3). Slight variations are noted, but this was mostly in the ship itself, rather than the overall coloring as set down by regulation. It would be impossible to list all the books of reference. This information, like life and learning, was gathered from many sources and in bits and pieces. Some references are mere notes in a ship's log.

PAINTING TIPS

It is best to avoid the glare of glossy finishes. Use satin or nongloss varnishes and flat paints for best results. Contemporary models are painted in flat colors. The glare of varnish is usually noted on the surfaces of ship models made prior to 1940, and is undoubtedly a result of the lack of selection, rather than the technique.

An old ship modeler (94 years old), who began his career in his youth, taught me the trick of "wet sanding" to remove the glare in restoring and building when the finish could not be removed. In this method, a wet and dry sandpaper of 120 grit is used with small quantities of water to float the residue away. He also taught me to use a matte varnish over the glossy type. This product can be found in most art supply stores.

Following are a few more points to remember when you are painting old-time ship models:

- ✪ An open gunport lid shows the colors of the interior of the ship. Use the same shades you used for the bulwarks and gunwales: red or a stone color.
- ✪ The black color of the lower wale was usually continued down to the waterline, especially where the wale rose in its line aft.
- ✪ When the color line cut across the gunport lid, it was continued without interruption. That is to say, you might find a gunport painted in two colors.
- ✪ All ironwork was painted black, in particular on navy ships. Merchant ships painted over everything encountered on the exterior hull. Interior painting varied. Their colors depended on what was in the paint locker. Bulwarks and toprails were usually shades of green or light blue. The caprail was varnished.
- ✪ Copper bottoms, which were first introduced around 1761, were in general use after 1785. Bright copper is fine if your model is being represented in the prelaunch stage or after an overhaul. Copper that has been in seawater for a time is tinted with green. Copper sheets or precut plates can be colored with shades of red and light brown by heating prior to application, if you are using this method instead of paint.

Table 8-1. General Colors—British Warships 1500-1860.

PERIOD	HULL	UPPER WORKS	INTERIOR	BOTTOM
1500-1610	Varnished oak; black wales; gunports same as hull	Geometrical patterns of bright colors	Red or varnished oak	White
1610-1703	Same	Blue or black; carved work gilded	Red with gilded carved work	White
1703-1745	Yellow or varnished oak; gunport lids same as hull; black wales	Same	Red	White
1745-1775	Same	Blue; gilded carvings	Red	White
1775-1798	Yellow with black wales or only the lower wale black	Black, with yellow or gilded carvings.	Red	Copper or white
1798-1813 *"Nelson fashion"*	Black with yellow band along line of gunports; lids black.	Black; yellow lines on the mouldings.	Stone; cabins pale green.	Copper
1813-1820	Black with yellow band edged in white on each line of gunports; lids black.	Black; no lines or carved work	Stone	Copper
1820-1840	Black; white band on each line of gunports; Thin white line at waterline; lids black.	Black; no lines	Green	Copper
1840-1860	Black; white band on each line of gunports; Red, green, or white waterline; black gunport lids.	Same	White; funnel (if any) black	Copper or red

Fig. 8-3. Museum quality and correct even to the colors is this model of the *Alfred*, 1776, first ship of the Continental Navy (Photo courtesy of the Naval Memorial Museum, Washington, DC).

Again I would stress a little research. The better known popularly modeled ships have been pretty well researched. The colors suggested by American kitmakers and noted in plans used by most scratch-builders can be trusted. The plans offered from commercial sources are, for the most part, accurate. Double-check, however, to make sure of the colors on the lesser known ships.

NINE

Holding It All Together

A little goes a long way.
Enough is better than too much.
—MAE WEST

"WHAT'S IN A NAME? A ROSE BY ANY OTHER NAME would smell as sweet." The words of Shakespeare still ring true. What are called *cements* by some are referred to as *glues* by another. A third party would refer to them as *adhesives*. Confused?

The trade names of glues literally run from A to Z. From Amroid to ZAP, all types are represented. Some are fast setting, some slow. They run from instant hold all the way to clamp it in place for 24 hours. Solvents, from water to unstable, explosive or inflammable compounds, are incorporated in the manufacture. Each has a need, each has a use. Not all are needed to build ship models.

Manufacturers use their own closely guarded, patented, trademarked, and compounded formulas. Quality might vary. The brand names referred to in this discussion are not necessarily the best. Make your own evaluation on what works well in a particular situation.

Begin with the text, *Adhesives and Glues—How to Choose And Use Them* by Robert S. Miller. You can secure a copy from:

FRANKLIN CHEMICAL INDUSTRIES
R.D. #1
New Ringgold, PA 17960

Many other volumes are also available. Most are technical volumes dealing with the technical aspects of bonding strength, chemical reactions, formulations, and actions. All have their place in the study of a subject.

Let's divide this discussion into two major classifications: *multipurpose glues* and *special-purpose glues*. Whenever possible, the product will be identified by brand name. Uses and formulation will be touched on lightly. Several advantages and disadvantages will be mentioned.

Not all points on this controversial subject can be covered without considering the factor of experience. Whatever the outcome, the test of what worked best will be time, and time alone. If it is still all together 100 years from now, then it was a good choice of adhesive.

MULTIPURPOSE GLUES

Multipurpose glues include white glue, wood glues, household cements, glues for plastics, super glues, and structural acrylic glues. Discussions on each of these types follow.

White Glue

This is the most popular woodworking glue used today. The designation is broad and inaccurate. The formula, developed in 1940, is a compound based on a synthetic polymer. The classification is wide and variable.

Most white glues are composed of a polyvinylacetate (PVA) emulsion. Simply stated, this is a water-based synthetic adhesive. To set completely, the water must evaporate. The glue, in its liquid state, can be thinned with water. It dries waterproof. Shelf life is virtually indefinite, as long as the solvent is contained by proper sealing and under normal temperatures. The temperature can be slightly below room settings, but avoid extremes of heat or freezing. Binding is completed when the glue hardens within the material holding the two surfaces together. Of course, the materials must be porous. Don't expect this glue to work on smooth, hard surfaces. There must be some surface penetration.

Clamping or holding in position is required. Setting time is approximately one hour. Humidity and evaporation will vary the time. PVA glues will harden at temperatures as low as 60° F. Complete hardening occurs in 48 to 72 hours.

A translucent residue will remain in the exposed areas of drying. The residue, although invisible to the eye, will be impervious to paints, stains, and varnishes.

Glue that has been thinned with water will penetrate to a greater depth. Under these conditions and depending on the amount of bonding material, it will be of a much weaker strength. Strength is not the important factor, however, when using water-thinned "white" glues to saturate rigging line and bind seizing.

This thinned formulation can end the frustration of coiling lines and fixing belayed hangings. Do your layout of saturated line on a piece of wax paper. After it is dry, peel off the paper and glue your coil or belayed line into position with a drop or two of full-strength glue.

The most common brand is Elmer's, one of the products of the Borden company. Glue-All, a type, sets faster than School Glue. The latter, made for the messy and a blessing to the mothers, washes out of clothes even if it has set completely. The stronger professional type, call Carpenter's Wood Glue, is not a true white glue.

Special Wood Glues

The so-called *yellow glues* are also water-based emulsions. Unlike white glues, they contain polyvinyl copolymers. They are referred to as *aliphatic resins*. Formulated with the woodworker in mind, Elmer's Carpenter's Wood Glue, Wilhold Woodworking Alipahatic Resin, and Titebond by Franklin are but a few of the glues in this classification.

Penetration of the fibers is deeper with wood glues, and the bonded joint is stronger than the white glues. Setting time is faster and less clamping time is needed.

Both white glues and aliphatic resins are thermoplastic, that is, they will melt when subjected to heat. White glues melt at a lower temperature. This is the stuff that gums up your sandpaper.

The yellow color of the aliphatic resins is added by the maker to enable cleanup with water before the solution sets. Since we as modelers don't need the strength of a carpenter making a chair, the slight thinning of the glue will not weaken the joint. Run a damp rag, rinsed and rung out often, over any joint that must be painted, finished, or stained. A good motto to remember is "wipe it wet, before she sets."

Household Cements

In the rather broad classification of household cements, we will lump low-cost cements that come in a tube. They are clear adhesives, somewhat water resistant, that work well on porous materials, such as china, plaster, wood, leather, etc. For the most part, formulation is polymer, vinyl, or styrene resin. Perhaps you are familiar with them by their trade names. 3M Super Strength Household Cement, Duro, and Ambroid are a few of the types commonly found in most stores.

These glues generally are classed as "airplane" glues. The solvent and its characteristic order make for instant recognition. Oil of mustard has been added, by law, to discourage the "sniffers." Also they are sold from a closed case or under the counter only to those of proper age.

The basic component in these glues is cellulose nitrate held in a dissolved state by the solvent acetone. You might remember using this glue on the porous balsa wood models of your youth. The most popular brands are Testors and Duro.

Acetone is a highly flammable compound with dangerous fumes. Since it is the solvent for these glues, it would be the thing to thin the consistency and clean up the spills. Be sure to use it in a well-ventilated area and avoid any open flames.

Once hardened after the evaporation of the solvent, these glues are impervious to penetrating paints, stains, and some varnishes. These compounds are not good gap fillers and tend to shrink after drying. Bonding is rapid; setting time is almost minutes. They are not strong glues.

Glues for Plastics

Glue not designed for plastics invite disaster. Plastics can range in states from a liquid to as hard as steel, depending on their formulation and combinations with other materials. The term *plastic* has become a broad and nondescriptive term. Each type requires a special adhesive.

Modelers who use plastic components and make plastic models know which type to use in their work. They are also aware that the solvent in the compound will mar the surface of the part on which they are using it. A careless drop on the finger, a brushed away spill, and the entire model can be marked for life. One enterprising modeler places his fingerprint on an exposed, but nonvital area of his ship model for identification. Nobody can ever deny that he made it.

To effect a bond, the glue must dissolve the surfaces of the parts to be united or add enough new material of a similar characteristic, then dissolve the surface. The glue must be compatible with the plastic that it is to unite.

Revell Plastic Cement is excellent for styrene plastic models. Testors, on the other hand, is available in a liquid form for polystyrene, ABS, acetate, Plexiglas and many other plastics.

Testors glues for plastics are available in a metal tube, a ''putty'' to fill seams and build areas. This company's wood cements are rated as ''regular, fast, and extra fast'' drying. The plastic glues are available in the same time-rated segments. I suspect it's the amount of solvent as well as the compounding that allows these ratings.

Pactra also makes glues to hold plastic models together, as do Microscale, Micro Weld, Plastruct Plastic Weld, Duro Plastic Glue, and the all-powerful Wilhold R/C-56 Modeler's Glue. The last product claims to be able to bond plastic, fiberglass, metal foil, and wood surfaces all to each other, as well as to themselves.

Basically there are two ways plastic glues work. Both rely on dissolving the material. The thicker types, after application, dissolve a slight portion of the surface and rely on the components to fill the gaps and bond the surfaces. Too much glue results in a

problem with cleanup and a danger to marring the details.

Liquid types have no filling power. The surfaces to be bonded must be in complete contact. They rely on dissolving the surfaces and bonding by common union. The whole process is not unlike welding metals. It is interesting that one maker has chosen the word *weld* in naming his plastic glue.

Acrylic plastics, as well as their cousins, require a close contact to bond. The usual setting time is within 10 minutes. Consider them completely cured in 24 hours. Most are not good gap fillers. Shrinkage during and after drying occurs after the solvent evaporates. The solvent, not unlike acetone, is to be used with caution. Have proper ventilation and again, douse the butts. Use acetone for cleaning up tools and work areas for spills.

Super Glues

Not by the virtue of their holding power are these glues named. In their early days, they were touted as being strong enough to hold up a ton of weight and set in seconds. With the passage of time, *cyanoacrylate* (CA) adhesives have not lived up to their reputations. All CAs are born of the same formula. The actual manufacturers produce and sell the glue in bulk. Most sellers, brand names you know, are simply repackagers equipped with a super advertising agency. They include Alteco, Krazy Glue, Superstick, Jet, Hot Stuff from Satellite City, and the various products of ZAP.

The clear liquid, discovered by accident in the late 1950s, is supplied in a tube, bottle, or syringe (for thicker varieties). Ready to use full strength, the temperature for reaction should be at least $60°$ F. The instant set is their reaction, interaction, with the hydroxyl ion in an alkaline solution. In plain terms, this is moisture on a microscopic level. Almost every surface has enough of this substance to effect a reaction. Should there be an overabundance, no reaction takes place. In other words, CAs will not bond on a wet or damp surface. A white residual remains if you use CA on a wet plank.

Excessive amounts of CA will affect the bond. Too much might nullify the reaction. Use it sparingly. One drop is enough to cover 1 square inch of surface.

Setting time is from 1 to 60 seconds. If that isn't fast enough, accelerators are available. No clamping, as such, is needed. Constant pressure, assuring surface contact, is enough. Full cure is complete in 48 hours. Setting time variables are imbalance of the substrate, temperature, humidity, and the amount of glue used. CA glues will weaken above 150° F.

Some makers claim that their products are waterproof. Others remain silent. Age and weather will slowly deteriorate the bond.

The surface contact is and should be as smooth and close as possible. The high viscosity of the product flows with speed between the surfaces and bonds completely. Metal will bond to metal, and incompatible materials will bond to each other as long as they have smooth surfaces and are in good contact.

Using super glues is easy. It is also fraught with danger. Since the bonding is so rapid, most jobs do not require clamping. Simply holding the parts or pieces together until they are stuck is enough. Once they are in position, place a drop of glue on the area to be glued. It is not good practice to bring the tip of the applicator into contact with the work. The capillary action acting on the free-flowing solution will soon flood the site. The rapid dispersal of the solution as a result of the high viscosity is the dangerous side effect.

Super glues are stupid. They will run as far as they can under and between two objects in close contact. They will stick anything to anything else under the proper conditions. The moisture on your fingers or the part to be glued are all the same to them. Flesh will bond to inanimate objects as well as to itself. Never use your fingers as a clamp. Don't get your clamp too near the area, or it might become part of the repair. Press or hold the parts together with a pointed, but blunted, metal object. If it gets "stuck," there is less surface to contend with in the separating.

Accidents can happen when you least expect them when you are using super glues. A drop spilled on the flesh is not a panic situation. It will not burn you. If it sets up, you begin to notice a hard skin layer forming on your fingertips. Don't worry, in time and without any help, it will all peel off.

A good soaking helps move things along. Soften the tissues and allow your natural perspiration, fats, and oils to get down into the area. This will release the bond between the two surfaces.

Super glue in the oral cavity is not as dangerous as you might have been led to believe. Neither is swallowing the solution. There isn't enough of the glue in an average container to effect a bonding. The larger containers are usually sealed with small openings, even after the cap is removed. There is too much moisture and coating on the mucus surfaces for the glue to work. It therefore shouldn't glue the throat shut. By the time it gets to the stomach, it is cured particles of glue and harmless.

The problems associated with accidental ingestion are usually in the mouth and lip area. In most cases, the injuries are more the result of uncontrolled panic than bonded surfaces.

Other solutions will loosen and dissolve super glues. Acetone is one. Most homes have acetone around in the form of nail polish remover. Some of the fancier and expensive brands are made up in special formulation. These are the nail polish removers that are sold as the "oily" kind. They are great for getting shed of super glue.

Cyanoacrylate solvents are available. Most shops that sell super glues also sell the solvents. Their names are similar sounding to the parent product. For example the makers of ZAP, a super glue familiar to most model builders, have named their solvent Z-7 Debonder. Their accelerator is named Zip Kicker. Golden West Fuels of Woodland Hills, California, makes an excellent solvent named Ultra.

These solutions, for the most part, are also flammable and should be used with caution. They are a nitroparaffin based solvent, Nitromethane. They have a flash point of 96° F, so don't get them, or yourself, overheated. Simple directions are on the bottle. Borden and several other manufacturers make a paste form that comes in a tube.

Removing super glues from the skin with cyanoacrylate solvents calls for patience. Apply the solvent to the skin areas with a soft cloth or cotton applicator. If the area is large, flow it on in small amounts. Wait a minute or two for the glue to dissolve. Now, slowly peel the skin away from the surface to which it is stuck. Keep repeating the process until you are free and clear. Wash the area well with soap and water to remove all residue.

If you are using the paste type, it is almost like an ointment. Paint it over the area with a swab or soft cloth. Again, wash well with soap and water when you are loose.

The applicators, by design because of the fast flowing liquids, are thin tubes. Occasionally they become clogged. Without thinking, you might wish to peel the dried-out glue from the tip of the tube with your fingers. Don't flick the tube to release the plug of dried glue. A drop might work its way free and go flying about. It could and has landed in people's eyes. The same situation could occur if you move the tube from the object to be glued too rapidly.

The natural instinct when something flies into the eye is to rub the eye. Don't! There is no need. In most cases the amount of super glue is so small and the amount of natural moisture so vast, that adherence of the inner eye structures does not take place. Your best course of action is to squeeze the eye closed hard. This action can, in most cases, produce an additional flowing of fluids (tears) between the eye and the lid.

Should there be a bonding of the eyelids, do not use force to pry them apart. Flush the area with luke-warm water to assist the loosening of any adhered fleshy parts and to remove any microscopic particles of set glue.

There may be a slight redness to the eye after this episode. If it hasn't gone away in half an hour or so, get professional help. Don't use eyedrops. Their soothing chemicals might not work under these conditions. The redness is a result of a chemical burn or allergic reaction.

The hardest thing of all in dealing with accidents involving super glues is not to follow your natural instincts. The natural reaction when you get stuck is to pull away. If you are going to work with or be around super glues, remember to forget natural instincts. The key phrase is simply, "don't panic." Always be ready for anything unusual. Safety with super glue requires preparation and a lot of common sense.

Gap-Filling CAs

Gap-filling CAs have been introduced. No more, like in the early days, need one use sodium bicarbonate dusted into the areas before adding the super glue. The invention was needed to cover the range of demand for a fast-working glue with greater strength than cellulose products. Gap-filling CAs are highly porous. They also could be the answer to "sloppy" workmanship. Better craftsmanship gets better results and greater satisfaction.

Trade names, again associated with the maker, are Super-Woody, Super T, and Zapgap. Deeper penetration is needed, as well as the ability to fill gaps and limited uneven surfaces. Special formulation is required. Woods contain acids and CAs need alkaline pH. The results are a thicker solution and a slower setting time. Unlike its thinner sister, it does not flow freely between the surfaces to be bonded. Application is made to the surface of one of the parts, and then the parts are placed in contact. Setting time might be as long as one to two minutes. Either clamp or apply a "spritz" of an accelerator.

Cyanoacrylates have a short shelf life. They will, in time, harden in the container at room temperature. The thicker gap fillers will harden even faster. To prolong its life, you might store the glue in the refrigerator. Always bring back to room temperature before use.

A few words on storage. To save sealing the glue by removing the tubing, place the bottle inside a sealed container. A larger jar works well. Moisture can get into the bottle and spoil the contents. Even the small diameter of the tube allows moisture to creep into the bottle. If the tube gets plugged, replace it. Don't try slipping a wire through. You are pushing the dried glue into the bottle. In addition, the moisture on the wire could set a reaction, and you now have a tube with a glued wire in it.

Structural Acrylics

A new product, a development of second-generation technology, is sold under the Duro trademark. It was developed by DuPont, and combines the strength of epoxy with the speed of cyanoacrylates. Excellent bonding is available between noncompatible materials. Porous and nonporous materials will bond. It has good gap-filling qualities, but is not as good as epoxy.

Unlike epoxy, structural acrylic is not a two-part glue, and the components are not mixed together. The activator is placed on one surface with a brush or eyedropper. The resin is applied to the other. Bonding takes place in a minute or two with full strength, and complete cure is accomplished in 24 hours. It is water-resistant.

The trade name of this wonder worker is Depend. The unusual characteristic is its ability to work on dirty or oily surfaces. Temperatures as high as 212° F have no effect on this product's bonding.

Depend fills that gray area between multipurpose and special-purpose glues.

SPECIAL-PURPOSE GLUES

Special-purpose glues include epoxy, hot-melt glues, plastic resin glues, resorcinol, wide and cosein glues, contact cements, silicone-rubber adhesives.

Epoxy

When you need strength, gap-filling properties, or bonding of detailed and different materials, then be content with epoxy. It became available in the early 1950s.

First, the disadvantages. Epoxy is expensive. Mixing is a nuisance. Anything left over is wasted. It does not work well, if at all, on metal-to-metal bonds. There is little, if any, flexibility. It is strong yes, but a little weak under "sheer" pressures. Cleanup is lengthy, and the solvents—acetone or lacquer thinners—are dangerous. It takes a lot of solvent to clean up mixing tools.

The chemical reaction, which occurs at 65° F, begins as soon as the components are mixed. The pot life is short. Bonding strength is determined by the proportions of the two components, the resin and the hardener. Too much of one or the other can affect the final outcome.

Epoxy glues are cured by chemical reaction between the resin and hardener. There are two basic categories of epoxy: polyamide and amine curing. The difference is the time it takes to harden completely.

Devcon is a polyamide. Hobbypoxy features four different setting time formulations. There are several other brand names. A trip to your hobby shop, paint store, supermarket, auto supply, hardware, or variety store will add to your knowledge and perhaps confusion.

Amine curing epoxy, unlike polyamides which take between 30 minutes and 2 hours to set and are not cured for 24 hours, are called fast-setting. They take 5 minutes to set.

The so-called "5-minute" epoxy, as well as all such rated glues, depend, not on how long, but how well you mix the resin and hardener. Uneven dispersal of the chemicals resulting in complete exposure to each other can result in improper curing. Both the slow and the fast cure in 24 hours.

Clamping is mandatory. The glues are very slimy and the parts will slide if not clamped in position. Hard clamping is not needed. Epoxy is a great gap filler and dries to a clear line. Use just enough pressure to ensure a snug fit, and clean up the globs early.

Mixtures vary from a light golden color to deep amber, depending on the maker. Exposed glues will darken with the passage of time.

Epoxies are good glues to use in construction and repairs. Bonding, where strength is not the consideration can be made with thinner solutions. After mixing, use a little acetone as solvent and thin to the desired consistency.

After a little experimentation, and perhaps failure, you will find what you are looking for to hold a part on a flat surface. A drop on the wheel of a gun carriage, a capstan, or a pinrail assured me that there would be no movement even on a varnished deck. Mix only what you can use at a given time.

Hot-Melt Glues

The newest and most controversial glue in the ship modeler's armament is back. Formulation is based on synthetic polymers, polamide, and polyethylene thermoplastics, which melt when heated. Sold in cakes, tubes, or plugs to be used in an electrically heated pistol-type applicator, they are gaining in popularity and stirring a storm of protest among some.

Melting under heat—200° F to 300° F—and solidifying on cooling, their bonding qualities are questionable over the long run. One disadvantage is that resolidification takes place in 60 seconds. You can extend the time by preheating the parts. The bond line, which is a thin opaque of neutral color, can't be sanded, but excessive material can be scraped away.

The act of reheating destroys the bond. That might be an advantage if you need to disassemble something. The heat might scorch or stain the work.

Personally, I can't recommend this glue for ship model work. The use is limited.

Plastic Resin Glues

These glues are seldom used. This relatively low-cost product comes in a powder form that is mixed with water and a urea-formaldehyde compound. The deep penetration will, when completely cured, form a bond stronger than the wood itself. It is completely water resistant. It is a good glue to use when making up a bread-and-butter hull that will become a working sailing model.

Resorcinol

Another, perhaps even better, glue for making bread-and-butter hulls is resorcinol, a two-part adhesive. It is a good gap filler and dries completely waterproof. The powder (catalyst) is simply mixed with the liquid resin. Follow the manufacturer's directions.

Allow a little longer clamping time than list if you live in a highly humid area. Clean up while the glue is wet. Resorcinol is a little more expensive than most wood glues, but well worth the price in ship model building.

Hide and Casein Glues

These wonder workers, relegated to the cabinet-maker's art, are products of nature. Hide glue has been around for generations, perhaps centuries. The early ship modelers used this glue; they had little else.

Casein glue is a natural product made from milk. The protein part of the milk, *casein*, is extracted and rendered into a powder. There are several trade names of this product; however, since it has fallen into disuse, you might need to ask around

Casein glue works well with woods that have oily or resinous components. Teak and pine can be held well with casein glue. There is limited use for this one in ship modeling.

Contact Cements

Made of a synthetic rubber, neoprene, and rendered into a liquid form, contact cement has been around since the 1930s. Different porous and non-porous materials bond fairly well together with contact cements. A good example of use is copperplating a ship model hull.

The name says it best, *contact cement*, and that's the way it works. Both surfaces are coated with cement and allowed to air-dry. The adhesive begins to harden by the evaporation of the liquid during the open period. The moment the parts touch, the bond takes place. A good bond takes place with hand pressure alone. If you need a little time to position that copperplate apply another light coat of cement prior to placement.

Included in the solvent will be varying amounts of water, methyl or ethyl ketone, acetone, toluene, and petroleum distillates. You can clean up an area with any of these chemicals. I use a little benzine to get the dried yellow cement off the copperplate, my fingers and tools.

Pilobond, Devcon, 3M and other contact cements too numerous to mention can be found in most stores. They are popular for gluing leathers and plastic ornaments to wood.

Silicone-Rubber Adhesives

If you need a glue that is waterproof, a great gap filler, and never dries hard, the silicone-rubber adhesive is for you. Think of it as a sealer around two hard-surfaced items. How about the fiberglass hull and the propeller shaft on your radio-controlled model? This glue is not only excellent to seal out the water, but its nonhardening characteristics absorb vibrations.

Devcon has one called "clear silicone rubber." Hosco's GOO, is another. DuPont has one, as well as the 3M company. Choose one. Allow it to air-dry and prepare yourself for the aroma of ammonia. Full cure is effected in 24 hours and that's as hard as she gets.

Expect to find this one in hobby shops or plumbing sections. This is a tub, tile, and caulking sealer.

You will need to use a glue of some type, even if you carve your model from a solid block. The choice, I trust, has been made a little simpler by this chapter. Not all of the glues, adhesives, and cements that were mentioned are available. The market changes too rapidly. The chemists and the compounders come up with new and better formulas faster than you can try them. Some mentioned are on your shelves or in the drawer, workbox, or area, this very moment. How you use them or how you will continue to use them is your choice.

Each adhesive has a specific and intended role in the building of your ship model. All were manufactured with a purpose in mind other than profit. Improper use, like anything else, will result in failure.

TEN

Construction of the Hull

I tell this tale, which is strictly true,
Just by way of convincing you
How very little since things was made
Things has altered in the shipwright's trade.
—RUDYARD KIPLING

SINCE THE DAWN OF TIME, THE BOAT BUILDER, OR shipwright, has determined the shape of the hull. It was his design, his workmanship, and often his own labor that produced the final product that went forth upon the waters. He saw to the cutting and shaping of the wood and the building of the ship, and directed the search for the tree limbs that grew in the shapes he needed.

Natural preshaped wood not only saved time, but was stronger by the very nature of its growth (FIG. 10-1). *Compass timbers,* as they were known, were often developed by deforming young trees. It wasn't long before the forests of England and the coasts of most countries were devastated through the removal of such timbers. In no time at all, the so-called stout ships of English oak were being built of imported wood. Wars were fought for the forests contained within a country's boundaries. One of the fastest growing industries in the American colonies, before they won their independence, was the export of timbers to England. It took over 2,000 trees to build an English ship of war.

Model shipwrights are not faced with this problem. Their task is on a smaller scale. Materials are easy to come by, and with modern tools, much easier to shape. Imagine what it would be like to search the backyard, woods, and forests for branches and twigs that matched the shapes you needed for your model.

Another, and perhaps greater, advantage over a master shipwright of old is the modeler's choice of hull. He can select the type of hull he wants to build. The modeler concentrates on the shape he wants, not the sailing ability or cargo-carrying capacity. He is free to choose the method of construction.

Basically, the shapes of hulls are divided into two classes: the *hard chine* and the *soft chine* (Fig. 10-2). The hard chine is a sharp coming together of the sides and bottom. This is the shape and design of the flat-bottomed dory, rowboat, or skiff. It is also the shape of the faster, high-powered ships and boats that must move through the water and "plane" the waves.

The soft chine is a smoother coming together of the two components to form the shape. This is the round bilge of ships designed for maximum cargo space. It remains the shape of many ships today. Soft chine gives the greatest capacity for cargo and allows the best unrestricted movement through the water.

There are occasions when the two chines are merged in the interest of design and shape. The naval architect might combine them by giving free vent

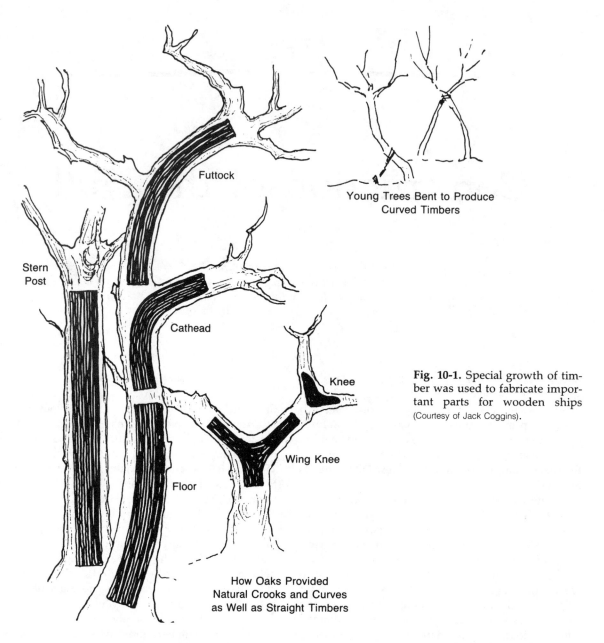

Futtock

Young Trees Bent to Produce
Curved Timbers

Stern
Post

Cathead

Knee

Fig. 10-1. Special growth of timber was used to fabricate important parts for wooden ships (Courtesy of Jack Coggins).

Wing Knee

Floor

How Oaks Provided
Natural Crooks and Curves
as Well as Straight Timbers

to his ideas. The shape and chine of the hull are important factors for the modeler to consider when choosing a building method.

SOLID-HULL BUILDING

The choice of hull-building method should be based on the size of the model, the material availa-

ble (or desired), your skill, and the desired results. In the solid-hull building method, a solid block of material is selected and the shape of the hull is slowly carved. It is not unlike sculpting. For the most part, hand tools are used. It is a slow and painstaking process. The shape is slowly carved to fit outside templates. Every modeler should carve a solid hull at least once (FIG. 10-3).

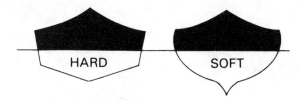

Fig. 10-2. The shape of the hull, its *chine,* is hard or soft (Courtesy of Moonraker Publications).

You can have the hull custom-made. This is an acceptable practice. Pattern makers are a vanishing breed. If you have a friend who is a ship modeler and loves to carve hulls, perhaps you can prevail upon him to do the work for you.

You also can buy solid hulls that have been preshaped by machine. This type of hull is furnished with kits. Several kit manufacturers will sell the preshaped hulls.

While we are on the subject of solid hulls as furnished with a kit, a short course in working this type of hull is in order. They are not ready to go with just a little sandpapering. If this is your first try, you should read the instructions that came with the kit. Study the blueprint carefully and note the position of the section lines.

✪ Plane the area where the keel will be attached. Be sure that it is square (FIG. 10-4).

✪ Next, install the keel, stem, and stern post.

✪ Cut templates from cardboard, posterboard, or

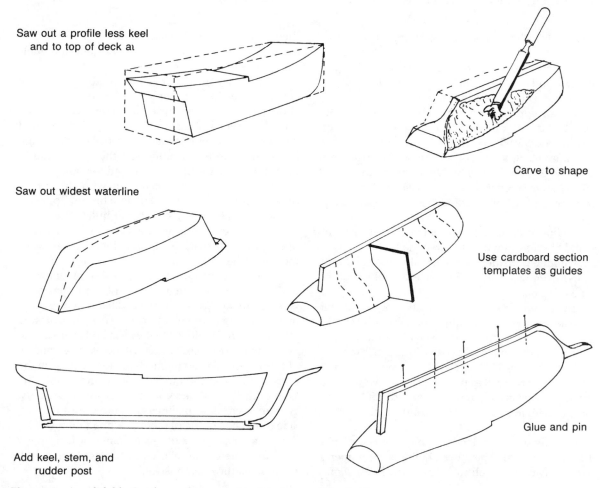

Saw out a profile less keel and to top of deck a

Saw out widest waterline

Add keel, stem, and rudder post

Carve to shape

Use cardboard section templates as guides

Glue and pin

Fig. 10-3. A solid block of wood is carved to the shape of the hull (Courtesy of Moonraker Publications).

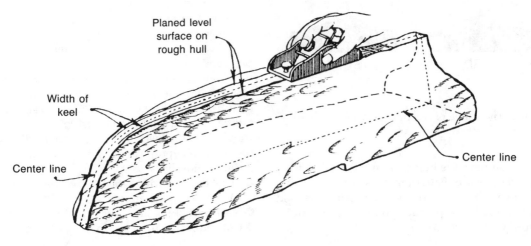

Fig. 10-4. Preparing a solid hull to receive the keel (Courtesy of Model Shipways).

bristol board to section lines, as traced from the plans.

○ Shape the hull and prepare the surface.

○ Locate and cut the top rail, waterway, etc. Remove material as indicated by the plan.

○ You can apply decking in one piece (FIG. 10-5). Scribed decking is often furnished with the kit or as individual planks. (See Chapter 9.)

An excellent source of reading and instructions for all types of solid-hull building, kit or otherwise, is *The Neophyte Shipmodeler's Jackstay*, by George F. Campbell, M.R.I.N.A. (Model Shipways, Bogata, NJ).

It is most difficult to find a piece of material in a solid block from which to carve the hull of a large-scale model. Consider the weight alone. A solid hull carved from wood in a large scale would be rather difficult to manage.

The popular means of construction of a solid hull is the *laminated* method, rather than the solid block. Not only does this reduce the weight, but also saves on the amount of material needed. This is called *bread-and-butter building* (FIG. 10-6). It is also much simpler to secure the material as precut boards of wood. The carving time is greatly reduced. Wood can be laminated (glued) in a vertical or horizontal manner (FIG. 10-7).

Carving out or hollowing the inside is a matter of choice. Several experienced builders recommend that you carve the hull to an even thickness along the sides, except at the attachment of the keel. The thickness needed at the keel is important in models such as racing sailboats.

The lighter weight that results also allows the wood to breathe. Thicker wood has a tendency to check (crack) from expansion and contraction. Solid hulls for larger scales should, therefore, be avoided if at all possible. Hollowing out also allows a design in construction to accommodate the special equipment and gear for radio-controlled versions.

A dramatic effect is achieved with the use of different colors of selected woods. This method is often seen in the carving of the half hulls. The use of different colors to indicate the waterlines was developed in the days of lifting and lofting from scale models rather than plans.

Planking over a solid hull is good training for the builder who wishes to gain experience in handling wood planking strips. With a solid backing, the shaping and fitting of the planks can be the concentrated effort. Planking is affixed to the solid and shaped hull.

Planking over a solid hull will necessitate removal of extra material to accommodate the thickness of the planks and keep the model in scale and true to the lines of the hull. When you are building from plans, be sure to check if the lines are measured to the inside or outside of the planking. A good plan will indicate the measurement. As a matter of fact, many museums prefer the solid planked-over type of hull for models they commission.

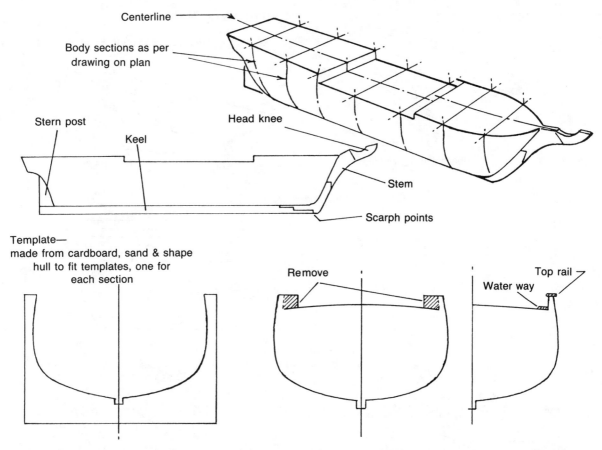

Centerline

Body sections as per drawing on plan

Stern post

Keel

Head knee

Stem

Scarph points

Template—
made from cardboard, sand & shape hull to fit templates, one for each section

Remove

Top rail

Water way

Fig. 10-5. Steps in accurate hull carving and preparation of solid kit hulls (Courtesy of Northshore Deadeyes, Ltd.).

THE BUILT-UP METHOD

In the built-up method, the hull is shaped by the addition of material. In the solid-hull method, material is carved or removed. The built-up hull is like getting back to ship construction. Some refer to this as the *hollow hull*.

The built-up methods should be correctly identified. Let's set the record straight. A *plank-on-frame* construction is a scaled version made in the way the original ship was built (FIG. 10-8). Each frame, or as close a representation to each frame, is built of all its component pieces and then attached to the keel (FIG. 10-9). The keel is also built up much like the real ship. The stem and stern (deadwood) areas are built like the original life-sized vessel. Several aspects might not be actually as the real ship was built, but it is as close a scale model of the original as the modeler

desires. You can compare yourself to a (model) shipwright working in miniature.

The exacting work and planning of building a plank-on-frame ship model will not be detailed at this time. The authors of the books alluded to in other chapters writing explain the requirements in great detail.

The plank-on-frame hull may or may not be planked over completely. A modeler should be proud to show internal construction details. Why would you wish to hide all the efforts and craftsmanship under a layer of planking?

As a compromise to hiding all your talents, you can plank the model to the waterline on one side only, or leave sections of planking off, to expose the frames from the waterline and at any area all the way to the keel. Plank the other side completely. When,

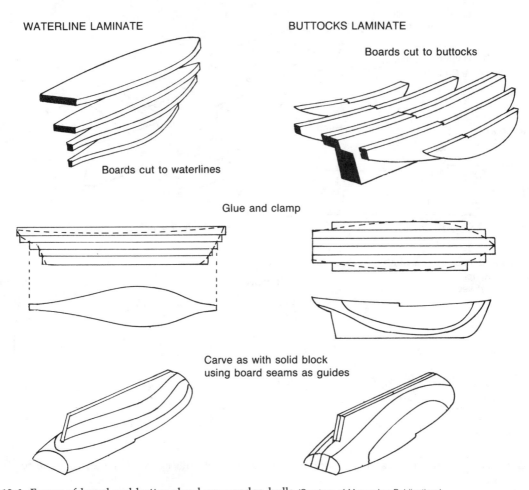

WATERLINE LAMINATE

Boards cut to waterlines

BUTTOCKS LAMINATE

Boards cut to buttocks

Glue and clamp

Carve as with solid block
using board seams as guides

Fig. 10-6. Forms of bread-and-butter glued-up wooden hulls (Courtesy of Moonraker Publications).

Fig. 10-7. A bread-and-butter hull completed using different woods for color (Photo by Steve Sagala).

Fig. 10-8. A plank-on-frame model of a brig of war built at 1:32 scale by Portia Takakjian (Photo by Steve Sagala).

or if, you build a display case, have one side installed with a mirror. The viewer will then be able to see the model in a full profile view. The other side will be seen reflected in the mirror. This has almost a three-dimensional, X-ray effect.

Only two kits come close to the plank-on-frame method: Bluejacket Shipcrafters has produced a model of the winner of the first America's Cup, the

America, and a revenue cutter of 1853, the *Jefferson Davis*, in kit form FIG. 10-10).

The preshaped frames are cut from built-up pieces of basswood, and the keel is formed from several pieces of the same material. The pieces of the keel, bow, and stem that will be assembled to form the base for the frames are also preshaped. The tip of the bow and the stern (taffrail) are preshaped solid

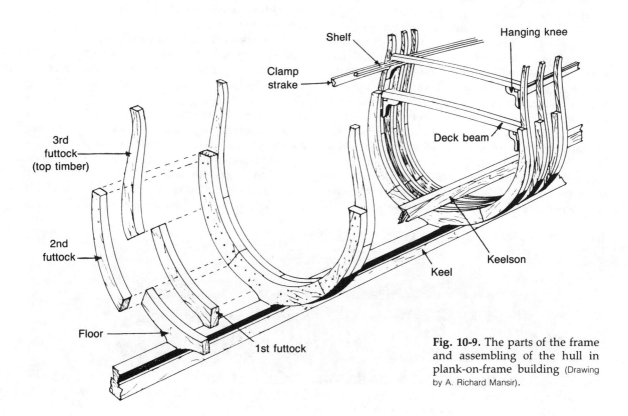

Fig. 10-9. The parts of the frame and assembling of the hull in plank-on-frame building (Drawing by A. Richard Mansir).

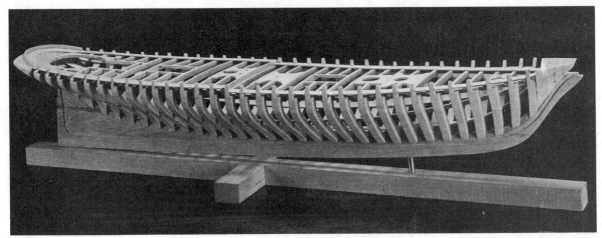

Fig. 10-10. The hull as assembled from the Bluejacket kit of the America's Cup yacht *America* (Photo courtesy of Bluejacket Shipcrafters, Inc., Castine, ME).

pieces of basswood. These models are not completely accurate in the number and thickness of the original ship's frames.

The manner of construction used in the Bluejacket kits is designed for the model shipwright who wishes to build a plank-on-frame model, but does not wish to devote the time and effort needed to scratch-build. I would rate it as another building experience, not unlike construction of a real ship. Here is an area to test your skills in assembling and woodworking. Undoubtedly you will be hearing more of this type of kit in the future.

Northeastern Scale Models, Inc., an American kit manufacturer and wood fabricator, has produced a series of half-hull "with exposed ribs," kits to be mounted on plaques. This is a limited series containing a few famous hulls, such as *America* of 1851, the Baltimore clipper *Alert*, the famous whaler *Charles W.*

Morgan, and the clipper *Black Hawk* (FIG. 10-11). Most of these kits are still in production under the name ''The Sea Classic Series.'' No rigging is intended to be added. The stub masts make a dramatic addition, and a little customizing can turn them into attractive conversation pieces.

The makers of ship model kits have perverted the term *plank on frame*. In reality, they should tell it like it is : *plank on bulkhead*. This version of the built-up ship model is not constructed with built-up frames. The ''frames'' are plywood bulkheads (FIG. 10-12). In some kits, the outlines are simply printed on the plywood. In others, they are die cut, while in a third they are cut out and almost completed for you. All are notched for assembly. Of course, the more labor involved the higher the price.

The number of bulkheads included in the design of these kits is in my opinion and I believe the

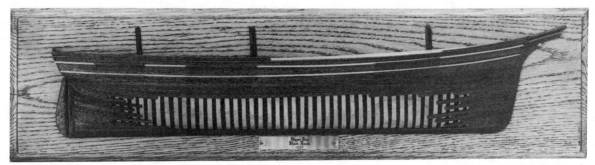

Fig. 10-11. Half-hull model of the plank-on-frame model as produced from the kit of the *Black Hawk*, 1857, by Northeastern Scale Models (Photo courtesy of Northeastern Scale Models, Inc.).

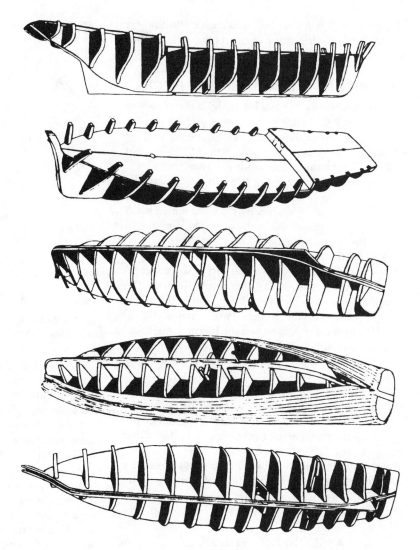

Fig. 10-12. Plank-on-bulkhead construction, referred to as a built-up, or hollow-hull, method (Courtesy of V. Lusci).

manufacturer's, sufficient to ensure the shape of the hull. The kit designer often will use as few as possible to save on the cost of material, especially in the less expensive kits.

The planks—thin wood strips—are to be placed over the bulkheads to form the hull. Again, depending on the designer and the cost of the kit, the planking might be a double layer of thin strips or a single layer of thicker strips. The double-planked hulls use a less expensive wood for the first layer. This underlayer is to be covered with a thin "show" wood. The completed model results in a hull that is completely covered by planking. It is a built-up hull. All mistakes

and errors of construction and patching can be concealed under the planking.

The sharks of commercial salesmanship have convinced many a potential model builder that it is a "breeze" to build a plank-on-bulkhead ship model. It isn't. Many a model has been relegated to the closet shelf while the builder gathered courage. To this day many are never finished.

The majority of kits of the plank-on-bulkhead variety are imported. The basic instructions, translated into English, are sometimes laughable; and often misunderstood. This is perhaps the reason for the profuse illustrations. You might not speak or read the language, but you can follow pictures. Building a model by following the pictures is the rule, rather than the exception.

CORRECTING ERRORS IN KIT PIECES

The foundation of your kit model is the plywood frames and keel. Some of the pieces, which are cut by powerful hydraulic cutting blades, are warped, or unequal. The longest piece, the keel, might be bent as a result of changes in humidity. If this "hogging" is evident by sighting along the part, you might be able to save it.

Wrap the part in kitchen plastic wrap with a small piece of cotton placed out of the way. Moisten it with water. Be careful because all you want is some moisture to fill the air spaces within the wrapping. You do not want saturation. Place the part under a weight on a flat surface. Leave it overnight. Remove the wrapping and air-dry completely under the same weight. Make certain that the part remains flat.

This method should loosen the binding glues and reshape the part. If you can't cure the warp, remake the piece. Aircraft plywood is available at most hobby shops.

Test to see that the bulkheads are cut the same on both sides of the centerline. Mark the centerline and trace the outline of the frame on a piece of paper. Fold the paper at the centerline. Hold the folded paper to the light. If the frame is "true" the lines should overlay one another. If there is too great a difference, discard this unit and make another plywood bulkhead. Wood kits are a forgiving medium (FIG. 10-13).

ASSEMBLING THE HULL

Assemble the hull frame with all parts perfectly perpendicular. Build a jig to hold the keel. Use a flat board with two parallel strips just far enough apart to hold the keel's length. Make them snug enough to attain stability and allow removal. Make the baseboard large enough to allow constant use of a carpenter's square (FIG. 10-14).

Start by placing the middle frame and then each successive frame, alternating in bow and stern directions. Set and glue the frames with the aid of a square and make each part 90 degrees to the other. Wait till the glue dries (overnight) before removing from the jig. Now you have a foundation to plank.

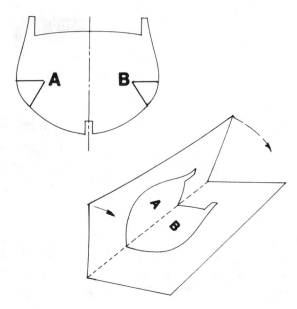

Fig. 10-13. Testing to see that the bulkhead is equal on both sides of the centerline (Courtesy of Moonraker Publications).

When all the bulkheads are secure, get ready for some sanding and truing of the frames. Select a piece of scrap wood long enough to straddle three frames and wide enough to supply a surface for sandpaper. I call this a *truing block* (FIG. 10-15). Wrap medium to coarse sandpaper (40 to 60 grit) around the block.

Be careful not to pull away the layers of the plywood as you sand or force the frames out of the 90-degree position. Stroke the frames in one direction, sighting the truing block to see that it makes contact with at least three frames on each stroke. Use a plank to test the surface for vital contact. If the plank lies flat on the surface, you have accomplished your purpose.

You might need to shim some skimpy areas. Fill the space with scrap strips of wood glued to the edges of the bulkhead (FIG. 10-16). Sand away the surplus with the truing block until the test plank lies flat.

Use a cutting edge—either a knife or a plane—to reduce frames that are too large to allow sanding. Keep the edge of the plywood square. Should you remove too much material, shim and true again.

The *canted* surfaces, at bow and stern where the plank curves to form the structure of the hull, must accept the plank on a flat surface. Remove some of the edge of the bulkhead, the sharp angle, with a

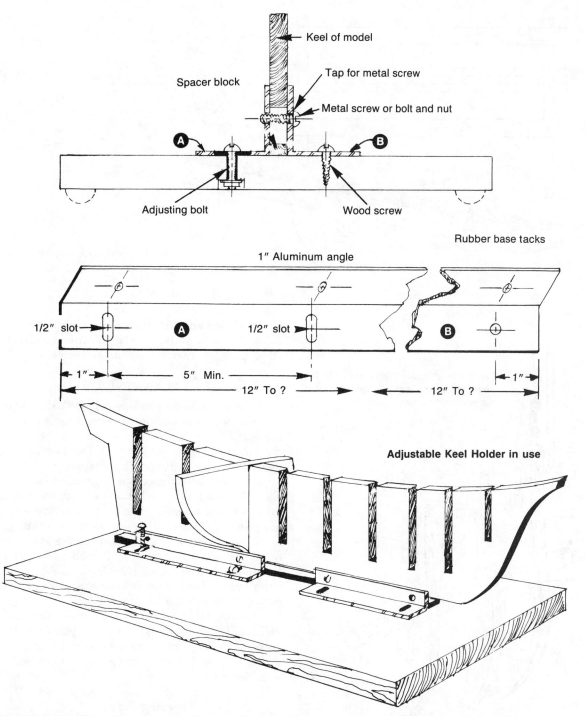

Keel of model

Tap for metal screw

Spacer block

Metal screw or bolt and nut

Ⓐ

Ⓑ

Adjusting bolt

Wood screw

Rubber base tacks

1″ Aluminum angle

1/2″ slot

1/2″ slot

Ⓐ

Ⓑ

1″

5″ Min.

12″ To ?

12″ To ?

1″

Adjustable Keel Holder in use

Fig. 10-14. A building jig to be made from simple materials to ensure proper installation of the bulkheads to the keelpiece (Drawing by A. Richard Mansir).

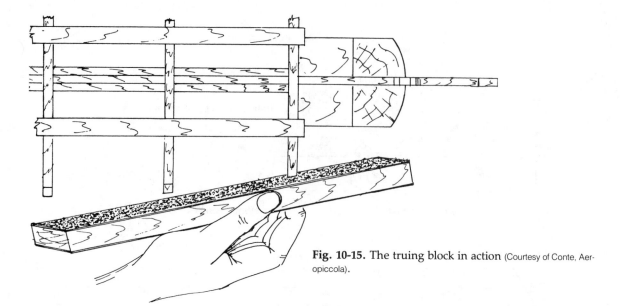

Fig. 10-15. The truing block in action (Courtesy of Conte, Aeropiccola).

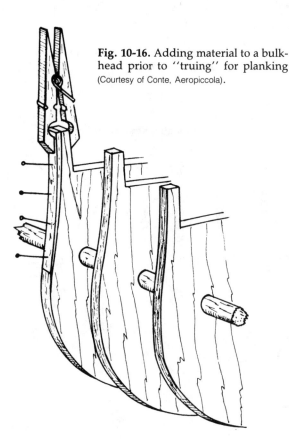

Fig. 10-16. Adding material to a bulkhead prior to "truing" for planking (Courtesy of Conte, Aeropiccola).

blade. Flatten and true the surface with the truing block. Keep the surface contact of three bulkheads when possible, two at the sharper angles.

PLANKING

Where should the planking begin? The "run" of the planks does not follow the waterline. It follows the *sheer line*, that is, the curve of the deck. The place most modelers begin planking is at the sheer or deck line. This plank is fixed without tapering.

Another school of modelers begin planking at the keel. The plank is curved and fixed into the *rabbet*, the groove cut in a piece of timber to receive the edge of a plank. It is best to cut the groove before planking.

Others begin with a garboard plank and lay the finish keel over it to form a pseudorabbet (FIG. 10-17). If you elect to begin your planking at the keel, the sheer line might or might not manifest itself in time as you work upward toward the deck.

You could start at both ends and meet in the middle. I do. I find it most difficult to fit a plank into the rabbet with the planks from the sheer crowding the fit. Tapering and placing stealers is also much neater with this method.

Tapering Planks

Wherever you start, plank each side alternately. Be prepared to taper the planks. There might be only

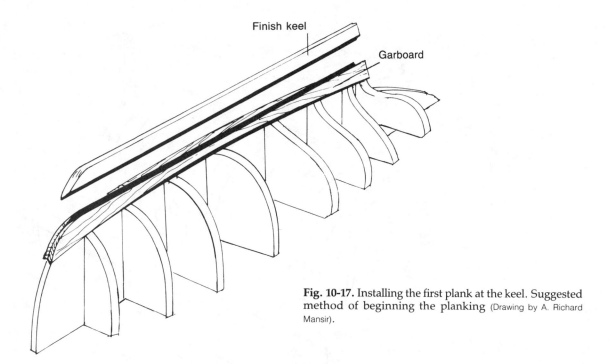

Fig. 10-17. Installing the first plank at the keel. Suggested method of beginning the planking (Drawing by A. Richard Mansir).

a little tapering at the center of each plank as sheer meets keel line. Tapering at the ends is mandatory. You are covering a curved surface with flat strips. You can compare the task to building a mandolin. The planks will overlap as you progress with the work. Eyeballing is a common practice, and removing the excess wood is a matter of experimentation, at least at first. You make it a science through the research and selection of an approved and time-tested method.

F.D. Conte, an Italian kit manufacturer, stated in his book, *Period Model Boat Manual* (Aeropiccola Company), ''It is useless to say that tapering is not an essential operation inasmuch as the perimetrical size of the frames decreases gradually at both ends of the ship (stern and prow).'' (SEE FIG. 10-18).

Preshaping Planks

The curved surface of the hull demands that the planks be preshaped by bending. The method of bending is your choice. You can bend a group of planks in a jig. The multiple bending jig (FIG. 10-19) is constructed of plywood. The base, side pieces, top pressure bar, and incidental parts are made of standard 1-inch pine board. The top pressure bar is held with a series of rubber bands. A bending jig can be as simple as a row of galvanized, aluminum, or other rustproof nails or screws (FIG. 10-20). Place the planks in the jig wet.

You can also use plank benders. Then hold each plank in position until it dries. A mechanical bender crimps the undersurface. Several varieties are avail-

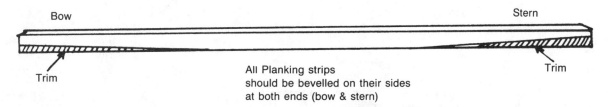

Fig. 10-18. Tapering sites on the plank (Courtesy of Northshore Deadeyes, Ltd.).

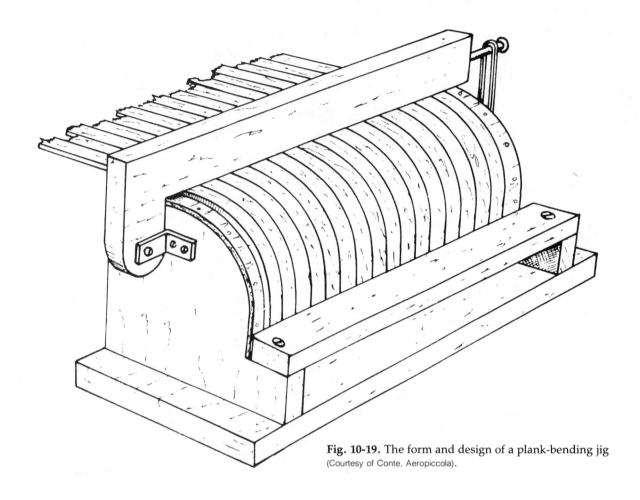

Fig. 10-19. The form and design of a plank-bending jig (Courtesy of Conte, Aeropiccola).

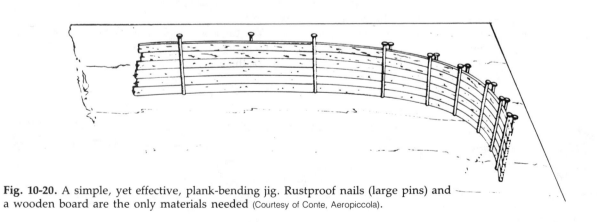

Fig. 10-20. A simple, yet effective, plank-bending jig. Rustproof nails (large pins) and a wooden board are the only materials needed (Courtesy of Conte, Aeropiccola).

able. Among them are plierlike hand-held models, roller wheels that bend the plank by crimping the underside as the handle is turned, and a plate with slotted areas to place the bending jigs. An electric model with a cam and spring holder is made by Aeropicolla of Italy.

You can cut small slits on the glued side of the plank where curved surfaces are of such sharp nature to endanger the plank. Bend planks by pressing two fingers against the thumb. The softer woods (basswood, pine, and thin hardwoods) will respond to this mechanical workmanship.

Heat, steam, and pressure are the best plank benders. Wet the planks in water for about 20 minutes. Bend them over a rounded surface (FIG. 10-21). If at all possible, heat the surface. The resulting steam will loosen the fibers.

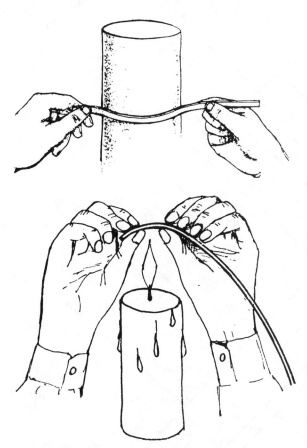

Fig. 10-21. Bending planks by hand with heat after soaking in water (Courtesy of Conte, Aeropiccola).

Holding Planks

Holding the plank in position on the model while the glue dries is a test of inventiveness. (See Chapter 19.) There are planking screws (gadgets) commercially available. Perhaps you would like to make a few for yourself. It isn't that hard. Charles Pipes of the Ship Modeler's Associates of Fullerton, California, deserves the credit for this idea.

The materials needed are a basic hardwood for the plate and a dowel or brass rod for the screw. Although the dimensions given in FIG. 10-22 can be varied according to the size you require for your work, the basic size is practical for all work. You can substitute for the Futaba Servo Mount screw any small screw of the proper size. Assembling remains the same.

The use of this tool is shown in FIG. 10-23. It is recommended that you drill a pilot hole before turning the screw into the supporting areas. The next plank will cover the hole after the planking clamp is removed.

Clamps (spring or C), rubber bands (not too many or too tight), dressmaker's or T pins, and whatever comes to mind can all be used. Remember that the plank is filled with stress and internal pressure. It wants to get flat again. Harder woods resist the most. The answer to perfect planking is planning.

Several texts are available to assist you in planking. The volume by C.F. Conte is a start. *Planking Model Ships* by A. Richard Mansir (Moonraker Publications Workbook Series) is informative. *Lusci's Ship Model Builder's Handbook* by Vincinto Lusci, a noted builder and developer of the Mantua Model (ship) kits, refers in detail to the building of kit models and has extensive chapters on planking. *Ship Modeler's Shop Notes*, (Nautical Research Guild, Inc.) has excellent information on all types of planking. All of these texts are still in print and available through hobby dealers, mail-order houses, and bookstores.

Bowing

There is a tendency for the planks to bow inward if insufficient bulkheads are used to form an underlying support. Bowing and buckling of the strips can also, and often do, occur as a result of climatic changes. Wood, no matter how thin, breathes. Thus, bowing inward or outward is not always a result of poor workmanship.

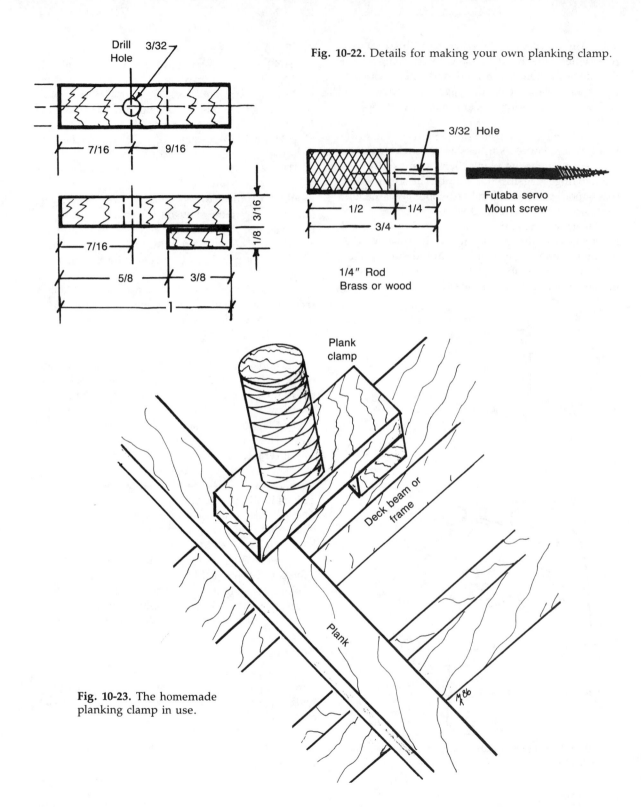

Drill Hole 3/32

Fig. 10-22. Details for making your own planking clamp.

7/16 9/16

3/32 Hole

7/16

3/16

1/8

5/8 3/8

1

1/2 1/4

3/4

Futaba servo
Mount screw

1/4″ Rod
Brass or wood

Plank clamp

Deck beam or frame

Plank

Fig. 10-23. The homemade planking clamp in use.

There is also no set time that this condition can occur. It just happens. Many a novice modeler has become discouraged with hollow-hull building as a result. If the problem occurs from poor construction, however, it can be corrected, even prevented.

The solution to the problem of bowing or concaved shaping of the planks is a matter of planning. First, look to the fixing of the planks. If this step is not done properly, it can produce disastrous results. Good gluing is mandatory. Treenails, or trunnels, which are wooden pegs, will add strength to the construction, but are not necessary at all joints. When kept in scale and using the proper spacing, they add to the model's appearance. Many modelers use small nails and lil pins instead. The fastening method is your choice.

There are specific rules for treenailing planks. The butted ends are staggered according to predetermined rules and adjusted to the lengths of the planks (as would be in real life) and the stealers. Spacing and location will be discussed in another section of this book.

Several kit manufacturers, especially those that make the less expensive kits, advocate the use of metal nails. Some makers and modelers feel that a row of brass nails in each plank at each bulkhead makes for an attractive model. I disagree. Also, the nails are not always needed for strength. (See Chapter 18.)

Secondly, you might wish to secure the frames in their 90-degree positions prior to planking. FIGURE 10-24 gives you an indication of how to accomplish this step.

A method to prevent buckled planking is to either add more bulkheads, or add wide strutlike braces or a filling material, such as blocks of balsa wood. The weakness of thin planks with no underlying supportive material can become a problem when you are cutting out gunports.

FIGURE 10-25 indicates a more advanced method of framing gunports and supporting planks. Use this method if you care to correct the designs in a manufactured kit. These are the methods used when a modeler begins *customizing* kits by redoing the original design or building methods of the manufacturer. The act of customizing begins when a modeler changes something in the building, adds parts that did not come with the kit, or replaces out-of-scale parts.

In several of the better designed built-up kits now available, the bow and stern areas of the models are built up to a solid and firm type of construction. The pieces, usually balsa or an easily workable wood or press-molded material, are fitted into the bow or stern areas and glued to the bulkheads. If your kit doesn't use this method, you can, and should, incorporate it (FIG. 10-26). The added solid material gives a firmer support to the planking. It also ensures a smoother curve when planking. This is a great help; if you are working on an apple-cheeked, bathtub-shaped bow of an early-period ship.

Sometimes fillers are a great help in shaping the tumblehome and strengthening the below-deck gunports. These sites suffer most in the "cutting through" when the gunports are made. You can glue extra pieces of wood between the plywood bulkheads to give added support in these areas. Consider it similar to framing a house and building in the window areas. This method lessens the difficulty of planking with nothing behind an opening.

DECORATIONS

In some of the model kits of period ships, the material designed to be used as the stern galleries or decorative carvings might be metal or simulated wood.

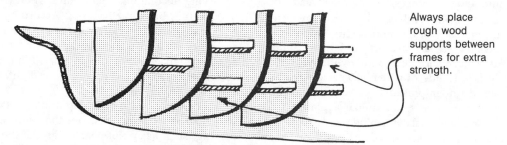

Always place rough wood supports between frames for extra strength.

Fig. 10-24. Reinforcing the bulkheads and maintaining proper alignment while building (Courtesy of Northshore Deadeyes, Ltd.).

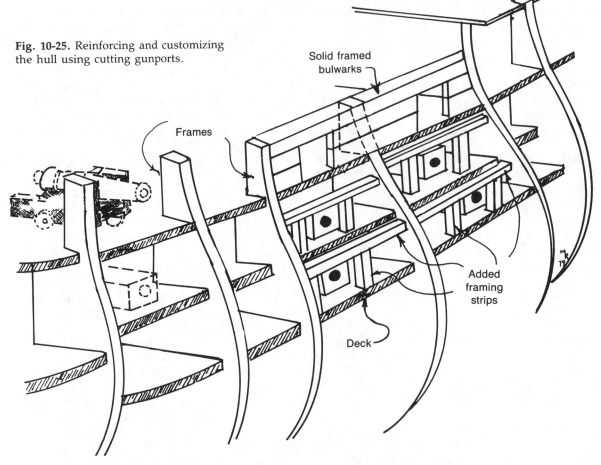

Fig. 10-25. Reinforcing and customizing the hull using cutting gunports.

Solid framed bulwarks

Frames

Added framing strips

Deck

Solid cast-metal taffrails, figures, and stern galleries are included in some of the better grade and higher priced kits. Metal decorations in most kits are usually cast brass or bronze. Some are rather crude. They provide an enormous time saving for the modeler who has not developed the skill of carving.

The multitude of figures and "gingerbread" of the ships of the seventeenth century, while lovely to look at, are the bane of the noncarving modeler.

The cost of metal castings is forcing some manufactures to replace decorations with synthetic wood materials. The decorative figures and wreaths are preformed under pressure, elevated from the molded material. This is not unlike a plastic kit. Sheets of molded material containing the decorations of the sides and bow areas are often supplied. They are to be cut from the sheet and then painted and adhered to the model.

If you build a kit and customize it, why not try to carve your own decorations? Should you decide to expend all that effort in carving the decorations, why not build it from scratch (FIG. 10-27)?

Carving Decoration

Carving decorations seems hard when you first think about it, but it really is not. According to the methods suggested by David Stevens of Brecksville, Ohio, there is a logical and easy approach. It is a fulfilling experience and results in a satisfying period ship model (FIG. 10-28). For your trial flight, David suggests the following steps.

✪ The choice of wood is most important. Use a good workable hardwood. Select one that lends itself to carving, such as apple, pear, or any of the close-grained hard fruit woods. The hours you are about to devote to carving demand the use of choice

CARVED BOW PIECE

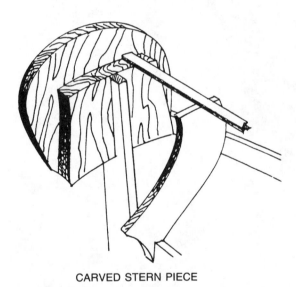

CARVED STERN PIECE

Fig. 10-26. Customizing the hull with fillers at the bow and stern areas (Courtesy of Moonraker Publications).

materials. Holly and boxwood have been modeler's woods for generations.

✪ Use the castings that came with the kit as your models. A pair of dividers is your most valuable tool to check accuracy and act as a guide to the removal of wood.

✪ The work will be done in either of two methods. Carving in the round, as with the figureheads and decorations at the stern, or as relief carvings, such

as wreaths, beakheads, etc. Relief carving is by far the easier method.

✪ Draw or trace the outlines (patterns) of the relief areas to be carved.

✪ Drill out the areas that will be removed (FIG. 10-29). Keep the depth constant by using a wood sleeve placed on the drill bit. The length of the drill protruding from the wood will keep the hole at the desired depth. A Dremel or similar hand drill or a drill press will speed the work.

✪ Chip out spaces in the area of larger removal. Use a router or steel bit to remove material.

✪ Use a sharp knife to carve and shape the relief aspects.

After a little experience duplicating the metal decorations that came with the kit, you might be so thrilled that you will become a scratch carver and do all the decorations on your masterpiece.

MINIATURES

A new school of modeling is becoming increasingly popular. Miniaturization is a form that takes more patience and less room than other kinds of modeling, as well as a lot of skill (FIG. 8-30). Some of the scales are 1:100. That is the average; many are smaller. Great models are being built in small scales in almost perfect duplication of the real ship. This work is done in the manner of the traditional piece-by-piece method or in the built-up scale model method. It is shipwright's work in microscale.

Should you wish to investigate this method, it is presented by the world's most famous miniaturist in written form. There are others, but *Shipbuilding in Miniature* by Donald McNarry (Conway Maritime Press) is still the bible of the microsized devotee. The book has been reprinted from the 1955 issue. Another, although not as complete, reading on the making of miniature models is the work of Mr. C. Monk, *Windjammer Modeling* (1954).

PLASTIC HULLS

Not truly a form of construction, but rather a shortcut in assembly is the use of plastic hulls. These hulls come in two types. The first, and the most familiar, is the one composed of preformed hull and pieces. They are mass-produced and sold as kits almost everywhere. The hull usually comes in two pieces, and the components are pressure-formed. All

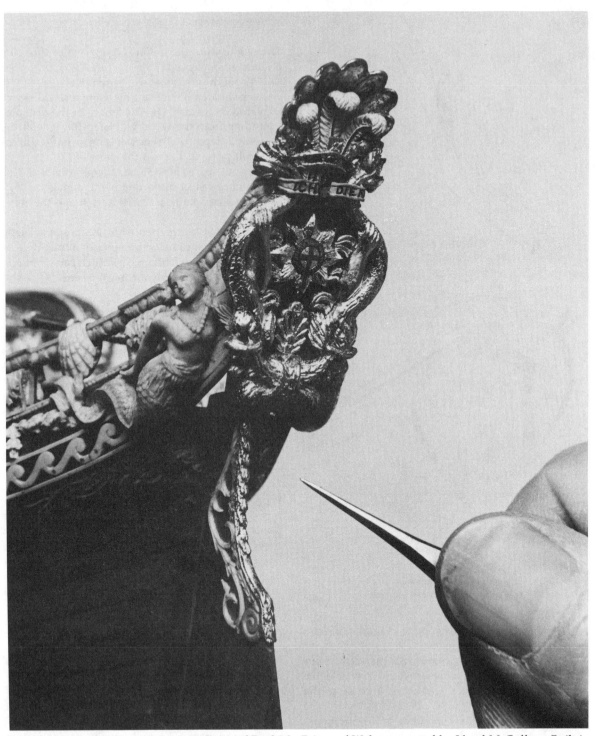

Fig. 10-27. Stern carvings of the State Barge of Fredrick, Prince of Wales, executed by Lloyd McCaffery. Built in a scale of 1:24, the skill of the modeler is shown in close-up (Courtesy of Lloyd McCaffery).

Fig. 10-28. The carving and the details of the bow of an 18-gun brig of war by Portia Takakjian (1:32 scale) are prime examples of the shipbuilder's art. Use of contrasting colors of natural wood gives added vitality. Note the use of treenails (Photo by Steve Sagala).

of the parts to make the model are styrene pressure-molded plastic.

Today's market offers detailed plastic ship models of all periods and description. The names of the ships are famous. A ship in the news is a model kit that will sell. The prices of the kits range from a few dollars to hundreds. The number of parts varies from a few to thousands. Perfect assembling and painting is the test of the modeler's skills. The model can be customized if so desired.

Customizing Plastic Kits

You can customize a plastic ship model kit by using only specific formed parts. In the case of a sailing ship, use only the assembled and painted hull. Customize the remainder of the ship, from the deck piece to the topmast. Lay a thin layer of wood planks over the deck. Reproduce masts, spars, and deck components in wood. Keep everything in proper scale.

Fig. 10-29. Drilling out the wood in preparation for carving a scroll (Courtesy of David Stevens).

This method is becoming favored by those who hate to build hulls but love to build ship models from a kit. For guidance, try the book *How To Build Plastic Ship Models*, by Les Wilkins (Kalmbach Books, Milwaukee, WI).

The masts and spars of a plastic model will sag and warp under the pull of the rigging, heat, and the ravages of time. Wooden masts and spars, however, will not slowly bend out of shape. If you wish to use these plastic components, you can strengthen them. The larger models have hollow masts. After assembly, you can stiffen the unit with a solid core. Use an inserted piece of shaped wood or pour a setting material such as epoxy into the hollow center. Use care.

Molded Hulls

The larger established American and European manufacturers of ship-model kits are offering molded hulls. The material is vacuum-formed plastic in most cases (FIG. 8-31). You can use the method of build-

Fig. 10-30. The stern carvings of a model of the *Berlin* by David Stevens (Courtesy of David Stevens).

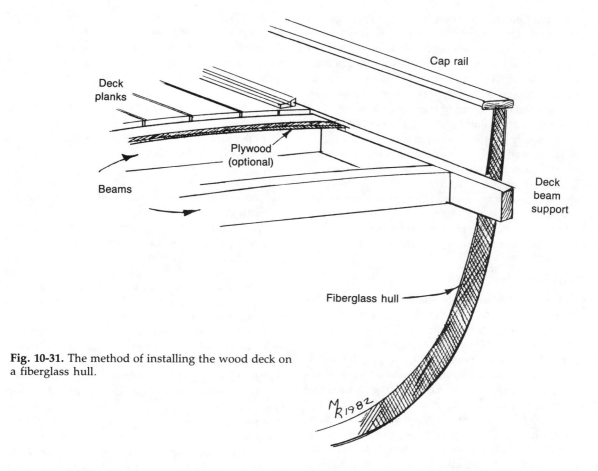

Deck planks

Cap rail

Plywood (optional)

Beams

Deck beam support

Fiberglass hull

MR 1982

Fig. 10-31. The method of installing the wood deck on a fiberglass hull.

ing in wood from the deck up for these kits, as well (FIG. 8-31).

Several manufacturers offer glass reinforced plastic (GRP) hulls for sale. For the most part, they are limited to military vessels, but many makers will build a custom hull for a client. You can specify a size in inches or as large as 10 to 12 feet. All hulls are in scale, and are as historically accurate as possible.

The sailing yacht devotee can select from several fiberglass, GRP, and heavy styrene vacuum formed plastic hulls. Scale versions of historic sailing ships also have been rendered using fiberglass for the hull and details. Wood was used to complete the models.

Better grade kits use (GRP) also. Everything, except the motors and radio-control gear, is usually included. The more gear included in the kit, the higher the price. Selections are based on desire. They do make attractive static models. You can, if you wish, convert your static version to movement by simply

restructuring the interior and adding the working gear.

Radio-Control Models

Large static models with plastic hulls can be used for action models. Reinforcing the hull is recommended. The plastic kits were not designed for the gear or to install radio control. You can make a radio-controlled version with a little customizing and watertight construction. Again, these kits can vary in completeness and quality. The selection of these types of ships is limited.

Radio-control enthusiasts can select a hull or a complete kit to construct a ship model. The type of material used to build the hull is not important, as long as it is waterproof. Excellent models are made with balsa hulls shaped over plywood bulkheads. To waterproof, use a fiberglass covering, epoxy sealing, or paints. Glue the wooden hull together or coat it with epoxy internally, and paint it on the outside.

Most manufacturers offer some version of a model or group of models for the radio-control market. The selection of models is limited to the manufactured units and kits. For the most part, radio-controlled kits are of warships or more modern vessels, and quaint working ships such as tugboats, fishing trawlers, and pleasure boats.

Plastic and fiberglass submarine hulls are becoming quite popular. these ''working models'' are constructed by the enthusiast who wants a submerging model. The models are radio-controlled versions. Components must be watertight. There is a high mortality rate in this form of ship modeling, usually because of small errors in construction.

Fabricating Hulls

The modeler who wishes to fabricate or is not able to find the manufactured plastic hull of the ship he wishes to build still has a choice. He can prepare a mold and build a fiberglass hull. There are three basic methods: the negative mold, the positive mold, and a combination of both, for models requiring internal and external structure details to be molded into the surface. This is a subject unto itself and will not be discussed at this time. It is, however, not a difficult method and is gaining in popularity.

Recommended reading, should you wish to construct your own fiberglass hull, includes *Building Fiberglass Ship Models From Scratch,* by Richard V. Humphrey (TAB Books), and *The Glassfiber Handbook,* by R.H. Warring (Argus Books).

There are many books on the subject of forming and working with plastics. These two are best suited for ship modelers. A trip to your local library will be of great assistance if you are not familiar with the medium. Learn it carefully. You will be dealing with dangerous components.

EXOTIC MATERIALS

Last, and by no means an improper method, is the building of ship models (hulls) from obscure materials. Ever heard of the use of bone? The famous prisoner-of-war models of the Napoleonic era, which were made of soup bones, human hair, and other materials, are an art form that is being revived. The material is true bone, ivory from the keys of old pianos, or ivory-tinted and -textured plastic.

The simulation and copying of the method is becoming popular. Many are simply pieces of these materials planked over a solid hull of carved wood. Collectors who have a taste for the unusual and bizarre, and have the money, have created this demand.

Paper and paper products are also used to build ship models. Although many would scoff at this method, it is an art form in itself, and in some cases is difficult to master. The use of hard-pressed board and the better known bristol board cards is also experiencing a revival.

Metal ship models have been made by enterprising and experimenting individuals. Several have used precious metals. A rendition of a period sailing ship on display at a gallery in New York is constructed of sterling silver. The workmanship is so fine and the scale has been adhered to with such complete faithfulness that the gallery owner does not know how to classify it. One faction says it is a sculpture, another an assemblage. I say it is a ship model that is a work of art.

Mystic Seaport Museum displays an unidentified ship of the line built of glass. The vessel is 21 inches long, 17 inches high, and 8 inches wide. The model was brought from France in 1852 by Capt. David Farnham.

Of the more than 50 models on display at Mystic Seaport, ranging in size from 7/8 inch to 8 feet long, several are of bone, glass, silver, fiberglass.

STYLES AND TYPES OF HULLS

It is not the purpose of this chapter to detail all the methods of hull construction mentioned here. There have been, and undoubtedly will be, volumes written on the subject. Rather than state which manner of building is best or favored over the other, I prefer that you, the builder, choose.

If you are a kit builder, you have a limited choice of ships to model. All you have to select from are kits that are available. The ships usually follow the trend of what is popular, current, or has a hull shape that can be altered slightly, resulting in another kit. You are limiting your freedom of choice to the offerings of the commercial world.

Did you ever stop to think that someone out there has built or is building a better *Victory* than you have? Why not channel your energy to a lesser known model? It can be just as challenging. Perhaps you can derive even a greater satisfaction from doing the work from the very beginning. The information is there; you just need to dig a little deeper.

If you are a scratch builder, you also, by your own choice, limit yourself to the ships you model. Research is tedious and often frustrating. Many scratch builders limit their choice to ships for which information is readily available. Many believe from this easy-to-obtain information that their version is the only and best rendition. Wrong.

INFORMATION

Let us explore the printed sources of information that already exist on the subject of hull building. Some of these sources are readily and easily available. Others are out of print and will take a little effort to find. I have taken the liberty of listing the books, pamphlets, etc. according to types of construction. In several issues of periodicals, entire articles have been devoted to the titles and authors of ship model-building volumes, both past and present.

The information contained in some of the writings might be only a few sentences. Some might run a chapter or two. There are very few complete, all-encompassing volumes devoted to a particular hull-building method.

The exceptions are books, writings, articles, and references to the building of "real" ships and boats. There is often too much information in these texts. If you have secured this information to use simply to build a ship model, you might find the subject overwhelming. You will need to redraw most plans and prints of a real ship to produce a ship model. Many of the parts used in the building of the hull are not needed in a model.

In researching books on building ship models, you will need to seek out the sections that cover building a ship model's hull. These sections are most often devoted exclusively to a single method of construction. The author will cover a vessel's history and how to build that particular model. Others will write and illustrate a combination of all things. The author usually has experience and the ability to set in print the knowledge gained. Authors writing about

the construction of the fiberglass hulls seem, for the most part, to stick to the subject exclusively.

General Reference

A few of the following volumes on methods of hull construction have stood the test of time and are still in general use.

Period Ship Modeling
R.K. Batson
Argus Books, Ltd.

Scale Model Warships
John Bowen
Conway Maritime Press

Waterline Ship Models
John Bowen
Conway Maritime Press

The Construction of Model Open Boats
Edward C. Freeston
Conway Maritime Press

Building Warship Models
P.C. Coker, III
Cokercraft

Block Ship Models
C.G. Davis
Edward Sweetman, Inc.

Ship Model Building
Gene Johnson
Cornell Maritime Press

Building Ship Models From Scratch
Kent Porter
TAB BOOKS, Inc.

Ship Modeling Hints and Tips
J.H. (Jason) Craine
Conway Maritime Press

How To Make Old Time Ship Models
Edward W. Hobbs
Brown, Son & Ferguson

Scale Model Sailing Ships
John Bowen
Conway Maritime Press

How to Make Old Time Ship Models (All methods)
Edward Hobbs
Brown, Son & Ferguson

Five Historic Ships From Plan to Model
George S. Parker
Cornell Maritime Press

Techniques of Ship Modeling
Gerald A. Wingrove
Argus Books, England
(advanced methods)

Neophyte Ship Modeler's Jackstay
Model Shipways
(How to handle the preshaped solid hull)

Plank-on-Frame References

Both plank-on-bulkhead and plank-on-frame methods are discussed in the following books and publications:

Period Model Boat Manual
F.D. Conte Aeropiccola

Ship Model Builder's Handbook
V. Lusci Mantua, Italy

Original versions were in Italian. The books have been translated and are written in clear and concise English and profusely illustrated.

A. Richard Mansir has written a series of publications devoted to various aspects of ship building. Among them is his soft-cover publication, *A Ship Modeler's Guide to Hull Construction* (Moonraker Publishing), recommended as another learning book.

The introduction to terminology and identification of the parts of the hull is, with a few minor errors, quite good. The illustrations are outstanding and many are in color. Most of Mt. Mansir's publications have been compiled into a book with hard covers and color illustrations, *The Art of Ship Modeling* (Van Nostrand Reinhold). It contains many models to view and many methods to study.

Keys to Successful Ship Modeling
Richard O. Roos
Moonraker Publishing
(Aero, a division of TAB BOOKS, Inc.) (A good beginners book for plank on bulkhead.)

The subject is also covered in a volume by Colin Riches entitled *Ship Models From Kits* (Conway Maritime Press, England). The text is easy to follow, and it is profusely illustrated. Go with the text and ignore the workmanship shown in the photographs.

Building in the true plank-on-frame method is covered in the following books. I have taken the liberty to identify some of the methods of plank-on-frame construction as proposed by the authors.

Plank on Frame Models
Volume I and Volume II
Harold Underhill
Brown, Son & Ferguson
Recommended reading on how to build the Brig *Leon*, including lifting and lofting frames. Applicable to plank-on-frames. Applicable to all plank-on-frame construction step by step. Vol.II covers Masting & Rigging.

The Built Up Ship Model
Charles C. Davis
Sweetman & Co. NY
Conway Maritime Press, United Kingdom
Am. Brig *Lexington*, construction in a step-by-step manner. Covers preshaping the frame before assembling.

Ship Model Builder's Asst.
Charles C. Davis
Sweetman & Co., NY
Conway Maritime Press, UK
Chapter on plank-on-frame construction and details of scratch-building in period ships.

The Colonial Schooner
Harold H. Hahn
Naval Institute Press
Chapters show a different method of frame building, using a jig and building upside down.

Ship Modeler's Shop Notes
Nautical Research Guild
Bethesda, MD
A must for all ship modelers. Covers much!

Building Model Warships
P.C. Coker
Cokercraft
For the modern (1900+) builder. All methods included, with a good section on plank-on-frame construction.

A Ship Modelmaker's Manual
John Bowen
Conway Maritime
The hull and fittings of the modern nonnaval ships.

The 32-Gun Essex: Building A Plank-On-Frame Model
Portia Takakjian
Phoenix Publications
Cedarburg, WI
Book form of the series of articles that were published in *Model Ship Builder*. A step-by-step instruction guide to be used with the author's plans.

There are special items to be covered in the construction of hulls that are mentioned in written volumes. The building of the half hulls and waterline type models might be of particular interest. John Bowen's book, *Waterline Ship Models* (Conway Maritime Press, England) deals with the subject in a straightforward manner.

Other Information Sources

You must not overlook periodicals. They are published on a continuing basis in many countries. You might wish to subscribe to the writings on building and researching ship models in several languages. I do. They offer interesting approaches and varied, as well as interesting, subjects. If you can read pictures, you are all set. If you can read the language, you are a wonder.

Not many discuss hulls as a separate subject. The construction of the hull might be a part of the series of writings concerning the building of a particular ship model. The hull is covered in detail. Most, if not all, of these writings assume that you are familiar with that particular method of building.

Read and study any method of model building that is different in any way. If you have never attempted that method, it might prove challenging. You should be familiar with all methods, even if you never intend to use them.

Following is a listing of the periodicals that are available for subscription. Identification as to contents will be indicated; however, the writings and information might vary with each issue.

Model Ship Builder
P.O. Box 128
Cedarberg, WI 53012
Bimonthly. The general format is dedicated to ship modeling in general. All phases of construction are discussed. Building hints and tips are given in each issue.

Scale Ship Modeler
7950 Deering Ave.
Canoga Park, CA 91304

Model Boats
Model & Allied Pubs.
P.O. Box 35, Wolsey House
Wolsey Rd. Hemel Hempstead,
HP2 4SS, England

Scale Ship Modeler (bimonthly) and *Model Boats* (monthly) are, for the most part, directed toward the radio-control builder. Articles deal mostly with the steel-hulled vessels of modern (1900 to date) ships of all nations and uses. Sailing ships and their construction are often included. *Model Boats*, offers information for the sailing yacht enthusiast. Occasionally, removable, full-scale plans for the ships under discussion are included.

Ships in Scale
23 Just Rd.
Fairfield, NJ 07007
Bimonthly. Similar in format and presentation to *Model Ship Builder*.

Model Shipwright
Conway Maritime Press,
24 Bride Lane, Fleet St.
London, EC4Y 8DR

North American Agent:
The Dromedary
6324 Belton Dr.
El Paso, 79912
Quarterly. The "best" in ship modeling periodicals. It covers all forms of ship-model construction, history, and methods. A must for all devotees of ship modeling.

Clubs, Organizations, and Guilds

Excellent sources of information, ones that are literally gleaned from fellow modeler's minds, are publications of ship model clubs and organizations. While there seem to be an abundance of clubs, not all publish a newsletter (which is no detraction of their strength of purpose).

Publications of some of the clubs spring up almost overnight. Waiting to see who will survive is interesting. Following are the strongest that have survived.

The Journal of the Nautical Research Guild
6413 Dahlonega Rd.
Bethesda, MD 20816

From its early days of publication in 1958 as a mimeographed offering, this publication has grown into one of the most accepted and accurate periodicals for ship modelers and devotees of ships and maritime history. the format is historical, and the accuracy of ship-model construction, when reported, is unquestionable. Ample illustrations are included. A few building tips are included on occasion. This quarterly publication is a must for dedicated and accurate modelers and historians alike.

Steamboat Bill
Steamship Historical Society of America
414 Pelton Ave.
Staten Island, NY 10310

This publication is for the devotee of the steamship. River vessels and commercial passenger-carrying ships are covered. The main interest seems to be the paddle wheelers of the past.

The Fife Rail
Nautical Research and Model Society of Chicago
620 Saddle Rd.
Wheaton, IL 60187

Similar in approach to the *Journal of the Nautical Research Guild*, with a few shortcomings. It is still published in Xerographic form. Much of the material is copied from other sources. Original articles by the members are quite informative. The binding is a stapled loose-page form. A better than average club publication. Many issues are continuations of a study program.

Broadsides
The U.S.S. Constitution
Model Shipwright's Guild of New England
P.O. Box 247, Lynn, MA 01903

This is the annual publication for members and friends of the organization. There is, as with most well-organized clubs, a monthly newsletter. This issue is the culmination of all the best from the newsletters and a few extra goodies besides.

The Newsletter of the Shipmodeler's Association of Fullerton, California
2083 Reynosa Dr.
Torrance, CA 90501

A good example of what a monthly club publication should be. Breezy, newsworthy, and complete with hints and tips. This one holds the reader's interest.

South Bay Model Shipwrights
1623 Ben Rd.
Los Altos, CA 94022

The writing is easy-going in this monthly club newsletter. There are ample suggestions on securing materials and information relative to good ship modeling.

Many other organizations also publish newsletters. Some clubs, however, just don't bother to tell anyone of their existence. Territorial recluses I call them.

Today's strongest most active club can be gone like a puff of smoke. Do you remember what happened to the publication of The North Shore Deadeyes of the Chicago area? This is still a strong organization, having overcome the loss of an excellent meeting place. The rebirth of their *North Shore Deadeyes*, a quarterly publication, is in the offing. Many of their educational offerings from issues of the past are reproduced on these pages.

If, by luck, you reside in the area of a club, sign aboard. You can then avail yourself of the members' advice and counsel, as well as the publications. Attending the meetings, especially the show-and-tell segment is an education in what you can do better. If you look around, ask at hobby shops, and look for meeting announcements in periodicals, you might find a ship model club in your area. If not, why not start one?

Without a doubt, there are many books and periodicals that cover the building of hulls. If the comments and controversy you read in the periodicals make you want to look up the references to see who is actually right, then all the better. That's what makes for better modelers. Nobody is always right, and no method is perfect. Perfect models are the result of research and preparation, as well as building.

ELEVEN

Decks and Above Decks

One must learn by doing the thing;
Though you think you know it,
you have no certainty until you try.

—SOPHOCLES

EVERY SHIP HAS A DECK; OTHERWISE IT IS REFERRED to as an open boat. Some decks are steel, some are wood, some are even fiberglass. Steel ships can have wooden decks. Seldom will you find a wooden ship with a steel deck, however. No matter what the material, if a ship is closed over, it has a deck, either full or partial.

The lines of the seams between the planks, and their respective waterproofing materials, are visible on the wooden-decked ship. They are caulked. This is one of the many little details with which a ship modeler must contend. The little details, properly attended to, make a simple ship model outstanding.

Details can become a chore unless you approach them in a logical fashion. You can overcome the difficulty in producing the clean, crisp lines of the deck seams. The butted ends of deck planks are not that difficult to simulate. Indicating the fastenings (treenails) at the butted plank ends and keeping them in scale are just more problems to solve.

There are several tried and true methods to achieve the *seam*ingly impossible tasks. Some you already know, but there are many newer and more experimental ways.

The easiest way is to install the deck as one complete, thin wood covering. This is the so-called *built-over* deck. A one-piece sheet of cardstock, wood, plastic, etc. is applied over the deck beams, false under-decking, or plywood bulkheads. This method of ''laying the deck'' is gaining in popularity.

SCRIBED DECKING

Commercially produced sheets of pre-scribed decking are available in two thicknesses: 1/32 inch and 1/16 inch. The pieces, usually basswood, are manufactured in sizes 2 and 3 inches in width and 22 to 24 inches in length. They are scribed with lines ranging from 1/40 to 1/2 inch apart.

A built-up decking is composed of strips of wood (planks) glued together with a contrasting darker wood glue. The scribed and constructed decking is found in most hobby shops or mail-order catalogs. Scribed mahogany, walnut, or teak plywood is available, but rather difficult to find.

Decking is applied, in most cases, as one piece fastened or adhered to the supporting structures. It is best to prepare a template. You can trace the pattern to the decking material, then cut and fit the part to the final size.

Fitting the decking to *cutouts*, areas that indent the edges of the pattern, is easier if the pattern allows for the cutout. For difficult areas or decks with sharper curves, the test fitting can be difficult. You can split the decking lengthwise at the area of the *king* plank (centerline). Test-fit each half to the cutouts and glue the completed deck into position. You can split decks with unusual or extremely curved patterns into several lineal pieces, if necessary.

You can darken the scribed lines with a contrasting color to indicate the caulking (SEE FIG. 11-1E.) Brush thickened paint (do not use stain) on lightly and rapidly in small areas. Then quickly wipe it from the planks while still wet. The color remains behind in the scribed line.

If desired, you can also indicate butted ends. FIGURE 11-1C shows one method. Add them in the proper pattern for a planked deck using one of two methods. You can use a blade to add a carefully cut line before the coloring, or you can use a sharp, pointed instrument to scribe the butted seam. The cut (scribed) line will assume the same coloring of the deck seams.

After complete drying of the color used to indicate the seam, lightly sand and/or scrape the deck. (FIG. 11-1F). Apply a coat of varnish or shellac after you have fastened the deck to the model and attached

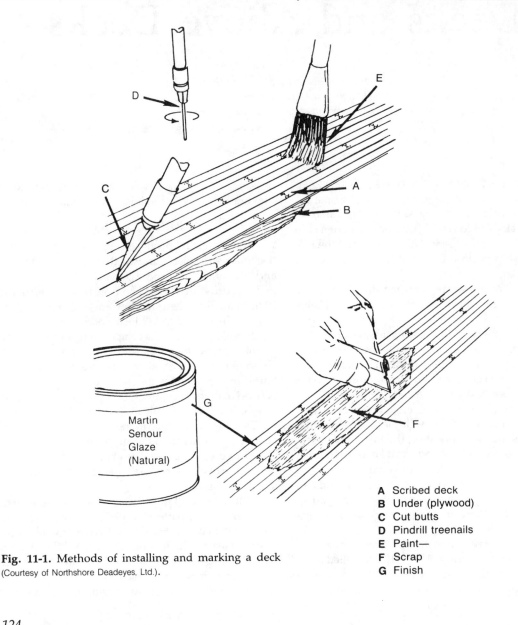

Fig. 11-1. Methods of installing and marking a deck
(Courtesy of Northshore Deadeyes, Ltd.).

A Scribed deck
B Under (plywood)
C Cut butts
D Pindrill treenails
E Paint—
F Scrap
G Finish

124

deck furniture. Some builders prefer to affix the deck to the model after the lines are prepared and do the coloring and final finishing on the model itself.

You can darken the lines with a pencil. Not all deck seams are black, however, so the use of a colored pencil would be indicated. Keep the point sharp and draw (pull) the lines. Do not push. A method of sharpening the pencil and a knife blade for scribing will be discussed later. You can draw the butted ends in the same manner after you cut the lines with a blade.

You can use a sharp, pointed pencil to indicate the treenails in the deck. Keep the point sharp by rolling it over a sandpaper block or use a draftsman's pencil sharpener. Lightly press the point into the material to indicate the treenails.

PRINTED DECKING

Many kits feature a printed sheet of decking, including most wooden model kits from Europe. The lines are black or dark colored. Some modelers are content to use this piece as they find it. Others use this furnished part for customizing by laying individual planks over it.

The method of customizing will be outlined later. The printed lines make an excellent guide for the planks. I suggest you check the size of the planks against the scale of the ship you are building. Often the lines are directed more for aesthetics than accuracy. The printed decking is also available from several commercial sources.

SCRIBING THE DECKING

You can make a scribed deck from a thin sheet of wood or plywood to suit your requirements. Before cutting the decking to the shape of the hull, scribe the lines with a sharp blade or a needle. Use a good, straight edge. I recommend a metal ruler. Use a divider to prick in the line spaces, ensuring even plank divisions. If you exercise a little care and do a great deal of planning, you will accomplish the task in no time. FIGURE 11-2 indicates the method of clamping and scribing a sheet deck. You can darken, or *contrast*, the seams using the method outlined previously. You can simulate the butted ends in the same manner. This method of scribing can be used on any material you choose that will accept a scored line and a contrasting color application.

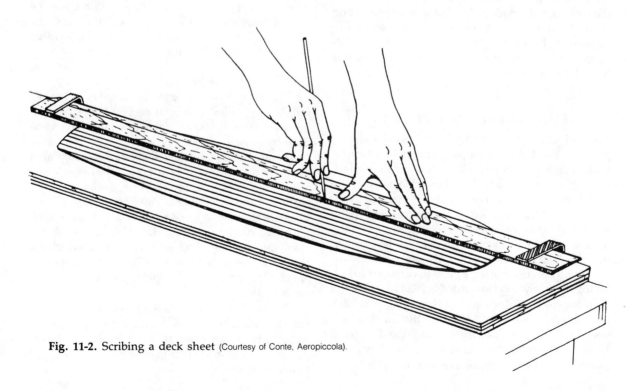

Fig. 11-2. Scribing a deck sheet (Courtesy of Conte, Aeropiccola).

Drawing the Lines

Ship modelers, in the early days before kits and manufactured deck pieces, drew the deck seams. The favored method included the use of India or other forms of waterproof, noncreeping ink. Wood was the material most favored. In some cases, a hard-surfaced posterboard or layered hard-surfaced board (bristol board) was applied as the overdeck on wood models.

The wood or other material was first sealed with shellac, varnish, or lacquer to prevent the ink from soaking or running. A straightedge and a bow pen were used to draw the deck seams on the surface. Butted ends and treenails were also drawn in ink. The deck was then cut, fitted, and affixed to the model. Old models with this method of deck seaming can be seen in most museums and collections even today.

To draw the seams with a pencil, first sharpen the pencil point to a flat wood-chisel shape using a piece of sandpaper glued to a scrap of wood, such as an emery board. Draw the lead tip across the surface to shape and maintain a sharp point. Keep the nonangled side against the rule.

To cut the seams in a wood board, you can use a No. 19 X-ACTO or Mascot blade sharpened to the same shape as the pencil. A No. 11 is excellent on the smaller scale models. The angle is sharpened on the right side of the blade (FIG. 11-3). I am right-handed so I keep the flat (left) side of my chisel-shaped, sharpened blade against the rule. In this way, I can scribe without waving. If you are left-handed, shape and sharpen the blade accordingly.

EDGING THE DECK PLANKS

Undoubtedly the method most used today is planking the deck with properly scaled wood strips. Each strip is laid individually and is cut to a length coinciding with the actual or planned location of the deck beams. The butted end pattern is planned in advance. The "deck planks" are laid according to the desires of the modeler in a complete fashion, or the deck is partially completed. Models can be planked in the revealing admiralty or dockyard model styles.

If you are customizing a kit, you can lay the deck on top of the plywood underdeck. (SEE FIG. 11-1A and B). If the deck is from a kit and is printed, you have the pattern in advance, including the hatches and deck openings. Cut away some additional material from the top of the bulkhead where the deck is attached to allow for the thickness of the planks.

Scratch builders also use this method. The thickness of the underdeck of plywood that is laid over deck beams or other material is incorporated into the design. Their combined thickness is calculated in advance of any construction. Nothing is more distracting or anger-provoking than to find your "thick" deck has caused the bulwarks to be too shallow and your top rail to be only a few inches above the deck. What protects the crew from falling overboard and how can they have a railing to lean on if the top rail is 24 inches (in scale) above the deck?

Deck planking runs fore to aft (FIG. 11-4). It is laid parallel to the centerline of the ship on either side of the king plank. The king plank is usually wider than all the other planks and is laid over the centerline of the ship. The outside planks are called the *margin planks*.

When a deck plank meets a margin plank at a curve, it is *joggled*. Historically there were several methods of joggling. Research will tell you which one was used during the time the ship you are modeling was built. Joggling avoids the sharp point, adds to the strength of the structure, and is in the approved shipwright provisional design (FIG. 11-5).

The angle at which the margin and the deck plank meet is called the *snipe*. The rule is "With the snipe (angle) more than twice the plank's thickness, the plank shall be joggled into the margin plank with a butt not less than half the plank's width."

Methods of Edging

Preparing the deck with simulated caulking before laying is done is one of several long-used and time-tested methods. The following ideas have been used by myself and others.

Paint. Some modelers with power equipment saw their own planks from a stock piece of a selected type of wood. Before ripping your planks, paint the surface of the wood block. Paint both sides if it is a large-scale model. A good black or dark brown semi-gloss enamel does nicely. Saw the planks off the blank in the proper thickness. The edges, which are the painted surfaces, are now caulked. The planks are ready to prepare and apply with the caulking already indicated.

Another method of simulating caulking is to prepare a stack of planks by clamping them together tightly. Brush, roll, or spray on the paint over the exposed edges. Use the paint sparingly and undiluted to avoid creeping.

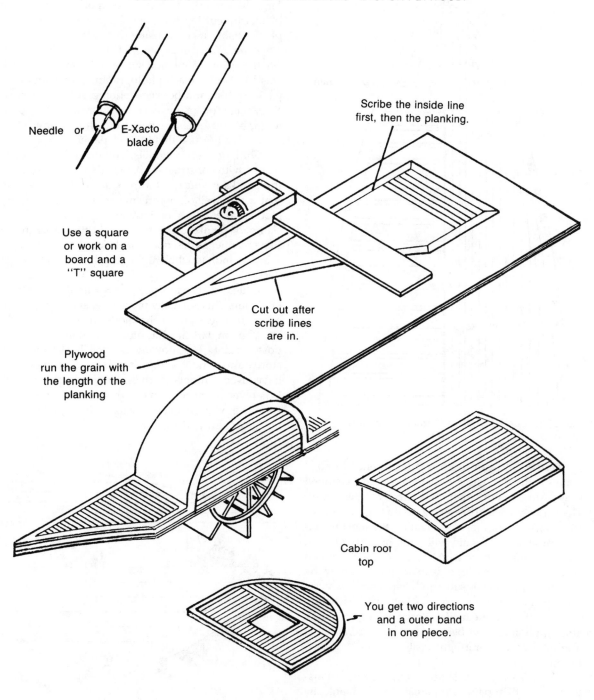

Needle or E-Xacto blade

Scribe the inside line first, then the planking.

Use a square or work on a board and a "T" square

Cut out after scribe lines are in.

Plywood run the grain with the length of the planking

Cabin roof top

You get two directions and a outer band in one piece.

Fig. 11-3. Scribing small decked areas on a model (Courtesy of Northshore Deadeyes, Ltd.).

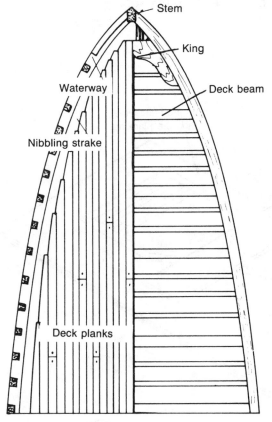

Fig. 11-4. A deck layout and terminology (Courtesy of Moonraker Publications).

Labels in figure: Stem, King, Waterway, Deck beam, Nibbling strake, Deck planks

is a larger scale model, cover both edges of the planks for a thicker seam line after assembly. Separate the planks by cutting the tape along the edges of the planks using a chisel blade (No. 11).

Paper. You can use a variety of materials to simulate the seams. A method suggested some years back was to use the black photographic paper found in packs of film and between photographic papers or X-ray film. Today, however, most film and other photographic materials are packed in aluminum-backed paper. Do not use this type of paper.

On larger scale models, you can edge the deck planks with construction paper. Paper both sides of the planks if you need a thick seam. Use any glue that works well on porous material. Carefully apply glue to the edges of individual, or stacked and clamped, planks. After drying, cut the paper in the same manner as described for electrical or plastic tape. Trim the individual planks to length and apply to the deck.

Glue. You can indicate seams with the use of colored glue. This is a tricky procedure, and I would suggest a test session off the model first.

You can darken white glue by adding dry-powder poster paint. This powder is available at most art stores and school supply houses. Some modelers have used lampblack, dyes, or tints such as RIT. Whatever your selection for color, the agent must be soluble in water and be able to be dispersed by mixing thoroughly in the glue.

Pencil. You can use a soft lead pencil to edge planks with color, either individually or as a clamped stack. Although the method is effective, it is messy. The lead has a way of filtering up during sanding or smoothing operations and staining the most inconvenient areas. The stain will often occur while you are surfacing the deck with varnish or other painted surfacing. The particles of lead are picked up by the solvent. If you use this method, I suggest you spray the top surfaces of your planks with a sealer before applying them to the model. Spray painting the deck after application and before sanding or scraping is also advised. Several light coats are best between sandings.

Tape. You can also simulate caulking with a material other than paint. Prepare a stack of planks by clamping. Firmly fix a strip of electrical or colored plastic tape on the edge of the stack of planks. If this

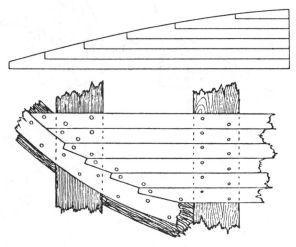

Fig. 11-5. A closer look at nibbing planks and the nibbing strake.

The color of the mixture in its liquid state is a dark gray if you are using black poster powder. Other mixtures will vary. A test drying is suggested before actual application.

Use generous amounts of the glue mixture to fix the planks—just how much will come with experience. Force each plank snugly against the adjoining plank, squeezing glue up between them along the edges and at the butt ends. If you work carefully, there should be no overflow of glue onto the surface of the plank.

Do not attempt to remove the excess glue while it is still wet. A damp rag can wipe away an accidental spill, but you must work fast before the color stains the material. In most cases, leave the mess alone.

After the glue is completely dried, scrape away the beaded excess. Do not sand the deck to remove the beaded glue. Scrape it. Remove all traces of surface glue. Scraping is sometimes, in my opinion, better than sanding. The deck is smoothed and the lines are crisp. You might like the results (FIG. 11-6).

Marker. You can use a felt-tipped marker to indicate seams. To avoid penetration to the deck side, the plank must be painted on the exposed side. You can use varnish, shellac, or Deft. Glue the unpainted side to the deck after marking. This is a tricky method; be careful how you do it. Experiment first.

Wood Filler. You can indicate seams by forcing dark mahogany wood filler into the seam lines of laid decking. To make your own wood filler, mix sawdust from the wood of your choice with a cellulose-based glue.

Leave a space the width of the caulking seam when you are gluing the planks to the deck area. Place a metal removable shim to ensure the correct width. Remove the shim after you apply each row of planking. Thin the mixture with solvent if needed. Force it into the seams with a spatula. Clean the excess away by scraping or using solvent. After the area is dry, you can sand it smooth. This method works well for smaller models.

Methods of Scraping

I prefer the following method to smooth wood surfaces and shapes. Scraping was used long before sandpaper came along and, according to one of my

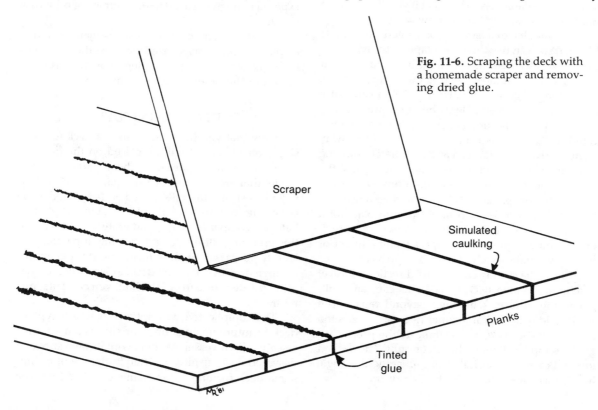

Fig. 11-6. Scraping the deck with a homemade scraper and removing dried glue.

Scraper

Simulated caulking

Planks

Tinted glue

sources, is still a preferred method by cabinetmakers and fine woodworkers.

FIGURE 11-6 shows a scraper in action. This tool is easy to make and can be purchased from wood tool catalogs. To make your own, select a piece of sheet metal or thin plate steel, under 1/16 inch thick. File or grind the edge at 90 degrees to the broad surface. A rolled edge should form, especially with grinding. Remove the edge, but do not sharpen. The "tooth" is what does the work. Tilt the blade in the direction of travel. Exercise caution to keep the cutting surface flat to the work. A nasty gouge can result from tilting.

Making your own scrapers allows you to design the widths and shapes you will need for each particular job. Wide blades, curved shapes, convex and concaved cutting edges—the possibilities are limitless.

One modeler uses 1/4-inch plate glass and pieces under this thickness to make his scrapers. He collects scrap pieces from his local glass and window installer. Other sources are hardware or building materials dealers. You can use thinner pieces for small jobs. The glass is held in a flat wood handle secured by epoxy. There is no need to sharpen this type of scraper, and the cost is so low that if you drop or chip one, you can simply throw it away.

Do you have a supply of dulled removable blades? You can use them as scrapers. Exercise caution. The discarded blades might be too dull to cut properly, but you must use them with care because the cutting edge is extremely thin. You can put a scraper edge on the blade as outlined previously.

The overall use and action of scraping, as indicated in FIG. 11-7, is common sense. Scrape away from the fixed objects, such as a deck hatch combing or cabin. This method prevents buildup against the structure and a difficult clean up afterward.

The bottom panel in FIG. 11-7, marked A through D, will show you how to hold the thin blade of a scraper mounted in a handle. As discussed previously, you can guide flat scrapers using a finger or two to maintain steady downward pressure.

Tilting the cutting edge in the direction of travel results in jumping (FIG. 11-7A). This can, and will, gouge the surface, sometimes beyond repair. The blade held in a vertical manner (FIG. 11-7B) cuts too deeply. FIGURE 11-7C and D indicate the proper angle for scraping either to the left or right. The dashed line indicates the vertical plane. Imagine the angle needed as always being in the line of travel.

DECKING MATERIAL

The method to use to indicate seams depends a great deal on the material used for the decking. The harder, close-grained woods, such as holly, will be easier to work with. Teak is too open grained, and in scale the grain is entirely too large.

Beech and birch are woods to consider for planking. They are somewhat hard and take a nice finish if prepared by scraping and successive sandings using finer grits. Basswood, the most commonly used, is the median wood. Relatively hard and inexpensive, it takes a nice finish. These woods stain well and can be used to simulate other woods, such as teak.

For treenails, if you wish to actually use them in your model for decking or planking the hull, I recommend bamboo. It draws well down to the fineness of a human hair. Place the bamboo in a predrilled hole, after dipping it in glue. Nip off the excess flush with the deck using a fingernail or cuticle clipper. I use sharp wire dykes for the larger and a small wire cutting tweezer for the finer plugs. Sand or scrape the exposed end, along with the decking. The final finish, varnish or shellac, penetrates deeper into the exposed end, giving it a darker, contrasting color than the deck.

Another method to simulate treenails is to drill or punch proper scale-sized holes at the butt ends of the planks. Force a contrasting color, such as wood filler into the hole. Sand or scrape when dry.

DECK FURNITURE

Now that you have established a deck for your ship, consider what will be placed on the deck.

Deck furniture consists of those parts of a ship model that are not part of the deck (FIG. 11-8). You will need strong fife rails placed at designated areas according to your model's plan. Cabins, skylights, hatches, companionways, and grates might fall into this grouping. Binnacle and steering apparatus can loosely be classed as deck furniture. If it penetrates through or rises above the deck, or is a structure that is not the deck or parts of the hull, you can call it furniture.

The complicated descriptions of which type of deck furniture belongs on your ship is a matter for research. Each vessel was built with its own specially designed deck furniture. Often in the life of a ship, some deck furniture was changed, other furniture

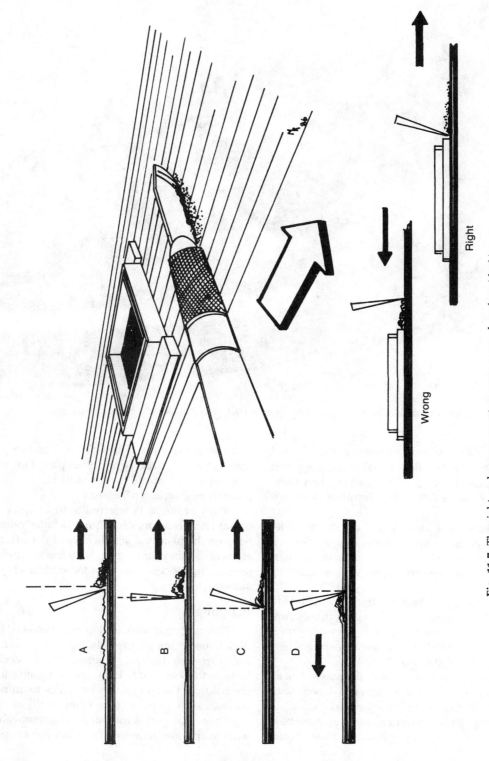

Fig. 11-7. The right and wrong way to scrape a wood surface (deck). Copyright 1980 by Lester W. Wilkins II. Reproduced with permission from the book, *How to Build Plastic Ship Models.* Published by Kalmbach Publishing.

Fig. 11-8. Bow and deck details of an 18-gun brig of war by Portia Takakjian (Photo by Steve Sagala).

added, and still other items removed at the whim of the captain or owners. Should you be modeling such a ship at a specific stage of her career, then there might be a variance in the deck furniture. Check it out.

Kit makers show location and construction details in the plans furnished with the kit. Scratch builders must rely on plans secured from commercial sources or drawings from their own research (FIG. 11-9).

There is nothing more distracting than to find improper deck furniture on a ship model that is supposed to be an accurate rendition, a piece of history. What would you think if you saw a steering wheel on a model of the *Mayflower*?

The same problem occurs with the masts. Not all masts are round. They are not tapered dowels with some things at the top to hold the next "stick" in place. Masts and spars aboard a sailing ship are built in modeling as they were in real life. They should

be built in the same careful fashion and in proper scale as the hull, deck, or any other part of the model. The subject of masts, spars, and rigging will be covered in Chapters 13 and 14.

Many of the texts referred to in Chapter 8 also contain details on deck furniture. Scholarly dissertations on the historical significance of deck furniture are available for your reading. Very few volumes written for ship modelers are devoted exclusively to this subject.

Planning

Planning your work undoubtedly allowed for the deck houses (cabins), fife rails, bitts, guns, and other deck furniture that will be adhered to the deck. *Adhered* is the key word. How are you going to glue them down? Certain glues won't stick to unfriendly surfaces such as paint. (See Chapter 9.)

Unless the part is intended to be removable, always keep some areas unpainted so you can adhere your deck furniture. Before varnishing or waxing a deck, lightly trace in the areas to which you will need to glue other parts. Wood glues must have porous surfaces to penetrate for strength and proper setting. Even the epoxy-based and super glues will pull away or separate after a time if there is no deep penetration. A layer of varnish or a nonpenetratable surface between parts will in time come undone or snap loose under the slightest pressure.

Hatches

The construction of hatches is not complicated. It is the seemingly endless methods that ship modelers use which makes it seem so difficult. A proper hatch belongs on a ship model as much as any other item. Needless to say, it should be in the proper period and of proper construction (FIG. 11-10).

Contrary to popular opinion, you do not need power equipment to build a hatch cover for a period sailing vessel. It is in actuality a grate. The operation of cutting the notches that fit together to make a grate, called *combing*, does not require complicated equipment. I will not discuss the use of a power saw for this task. Note, however, that the Unimat woodworking options even feature a combing attachment.

Following are two methods for hand sawing or making grates. One, shown in FIG. 11-11, is a little tricky in my opinion. The other method (FIG. 11-12) is simpler and results in less picking, repairing, and splitting. Both ideas are for the individual modeler who does not have power saws.

A little hint for making very small scale grates, or other items of deck furniture follows. This is a case of actually making square holes out of round ones.

Fig. 11-9. The deck furniture of the *Calypso* (Photo courtesy of Association des Amies des Musees de la Marine, Paris).

Fig. 11-10. Types of deck hatches and skylights (Courtesy of Moonraker Publications).

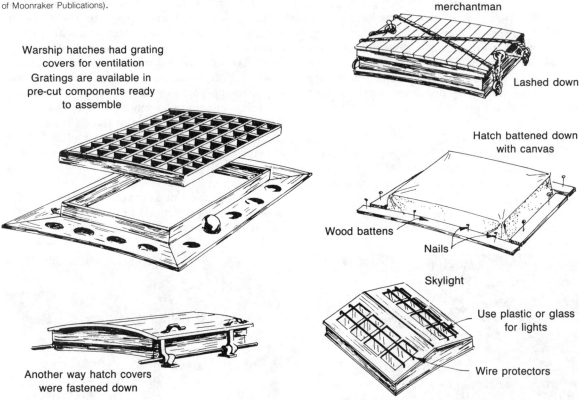

Warship hatches had grating covers for ventilation Gratings are available in pre-cut components ready to assemble

Hatch cover for merchantman

Lashed down

Hatch battened down with canvas

Wood battens

Nails

Skylight

Use plastic or glass for lights

Wire protectors

Another way hatch covers were fastened down

Master modeler Henry Bridenbecker of California earns my thanks for the suggestion. He calls it his "square deal."

You can vary the size of the hole very easily by varying the size of the tool you are about to create. Use a nail, rod, or other item of the proper diameter to secure a square hole. The material need not be tool-hard steel, but it should not be too soft to do the job. A good hardwood dowel will work. For purposes of illustration, we will make a 1/32-inch-diameter hole.

Select a brad 1/32 inch in diameter and remove the head with a hacksaw, as indicated in FIG. 11-13A. File the point of the brad to a squared sharpness (B). The trued-up point will be in the shape of a pyramid.

Attach the handle (C), which is nothing more than a squared stick, to the prepared brad shaft. It is imperative that the squared sides of the handle line up with the sides of the pyramid.

To make square holes out of round ones is a matter of small skill and much planning. Follow the rationale of the method in FIG. 11-13D.

Lay out the squares on the surface of the material. Pierce each indicated site with a sharp center punch. Drill a 1/32-inch hole completely through. Insert the point of the tool and tap gently, but firmly.

This little tool, of which I have several in assorted sizes, is also handy for making square holes in other items of deck furniture. FIGURE 11-14 shows an example of the square holes for the insertion of turning rods in a capstan and an old-period windlass respectively.

Ladders

Ladders are often a problem for ship modelers. The ones that come with the kits can be out of scale or get broken. Then you need to find another one or make your own.

You can construct a simple jig to hold the steps in place while the glue dries. Draw the angle of the insertion grooves on the side, saw and clean out the grooves carefully, and you have built your own "scratch" ladder.

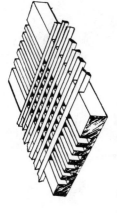

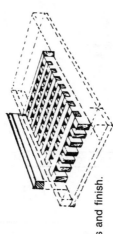

3. Glue in transverse members of grating.

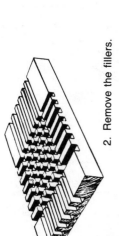

2. Remove the fillers.

1. Cut grooves spaced to the width of the grating openings. Fill the grooves again with scrap stock for support while cutting transverse grooves to one-half the depth of the first.

4. Cut away excess material; add facings and finish.

Fig. 11-11. One method of making grates for deck hatches (Courtesy of A. Richard Mansir).

4. Shape to deck chamber.

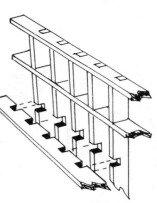

3. Interlock strips, glue.

Fig. 11-12. Combing the deck hatch strips with a saw to make gratings (Courtesy of A. Richard Mansir).

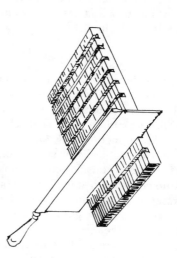

1. Clamp together strip stock.
2. Saw half through.

135

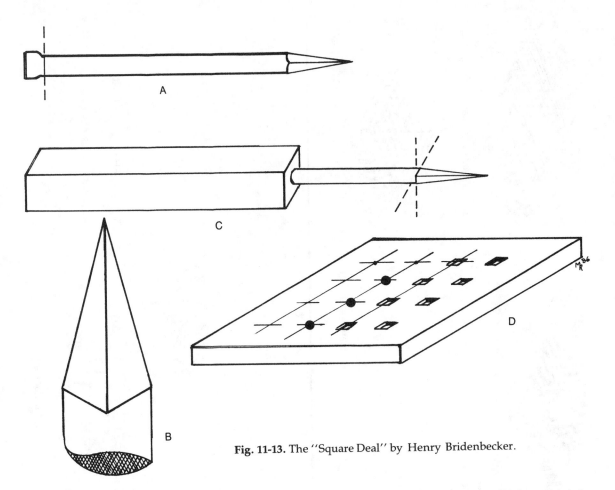

Fig. 11-13. The "Square Deal" by Henry Bridenbecker.

If that method is too much trouble, A. Richard Mansir has a quick and easy way to make ladders. His idea is shown in FIG. 11-15.

BOATS

The time devoted to construction of an accurate and detailed historical ship model is often spoiled by the lack of attention to the construction of the ship's boats. They should be given as much, if not more, attention as the model itself. Many a ship modeler does not even bother with ship's boats. They are omitted from many kits. When you consider the time needed to construct a ship model, you should not mind reserving a few hours for the building of the ship's boats. If you are going to do a complete job, include this vital feature.

Boats go on ships. They are a vital part of the communication system and transportation of goods, supplies, and men to and from the ship. Ship's boats have been found throughout history, and they still play a vital role today (FIG. 11-16). Each has a name and a function. Today, the names remain although the materials from which they are built has changed. Steel and other metals have supplanted the time-honored wooden boats. It is doubtful that the wooden boat will ever disappear, however. It will be here as long as there is wood available to construct a boat.

Like ships, boats have parts, and the parts have names. A little knowledge of the names of the parts can always come in handy (FIG. 11-17).

Types of Boats

The most often modeled ship's boats are from the warship. The smallest carried aboard was the dinghy or jolly boat, ranging in size from 12 to 16 feet. By

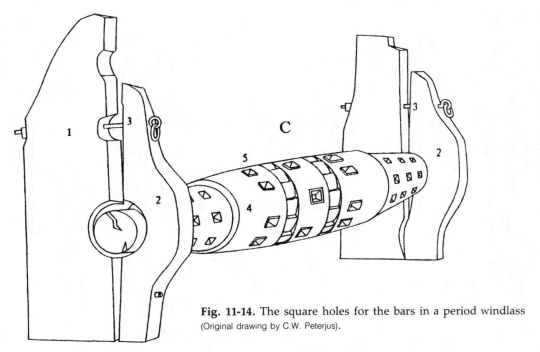

Fig. 11-14. The square holes for the bars in a period windlass (Original drawing by C.W. Peterjus).

contrast, the largest was the longboat or launch. This was carried aboard the larger ships and towed behind others of the fleet. All were boats to do the ship's work and carry supplies and personnel.

The sizes of ship's boats were carefully denoted and adhered to by tables and regulations. A little re-

search among the archives of national naval records will indicate what actual length, beam, and oar power was assigned to each named boat (FIG. 11-18).

Not all ships were capable of carrying a longboat. Most did carry a *pinnace*, however. It was speedy. This second largest boat of the navy carried supplies,

1. Stack up steps with spacer blocks and clamp together

2. Glue on one side

3. Saw steps and spacer blocks to width

4. Add second side

5. Finish front and back

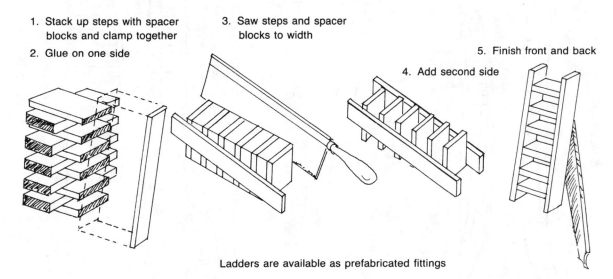

Ladders are available as prefabricated fittings

Fig. 11-15. A quick method of making a ladder using a saw and spacers (Courtesy of A. Richard Mansir).

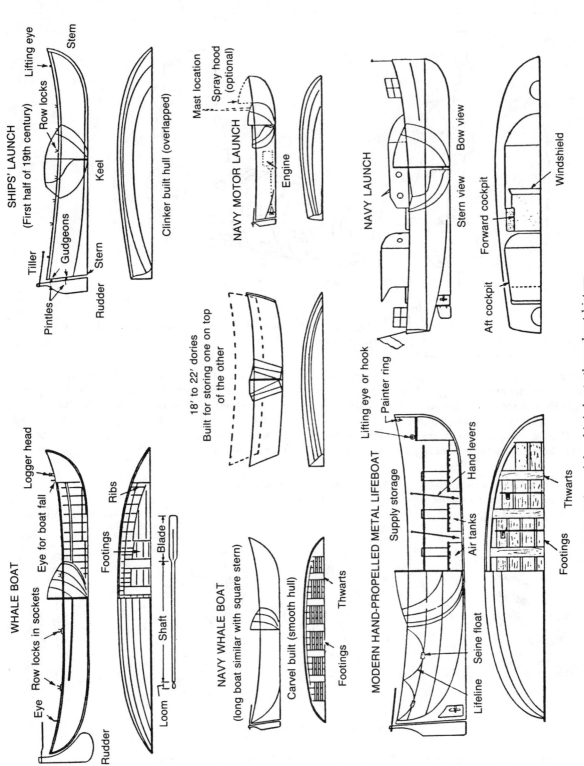

Fig. 11-16. A few of the ship's boats throughout history.

SHIPS' LAUNCH
(First half of 19th century)

Lifting eye
Stem
Row locks
Tiller
Keel
Gudgeons
Stern
Pintles
Rudder

Clinker built hull (overlapped)

NAVY MOTOR LAUNCH

Mast location
Spray hood
(optional)

Engine

NAVY LAUNCH

Stern view
Bow view

Aft cockpit
Forward cockpit
Windshield

18' to 22' dories
Built for storing one on top
of the other

WHALE BOAT

Logger head
Eye for boat fall
Ribs
Footings

Eye
Row locks in sockets

Rudder

Loom
Shaft
Blade

NAVY WHALE BOAT
(long boat similar with square stern)

Carvel built (smooth hull)

Footings
Thwarts

MODERN HAND-PROPELLED METAL LIFEBOAT

Lifting eye or hook
Painter ring
Hand levers
Supply storage
Air tanks

Lifeline
Seine float

Thwarts
Footings

138

1. Breasthook
2. Bow sheet
3. Wash board
4. Gunwale
5. Thwart
6. Thwart Knee
7. Thwart Stringer
8. Mast
9. Hanging Knee
10. Stern Thwart

11. Stern Bench
12. Gunwale
13. Wash Board
14. Backrest
15. Stern Sheet
16. Transom
17. Sternpost
18. Stern Knee (deadwood)
19. Floor Boards
20. Bilge Stringers

21. Lifting Ring
22. Snotter
23. Keelson
24. Hog Piece
25. Keel
26. Stem Knee
27. Apron
28. Stem
29. Frame Timbers

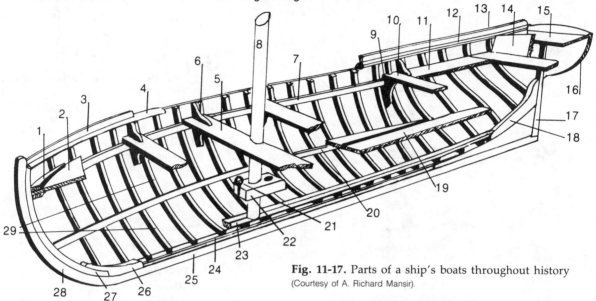

Fig. 11-17. Parts of a ship's boats throughout history
(Courtesy of A. Richard Mansir).

officers, and men, and was favored for combat and "cutting out" operations. It could be armed with a carronade. Two or more small guns, swivel mounted, were not unusual. A little light reading of any sea or pirate adventure with some good wartime activities will quickly identify the pinnace.

Historically the pinnace belongs to the 1700s. It was a British innovation and served well in that country's navy. The American colonists adopted it, as did most seafaring nations. The pinnace was used until the late 1800s. Later, both American and British forces changed to *cutters*. The design remained the same, as did the structural concept. There were a few changes. It is safe to assume that this was the same ship's boat well into the nineteenth century.

A plan of the pinnace is reproduced in FIG. 11-19. Please bear in mind that this is a general plan and is not intended to represent all pinnaces of the times discussed.

Plastic Boats

There are two methods of securing ship's boats for your model: you can buy them ready made, or you can build them. Several methods and various materials can be used to build them.

Metal boats, either white metal or Britannia metal, are available in all sizes and many scales. Commercial sources are mail-order houses, hobby shops, and most, if not all, American kit manufacturers.

Plastic boats cast in polyester resin, vacuum-formed styrene, fiberglass, and various man-made materials are on the market. They, too, are made by most kit manufacturers in scales that can be used by the average modeler.

You can make your own boats using casting resin and silicone rubber molds, which you can also make. Such a method is discussed in Chapter 19.

Carving a master model over which the silicone rubber mold will be formed will not be discussed at

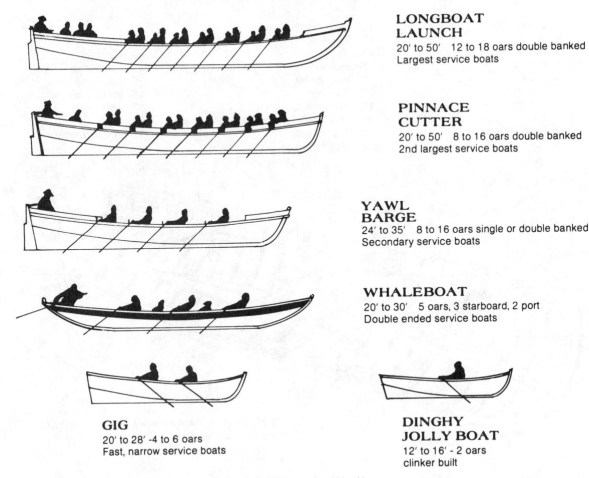

LONGBOAT
LAUNCH
20' to 50'   12 to 18 oars double banked
Largest service boats

PINNACE
CUTTER
20' to 50'   8 to 16 oars double banked
2nd largest service boats

YAWL
BARGE
24' to 35'   8 to 16 oars single or double banked
Secondary service boats

WHALEBOAT
20' to 30'   5 oars, 3 starboard, 2 port
Double ended service boats

GIG
20' to 28' -4 to 6 oars
Fast, narrow service boats

DINGHY
JOLLY BOAT
12' to 16' - 2 oars
clinker built

Fig. 11-18. The ship's boats of men of war (Courtesy of A. Richard Mansir).

this time. I recommend you use the solid-hull method. The simplest method is to buy the master models ready made.

Wooden Boats

Building wooden ship's boats can be involved and detailed. There are several excellent ways to accomplish the task. One method is to build the boat in the same planned manner as you would a plank-on-frame ship. You can use a building jig for this method, which is almost identical to the methods of Harold Hahn and Harold Underhill. Their books contain good step-by-step methods to follow.

You also can carve the boat from a solid block of wood. You can speed this process by using the lift method discussed in Chapter 10. If you plan to in-

vert the boat on the deck, there is no need to hollow the interior. If the boat is to be one of modern design and covered with a canvas protection, you can incorporate this feature in the design. Carve the details of the canvas cover and use a piece of cloth—painted of course—to simulate the cover. Attach rope lifelines and fastenings to the boat.

A. Richard Mansir, in his book *Art of Ship Modeling*, introduces another method (FIG. 11-20). It is a combination of the built-up method and the solid-hull unit. This application is also used by the ship modeler who combines the solid-hull and plank-on-frame methods in building a pseudo-Admiralty type of model. This method was not discussed previously. Use your imagination to determine how you could use it to build a ship model, as well as a ship's boat.

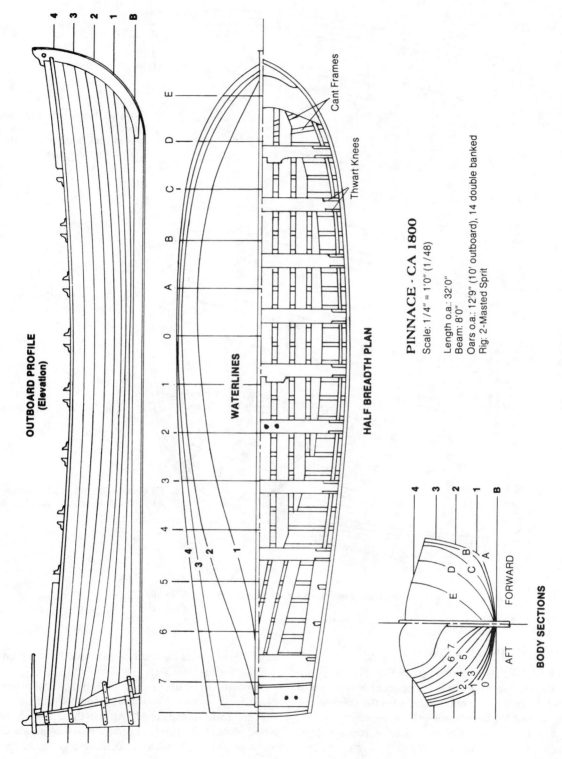

OUTBOARD PROFILE
(Elevation)

WATERLINES

HALF BREADTH PLAN

Cant Frames

Thwart Knees

PINNACE - CA 1800

Scale: 1/4" = 1'0" (1/48)

Length o.a.: 32'0"
Beam: 8'0"
Oars o.a.: 12'9" (10' outboard), 14 double banked
Rig: 2-Masted Sprit

BODY SECTIONS

FORWARD

AFT

Fig. 11-19. The plan of a typical pinnace (Courtesy of A. Richard Mansir).

141

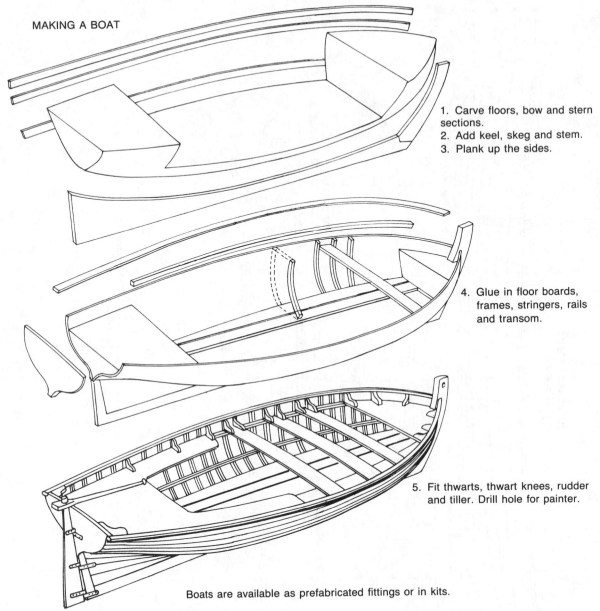

1. Carve floors, bow and stern sections.
2. Add keel, skeg and stem.
3. Plank up the sides.

4. Glue in floor boards, frames, stringers, rails and transom.

5. Fit thwarts, thwart knees, rudder and tiller. Drill hole for painter.

Boats are available as prefabricated fittings or in kits.

Fig. 11-20. A method of construction of a ship's boat (Courtesy of A. Richard Mansir).

Building a Wooden Boat

I would, with the help of the North Shore Deadeyes, like to present yet another way to build a ship's boat. This method combines the commercial product with a little home-grown ingenuity.

Let's begin with the materials. A form-molded plastic or presswood boat, or a carved master block

mold is used. You can obtain this mold from a commercial source or a kit.

Wood will be needed. Although the dimensions given here will be for a boat 3 inches or less, no specific scale is indicated. Adjust the sizes of the wood pieces to conform to the scale of boat indicated for your model. You can substitute any wood that suits your fancy. Those indicated are personal choices. The colors lend themselves best to indicate a dark ship's boat with a weathered and used look.

RIBS—1/32″ square basswood
PLANKING—1/32″ × 1/16″ mahogany
KEEL—1/16″ square mahogany or walnut
STERN—1/16″ square mahogany or walnut
FLOOR BOARDS—1/16″ × 1/32″ mahogany
RAILS—1/16″ × 1/32″ mahogany
OARS—Flat toothpicks (or carve your own)
OARLOCKS—1/32″ square basswood

Do not use metal oarlocks unless they were used during the period of your ship's construction. The finish can be dark walnut stain covered with a flat finish varnish, contrasted by the proper color of paint.

Use the glue of your choice. I recommend white glue or carpenter's water-based glue.

To begin construction, see the overall details in FIG. 11-21. FIGURE 11-22 shows the placement and identification of the parts that are referenced in the instructions.

✪ Remove the keel, stern, and other protruding shapes from the commercial product. Avoid a com-

pletely round bottom on any master mold. Sand the mold smooth.

Wax the form. A waterproof coating will prevent the adherence of glue spills. Super glues might penetrate the coating.

✪ Mount the form in an inverted position on a 1-×-6-×-4-inch pine board (FIG. 11-21). Glue at stern and transom. If the mold is for a double-ended boat, block to a level position (keel). (SEE FIG. 11-22, #1.) If your plans call for the construction of more than one boat, you might wish to elevate the form from the wood mounting board.

✪ Drill 1/16-inch-diameter holes 1/2 inch deep around the circumference of the boat, tangent to the sides at all desired rib locations.

✪ Drill a 3/32-inch-diameter hole to a depth of 1/2 inch at the bow parallel to the rake of the stern.

✪ Soak and preshape 1/32-inch basswood ribs over the mold form. Place the ends well into the predrilled 1/16-inch rib holes. Keep the ribs tight to the form. If you do not plan to make other boats using this jig, you may glue the ends into the holes.

✪ On square-sterned boats, the aftmost rib must extend 1/64 inch beyond the form. (See #2.)

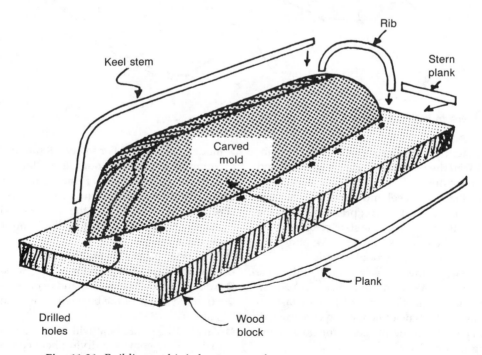

Fig. 11-21. Building a ship's boat over a form (Courtesy of Northshore Deadeyes, Ltd.).

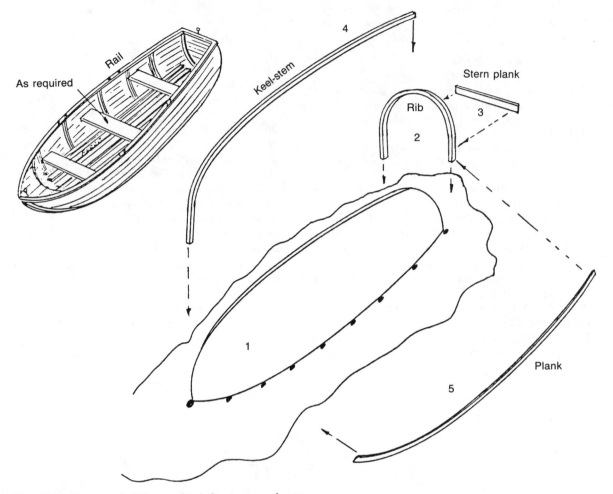

Fig. 11-22. Steps in building a ship's boat over a form.

⊗ Glue the stern planks horizontally to the aft rib. (See #3.) Trim the rib to shape after it is secure and dried in position.

⊗ Soak and shape the keel and stem. You can use one piece for both parts if you prefer. Glue to the centerline of the ribs. Insert the stem piece well into the 3/32-inch hole at the bow (See #4) and stern of the boat, if the boat is double-ended.

⊗ Begin planking at the gunwale parallel to the pine board and work toward the keel. (See #5.) You can lay on the planks in clinker, or *lapstrake*, fashion depending on the type of boat being constructed.

⊗ Trim, shape, and fit the planks at the bow before attaching to the ribs.

⊗ When the glue is dry, sand and stain the boat model on the form. For safety, all sanding and hull trimming should be done on the form.

⊗ Remove the boat model from the form by cutting the ribs at the level of the board.

⊗ Shape the caprail from the 1/16-×-1/4-inch mahogany piece. Test-fit before you mount the part on the gunwale.

⊗ Glue floor boards inside the boat.

⊗ Glue the caprail in position.

⊗ Add the rudder, stempost, and oarlocks (or *tholes*).

⊗ Stain the inside of the boat with a walnut or other stain.

⊗ Varnish the entire boat with two coats of flat varnish. Allow complete drying between coats.

⊗ Add davit hardware, eyebolts, blocks, etc.

144

Fig. 11-23. The oar, its nomenclature and specifications from the ship's boats of men-of-war (Courtesy of A. Richard Mansir).

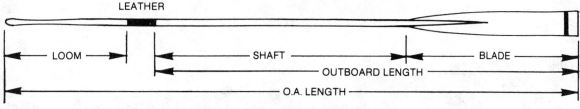

OARS
Oar Specifications

Length Outboard	1.25 x Beam of Boat
Length Inboard	.35 x Beam of Boat
Length of Blade	.30 x Length of Oar
Width of Blade at Tip	Six Inches (6")
Diameter of Shaft	1/48 Length of Oar

LEATHER

LOOM   SHAFT   BLADE
OUTBOARD LENGTH
O.A. LENGTH

Scale: 1/2" = 1'0" (1/24)

○ Shape flat toothpicks, rounded to form the shaft and loom. Follow the rule for length according to the oar specifications (FIG. 11-23). Stain the oars a golden oak. Do not varnish.

○ Add other accessories before you mount the boat to the ship model. FIGURE 11-24 indicates some of the items you might wish to stow aboard.

A variation on the theme just discussed, perhaps a more scientific approach, is a boat-building tech-nique perfected by Portia Takakjian (FIG. 11-25). The details of how the boat is built are left to your interpretation.

If this illustration confuses you, you might want to secure a copy of *The Construction Of Model Open Boats* by Ewart C. Freeston (Conway Maritime Press). For another method, see Moonraker Workbook Series No. 2, *How To Model Small Open Boats* by A. Richard Mansir (Moonraker Publishing).

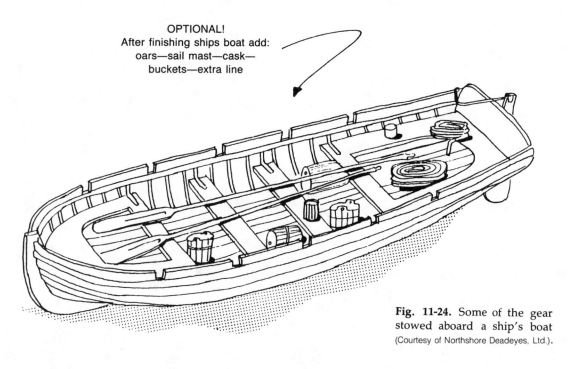

OPTIONAL!
After finishing ships boat add:
oars—sail mast—cask—
buckets—extra line

Fig. 11-24. Some of the gear stowed aboard a ship's boat (Courtesy of Northshore Deadeyes, Ltd.).

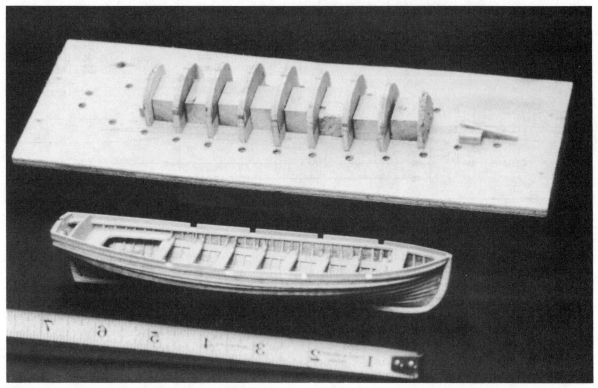

Fig. 11-25. The boat-building jig of Portia Takakjian (Photo by Steve Sagala).

TWELVE

Making Masts

Hindsight is always 20 / 20.
—BILLY WILDER

THE MANNER OF SIZING THE RIGGING BASED ON the beam of the ship, the diameter and length of the mast, and the thickness of the mast's stays will be touched on later. Texts, authors, and sources will be mentioned and often quoted. While these examples are by no means the only authorities, they are a good start.

The general term *masting a ship* refers to the placement of the mast. How far from the bow the first mast (foremast) will stand is carefully calculated. How far apart the others (if any) will be placed in order to impart the greatest power in pushing the ship through the water then can be determined.

In the early days of sailing, the ships were small. As their size increased, the master shipwrights, in need of space, rounded the bows in proportion to the increase of the beam. Their knowledge of hydrodynamics was limited. The ''apple-bowed'' craft were the result, In the years that followed, the search for speed over cargo-carrying capacity brought the sharp-bowed clipper and Baltimore clipper shapes into vogue.

The early shipbuilders placed the foremast very near the bow. Later designers began moving it progressively sternward as sharper bows and speeds increased. The changes in design were necessary because the placement of the sails played an important part in the sailing qualities of the vessel.

The same hydrodynamic applications applied to the beam of the ship. A wide hull carries more cargo, but moves slowly through the water with some difficulty. Shipbuilders thus began to make the hull longer and more narrow, which resulted in increased speed. This change in design was undoubtedly a result of advancing knowledge in construction methods (FIG. 12-1). The added bonus to a larger and longer vessel was increased cargo space. It wasn't long before the composite hulls of steel and wood soon gave way to the all-steel hull.

Masting and rigging also changed with these advances in the modern shipwright's applications. Masts were soon made of steel, and hemp was replaced by wire rope. The terms changed. The shipwright became a designer. The designer became a naval architect.

As you can see from this history, there is a need for a standard of measurement to check the accuracy on the masting of our models. A person who is knowledgeable on this subject can spot obvious errors, but they can be a source of embarrassment to the novice. Take note of the so-called ''scale-model'' kits. If the illustration or plan shows a mast that is longer than the ship's hull itself, it could be very wrong. If the main yard is more than twice the width of the ship's hull, it is wrong. I believe that the manufacturers design the models this way to make

147

Fig. 12-1. Model of *La Loire*, a four-masted bark of France (Courtesy of Association des Amies des Musees de la Marine, Paris).

them look larger than they are and to make the ship seem better looking in catalogs and on box lids. The finished item looks good on display—wrong in accuracy, but good looking. Not all kits are in this classification, however.

Now take a look at some of the models built from scratch according to plans secured or drawn by the builder. Take a quick eyeball measurement of the structures mentioned.

LOCATION OF MASTING

There must be some point at which to begin to determine the accuracy of a ship's masting. The measurement was taken from the plan. A line was drawn from the aft section of the stem, not including the cutwater. Another line was drawn from the forward area of the rudder post. These lines were drawn perpendicular to the baseline, which is the reference line drawn below the keel and in a vertical plane like the waterlines. The drawn lines were known as the *forward* and *after perpendiculars*. The measurement taken along the top deck between these lines was the length that was used to compute the tonnage. Several such formulas were used over the years. Although the calculation of the tonnage had its part in the masting and rigging of a sailing ship, it will not be discussed at this time.

The location of the mast was calculated in percentages of the deck's length. There was no set formula to determine where the foremast would be placed, nor was there one to set the distance of the next mast. These locations were based on methods that evolved over the years. For example, in 1747 the *Black Prince*, a West Indiaman of 440 tons, had the foremast set at .112 percent of the distance between the perpendiculars (FIG. 12-2).

The famous *Lexington* of 1775 set her foremast at .166 percent of the distance. The American Baltimore clippers of the 1800s were masted at .19 and .22 percent. In 1839, the American shipbuilder Donald McKay masted his ships at .14 percent of the distance.

Note that these percentages of the distance along the deck varied over the years and, most importantly, with the type of vessel. Ships, brigs, schooners, sloops, and the like were all masted for the sailing qualities imparted by the location of the mast and the drive of the sails. Designers considered the placement, taking into consideration the center of gravity of the ship. The facts of the tonnage, how she was loaded and in ballast, were influencing factors.

The average modeler is not interested in how his model sails. His prime interest is accuracy.

The rake of the masts has very little to do with the sailing qualities of the ship. This fact was proven over the years. In the Baltimore clipper, the rake of the mast was carried to supreme absurdity (FIG. 12-3). Many thought it was the rake that gave her the speed. It was, of course, the entrance of the hull in the water and the spread of the sails over the hull. It is the rake of the masts, however, that gives the Baltimore clipper her identifiable characteristics.

To ensure the accuracy of the rake on your model, you can check the tables established for the rake of

Fig. 12-2. The sail plan of H.M.S. *Black Prince* of 1747, an Indiaman of 440 tons.

149

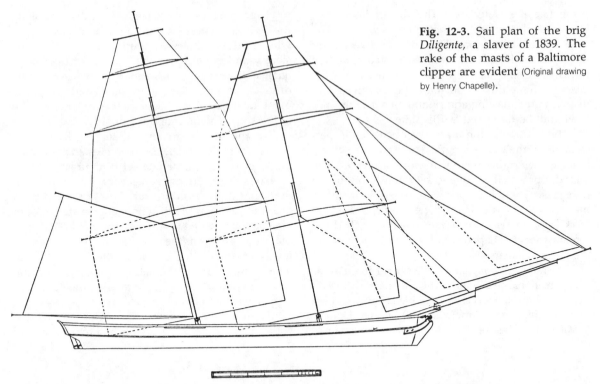

Fig. 12-3. Sail plan of the brig *Diligente*, a slaver of 1839. The rake of the masts of a Baltimore clipper are evident (Original drawing by Henry Chapelle).

masts aboard specific ships over the years. Such a source would be the book *Baltimore Clippers* by Howard Chapelle (Edward Sweetman Co. Largo, Fl.)

There were tables for every aspect of a ship's construction and operation. To save you a little time in masting your Baltimore clipper, note that the rake of the foremast was between 7 and 11 degrees; the mainmast 8 to 12 degrees, and the bowsprit (sleeve) 3 to 4 degrees. The name of the ship and the period of her building might have a strong bearing on the angle of the rake. Be careful and do your research.

The location of the masts that would be stepped along the length of the deck also evolved over the years. The overenthusiastic modeler can, if not careful, wind up with lofty spars and an inaccurate model unless he takes into account another consideration. I refer to the use of measurements for the length of the masts without consideration of how far they step inside the hull. This second measurement is necessary for proper construction of the lower mast.

The length given in plans is the length of the entire mast, both above and below decks. All the other masts (topmasts, gallants, etc.) that would be affixed to the lower portion are then added in the measured

proportions above the deck. Check the measurement known as *the depth of the hold*. It is usually indicated on the ship's draft or the better model plans. You can measure this distance to be sure on most plans. Now it is an easy measurement to find the distance from the *keelson*, or where the mast is stepped, to the deck. Mark this distance on the mast. This mark should coincide with level of the deck after you step the mast on your model.

A mast is not a straight pole; it is tapered. The sides and the construction of stepping at the *fid* (or bottom of the mast), the shape at the attachments of the mastheads and partners, even the tapering, all need to be carefully worked out. As an example, you can calculate the taper as follows: Divide into four equal parts the length of the mast from the deck to the top of the hounds (lower side of the masthead). Then apply the proportions of tapering to each quarter (FIG. 12-4).

DOUBLING DISTANCES

The *doubling* or *masthead*, is the amount of overlap of the top of one mast and the bottom of another. As you might have guessed, it is also a distance fixed

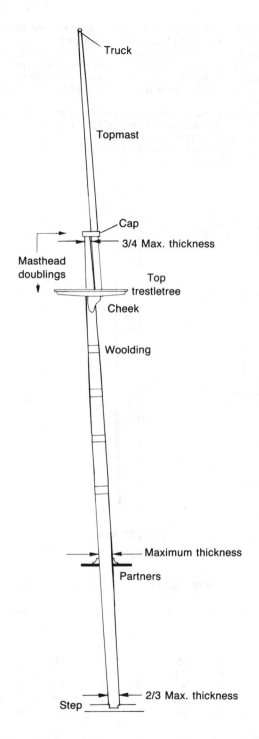

Truck

Topmast

Cap

3/4 Max. thickness

Masthead
doublings

Top
trestletree

Cheek

Woolding

Maximum thickness

Partners

2/3 Max. thickness

Step

Fig. 12-4. The parts of a mast and top (Courtesy of Moonraker Publications).

by table and custom (FIG. 12-5). The distance of the doubling in the early vessels was not as great as the ships that followed. The longer the mast, the greater the doubling distance. Adherence to this formula gave the mast a steady strength. Compare the *Mayflower* doublings to the *Victory's*. The doublings in a clipper are almost unbelievable. Added length gave added weight, with which the designers had to contend.

Note that the doublings were different in each country. A ship's home country could be identified by the manner in which she was masted and/or rigged. Countries often copied the designs of the hull shapes from one another. They varied their masting and rigging very little, however.

American and Swedish ships built prior to 1800 usually carried a masthead, on the main, that was one-sixth the length of the lower main. The fore masthead was nine-tenths the main, and the mizzen was three-fourths the length of the main. Let's assume that the ship we are building has a 60-foot mainmast. The masthead would then be 10 feet. If she were French, it would be 8.57 feet, and if she were Danish, 7 1/2 feet.

The measurements changed after 1800. The longer the masthead, the stiffer the total mast. The established figures were again changed to account for the added weight. The length of the masthead became a measurement of a proportion of the lower mainmast (FIG. 12-5). In 1843, the United States Navy established set rules and regulations for masthead length based on a proportion of the spars.

As every builder and devotee of sailing ships knows, there was a top at the masthead. This platform held the shrouds, fixed the upper masts, and gave a work or fighting area, as well as a secure location for a lookout. The structures that went into the making of the tops were built to rigid standards and measurements. The length of the hounds, the size of the trestletrees, and the length of the cheeks were set down. Every ship had its own characteristics for mast construction. The period of time of shipbuilding dictated the type of mast construction.

MAST LENGTH AND DIAMETER

The length and diameter of the masts were based on the measurement, or a portion of the measurement, of the beam of the ship. Mungo Murray set down the proportions of the masts and yards of the

To Use This Chart:

1. Measure the beam of the ship at the widest point. For example: Beam equals 25'

2. Determine era of vessel and use only the columns so marked. ex. 1650

3. Determine height of mainmast—multiply the number under the era opposite entry "A. LOWER" in the MAINMAST column by the beam. ex. 2.4 × 25' equals 60'

4. To find the height of any other mast or yard multiply 60' times the decimal fraction in the appropriate box. ex. the fore topmast entry under 1650 is .42; .42 times 60' equals 25.2'. Hence the fore topmast of the ship will be 25.2' long. ex. the length of the lower mizzen (cross jack) yard would be .50 × 60' equals 30'.

Remember that the dimensions given are but mean averages for the general run of ships in these periods. The mast dimensions of a particular vessel could vary from those shown depending on type, nationality, or dozens of other factors.

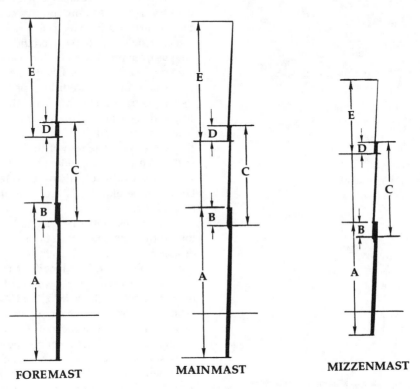

FOREMAST   MAINMAST   MIZZENMAST

MASTS		MAINMAST			FOREMAST			MIZZENMAST		
as fractions of lower main mast	1650	1750	1850	1650	1750	1850	1650	1750	1850
A LOWER	2.4 × Beam	2.28 × Beam	2.1 × Beam	.80	.90	.96	.75	.84	.86
B LOWER DOUBLINGS	.06	.13	.23	.05	.13	.18	.08	.095	.17
C TOPMAST	.52	.58	.77	.42	.57	.77	.34	.43	.60
D TOPMAST DOUBLINGS	.05	.06	.27	.05	.06	.15	.08	.095	.19
E TOPGALLANT MAST	.26	.31	*.91*	.21	.29	.86*	—	.22	.66

*Topgallant, Royal and Skysail on a single pole

Fig. 12-5. Dimensions of spars (Courtesy of Moonraker Publications).

ships of the period in 1765. As do most, he began with the main and its masts. His tables were for naval vessels and were based on the number of guns carried. Undoubtedly this was the influence of the British rating systems.

Mainmasts and foremasts in ships down to 60 guns were 1 inch in diameter per yard (36 inches) of length, which was taken to mean the entire length of the lower mast. Mainmasts and foremasts down to 50 guns were 27/28 inch in diameter for every yard of the entire length of the mainmast. Mainmasts and foremasts of 24-gun ships were 12/13 inch in diameter for every yard of the mainmast.

Murray used the mainmast's measurement to establish the basic diameter on which all other calculations were made. Remember, the length of the mainmast was fixed by the beam of the ship. It is then logical to assume that the diameter would vary for the size of the vessel also. All the other measurements were the same from there on out for the topmasts that were fixed above the lowers.

The mizzenmast was not calculated by the number of guns aboard. This mast was fixed at 15/22 inch per yard of the lower mainmast. The mizzen topmast was 5/6 inch per yard; the bowsprit, 1 1/2 inch per yard; and the jib boom, 7/8 inch per yard. I admit the term *yard* is confusing, but up till now we were talking about a measurement of length. Murray also used this measurement to calculate the portions of the heads and hounds of the mast, the tops, the caps, the trestletrees, the crosstrees, the yards, and the spars.

Murray's approach even extended to the width and breadth of the tops. As an example:

$$\text{Mainmast top} = \frac{\text{Ship's beam} \times 75}{100}$$

$$= \text{Length in yards}$$

$$\text{Foremast top} = \frac{\text{Mainmast} \times 86}{100}$$

$$= \text{Length in yards.}$$

Another method to calculate the dimension of mast tops, and in many cases a simpler approach to

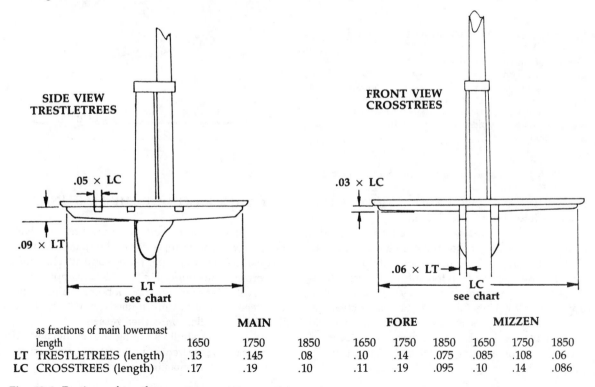

as fractions of main lowermast length		**MAIN**			**FORE**			**MIZZEN**	
		1650	1750	1850	1650	1750	1850	1650	1750	1850
LT TRESTLETREES (length)		.13	.145	.08	.10	.14	.075	.085	.108	.06
LC CROSSTREES (length)		.17	.19	.10	.11	.19	.095	.10	.14	.086

Fig. 12-6. Portions of trestletrees (Courtesy of Moonraker Publications).

PROPORTIONS OF BOWSPRITS

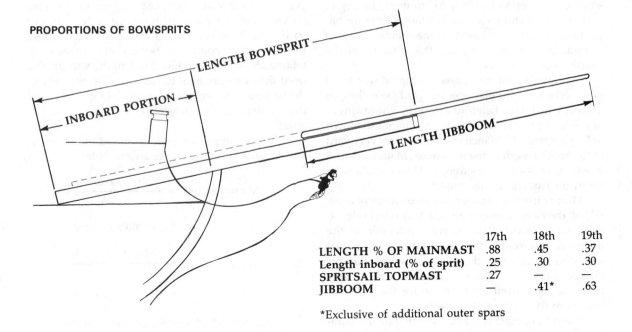

	17th	18th	19th
LENGTH % OF MAINMAST	.88	.45	.37
Length inboard (% of sprit)	.25	.30	.30
SPRITSAIL TOPMAST	.27	—	—
JIBBOOM	—	.41*	.63

*Exclusive of additional outer spars

PROPORTIONS OF BOOMS AND GAFFS

The proportions of booms and gaffs defy generalized formulas. While most of the time gaffs were shorter and lighter than booms, and both spars tapered from thickest at the mast, the reverse of these practices also occurred. These illustrations are more or less typical of fishing schooner spars of about 1850.

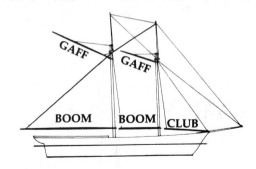

Fig. 12-7. Portions of bowsprits and boom and gaffs (Courtesy of Moonraker Publications).

the subject, was the United States Navy Rule of 1840. I offer a few examples to illustrate.

The main top was equal to one-half the breadth (beam) of the ship as measured from its molded side. The foretop was nine-tenths the breadth of the main top. The mizzen top was four-fifths the breadth of the foretop. The lengths of the tops were all, if measured by the 1840 USN Rule, two-thirds their breadths.

There were also set ratios and measurements to construct the crosstrees and trestletrees. FIGURE 12-6 is a chart for making trestletrees and tops in proportion.

OTHER PARTS OF THE MASTING

The spars, boom, gaff, jib, bowsprit, etc. had standard ratios and proportions. The spars also must be constructed with proper fittings and attachments. The formulations offered in FIG. 12-7 are approximations. Note that there were no jibbooms prior to the seventeenth century. Unfortunately, however, I have seen them installed on earlier vessels.

If you want to build a sailing ship model and do not want to do research and calculations, you can refer to FIG. 12-8 for masting proportions.

PROPORTIONS OF YARDS

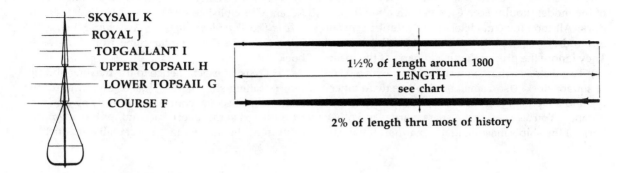

SKYSAIL K
ROYAL J
TOPGALLANT I
UPPER TOPSAIL H
LOWER TOPSAIL G
COURSE F

1½% of length around 1800
LENGTH
see chart

2% of length thru most of history

YARDS		MAIN YARDS			FORE YARDS			MIZZEN YARDS		
as fractions of lower main yard		1650	1750	1850	1650	1750	1850	1650	1750	1850
F	COURSE	2 × Beam	2.25 × Beam	1.9 × Beam	.85	.88	.88	.50	.60	.61
G	TOPSAIL	.50	.70	.91	.43	.62	.80	.25	.30	.56
H	UPPER TOPSAIL	—	—	.83	—	—	.73	—	—	.51
I	TOPGALLANT	.25	.47	.66	.22	.41	.58	—	.24	.40
J	ROYAL	—	—	.63	—	—	.55	—	—	.38
K	SKYSAIL	—	—	.50	—	—	.44	—	—	—

Fig. 12-8. Portions of yards (Courtesy of Moonraker Publications).

Jig for shaping spars

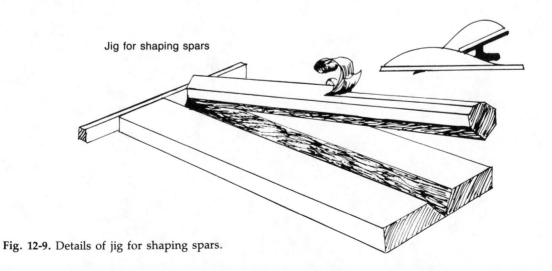

Fig. 12-9. Details of jig for shaping spars.

The beauty of a properly constructed mast, yard, boom, and gaff is an indispensable part of sailing-ship modeling. The construction of these vital parts of the model should receive greater attention than it does. All too often, modelers are content to install a round dowel, slightly tailored, and call it a mast. They ignore the proper shape and parts of the mast.

To construct a mast, you should start with a piece of square stock. Use a small block plane to do tapering and shaping. A jig, (FIG. 12-9) can be of great assistance. You also can shape spars, yards, and other parts of the ship's masting in this manner. If you are a kit builder, you can shape round dowels that came with the kit.

Charles G. Davis first published a book in 1926. Recently republished by Conway Maritime Press, its title is *The Ship Model Builder's Assistant*. Much of the information in this chapter came from Mr. Davis' book.

There is an exact science to the masting and rigging of sailing-ship models, just as there was for the real vessels. Become your own authority by using the texts quoted in this book. Each author has attempted to present the subject in an acceptable manner.

THIRTEEN

Proportions for Rigging

An expert is a man who has stopped thinking.
Why should he think? He is an expert.

—FRANK LLOYD WRIGHT
(1869-1959)

WE MUST GIVE SOME THOUGHT TO THE THICKNESS of ropes and lines. What has gone into the building of a "kit" model and even the work of a scratch model can become infected with the ideology "if it looks good it's O.K." Following is one of the actual methods of sizing the standing and running rigging of the life-sized ships that we model. It is hoped that the following presentation will enable you to determine the actual size of the rigging represented by your ship model. These facts will then enable you to transpose dimensions into the scale you are using.

I hope that as you get further into this subject, you will not become discouraged or confused. The purpose of this exercise is to introduce the novice and reintroduce the informed to some of the rules and regulations of proper rigging for a scale ship model. While this presentation will by no means be complete, the sources quoted might stimulate you to continue your search for truth and accuracy.

PRINTED SOURCES

There is always a way to do it right. If the right way continues to be applied, then it becomes a rule. That's what the builders of the real sailing ships thought through the ages. They were a little sloppy about keeping records prior to the early sixteenth century, however. Many could not read or write. Most of the information was passed on by word of mouth,

often from father to son. We owe most of our records to men like Samuel Pepys, Dean Humphries, and those who came after. They, through their own desires or under orders, began collecting the manuscripts, plans (drafts), and illustrations. Some were of the years preceding their time; most were of their day. Many are now preserved in the libraries, archives, and museums of England, France, Spain, and other countries.

The average modeler cannot always avail himself of these works in their original forms. Copies from the museums are not always clear or complete. They are useless to the modeler who does not know how to redraw them or translate the language. Fortunately, the major works, in text form, have been reprinted over the years and are currently available.

The most widely accepted volume is *Seamanship and Sail Making* by David Steel. This work was first published in London in 1794. It is now commonly labeled *Steel's Elements of Masting, Sailmaking and Rigging*. This volume is currently published by Edward Sweetman Co.

Facsimiles of the original editions of *Steel's Naval Architecture* and his other volume on masting and rigging are available at a "collector's" cost from:

SIM COMFORT ASSOCIATES
127 Arthur Rd.
London, England SW19 7DR

The books are written in the language of the times and undoubtedly were intended for use by master riggers, shipwrights, and mast builders. The information contained therein is most useful to modelers and historians of period ships. This is undoubtedly the reason for the book's continued availability and high status. Large fold-out plates show the parts that were needed and the sizes, in comparison, of the masts and spars. The tables are rather complete for the masting and rigging of various ships. Included are not only naval, but also merchant ships.

A contemporary volume published in 1979 by Naval Institute Press (USA) and Conway Maritime Press (England) is one destined to become the bible of the modeler. *The Masting and Rigging of English Ships of War, 1625-1860* primarily covers British warships. James Lees has done a creditable job in preparing his study.

Between these two extremes of time in the publishing world you can find many other writings devoted to the masting and rigging of sailing ships. Although some have been questioned as simply copies or abstractions of known or established works, many have advanced the art. They are too numerous to mention here. Some have been alluded to on previous pages. It behooves the serious ship modeler to become acquainted with what might turn out to be constant companions in the advancement of his skills.

SIZING RIGGING

One of the hardest things to explain when viewing some models is that the rigging just doesn't look right. The fault often lies in the fact that the rigging has been overstated—that is to say, it is too thick. Often this is the result of the kit manufacturer who includes too little line of graduated sizes, or the modeler building from scratch who does not understand the rules of rigging.

It is best to understate all the rigging, both standing and running, and especially the ratlines, for a better balance. I said *understate*, not *undersize*. You will find that understating will give you a more comfortable viewing sensation. It will also allow you the luxury of graduating your lines as you work aloft from the deck to the royals.

Several aspects of the rigging can be graduated in a set table. TABLE 13-1 is presented as a quick reference to size. It is not to be considered an actual rule

for a modeler's use. None of it means anything unless there is a strong urge for perfection and instruments to measure accurately.

The measurements for seizings and other small additions are too tiny on a scale model. Here the modeler who is not into such details will need to use the ''if it looks right'' method.

The sizes of the lines should be mentally graduated into four classes or groups. These areas are the same as the standing rigging: lower, top, top gallant, and royal. The sizes of the running rigging will be in the same proportions as the real-life sizes, as determined by calculation. Remember that the closer to the deck the rigging is, the thicker the line. The exception is the lines that work the sails, i.e., bunts, leech, clew, etc. Their thicknesses are constant. Keep in mind the actual size of the rope and the hand that held it.

There are tables and rules concerning the running rigging. This was the guide for the rigging master and boatswain. It should be your guide. In your research keep in mind that during times of repair and maintenance changes were made to the rigging. The sizes of the rigging were determined by the captain or boatswain. When a vessel was refitted, the rigging would be changed. Ships began with one rig and were refitted with another. A fore-and-aft rig could become a square rigger, or vice versa. The *Kate Cory*, of whaling and Civil War fame, is a good example (FIG. 13-1). Modeling the ship is not enough. You should identify the period of her life that you are modeling and present the rigging accurately.

MEASURING ROPE

What is confusing in books on rigging is the representation of one dimension in terms of the other. The measurement of the rope is often given in the circumference or diameter of a set standard. If at any time you need to change from one measurement to the other, you will need to convert from circumference to diameter and vice versa. To convert from circumference to diameter, divide by 3.14159. Conversely, to find the circumference when the diameter is known, multiply by 3.14159. If you don't want to get too picky with your tolerances, then simply divide or multiply by 3.

TABLE 13-2 was designed to assist in the estimated selection and sizing of the running rigging in a par-

RIGGING SIZE TABLE

Circumference In Inches	Diameter In Inches	Scale Diameter in .000 3/32:1	1/8:1	3/16:1	1/4:1
½	.16	.001	.0015	.002	.003
1	.31	.003	.003	.004	.006
1½	.47	.004	.0045	.007	.009
2	.63	.005	.0065	.010	.013
2½	.79	.006	.008	.012	.016
3	.95	.007	.0095	.015	.019
3½	1.11	.009	.0115	.017	.023
4	1.27	.010	.0135	.020	.027
4½	1.43	.011	.015	.022	.030
5	1.59	.0125	.0165	.025	.033
5½	1.75	.0135	.0185	.027	.037
6	1.91	.015	.020	.030	.040
6½	2.06	.016	.0215	.032	.043
7	2.23	.017	.0235	.035	.047
7½	2.38	.018	.025	.037	.050
8	2.55	.0195	.0265	.040	.053
8½	2.70	.021	.0285	.042	.057
9	2.86	.022	.030	.044	.060
9½	3.02	.0235	.315	.047	.063
10	3.18	.0245	.033	.049	.066
10½	3.34	.026	.035	.052	.070
11	3.50	.027	.0365	.055	.073
11½	3.66	.0285	.038	.057	.076
12	3.81	.030	.0397	.060	.080

Table 13-1. Rigging Size Conversion for Popular Scales.

ticular scale. Please remember that the sizes given are in the diameter of the rope.

There is another way to determine sizes of rope. If you do not plan on making your own rope with a "rope walk," which will be discussed later, you can size commercial line with a simple method devised by Noel C.L. Hackney. I have taken the liberty of expanding his method.

Let's establish a definition. This is official, coming from the United States Bureau of Standards. "The diameter of a thread (line) is the number of hanks to make a skein. Hanks are defined as the turns of materials of a specific weight equal to a given length to become a skein. A skein is a quantity of yarn, thread, silk, wool, etc., wound a specific length then doubled and knotted." Consider that a No. 40 cotton, No. 24 waxed linen, and No. 110 synthetic line are all the same thickness.

If you measure with a device that applies pressure, you will crush the material. It is difficult to know

when you have the correct reading. If you use a micrometer, you can stiffen the thread with a drop

Table 13-2. Size of Model Ropes in Popular Scales.

Size of Rope in real ship Diameter in inches	Size of Model Rope Diameter in Millimeters (1 Millimeter = .0393 inches) 1/8" - 1'" 1/96	3/16" - 1'0" 1/64	1/4" - 1'0" 1/48
1/4"	.07	.10	.13
1/2"	.14	.20	.27
3/4"	.21	.30	.40
1"	.28	.40	.53
1 1/2"	.42	.60	.80
2"	.56	.80	1.07
2 1/2"	.70	1.00	1.34
3"	.84	1.20	1.61
3 1/2"	.98	1.40	1.88
4"	1.12	1.60	2.15

Fig. 13-1. The model of the whaler *Kate Cory* as a brig (Model and photo by Jim Roberts).

of super glue and measure the stiff, hard thread directly.

You can also measure by eyesight. You will need a ruler and perhaps a calculator. Select a dowel of 1/4-inch diameter. Mark off 1 inch on the surface. You will be taking a reading based on the number of turns per inch (tpi). To save wear and tear on the eyes and nerves, divide the inch into multiples with which you are comfortable. Segments of 1/4 inch are ideal. Simply multiply your count by four to get the tpi.

Wind the thread of unknown size around the dowel. Make each turn lie snugly against the next. Do not pull too tautly, or you will change the diameter of the line. When you have covered 1/4 inch, count the number of turns and multiply by four to get the turns per inch: 32 turns (counted) × 4 = 128. Divide the number of turns per inch (128) into the basic unit of one inch to get the size of thread. In this case, the answer is .0078 inch.

To convert to metric, multiply the answer by 2.54. The answer is .198 mm, or rounded off for shopping purposes, 2 mm.

Now all you have to do when you need more is find and buy the size you have determined is the one you are using.

If you know the life-sized rope, you need to render it to scale. To calculate the full-sized rope equivalent, you need to convert this measurement, which is the diameter, into the circumference. Divide by 3.14159 for both inch and metric conversions. If you know the circumference of the life-sized rope, then reverse the process.

Let's get into scale. Substitute numbers for the unknown variable:

A = tpi, or circumference of the life-sized rope.
S = scale of your model.
Size = 1/A × 22/7 (3.14159) × S

DEVELOPMENT OF RIGGING SIZES

Everything has to have a beginning. The measurements that were used to set the standards and tables for masting and rigging a sailing ship had a beginning. It was the hull of the ship itself. The sizes of the mainmast and the mainstay, for example, were established by the beam of the ship. A fractional part of the widest portion of the ship was used as the gauge to determine not only the length of the lower segment of the mainmast, but also the thickness of the stay which held that particular mast. All rigging measurements then were based on this measurement. The same was true for all the other masts and portions of masts on any particular vessel. This ratio was changed slightly over the years.

From 1650 to 1750, the height of the lower portion of the mainmast was equal to 2.4 times the length of the beam. Each of the remaining masts were then a percentage of this figure.

To illustrate, the main topmast's length was 52 percent of the length of the lower mainmast (.52 times that length); the topgallant mast of the mainmast was 26 percent. Even the doublings were calculated. The lower doubling of the masts, lower and gallant, was 6 percent; the topmast, 5 percent. The percentages and ratios were continued in set readings for each mast and yard. The measurements were established as tables for each particular vessel.

The measurements were changed in 1750 to 2.28 times the length of the beam and again in 1850 to 2.1 times that length. The formulations changed, some only slightly, through the years. As rigging knowledge advanced, so did the length and construction methods of the masts, and correspondingly the sizes of the rigging.

Naval vessels demanded a different type of masting, and therefore a different proportion of rigging than merchant ships. The statistics of smaller sailing ships, such as coasters, fishing boats, cutters, etc., have been recorded and preserved, for naval ships much more than for those of merchant service. The designers and builders of sailing ships prepared, or had prepared, tables of sizes to follow as they built their specific ships.

I suggest that you check if masting and rigging tables for your model are available. You can do no better than to follow the tables of the real ship in masting and rigging your model. If they are not available, consider making your own tables. Base them on the methods outlined in accepted and time-proven texts, such as those mentioned previously.

Several such books, while not primarily intended as volumes on masting and rigging, do contain useful information. I refer in particular to the work of Charles G. Davis, *The Ship Model Builder's Assistant*, recently republished by Conway Maritime Press. Go back to the index in Davis' book after you have read the text.

The diameters of the masts were proportional to the length. This measurement also varied over the years. Search out the information of the period in which your ship was constructed.

As a quick example, up to 1670 the main (lower) mast diameter on a British warship was 1 inch for every 3 feet of the length. From 1670 to 1773, it became 15/16 inch for every 3 feet; from 1773 to 1794, 9/10 inch; after 1794, back to 1 inch for every 3 feet.

If you're not into the setting down of information and do not wish to go to all that bother, then use the following garnished graduations.

With only a few exceptions, you can work out the sizes of both the standing and running rigging in relation to the size of that mast's stay. Please feel free to elaborate and extend your knowledge of masting and rigging based on this fact alone. What follows is only a superficial set of rules to help your model at least look right, even if it isn't accurate enough to be classed as a true scale model of so-called museum quality.

Standing Rigging

Stays. The largest of the standing rigging lines was the mainstay. It was rated as having a circumference equal to one-half the greatest diameter of the mainmast. The mainstay, thus, would be equal to one-sixth the diameter of the mainmast. The stay for the topmast of the main would be one-half the size of the lower stay. Next, as you can almost anticipate, the topgallant stay was one-half the topmast, and lastly the royal stay was one-half the size of the topgallant. You can see that a pattern is emerging.

What holds true for the lower mainmast stay also holds true for all the other lower mast's stays on the ship. Thus, you can rig your model knowing that each stay is one-half the size of the stay below it. You can quickly see that each mast will need four graduations of lines, depending of course on the period and diameter of the mast under consideration.

If you remember that the stays run fore and aft and the shrouds run side to side, you will be able to select the lines more easily. Also note that the standing rigging ranged from a deep brown to black in color. It was tarred.

Shrouds. The lower main shroud was six-tenths the size of the lower mainstay. If you do not wish to measure that closely, then take it as half the thickness. Each lower foremast shroud was the same size as its appropriate stay. The mizzenmast shrouds were eight-tenths the size of the mizzenstay. Moving upward, we find the fore and main topmast shrouds were sixty-six hundredths—again you could settle for half—the size of the lower shrouds. The mizzen topmast shrouds were the same size as the mizzen topmast stay. All the other masts followed, with their measurements of the topgallant shrouds the same as for the topgallant stays.

As you could have predicted, there were set tables for the number of shrouds carried aboard a vessel. Each period of time had a designated number and each sea-faring nation had its own tables of standard rigging (TABLE 13-3).

Measurements of Rigging Parts

So much for a quick sizing of the standing rigging. These were not the only proportions set down for the various parts of the standing rigging by a long shot. The makers and recorders of the rules of rigging had a formula for every part that made up the rigging. Leaving nothing to chance, every part was identified by size. Wooldings, gammoning, collars, pendants, and backstays for all the parts of the rigging from bowsprit to bumpkin were named and sized. Look at FIG. 13-2, which illustrates the rigging on the mast of the H.M.S. *Victory* (from the book *Anatomy of Nelson's Ships* by C. Nepean Longridge, Naval Institute Press, Annapolis, MD) and you will see what I mean.

As an example of how these boring facts might assist you in your rigging, let's take a look at one item, the thickness of the lanyards that lashed the deadeyes. They had to conform to their respective sizes. The size was the same at all shroud locations: one-half the thickness of the appropriate shroud for that particular mast.

The same rules of thickness applied to the thickness of the lanyards that lashed the stays. The exception was the lower stay lanyards, which were

Table 13-3. Number of Shrouds Denoted by Centuries.			
MASTS	**17th**	**18th**	**19th**
Foremast	9	7	6
Main mast	10	8	7
Mizzen mast	5	5	5
Fore topmast	4	4	3
Main topmast	5	4	4
Mizzen topmast	3	3	3

one-third the lower stays. All the rest were one-half the thickness of their respective stay measurements.

Hint: the distance that was recommended between deadeyes was equal to 1 1/2 the diameter of the deadeye. This is again a rule of thumb, but it does make spacing a little more attractive. More importantly, it allowed room to adjust the tension of the shroud or stay. Some ships only used one diameter; others, more. A little investigation is needed.

Should you like to begin your education at the very beginning, say in the period between 1600 and 1720, then get a copy of *The Rigging of Ships In The Days of The Spritsail Topmast 1600-1720* (Cornell Maritime Press, Rockville, MD). This classic reference volume, written by R.C. Anderson, covers the rigging methods of several nations for the years mentioned. The work was originally printed in 1927. It explains the intricate parts and rigging of ships in the beginning days of sailing high adventure.

Running Rigging

What about the running rigging? Were there established rules for the sizes of the lines, as there were for the parts and sections of the standing rigging? Yes! It can get to be a little hairy. So I will give only a few examples. I leave you to conduct the in-depth study.

Following, in a rather brief form, are some of the parts and sizes of the running rigging of the main yard. Remember that the figures are based on the size of the mainstay. The choices of the parts of the running rigging were selected at random for illustration purposes only. Truss pendant, nine-twentieths; lifts, one-third; footropes, one-fourth; footrope lanyards, one-tenth; bunt line (legs and falls), eighteen-hundredths; Clue garnets, one-fifth; sheets, four-tenths. You can find all this spelled out for you in

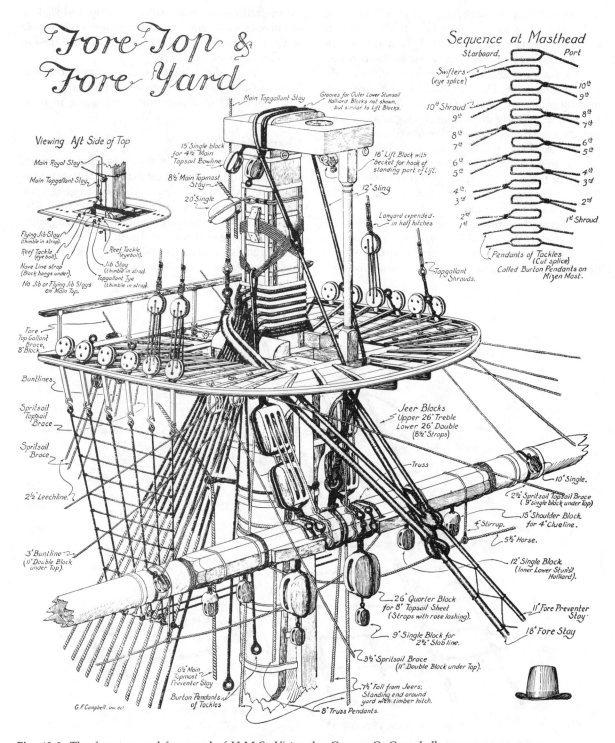

Fore Top & Fore Yard

Sequence at Masthead

Starboard.   Port

Swifters (eye splice)

10th Shroud

9th

8th

7th

6th

5th

4th

3rd

2nd

1st

10th

9th

8th

7th

6th

5th

4th

3rd

2nd

1st Shroud

Pendants of Tackles (Cut splice) Called Burton Pendants on Mizen Mast.

Viewing Aft Side of Top

Main Royal Stay

Main Topgallant Stay

Flying Jib Stay (thimble in strop)

Reef Tackle (eye bolt).

Nave Line strop (Block hangs under).

No Jib or Flying Jib Stays on Main Top.

Reef Tackle (eyebolt).

Jib Stay (thimble in strop).

Topgallant Tye (thimble in strop).

Main Topgallant Stay

Grooves for Outer Lower Stunsail Halliard Blocks not shown, but similar to Lift Blocks.

15" Single block for 4½" Main Topsail Bowline

8½" Main Topmast Stay

20" Single

16" Lift Block with becket for hook of standing part of lift.

12" Sling

Lanyard expended in half hitches

Topgallant Shrouds.

Fore Top Gallant Brace, 8" Block.

Buntlines

Spritsail Topsail Brace

Spritsail Brace

2½" Leechline

3" Buntline (11" Double Block under Top).

Jeer Blocks
Upper 26" Treble
Lower 26" Double
(8½" Strops)

Truss

10" Single.

2½" Spritsail Topsail Brace (9" single block under Top)

15" Shoulder Block for 4" Clueline.

4" Stirrup.

5½" Horse.

12" Single Block (Inner Lower Stun'sl Halliard).

11" Fore Preventer Stay.

18" Fore Stay

26" Quarter Block for 8" Topsail Sheet (Strops with rose lashing).

9" Single Block for 2½" Slab line.

3½" Spritsail Brace (11" Double Block under Top).

6½" Main Topmast Stay

Burton Pendants of Tackles

G.F.Campbell. inv. del.

7½" Fall from Jeers; Standing end around yard with timber hitch.

8" Truss Pendants.

Fig. 13-2. The fore top and fore yard of H.M.S. *Victory* by George C. Campbell (Courtesy of Argus Books).

163

James Lees' *Masting and Rigging of English Ships of War 1625-1860* (Conway Maritime Press). The colors of running rigging varied from the light hemp of new rope to the gray of weathered and exposed rope.

To many modelers, the tying of the ratlines is the most troublesome. The most sought-after shortcut is making or buying ready-made lines (shrouds) with the ratlines already in place (FIG. 13-3). As one who has gone the route, including the use of a shroud line tying board, I urge you not to attempt this off the ship unless you can maintain complete accuracy in the length of the lines (FIG. 13-4). It is best to tie the ratlines on the shroud lines after you have already installed them on the model.

To space the ratlines, you can insert an index card (white preferred) behind the installed shrouds. You can, if you wish, scribe the card's surface with a drawn graph. Indicate the spaces that would be used for the ratlines on your particular ship and stick to the proper scale. The shrouds are completely visible against this background and the spaces to tie the ratlines are at once apparent.

The method of tying the ratlines is one of choice. I prefer the clove hitch with the ends seized.

Chapter 14 discusses running rigging in more detail.

Changes in Rigging

There is one point that I wish to stress strongly. Check carefully on the period that your ship was constructed. There were many changes in rigging, both standing and running, as the years rolled by. The early ships of the 1600s were endowed with a generous abundance of stays and shrouds. There seemed to be ratlines everywhere, not to mention the complications of the spritsail masts.

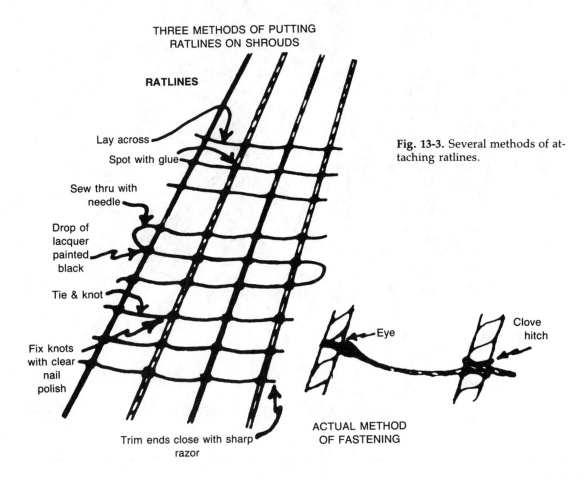

THREE METHODS OF PUTTING RATLINES ON SHROUDS

RATLINES

Lay across
Spot with glue
Sew thru with needle
Drop of lacquer painted black
Tie & knot
Fix knots with clear nail polish
Trim ends close with sharp razor

Eye
Clove hitch
ACTUAL METHOD OF FASTENING

Fig. 13-3. Several methods of attaching ratlines.

As the knowledge of masting and rigging increased with the use of better engineering principles, the rigging changed. It seems that the stronger the structure and the clearer the ideas, the less the rigging. Many plans vary in the number of stays and shrouds.

Not surprisingly, there were tables for the numbers of shrouds for each mast. The numbers varied with the size (tonnage) of the ship and the beam measurements. These, as you recall, denoted the height (length) of the masts.

I wish to stress the same point for the running rigging. Check the period.

You might find that a careful examination of many models on display, both in public and private, are inaccurate in their rendition of rigging. The later sailing ships, for example, often were rigged with chain lifts and braces. Mast yokes and boom structures were of iron. Ships of the latter days of sail had steel masts. Clipper ships, which represent the height of the rigging art, had the most advanced and complicated rigging.

The clipper ship's rigging, and all its complications, is detailed in Harold Underhill's book *Masting and Rigging the Clipper Ship and Ocean Carrier* (Brown Son & Ferguson, Publishers). A companion volume is his *Sailing Ship Rigs and Rigging* (Brown Son & Ferguson). This book contains a useful glossary concerned with masts, spars, sails, and rigging (FIG. 13-5).

AN EXAMPLE

Earlier I mentioned making your own tables. I would like to show you an example. Remember that the ratios started with the mast's (spars) diameter and were related to the circumference of the rope. The diameter is equal to the circumference divided by 3.14159. You can use 3 for your figure if you don't need to be extremely accurate.

TABLE 13-4 gives measurements for part of the standing rigging of the *Washington*. The model is, as you might suspect, not from a kit. It is also not the *Washington* of 1837, which was a brig.

My decision to model this ship began with the information found in the United States Navy's publication *American Ships of the Line* (Naval History Division, United States Navy Department, 1969). The ship served in the Mediterranean from 1816 to 1818. It was an American 74-gun ship and looked like an interesting project.

Table 13-4. Standing Rigging of the 74-Gun Ship of the Line, *Washington*, 1815 (based on tables of USN 1826).

Rigging Location	
Fore shrouds	11.50
Main shrouds	11.50
Mizzen shrouds	8.00
Fore stay	17.00
Main stay	18.00
Mizzen stay	12.00
Fore spring stay	12.75
Main spring stay	14.00
Fore topmast shrouds	6.75
Main topmast shrouds	6.75
Mizzen topmast shrouds	5.33
Fore topmast stay	10.25
Main topmast stay	10.25
Mizzen topmast stay	7.25
Fore topmast spring stay	7.50
Main topmast spring stay	7.50
Mizzen topmast spring stay	5.50
Fore topmast back stay	9.25
Main topmast back stay	10.00
Mizzen topmast back stay	7.00
Fore topmast breast back stay	8.00
Main topmast breast back stay	8.75
Mizzen topmast breast back stay	6.00
Fore topgallant shrouds	5.00
Main topgallant shrouds	5.50
Mizzen topgallant shrouds	4.00
Fore topgallant back stays	6.50
Main topgallant backstays	7.00
Mizzen topgallant backstays	5.25
Fore topgallant breast back stay	5.50
Main topgallant breast back stay	7.00
Mizzen topgallant breast back stay	4.00

**Ratio/Proportion
of spar Diameter
Circumference
(In Inches)**

The United States only built 15 ships of the line. We gave away the first one, *America*, to the French for their assistance in our war against England. Since they were all 74-gunners, except the *Pennsylvania*—a 120-gunner—the rigging and masting tables I made

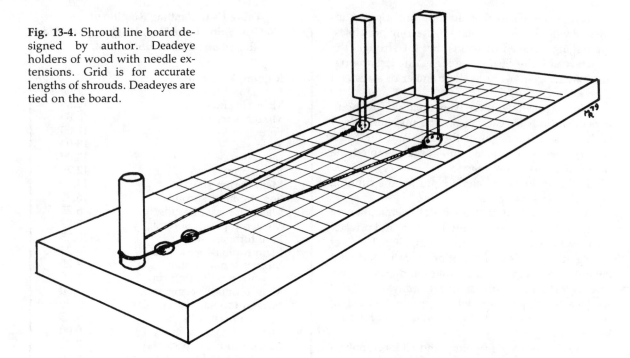

Fig. 13-4. Shroud line board designed by author. Deadeye holders of wood with needle extensions. Grid is for accurate lengths of shrouds. Deadeyes are tied on the board.

could be used for the upcoming ships of my ''someday'' fleet.

The tables for masting the *Washington* were an interesting challenge. I made them using the format of tables I found in the textbooks previously mentioned. I completed the tables for the masting and spars first, in order to prepare the standard sizes for TABLE 13-4.

Perhaps you are not into research as I am. I personally find it enjoyable. Building ship models for the sake of building alone loses its pleasure. I also enjoy sharing this knowledge. If you are of a similar persuasion, then have a shot at proper masting and rigging. Knowledge, like love, is more enjoyable when shared with others.

Fig. 13-5. A "bare-poled" model of the *Cutty Sark.*

FOURTEEN

Running Rigging

*A life spent in making mistakes is not only more honorable
but more useful than a life spent doing nothing.*
—GEORGE BERNARD SHAW

THERE IS SOMETHING INSPIRING ABOUT A "TALL ship." Rising from the decks high into the sky are the masts and yards with what seem to be miles of rigging (FIG. 14-1). If the real thing is awe inspiring, what about a model? A model of a tall ship is nonetheless amazing to the viewer. It, too, seems complicated.

Is there an order to all this? Could a group of men control a ship using all that confusing ropework? If you are a student of sailing ships, then you know the answer.

The standing rigging is logical. It holds the masts erect, and strengthens and maintains their positions. Each rope or wire is there for the purpose of bracing. The term *stay* seems to say it all. These lines are for the most part fixed. Those that are adjustable have mainly to do with tension and tautness. They are immobile.

What then of the *running rigging*—the working rigging that controls the mechanisms of sails and uses the wind that drives the ship? Is there an order and pattern to it, too?

SHIP HANDLING

Men who sailed aboard engineless ships learned their skills while they worked. They grew up in ships, often starting their careers in their preteen years. Over the years an order, a sense of feeling in ship handling, developed. A boy who lived on a ship as the days became weeks and the weeks became years came to know her as an intimate friend. As his knowledge grew, so did his responsibility—his rank as it were.

Over the centuries, the methods of ship handling slowly evolved. Everything about it was based on a common-sense approach to established patterns of "running" a ship. The sail-handling gear that led to the deck—most did—led to the pins in an orderly and constant manner. The pattern varied in the larger ships, some having more lines for working the sails than others. Some grouped the course gear to pin patterns on each side around the bole of the mast; others to main pinrails. Once the style of the ship was set up, it was rigidly maintained. Nothing was done in a haphazard fashion, but nothing was marked. Who could read marks in the dark?

A sailor knew the ship's gear by feel. He could tell from the manner in which the sail was made how she would be bent even in the dark. All sails were *roped*, that is, sewn with a strong hemp along the edges. The hemp was always sewn on the after side of a square sail. Fore-and-aft sails had the hemp sewn on the port side. A seaman always knew which direction the canvas must go, even in the dark.

Sailors already aboard taught the new hand the lines and ropes from the moment he came aboard.

Fig. 14-1. The main mast of the *Balcutha*, now berthed in San Francisco (Photo by John Margine, 1985).

He was taught to follow orders almost by instinct, without explanation and with a minimum of words. When men leapt into the pitching rigging and fought their way aloft to battle a wildly flapping and thundering sail, everyone knew exactly what they were doing and how to go about it. The entire operation was based on a system of order. There was a name for each item and pin, a definite lead for everything.

Ship handling hasn't changed much over the years. A sailor from the *Mayflower* could, after a few moments of looking things over, be at home on the U.S. Coast Guard training ship *Eagle*. The slight variances of the number of lines, yards, masts, or style of rigging are soon mastered by a knowledgeable seaman.

Sailing gear was grouped according to action. Clew lines, buntlines, leechlines—all were known or learned (FIG. 14-2). When a command was given, a sailor knew which rope would bring the proper response. Clew lines hauled up the corners of the sails.

Buntlines hauled up the great body of the sail in the middle and, on the larger ships, at more than one point. The leeches pulled up the sides. From down on the deck, the ropework had to be handled in a brisk fashion to "spill the wind" and furl the sail to the yardarm. The help of the ropes from below made the sails more manageable to the men in the tops.

As the buntlines came up, the men raced up the ratlines to fight the sail into submission. When the cry "All Hands!" was given, it was too late to grope for proper belaying pins. Sailors knew which were the braces to swing the yards, which were halliards to hoist, or tacks to position. The life of the ship depended on it.

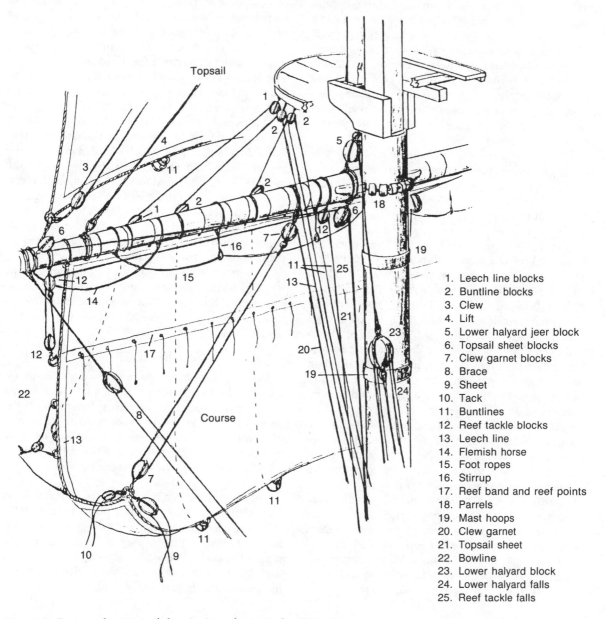

1. Leech line blocks
2. Buntline blocks
3. Clew
4. Lift
5. Lower halyard jeer block
6. Topsail sheet blocks
7. Clew garnet blocks
8. Brace
9. Sheet
10. Tack
11. Buntlines
12. Reef tackle blocks
13. Leech line
14. Flemish horse
15. Foot ropes
16. Stirrup
17. Reef band and reef points
18. Parrels
19. Mast hoops
20. Clew garnet
21. Topsail sheet
22. Bowline
23. Lower halyard block
24. Lower halyard falls
25. Reef tackle falls

Fig. 14-2. Parts and names of the rigging of a typical sailing ship (Courtesy of Jack Coggins).

MODELING RIGGING

Very few modelers have ever sailed aboard a sailing ship, let alone handled one. For most modelers, sailing has been in the mind. We read and dream of what it must have been like.

Many of us are quite knowledgeable about sailing ships and their rigging. This know-how came to us, like for the seaman of bygone days, through learning our skill. First we followed the plan that came with the kit. Then a sense of dissatisfaction grew. It didn't look quite right. We went to all the sources of information that might help us become better ship modelers. New words crept into our expanding vocabularies. New thoughts and ideas became second nature. After a few days aboard a ''real'' ship, we could handle her properly, under the eye of a good boatswain's mate.

The books that describe the adventure of service aboard a sailing ship are many. Their descriptions, though, while exciting, are sometimes filled with inaccuracy. I would rely more on the volumes devoted to handling ships under sail than on the incidental description given in an adventure novel.

The Visual Encyclopedia Of Nautical Terms Under Sail by Basile W. Bathe (Crown Publishers, N.Y. 1978) is a fine volume for learning terminology and sail handling. Of recent vintage, *Seamanship In The Age Of Sail* by John Harland (Conway Maritime Press, London or Naval Institute Press, Annapolis) is complemented with the excellent drawings of Marc Meyers. This is without a doubt the most detailed reference to date concerning the sailing ship. It includes information on how to handle emergencies and loss of masts and rudder, as well as how to move a sailing ship by combination of wind, sail set, and muscle.

Aside from all this nostalgia, this discussion concerns the running rigging of ship models. If you are producing a true scale model, then your rigging should be as close to the actual ship as possible. Although you do have a pattern to follow, it should be the best you can do, all facts considered. If you are content with the rigging plan as furnished in your kit, so be it. If you are customizing your kit or scratch building and doing extensive research, so much the better. What is presented in the following paragraphs will be a learning experience for some, a review for others, and a cause of concern for a few.

RIGGING TERMINOLOGY

Let's begin with fundamentals. To do some work, a rope must do something other than be tied around an object. It must make something move, pull something one way or another, and in general serve a useful purpose. Of course, you are well aware that a *rope* on land is a *line* on a ship. A *map* for a traveler becomes a *chart* to a sailor. It isn't a *window*, it is a *porthole*; the *floor* is a *deck*. Without involving you in rhetoric, let's talk about running rigging.

Basically, running rigging consists of a rope, a block or series of blocks, a fixed end, and a loose end. The loose end is usually where the sailor can be found, pulling. The loose end is called a *fall*; the fixed end is referred to as bend (FIG. 14-3).

Lines and sails are *bent* or fastened (FIG. 14-4). A *fairlead* is a device to ensure that the line runs true in its direction of pull (FIG. 14-5). A *purchase* is the power or advantage gained by applying the mechanics of a block and tackle to an object. It is this idea that makes up the science of running rigging. A *tackle* is a set of two or more blocks through which a line (rope) is rove for lifting a weight, or as stated, applying purchase. That weight of course includes yards, sails, cargo, and guns.

Try to visualize what the rigging had to do, how it would work, and what would happen if you were on one end hauling. What effect would the movement of the rope eventually have on the object to which it was attached?

BLOCKS

Let's pause here for a short dissertation on blocks. A *block* is a machine. It is a frame (shell) fitted with one or more sheaves (pulleys) and a pin (axle) around which the sheave revolved. The entire unit was enfolded in a strap (strop) to fix it at its place of work. The entire mechanism could be made of wood or metal, depending on the need or era of its construction (FIG. 14-6).

Blocks are given different names, depending on their shape, purpose, or place aboard a ship (FIG. 14-7). They are termed single, double, treble, or fourfold according to the number of sheaves contained within the body. It wasn't the weight of the object that denoted the number of sheaves needed, it was the power that had to be applied.

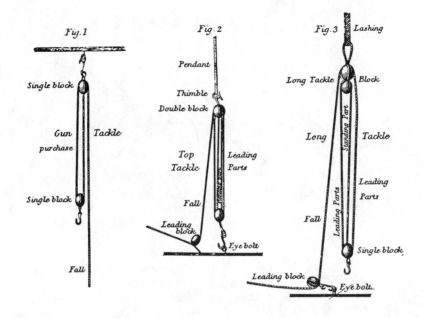

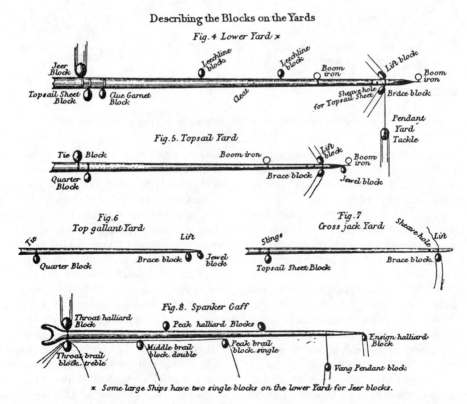

Describing the Blocks on the Yards

Fig. 4 Lower Yard ✕

Fig. 5. Topsail Yard

Fig.6
Top gallant Yard

Fig.7
Cross jack Yard

Fig.8. Spanker Gaff

✱ *Some large Ships have two single blocks on the lower Yard for Jeer blocks.*

Fig. 14-3. Block and tackle with applications as shown by a plate from *Young Sea Officer's Sheet Anchor* by Darcy Lever (Courtesy of A.W. Sweetman Publishers).

BENDING SAILS

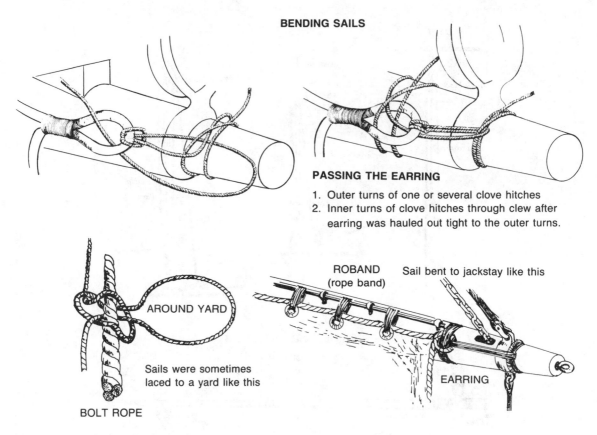

PASSING THE EARRING

1. Outer turns of one or several clove hitches
2. Inner turns of clove hitches through clew after earring was hauled out tight to the outer turns.

AROUND YARD

Sails were sometimes laced to a yard like this

BOLT ROPE

ROBAND (rope band)

Sail bent to jackstay like this

EARRING

Fig. 14-4. Bending sail, the methods of attaching sails to yards (Courtesy of Moonraker Publications).

Sizes. The size of the block was determined by the ratio of the number of sheaves to the thickness of the rope. The size of the sheave was, of course, dependent on the thickness of the rope.

For example, in the seventeenth century the sheave was constructed at 2 3/4 times the circumference of the rope. Of course, there were exceptions and the ranges changed over the years. Among the exceptions was the set of "rules" established by unofficial adoption in the country of origin. During the seventeenth and early eighteenth centuries, the English changed from the 2 3/4 measurement (nine times the diameter) to six times the diameter of the rope. American blocks were built at eight or nine times the diameter. The earlier the period, the larger the rope and the bigger the block. They ranged in size from 8 inches (the length of the shell) to 30 inches, and weighed up to 100 lbs. or more. By the 1800s there were over 800 different sizes of blocks used on a full-rigged ship. The proper blocks were required, and no expense was spared to see that they were aboard (FIG. 14-8). The blocks were a major item in the cost of outfitting a ship.

The evolution of blocks from crude wood ones, some not even sheaved, to all-metal, nylon-sheaved ones encompasses a long period of time. However, the basic purpose of blocks remains the same. Their function is to operate the ship in as efficient a manner as can be done by the sheer power of men and muscle. As time progressed, auxiliary power was used. The donkey engines appeared on deck. If so much care and consideration was given to the design and construction of special blocks to run a sailing ship, should not the same efforts be made to ensure that a model of such a ship contains the proper shapes and sizes of blocks? Making a scale model of a sailing ship means making scale blocks to equip that model.

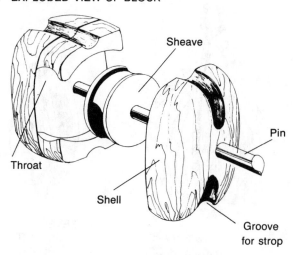

Sheave

Pin

Throat

Shell

Groove
for strop

Fig. 14-6. The parts of a block (Courtesy of Moonraker Publications).

There is really no problem with keeping your blocks in scale. The measurements from real sizes, if not calculated from rope diameters are available from books (mentioned later in this discussion). In keeping with the sizes and graduations of the ropes (lines) used in ship modeling there can be a variance. If you are the type who insists of accuracy down to the hundredth inch or millimeter, then whip out your micrometer and have at it.

Construction. There are several ways to make blocks. The method that becomes the most problematical in smaller scales is that of making each one individually. Unfortunately, you need to make them that way sooner or later. Here are two methods of making blocks in a ''mass-produced'' manner.

In the first method, you will start from a solid block (length) of wood. FIGURE 14-9 is almost self-explanatory. In logical fashion:

❂ Lay out the blocks by length and width and in scale on the wood (A).
❂ Cut the grooves for the strops (B).
❂ Drill the sheave holes (C). The illustration shows one, but you can take it from there.
❂ Shape the block (D). I do mine on a jigsaw after tracing the outlines.
❂ Separate blocks from the wood length (E).
❂ Shape, stain or finish, strop, and mount (F). There you are ready to rove with line.

Fig. 14-5. Attaching cleats and fairleads to the shrouds (Courtesy of Northshore Deadeyes, Ltd.).

BLOCK TYPES

TWO SHEAVED
FIDDLE BLOCK

SEVENTEENTH
CENTURY
BLOCK

SHEET BLOCK
WITH
SISTER HOOKS

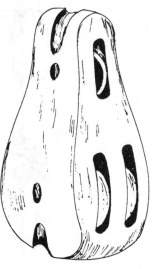

TRIPLE SHEAVED
FIDDLE BLOCK

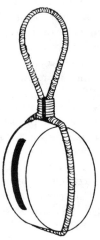

A single strop for a
block was most common
consisting of a hoop
made by splicing the two
ends of a short length of
rope together. The hoop
went round the block and
was seized leaving a loop
or becket for further
attachment.

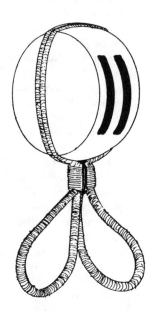

Double Stropped Block
might have the two
bights laced together
around a spar.

Long and Short End
Strop might be used to
fasten a block to a spar.

Monkey Blocks were
nailed to the top edge of
a yard as leads for the
buntlines.

Fig. 14-7. Types of blocks (Courtesy of Moonraker Publications).

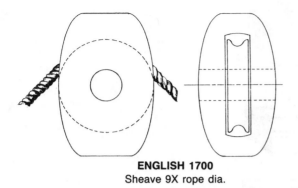

ENGLISH 1700
Sheave 9X rope dia.

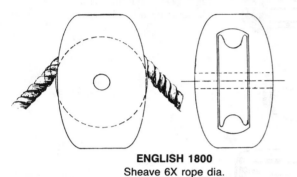

ENGLISH 1800
Sheave 6X rope dia.

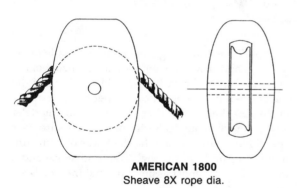

AMERICAN 1800
Sheave 8X rope dia.

Fig. 14-8. Ratio of the sheave to the diameter of the rope (Courtesy of Moonraker Publications).

The second method is for the more fastidious, or in cases where you wish to install a working sheave (FIG. 14-10). The steps of construction are basically the same as shown in FIG. 14-9, except that you use a laminated (built-up) method instead of a solid piece of wood. The area for the sheave is established by the open space. Add grooving for the strops after you have shaped the blank. Then add the sheave. FIG-

URE 14-11 shows a way to construct heart-shaped blocks for deadeyes.

The average ship-model kit does not have enough blocks in proper scale or design. The blocks are mass-produced in either of several woods or some form of metal.

Manufacturers of kits give very little, if any, regard to the period or type of construction. Few attempt to use blocks of that particular period. I have seen rope-stropped blocks on modern (1900+) ship models where metal hooks should have been used. The manufacturer used the same blocks in period, as well as modern, sailing ship kits.

Types. Use the proper blocks at the proper locations as far as possible. Use sister blocks at the lifts. Two single-sheaved blocks tied together would be all right for a jury rig or if you ran short on a long voyage. In some instances, such blocks were constructed for this use. No boatswain would condone improper blocking on his ship, however.

Do you know where a fiddle block should be used? A cat block? Have you used a monkey block on your models? Use of the many types of blocks should be as carefully thought out as the placement of the rigging. Therefore, a little research is indicated. Since David Steel published his work in London in 1794 (*The Elements and Practice of Rigging and Seamanship*) the practice of rigging has remained fixed by a set of guidelines and rules. These were not hard and fast rules, however.

One of the best rules came from Steel himself, who said, ''There is no one undeviating mode which is pursued in the progressive rigging of ships.'' What is the correct rigging of a true scale ship model if there is no set rule on the constant maintenance of rigging?

As the years passed, improvements came about. By 1848 Capt. George Biddlecombe, master in the Royal Navy, published his work, *The Art of Rigging* (Reprinted by Sweetman & Co., Largo, FL). None have taken the place of the masters of this art. The writings and drawings of Harold Underhill and David MacGregor, cover the modern type of clippers and merchant schooners.

Rigging began to change with the newer, faster, and better designed sailing ships. Fincham's work on the masting and rigging of the period of 1855 has recently been republished.

Devotees of period sail should include in their library the works of R.C. Anderson's classic, *The Rig-*

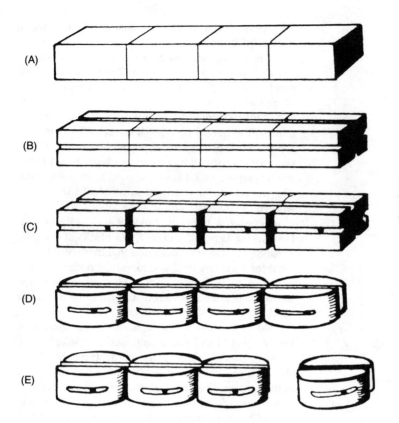

(A)

(B)

(C)

(D)

(E)

Fig. 14-9. Making your own blocks from a block of wood.

ging in the Days of the Spritsail Topmast 1600-1720 (Conway Maritime Press, England, or Cornell Maritime Press, Centerville, MD). The works of the masters will continue to be revitalized. A dedicated and improving modeler should be no stranger to these and future works concerning the subject of rigging.

SIZE AND PLACEMENT OF RUNNING RIGGING

Is accuracy needed in the size or thickness of the ship's running rigging? Consider the scale you are using. Consider also how thick a line is in that scale. Consider the size of the human hand in that scale. Try to remember what you have read on this subject.

The cables that hauled the anchor were huge. Bringing them (up) aboard called for an ingenious method of rope handling. The use of a purchase and nipper lines will not be discussed at this time. It is an interesting, subject, though, so check it out.

A rule of thumb is the statement "If she's under an inch, then she be a line, bigger than that, I calls

it a rope." The foregoing statement was made to me by a rare, and now gone, individual who had worked a sailing ship in the early 1900s. He told me of the power in a rope, "proper laid, proper rove," no matter the size. Remember that you are a scale modeler and remember your scale. If you are not sure, it is a good idea to understate the thickness of your running (and standing) rigging. Common sense and a little study will almost assure you that the line is accurate.

Several draftsmen of plans for the ship modeler have gone to great lengths to show the proper and acceptable rigging of the ship they have drawn. The belay points of any particular ship are important enough to be taken into consideration.

The late Frank Channing was undoubtedly one of the authorities on the whaling ship. His belaying plans are classics. The belaying points of the sailing ships that have survived and can be viewed today are not to be challenged. The belay points were taken from the ship itself or were determined through research when the ship was restored. If you are build-

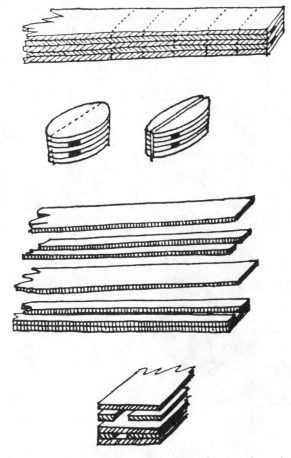

Fig. 14-10. Making blocks with laminated strips of wood.

ing a ship model of a restored vessel you owe it to yourself and the final product of your labors to be accurate in rigging.

For example, a kit of the *Wasa*, with all the restorative data to draw from, can be improved with proper rigging. A little research is all that you need. Most

''legendary'' modelers of today are most helpful. They want your model and modeling skills to be correct and proper, so don't be afraid to ask.

Suppose that you haven't the time or the desire to go this route. You are in a hurry, yet you know that there should be some semblance of order aboard your ship. O.K., since it is your ship, you can now become the boatswain. From your plan, you have rigged the standing rigging—stays and shrouds all in place, deadeyes even, and nice and taut.

You have hung the yards following whatever method you choose. You have bent the controlling (running) rigging and guided the lines through the tops down to where they will reach the pins. You have hoisted the yards into position and used the lifts to guide them steady. Braces are there to turn the yards. Where should these lines be tied?

The line should go to the nearest pin by the most direct route. In other words, belay your lifts for each yard in the same area. Work from the center pin outward as you advance up the mast—first the main, then the gallant, topgallant, etc. (FIG. 14-12).

Buntlines, clew lines, etc. usually come in pairs, one on either side of the mast outboard on the yards. Belay them in the same manner as you did the lifts, buntlines, clews, etc. Try to make sure that each line will work without fouling any other line.

What of the braces, sheets, downhauls, etc? They go to the pinrails along the gunwales. Keep an order to their belay points. The braces first, followed by the sheets and tacks. Each as you have noted come in pairs, one on each side of the ship, each serving as an antagonist to the other. One pulls while the other secures; the wind does the rest.

Your instinct can't always supply the best methods in this area. A little extra block, tackle, and purchasing will be needed in this department. A brace, in order to work, might need to be fairled

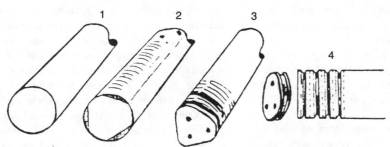

Fig. 14-11. Making heart-shaped deadeyes (triangle) from a dowel.

through a series of blocks to turn a yard. This is especially true the farther up the mast you go. However, she is your ship and you can rig her any way you want.

How should these lines be known? They need to have names. Each line aboard a ship was named for its use and where it did its work. Let's say you are told to haul on the foregallant buntline. I doubt if you would race to the mizzenmast and get ready. Now try another. "Haul the main lee brace," should find you at the mainmast and on the double. The site at which the line is "bent" and to which yard it is attached will get your mind set. What location and at what mast will tell you what line you will be working.

There are over 700 of these lines aboard the U.S.C.G. *Eagle,* and every cadet knows them by heart his first week at sea. It is an essential part of his training (FIG. 14-13). It is more than a test of memory. It is seamanship. His life and that of his shipmates might be tested by his knowledge.

Running rigging is primarily for the handling of the ship. Sails and the manner in which they are "handled" was alluded to previously. Understandably, if your ship model is without sails, then the lines and their positions just described would not be needed. They were "sent down" and unbent when the sails were removed, as were some of the yards. The tackle would be taken down and stored.

The way that a ship model is rigged is a matter of choice to the modeler who builds it. Each modeler is an individual (FIG. 14-14). Each model is a statement of individuality. I think that a model of a sailing ship is naked without its sails, unless of course, it is

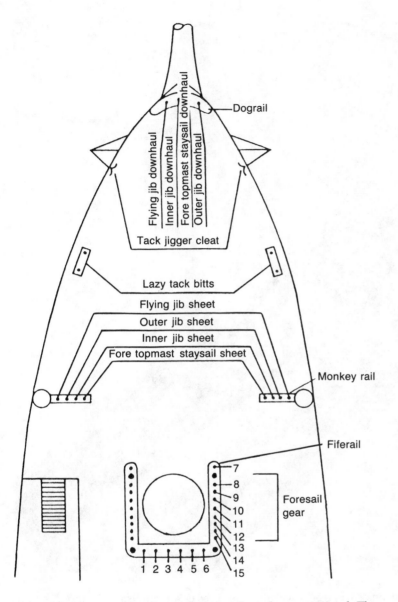

Fig. 14-13. A page from the handbook *Eagle Seamanship*, 2nd Edition, issued to cadets when they come aboard for training (Copyright © 1979, U.S. Naval Institute, Annapolis, MD).

Labels in figure:
- Dograil
- Flying jib downhaul
- Inner jib downhaul
- Fore topmast staysail downhaul
- Outer jib downhaul
- Tack jigger cleat
- Lazy tack bitts
- Flying jib sheet
- Outer jib sheet
- Inner jib sheet
- Fore topmast staysail sheet
- Monkey rail
- Fiferail
- Foresail gear
- 1 2 3 4 5 6
- 7 8 9 10 11 12 13 14 15

1. fore royal sheet
2. main royal staysail downhaul
3. gantline
4. main topmast staysail downhaul
5. main topgallant staysail downhaul
6. for royal sheet
7. lower topsail sheet
8. clew garnet
9. fore lift
10. fore leechline
11. fore inner buntline
12. fore outer buntline
13. upper topsail sheet
14. topgallant sheet
15. spare

represented as in port or some other situation where sails would be in error. A ship with sails seems to want to move. A ship model used in a diorama is a good example. Most models, however, wind up in cases or on static display. Why so many are "sans sails" is a source of irritation to me. Museums in particular are the greatest offenders.

REFERENCES

The rigging of sails is as precise a task as the construction of the model itself. Scale must be main- tained. The use of the proper lines and the fairleads, attachments such as bullseyes, lizards, cringles, etc., will depend on the period of the model. The texts mentioned previously will be more than helpful. Another is the *Young Sea Officer's Sheet Anchor* by Darcy Lever (Sweetman & Co., Key Largo, FL), a standard of the world of sailing ships since 1819. This text was used as a guide in the restoration and rerigging of the U.S.S. *Constitution* in 1928. Other books concerning rigging have been referred to in other areas of this book.

Fig. 14-14. Unnamed topsail schooner showing details of rigging (Photo courtesy of American Marine Model Gallery).

Most books about period ship modeling cover rigging. No favoritism or classification is intended here. I would, however, like to mention a few names for your consideration. In addition to those already mentioned, read the works of R.C. Anderson and his contemporary, R.K. Batteson, for the sixteenth and seventeenth centuries. These names are respected worldwide. Clyde Millward and Noel Hackney join their ranks.

For the eighteenth century, look for the works of Longridge, including *Anatomy of Nelson's Ships* (Na-

val Institute Press, Annapolis, MD) and *The Cutty Sark, The Ship and the Model* (Argus Ltd. England). Nineteenth century and contemporary information is available in the works of the controversial and legendary Howard Chapelle, the prolific Charles Davis, Hobbs, after Petrejus of Holland, Ben Lankford, and Eric Ronnberg, both Sr. and Jr.

Several of the books and information sources mentioned are now "out of print." They are available from dealers of used books, as well as libraries. Rare book dealers who specialize in nautical publications can be of great assistance. These books are not that rare, and many are undergoing reprinting.

I know that not everyone has the opportunity to meet and talk with ''experts'' or fellow modelers. However, a book is often as good, and many times is better. It can be referred to over and over. Read and try to own as many as you can on the subject you have chosen.

Details of a model of the H.M.S. *Vanguard*, the flagship of Admiral Nelson at the Battle of the Nile in 1798. This scratch-built model, built by Alfred Oxspring to plans secured from the National Maritime Museum in Greenwich, England, is an outstanding example of the shipbuilder's art. The model is the centerpiece of The Vanguard Collection, which belongs to the Vanguard Group of Investment Companies in Valley Forge, PA.

(Photos courtesy of Vanguard Group of Investment Companies.)

(Photos courtesy of Museum of Church History and Art, Salt Lake City, UT.)

(insert)The opening in the side of the *Enoch Train* depicts a day aboard the ship bringing settlers to America. The carved figures are by Curt Grinaker of Salt Lake City.

This 3/8 scale model of the *Enoch Train* by Jim Raines is on display at the Mormon Church's Museum of Church History and Art in Salt Lake City, UT.

(Model and photo by Lloyd McCaffery.)

This model of the infamous H.M.S. *Bounty*, in a scale of 1 inch = 16 feet, is based on original plans taken from the ship prior to her voyage on the Pacific. The open hull shows interior details.

(right) This model of a Chinese junk, produced from a kit by Amati, is an example of detailed customizing.

(below left) The whaleboat of the model of the *Kate Cory*, seen in the background, and all the tools of the whaler's trade carried aboard.

(below right) This model of Prince Frederick's state barge (1732) shows carving at its finest detail. The model, in a scale of 1/2 inch = 1 foot, is gold leafed on the starboard side. The port carvings are in natural wood. The model won First Place in the Small Craft Class competition held every 5 years at the National Maritime Museum in Greenwich, England, where the actual barge is preserved.

(Model and photo by Rick Evans.)

(Model and photo by Jim Roberts.)

(Model and photo by Lloyd McCaffery.)

(Model and photo by Rick Evans.)

The famous Stuart yacht, *Mary*, produced from a kit with added sails, makes an interesting model with fine detail and decorations.

FIFTEEN

Sails for Sailing Ships

For a ship is the noblest of all men's works—
A cunning fabric of wood, and iron, and hemp,
Wonderfully propelled by wings of canvas,
And seeming at times to have the very breath of life.

ANONYMOUS

A MODEL OF A SAILING SHIP WITHOUT SAILS LOOKS naked. It sits there on its display stand or in its case looking to all the work like a skeleton. On the other hand, a model with sails looks like it wants to move. The waterline model in a diorama, even one in a bottle, when wearing sails is alive.

Marine paintings show sailing ships with sails. A good rendition of a clipper, all sails set, spray flowing from the bows as she cuts the water, "bone in her teeth," is exciting. Why then do modelers insist on continuing to display their models in this fashion?

The excuses, if you wish to call them that, are many. I have heard the old chestnut, "It hides all the work I did on the rigging." Not true if you consider the extra rigging that is needed when you are bending the sail to the yard. Perhaps it is the extra rigging of tackle that the modeler doesn't understand or want to do (FIG. 15-1).

To add insult to injury, the modeler then displays his bare-poled beauty incorrectly. He hauls the yards to full lift, no sails, and squares them off. This is a gross error. If you take all the time to build a sailing ship model in scale, then why not show her as she would be in real life? The yards with sails sent down would be in a stored position. They would be at trestletree or mast doubling level. Some would even rest on the tops. Exceptions are the latter day sailing ships with iron truss and chain sling arrangements, mer-

chant ships, and clippers. Again comes an excuse, "It doesn't look good. They are all crowded in the middle."

How about a compromise? If you wish to show your model in the bare-poled attitude, make her look like she is in for refitting or at the shipyard waiting for sails. Unship an anchor—pay out a little cable and allow it to rest on the bottom of the display case or on the stand. This gives the effect that she is not simply adrift. Instead of fancy brass or wood pedestals, build a way under the model. Crosspieces of timber, a slanted underrail, and maybe a prop pole or two would also give the not-quite-ready-for-launch look. Then you can lower the yards to the proper position and your model will look complete—at rest, but ready.

If you don't care to indulge in research, then why not rig your model in any of the many ways that sails would be found aboard a ship? Other than being stored in the sail locker, they could be displayed from full press (all sails set) to furled completely. You might rig her in any of the various stages of sail handling. How about simply showing the sails hung out to dry?

DRYING SAILS

Each type of sailing ship developed its own technique for drying sail. Most of the time this was done in port or at the quay. You could identify the type

Fig. 15-1. Sails as installed by Maury Drummond on his scratch-built model of H.M.S. *Victory* (Courtesy of Maury Drummond, Jr.).

of ship by the way she dried her sails. There were basically two methods, other than simply "loosing sail:" "hauling out to bowline," and with "buntlines hauled up."

The only exceptions to the rule were the whalers. These independent types follows nobody's rules. They were the only ones who dried their sails with the yards at full hoist. All other ships did not expend the effort to raise the yards. Keep this fact in mind if your model is a whaler (FIG. 15-2).

Detailed descriptions of the two methods can be found in many of the old texts. The best references are photographs. Many were taken in harbors around the world to record the types of ships that visited.

Navy ships, which had an abundance of manpower, proceeded in an orderly manner and presented a neat appearance. Yards were placed in the lowered position. Garnets and clew lines were hauled up, and the lower sheets and tacks allowed to hang loosely down the masts. Buntlines were

hauled up. All remaining tackle hung loosely in a neat and military fashion. "Hauling out to bowline" resulted in the sails strung forward from the yard by the bowline. These lines were unbent from their usual position at the bridles and attached to the buntline cringles (FIG. 15-3).

The twentieth century windjammers had their method. The small crews aboard and the fixed position of many of the yards, one dependent on the other, developed a buntline raising, as it were.

SAIL HANDLING

If you wish to create a flood of conversation concerning your models, set your sails and brace your yards in the many acceptable, but little known positions of sail handling. The usual method of display is with all sail set and the yards at a 90-degree angle to the masts. Conditions of such nature were rare at sea. Most winds were from various points abeam and the sails set and braced for better advantage. Tilt your

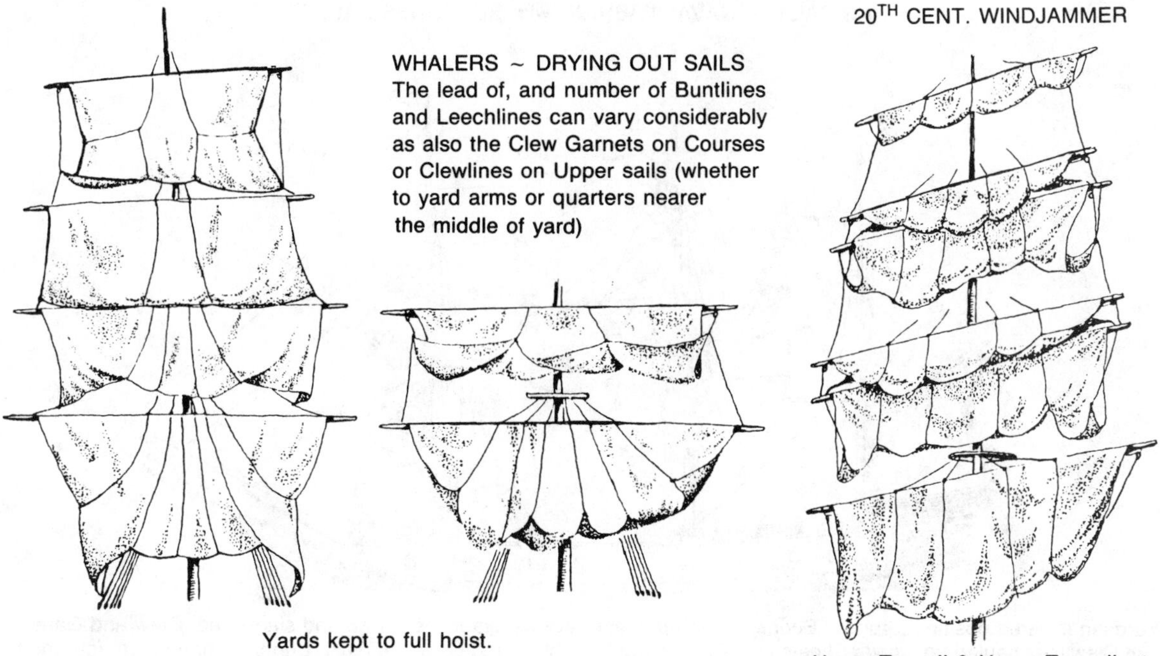

WHALERS ~ DRYING OUT SAILS
The lead of, and number of Buntlines
and Leechlines can vary considerably
as also the Clew Garnets on Courses
or Clewlines on Upper sails (whether
to yard arms or quarters nearer
the middle of yard)

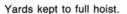

Yards kept to full hoist.

Upper Topsail & Upper Topgallant
yards lowered. Lower Sheets
and Tacks, and Lower Topsail
Sheets detached.

Fig. 15-2. The manner in which vessels dried sails (Courtesy of George C. Campbell, Model Ships and Boats).

model slightly to the lee side for an added dramatic effect (FIG. 15-4).

In several stages of maneuvering, called *tacking* or *wearing* ship, the positions of the yards and the sails would be in direct opposite brace. They would even billow out at opposing angles. For even stranger sail settings, check out the movements of "box off" (FIG. 15-5) and "A-Box" (FIG. 15-6). You are familiar with the command of "heave to" (FIG. 15-7). Can you set the yards and sails in the proper position?

The latest book out on sail handling is *Seamanship in the Age of Sail: An Account of the Shiphandling of the Sailing Man of War, Based on Contemporary Sources* by John Haraland (Conway Maritime, England, and Naval Institute Press, Annapolis). It is going to become a classic. Those already in the classic class are *The Visual Encyclopedia of Nautical Terms Under Sail* and *The Lore of Ships*. Both were published by Crown & Co. of New York. Unfortunately both are out of print. Check with your library or rare-book dealer.

If all the terminology throws you, a good dictionary is always handy. There are several encyclopedias

and dictionaries devoted to the subject. *A Dictionary of Sea Terms* by A. Ansted (Brown, Son & Ferguson) is back in print. Nautical terms and words used through the ages and stages of sail are arranged in alphabetical order. Illustrations and explanations of each are given.

CREW

A ship under sail must have a crew. Unless your model is the *Mary Celeste*, I would suggest at least someone at the wheel.

O scale railroad figures (HO and N for the smaller scales) repainted for the period of your ship make nice added touches. They show you care what happens to your ship.

Carving your own figures in scale and positions of action is a thrill you should experience at least once in your modeling lifetime. If you can do a figurehead, why not a figure? Check out a book on whittling or take a long, hard look at the illustrations provided here. (See Chapter 10.)

DRYING SAILS ~ NAVAL FASHION with BUNTLINES HAULED UP

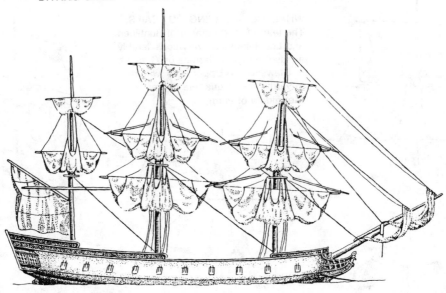

Yards in lowered position. Stunsail Booms triced up. Reef Tackles, slablines, let go and slackened. Clew and Garnets and Clewlines hauled up. Lower Sheets and Tacks hang loosely up and down the mast. Buntlines hauled up. Intermediate Staysails hang loosely.

DRYING SAILS ~ NAVAL FASHION, HAULING OUT TO A BOWLINE

Yards in lowered position. Stunsail Booms triced up or removed. Topsail Bowlines unbent from Bridles and attached to Buntline Cringles and hauled out. Tacks and Sheets disconnected from Lower Courses and hung temporarily from the Tops, with Clew Ropes bent in their stead and hauled out. All Buntlines, Reef Tackles, Clew Garnets slackened. Topsail Clewlines, Top Gallant Sheets steadied taut.

Fig. 15-3. Drying sails navy fashion (Courtesy of George C. Campbell, Model Ships and Boats).

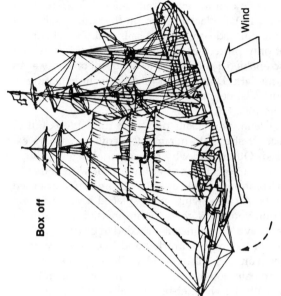

Box off

Wind

Fig. 15-5. A ship at "Box off" (Courtesy of Spectre Books).

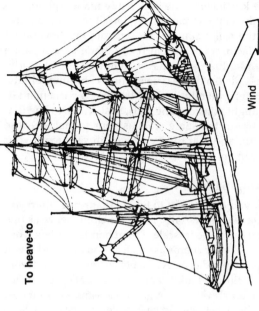

To heave-to

Wind

Fig. 15-7. The ship has been commanded "to heave" (Courtesy of Spectre Books).

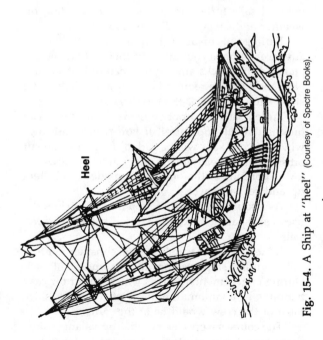

Heel

Fig. 15-4. A Ship at "heel" (Courtesy of Spectre Books).

A-box

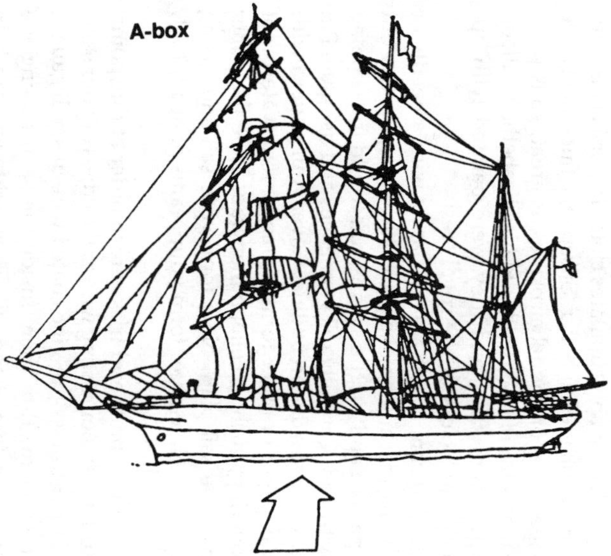

Fig. 15-6. A ship at "A-box" (Courtesy of Spectre Books).

SAILS

Where do you get the sails to put on a ship model? They are included in a few of the better kits. Some kits include the sails ready made; others furnish the cloth as part of the kit. One manufacturer sells the sail makings as a separate kit. Several kit manufacturers sell them ready made as a separate item. Mantua-Sergal has a complete line of ready-made sails (sold separately) for its ship-model kits. Although you might not be building a particular kit, you might consider the sails. Just check to see that they are in the same scale as your model, or close enough, and that there are enough sails to fill your requirements.

Making Sails

If you don't want to follow that route, then you will have to make sails. Keep the cloth weave as fine as you can to be in scale. Linen handkerchiefs work well. Make the seams as small as you can, and if you can't stitch, indicate. A fine pencil line is great. Avoid the "printed look" and use a dark brown or brownish-grey pencil. A good seamstress is your best ally. The panels should be in scale, as well as the lines and tackle (FIG. 15-8).

Have you considered using material other than cloth for making sails? Painted aluminum foil is easy to work with and simulates cloth. Paper-backed aluminum foil is even better. Silkspan, a fine-quality rice paper used on model airplanes, is great; so is plain paper. One of my friends did his Elizabethan galleon with paper sails, and they were painted with appropriate colors of the royal crest.

You can, if you are not handy with a needle or sewing machine, make your sails with glue. Lay out a pattern and cut the sails as you would for seaming by thread. Carefully roll your edges and use glue. Pin each sail to a drawn outline. Cover your pattern with wax paper or other form of transparent waterproof covering, such as cellophane wrap. Tape the paper over the sail plan. Now form your sail and, using thinned white glue, form your seams at head, foot, and leeches.

A few hints and tricks are in order at this point. Add a stiff, nonrusting wire to the edges of your sails. Copper-, brass-, or zinc-coated wire in small gauges is excellent. Run them inside the seams along the leech and foot of the sail. These stiffeners can help billow or hold a sail at "fill." When you come to the clew, leave some wire exposed and form it in a loop to simulate the cringles to attach the working tackle. Three or more blocks often attach here (FIG. 15-9).

As you know, every sail had a rope around the edges. It was placed astern on the square sails and to the port side on the stay sails and jibs. This rope not only protected and strengthened the sails, but also enabled a good sailor to bend sail properly even in the dark. Don't forget to add this little feature to your sails, be they cloth or paper. Keep the rope in scale. (SEE FIG. 15-10.)

Clean, white sails on a ship model look out of place. If she is on her maiden voyage you are excused. Otherwise, why not consider staining them to an "at sea" (for some time) color with coffee or tea solutions, weak dyes, or thinned water-based paints. A clean, white patch placed here and there among your sails gives the impression of a ship at sea. Leave 'em a little bit wrinkled to give the appearance of having been furled and loosed many times over. You might also consider a little weathering look in the paint job of your model. It would be in keeping with the weather-beaten sails (FIG. 15-11).

Sets of Sail

Furl the sails. The ship model can be displayed with all sails furled or just a few, depending on weather and sailing conditions (FIG. 15-12).

Furling sails made of cloth can be planned for in advance. Perhaps you can make them off the model, and add the blocks and rigging before installation. No panels will be required or indicated. Follow the steps shown in FIGS. 15-13 AND 15-14.

Furled sails need not be made as full sails. The bulk is difficult to control. If you plan in advance which of your sails will be furled, then you can cut off some of the ready-made material or cut down on lower portions of the ones to be made. Haul them up and set them wet.

As a substitute for cloth, you might consider the use of silkspan. It makes fine furled and full-shaped sails.

If the model is a warship, then consider fighting sail. Fighting ships seldom fought under full sail. During engagements, canvas was reduced for easy handling by a minimum number of crewmen, since most of the crew would be at the guns.

The courses were clewed up. Topgallants sometimes were loosely furled and lowered to the caps.

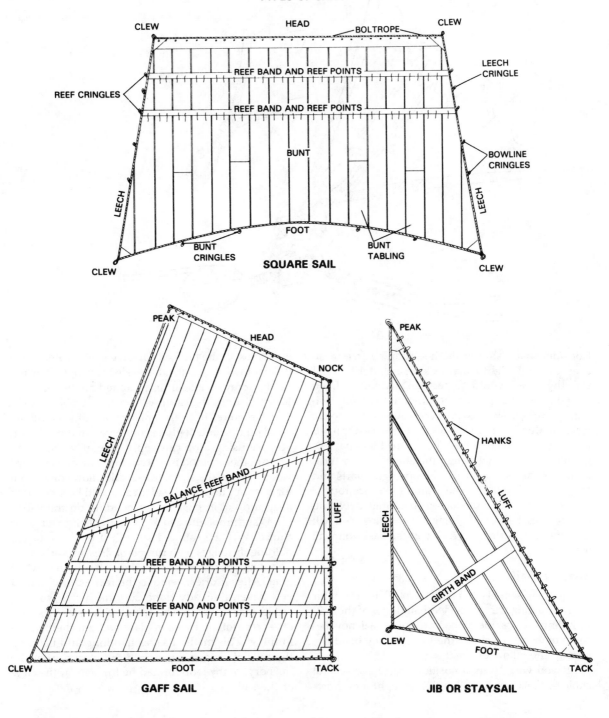

Fig. 15-8. Types of sails, the names of the parts, and how to make them (Courtesy of Moonraker Publications).

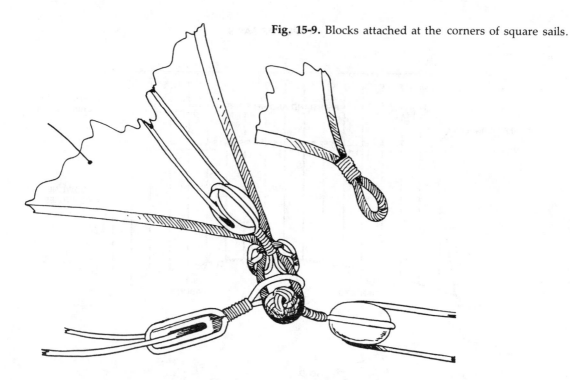

Fig. 15-9. Blocks attached at the corners of square sails.

Consider that a ship of the line running free in an average wind might make six knots. Under fighting sail, the speed would be perhaps two knots. Even close-hauled at a speed of one knot, it took only two minutes for the ships to pass each other on opposite tacks. In this short time, it was only the best trained gun crew that could, if they fired as the bows passed, get off a second shot before the enemy was astern. If your model is displayed with open gun ports and guns run out, fighting sail would be a nice touch.

Look at some of the famous paintings depicting battles at sea between fighting sailing ships. You will find ample material on which you can base your sail installation.

Shaping Sails

Shaping sails is not a difficult job. The reason for the nonrusting wire in the leech and foot of the sail, including the jibs, mentioned previously will now become obvious. To shape the sails, simply bend the wire to the billow desired.

If you wish to fix a position, you have several choices. Sails can hang limplike in light airs; how-ever, most of the methods involve using water. A solution of white glue that has been thinned with water can be sprayed or sparingly painted on the material. When it dries, the cloth will set stiff. Unlike starch, which requires heat, the amount of stiffness will depend on how much glue is dissolved in the solution you are using. You can apply several coats.

Another method is preforming. Make a semihard wood block in the shape of the sail. Allow some room for overlapping. The head area should be straight to keep the sail in position for bending on the yard.

Waterproof the block by any method of your choice. Wet the sail and smooth it over the block, holding the edges with rustproof dressmaker's pins. This might be the time to use the water-thinned white glue. After it dries, remove the formed sail and, if you haven't already done so, attach the working tackle. I try to have my buntlines, clews, leeches, and other controlling ropes in place and attached before forming. This method saves handling and bending the sails after forming. Attach the blocks, after the sails dry, at the loop formed by the wire at the clew of the sail.

Furling Sails

You can furl sails after you place them on the model. Attach the working tackle simply, and very gently use the lines to furl the sail. Identify the lines with little paper tags at the ends (FIG. 15-15), so you know which line to work. After you install the yard on the model, you can find the marked line among the maze of lines and belay to the proper pin. You will, of course, bend your sail to the yard before installing the yard on the mast.

A little gentle assistance with a pair of tweezers helps. Pull the cloth into position and shape with water. Assist gravity and shape the sails as if this force of nature were acting on the cloth.

After they dry in position, some sails might require additional setting. I first use a fine mist of water and then hair spray. The cheap, stiffer setting brands are the best. Macho types can call the hair sprays lacquer (in many cases that's what it is anyway), or use clear, spray plastic paints or varnishes.

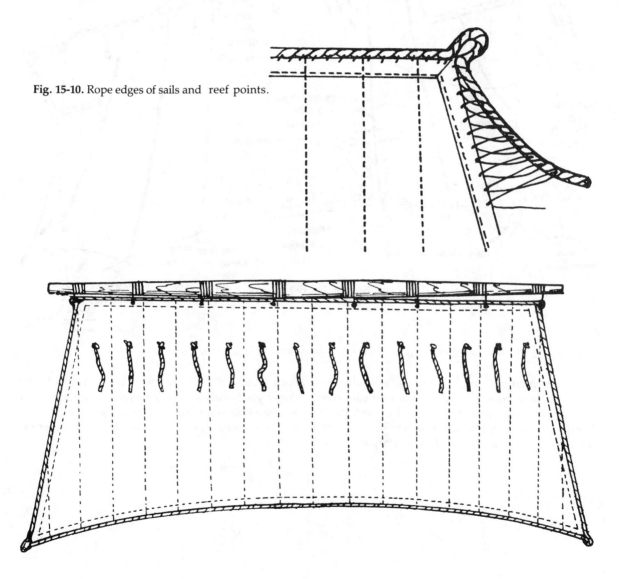

Fig. 15-10. Rope edges of sails and reef points.

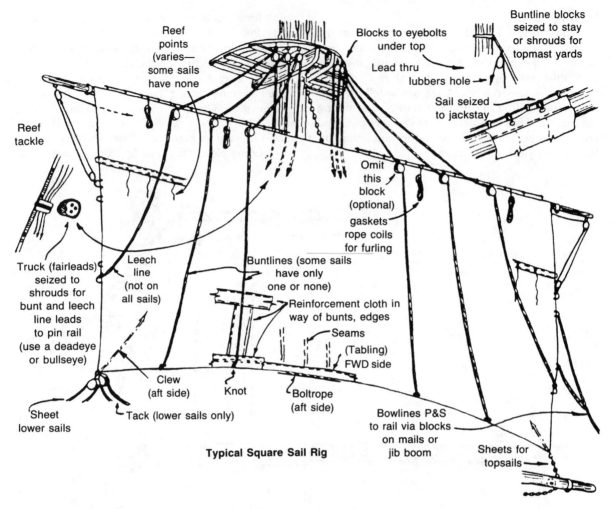

Fig. 15-11. A few tips on giving sails a "working" appearance (Courtesy of Model Shipways).

Use a minimum amount, just enough to do the job. In a short time, harsh chemicals will hurt cotton or flax, and destroy paper. Shellac is also used, but it dries with too high a shine. Use nongloss sprays. Watch out for the rigging and avoid droplet forma-tions. Add paint to the stiffening solutions if you doubt your skill as a spray painter. When you have reached this stage, there is no turning back.

Your model is now completed. She is under sail with sails.

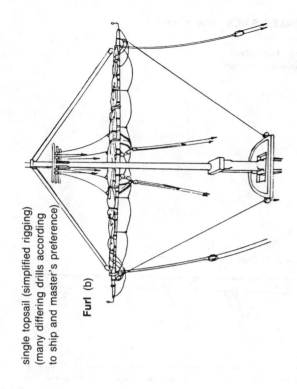

single topsail (simplified rigging)
(many differing drills according
to ship and master's preference)

Furl (b)

lift

buntlines

clewline

brace pendant

Furl (a)

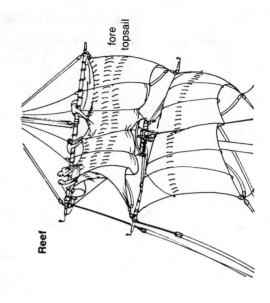

fore
topsail

Reef

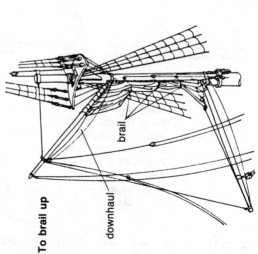

brail

downhaul

To brail up

Fig. 15-12. Sails in stowed positions
(Courtesy of Spectre Books).

195

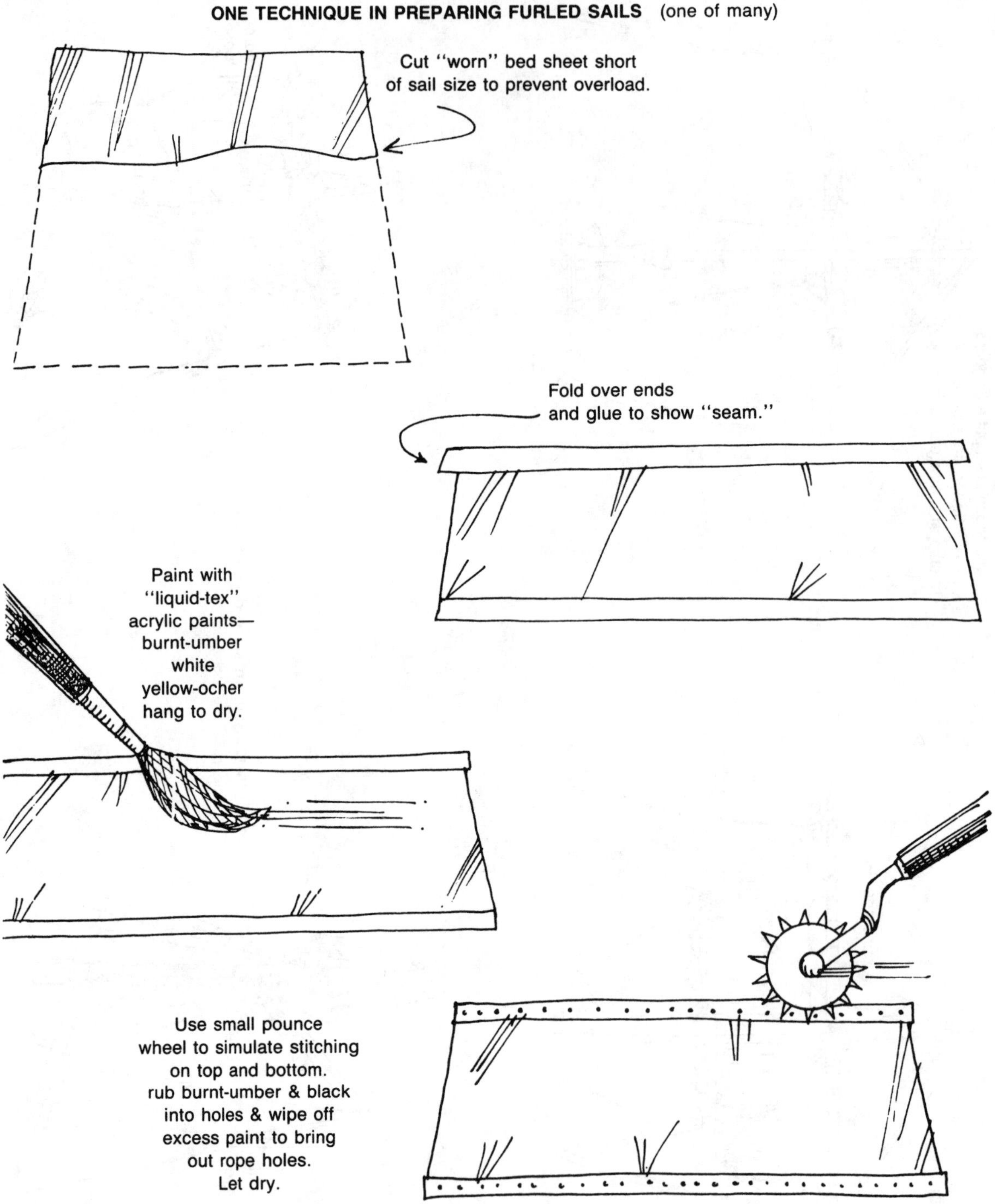

ONE TECHNIQUE IN PREPARING FURLED SAILS (one of many)

Cut "worn" bed sheet short of sail size to prevent overload.

Fold over ends and glue to show "seam."

Paint with "liquid-tex" acrylic paints—
burnt-umber
white
yellow-ocher
hang to dry.

Use small pounce wheel to simulate stitching on top and bottom. rub burnt-umber & black into holes & wipe off excess paint to bring out rope holes. Let dry.

Fig. 15-13. A technique of preparing to bend furled sails without the bulk of a full sail (Courtesy of Northshore Deadeyes, Ltd.).

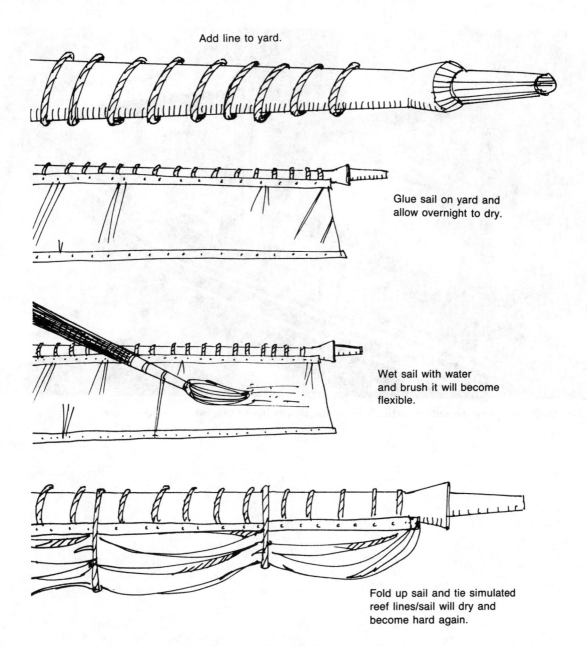

Add line to yard.

Glue sail on yard and
allow overnight to dry.

Wet sail with water
and brush it will become
flexible.

Fold up sail and tie simulated
reef lines/sail will dry and
become hard again.

Fig. 15-14. Adding the gravity pull and giving a furled look to your sails (Courtesy of Northshore Deadeyes, Ltd.).

Fig. 15-15. Adjusting the sails by actually using the proper lines (Model and photo by John Magine).

SIXTEEN

Anatomy of the Gun

*The great thing in this world
is not so much where we are,
but in what direction we are moving.*
—OLIVER WENDELL HOLMES

DO YOU KNOW WHAT THE NAME OF THE BALL ON the end of a cannon is called? If you call it the *button*, you are correct. There are other names for this part of the gun. Do you know them? Everyone knows where the muzzle is. Most can tell you the location of the breech. What about the other parts of the gun?

HISTORY OF GUNS

Before the introduction of the cast gun, about the end of the fifteenth century, artillery was "built-up." Wood staves were used in the early days. Sometimes they were lined with workable metals such as copper or bronze. Then the practice of welding iron rods together came along. Both types were hooped for added strength. Crude and unreliable, they soon disappeared with the advent of casting.

The idea of casting was slow to catch on. In 1332, the Moors cast a culvin rated at 4 pounds. This was accomplished only two years after gunpowder was first used to hurl a projectile. The "built-up" guns continued for some time until the secret of casting became common knowledge. Records show that some iron guns were cast in northern Europe at Erfurt in 1377. The Moors did their casting in Spain. By the late fifteenth century, gun foundries were well established in southern Europe. Most countries imported their guns from there.

Perhaps by custom, perhaps design, the shape of guns was established. Guns were cast with reinforced rings in place of the hoops. Casting was done in one piece. If you look at a gun standing on its end, muzzle up, you will notice the similarity to an architectural column. The designers then decorated the guns with wreaths, crests, mottos, and symbols. Guns were a tribute to the foundryman's art, pleasing to the eye and honoring the ruler of the period.

In 1756, John Mueller, master gunner of Woolwich, and an authority on weaponry, wrote a paper on the uselessness of ornamental guns. In describing the gun, he said that they were ". . . all taken from Architecture." His philosophy was practical, and the gun became a weapon instead of a showpiece. He discarded the designs of the traditional guns from the days of Queen Elizabeth, which had been adopted by Cromwell and were used well into the eighteenth century. Mueller improved on the formulas for gun design established in 1730 by Surveyor-General Armstrong.

TERMS

The history and development of the naval gun is a fascinating study. Volumes are dedicated to it. Our purpose is to study the anatomy of the weapon's external features. Before we explore the topographical features of the gun, however, you need to know a few terms.

Caliber is a term often used but seldom defined. It is the diameter of the bore, and also expresses the length of the bore. For example, on a 30-caliber gun the length of the bore is 30 times the diameter of the bore. Guns were fortified according to their bore.

Divisions of light, medium, and heavy guns required different amounts of metal for fortifying. The gun designers used the bore and the caliber to set tables and standards for the amount of metal to be used in the walls. The heavier the shot, the thicker the wall. This standard was undoubtedly related to the amount of powder used to propel the shot.

I will not attempt to cover periods, ratings, weights, or styles of guns used over the centuries. Reference will be restricted to the gun in general.

The *muzzle*, the business end, is the place to start. The first area was known as the *muzzle face*. Behind this area, a carryover from the days of the *bombard*, was the *reinforcing molding*. This takes us to the "swelling of the muzzle" (FIG. 16-1). There are several other names associated with this area. Some called it the *bell*. Others referred to it as the *swell* or the *flare*. From France came the term *la tulip* and the plural, *tulips*. The area must have reminded others of their favorite flower and they called it *lilly*. In the sixteenth century it was the *cornice*.

Next the first ring. The area has now narrowed. Quite naturally it was known as the *neck* of the muzzle. The *astragal* (FIG. 16-1), a convex architectural molding, was added as a ring. Some designer

thought it gave additional strength. The astragal of the muzzle was flanked by fillets. Often a fillet was in the form of a hollow molding. This molding was referred to as a *cavetto*, which was also a concave molding used in architecture. After the early part of the nineteenth century, the astragal was replaced by a flat ring or band. In no time it was omitted altogether.

The area between the muzzle ring and the second reinforce ring was known as the *chace*, sometimes spelled *chase*. Included in the area was the *chase astragal*, which is accompanied by the fillets. The short distance between the chace astragal and the second reinforce ring was called the *chase bridle*. It is there that the first *ogee*, or tapering, was found. This is another architectural term meaning a molding with an S-shaped curve in its profile. You can think of the ogee as a step upward or downward in the thickness of the gun.

The second reinforce (FIG. 16-1) was the area containing the *trunnion*. Some guns had no rings located here. Instead they simply had a bevel or hollow curve instead of a shoulder. If there was a ring cast, its forward edge coincided with the edge of the reinforce. The ogee of the second reinforce ring was actually on the chace girdle. A cavetto might have been present instead of an ogee. Sometimes a narrow cavetto separated the ring and the ogee. A flat ring was used after the nineteenth century.

The locations of these units were set by the standards of 1730 in the British navy. These standards were more or less used by all nations. The 20-caliber

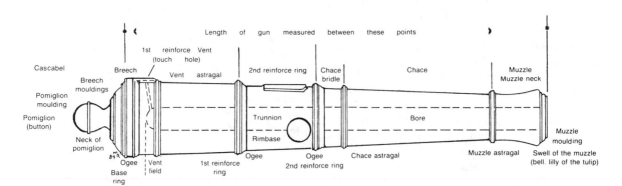

Fig. 16-1. The parts of a ship's gun.

(length) guns had the following outside proportions:

1st reinforce = 2/7 of the gun's length
2nd reinforce = 1/7 the length plus 1 caliber
chace = 4/7 the length minus less 1 caliber
trunnions = 1 caliber (approx.) in diameter

The trunnions, or arms, projected from the side of the guns. In 1756, Mueller raised the trunnions to the center of the bore to lessen the strain on the gun carriage.

Prior to the fourteenth century, guns had no trunnions. Mortars were the exception. They had the trunnions in the breech (cascabel). Location of the trunnion varied with the type of weapon. They usually were placed one-half caliber behind the second reinforce ring, but some were located three-sevenths the length of the gun from the hind edge of the base ring. The French placed them farther back, about one caliber behind the ring.

Mueller raised the axis of the trunnions from their traditional place (FIG. 16-2), which coincided with the lower surface of the bore. He also moved them to a position that was three-sevenths the gun's length, which stopped the tendency of the gun to "buck."

A notable exception, in addition to mortars, were carronades (FIG. 16-3). The axis of the trunnion sometimes was located at the lower surface of the gun itself. Often, two lugs were cast into the underside of the carronade, instead of a trunnion being used.

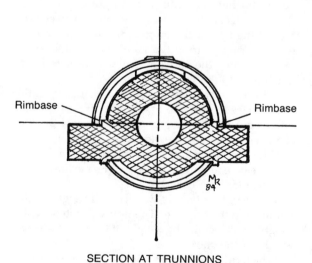

SECTION AT TRUNNIONS

Fig. 16-2. A section at the trunnions of a ship's gun.

Dolphins, those handlelike projections on early guns, were cast into the guns above the trunnions. They allowed the piece to be lifted onto and off of the carriage. This feature was not common on sea cannons. Early sea guns were simply taken from the army stores and placed aboard. Other names given to the dolphins include loops, lifting rings, handles, "D" rings, and from the olden days, ansae.

The *first reinforce* area included the vent, or *touch hole*. It extended from the first reinforce ring to the base ring. The first reinforce ring was identical in design to the second reinforce ring. Some guns omitted this ring altogether. The barrel was then cast smooth from the base ring to the second reinforce.

Vent moldings usually were cast in the same form as the muzzle and chace rings. The common form was the astragal and fillet design until the end of the eighteenth century.

The *vent field* did not show on the outside of the gun. This vital internal area played an important part in the design of the bore. It was in this small section that the first burning of the powder took place. It was usually as thick as the base ring and extended from the forward edge of the vent astragal to a point coinciding with the bottom of the bore (end). A flat area was cast on the upper surface of the gun at the vent hole. This flat base, or table covered the area from the base ring to within 1/4 inch of the vent astragal, sometimes joining it. The vent patch was usually as thick as the base ring. The vent hole was bored through the *vent patch*. Not all guns had this feature.

The all-important touch hole, or vent, extended from the top of the gun to the base of the bore, or the *powder chamber*. The gun was filled with powder from the chamber to the vent hole. The chamber was touched off to fire the gun.

Later guns had flintlocks and powder pans. The familiar fuse did not come along until later. Some of the cannon had two vents. One was not bored though, but held in reserve. After a period of time, the first hole would be closed and the second opened for business.

During this same time, the vent hole's location was changed to the breech. The cascabel was eliminated and the breech end flattened. A fuse was added, and the powder burned directly to the chamber.

The *base ring* (FIG. 16-4), a final, thick, hind end ring, was placed one caliber back from the bottom

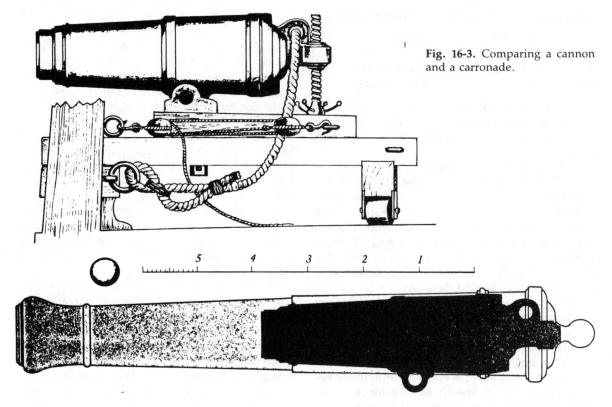

Fig. 16-3. Comparing a cannon and a carronade.

end of the bore. Its form was the same as the reinforce rings, including the ogee. It marked the end of the breech.

Technically, the *breech* of a gun lay between the bottom of the bore (internally) and the back end of the base ring. Breech moldings varied in width and number. Basically, there were two or more, depending on the size (weight) of the gun.

We are now literally at the end of the gun, wherein was the familiar and identifiable ball. The end of the gun was included in the area known as the cascabel (FIG. 16-4). It extended from the base ring, included the breech area and all its moldings, and ended at the tip of the button. This knob had several other names, which might pop up from time to time. They are *knop, pomelion, pommiglion, pomme, pom,* and the *knob.* Please do not get confused. The *area* is called the cascabel. The button is often erroneously referred to by the name of the area.

DIMENSIONS

Now that you have become familiar with the ex-

ternal features of the typical gun of the Broadside Era, following are a few more terms and facts. This potpourri of information is included as a teaser to induce you to further your education in guns.

The *length of the gun* was measured between the area of the face of the muzzle and the hind end of the base ring. During the latter part of the seventeenth century, the measurement was taken from the touch hole to the muzzle face.

The *length of the bore* was the distance from the muzzle face to the base of the bore. It was the hollow length inside the gun. If there was a powder chamber, its length was added to the total.

The *thickness of the metal* (walls) included the area from the bore to the outside edge. The moldings were not included.

The *weight of the gun* was its total weight. It did not include the carriage. The gun was rated by the weight of its metal. The weight of the metal was the weight of the shot.

The term *windage* does not refer to any allowance made for drift of the shot as a result of the wind. Unlike for the Kentucky rifle, on a ship windage refers to the difference between the diameter of the bore and the diameter of the shot. This distance, or clearance, varied through the centuries. As the science of artillery improved, it became better defined and smaller in measurement. There was less "blow-by."

The study of the naval weapon is endless. There are hundreds, perhaps thousands, of volumes on the subject, written in almost every language. The books cover, in detail, the periods from the first powder-driven projectile to modern ship's guns with all their computer-operated gear. There is one book that I consider the basic book of facts: *Artillery Through the Ages* by Albert Manucy (United States Government Printing Office, Washington, D.C.) This booklet printed for the National Park Service is still available. It is, as the subtitle states, "A Short Illustrated History of Cannon Emphasizing Types Used in America." It should be in your library.

ANATOMY OF THE GUN CARRIAGE

The weapon, a gun made of cast iron or bronze, was massive. The weight was enormous because of the amount of metal used. Six-pounders weighed a ton; 42-pound rated cannon weighed 6,500 pounds. They were all weapons for use at close range. Even the mighty 32-pounder had a range of only 2,900 yards. Accuracy was poor.

The fit of the ball to the bore was poorer still. Cannon were cast, not often milled (drilled), and pitted by wear and chemical action of the gunpowder. The windage allowed the ball to bounce along the bore. This was the type of gun used by navies from the thirteenth century until the American Civil War. Ship's guns were, with the exception of mortars and swivel guns, mounted on carriages.

Fig. 16-4. Moulding details of the breech.

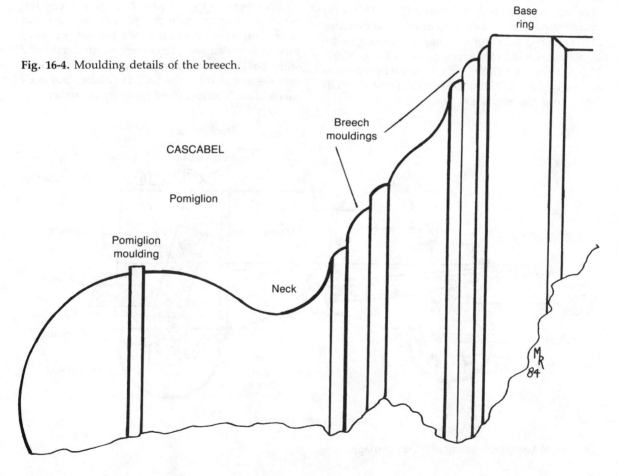

Dimensions and Materials

Wooden carriages were used. Most were of the four-wheeled variety. The two-wheeled carronade, with the slide mount, and the bed of the mortar were the exceptions. Formulas were established for the construction of wooden carriages.

Basic proportions, established by measurements of the gun, denoted the size of the mounting (carriage). Measurements were taken at the distance from the trunnion to the base ring, the diameter of the base ring, and the diameter of the second reinforce ring. The caliber was the fourth measurement. This quadrilateral figure, which served as the key, was rather complicated.

It was Mueller who established the specifications for gun carriages from the 3- to 32-pounders aboard English ships. Most nations followed this example. If your interest in the details compels you to further research, I recommend the books and papers of John Mueller, *Treatise of Artillery* (London 1756). This is the prime source of information regarding such weapons of the eighteenth century. Earlier periods of gun design are covered in the writings of Sir Jonas More, *Modern Fortification* (1673). American and later periods are discussed in L.L. Bruff's work, *A Text-book of Ordinance and Gunnery* (New York, 1903).

The woods used in the construction of the carriage were different. Selection depended on the country and the favored method of construction. The French colonials in America used cedar; the Spanish favored mahogany. British specifications until the mid-eighteenth century used dry elm for the cheeks and transoms. It was their contention that this wood, seasoned and dry, would not split under the impact of firing.

Oak, especially young oak, soon gained favor. By the end of the period and until the introduction of the wrought-iron carriage of the Civil War, this was the material used. The cheeks (side pieces) were the thickness of one caliber. Understandably, the larger the gun, the more massive the carriage.

Building a gun carriage was a matter of assembling large wooden structures with great care. Building a four-wheeled carriage, also known as a *truck*, required the skill of a true craftsman (FIG. 16-5).

The cheek of the Spanish carriage was one single plank. Construction of Spanish carriages was more complicated than those of other nations. They used no threaded bolts. Keys were inserted at the end of the bolt. Often a decorative washer was bradded over the end (foot) of the bolt. Decorative ironwork was added. Mortises were carefully constructed to

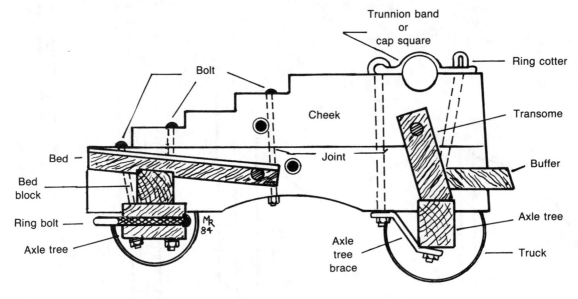

CENTER LINE SECTION

Fig. 16-5. A centerline section of a gun carriage.

hold the parts of the Spanish carriage together. If your ship model is of a Spanish ship, research the guns and carriages used aboard.

Wheels

Gun trucks (wheels) were not always constructed of wood. Early guns, usually those taken from the army to serve aboard ship, had cast-iron wheels. Needless to say, these wheels were soon replaced. Some had an iron tire, which was sweated on at the blacksmith's shop in the same fashion as for a wagon wheel (FIG.16-5). The majority of the trucks were wood edged. Iron tires destroyed wood decks in a very short time, especially if the ship saw a lot of action or participated in excessive "gun drills."

The axles were often protected by the insertion of metal thimbles or bushings. They saved the spindle much wear. Incidental internal construction varied among nations. The Spanish and French lined the top of the spindle with copper. The British, and of course Americans, lined the bottom. In short order, iron ferrules were fitted to the outer ends of the axles. That took care of the wear and allowed for lubrication. Ball bearings and bushings were a long way off.

Both the Spanish and the French used a set of *axletree bars* (braces) made of wrought iron. They strengthened the axletree and reduced wear on the spindle. They kept the structure from moving in a forward or backward manner against the strain of movement by the handspikes.

On a 24-pounder, the fore trucks (wheels) were 18 inches, the rear trucks were 16 inches. This difference in size compensated for the slope of the deck and gave some added resistance to the recoil, but not much. Most of the recoil was taken up by the breeching rope. Aboard smaller ships there was not much room for recoil.

The actual size (diameter) of the truck was made to suit the ship. Considerable variance was allowed. The carriage had to be level at the bulwarks. The relative diameters of the front and rear trucks were adjusted to suit the deck camber.

Trucks were built of two circles of wood riveted together. Eight or more rivets would be used. The grains of the two pieces would be placed at right angles to each other. The whole unit would then be protected (bound) by the iron tire. The truck resembled the rim of an early-model automobile wheel.

Parts of the Carriage

The cheeks of the carriage were built of two or more sections of wood. Points of contact between the edges were known as *joints*. These sites were sometimes mortised, but not often. Fastenings of metal bolts passed through and secured the units. Steplike construction cut in the top side of the cheek enabled the gun crew to have a fulcrum for their handspikes. A fulcrum was mandatory to accomplish the changes in elevation and aiming. The rear extensions of the cheeks were known as *horns*. Leverage was applied there to "train the gun." Long bolts with threaded ends passed through the cheek parts and were fastened with nuts and washers on the under side. The forward bolt, containing the cotter of the cap square (trunnion band), and the two rear bolts, forming the eyebolts of the cap square, also secured the axletrees.

Inside the carriage were the additional parts to which the cheeks were fastened (FIG. 16-6). Aside from the axletrees, which held the trucks, there were four more parts. Contrary to popular belief, especially among kit manufacturers, this was not one solid bed frame. The gun carriage was open under the main area of the gun. If you will take careful note, you will see that the cheeks form an angle. They were slanted toward the muzzle; they were not parallel. If you want accuracy, you should build your gun carriage as carefully as you build your hull. If you want a gun carriage that looks good, at least slope the cheeks.

At the forward end of the carriage, the strongest part, other than the axletree, was the transom (FIG. 16-7), sometimes spelled *transome* in the British texts and drawings. A bolt passed through the cheeks and the transom to hold the parts together as a tight unit.

Extending forward of and below the transom was the *buffer*, (British) or *breast piece*. This piece can be compared to an automobile bumper. The buffer extended beyond the carriage at the forward end to bump or buffet against the bulwarks when the gun was run out for firing. The edges often were faced with leather. This unit was secured to the transom by two bolts at either forward edge. Also note that there was a slight inward angle given to the cheeks at the forward edge of the carriage. This angle was so slight that it is not worth worrying about.

At the rear of the carriage is the assemblage that formed the actual bed (FIG. 16-8). Resting on the rear

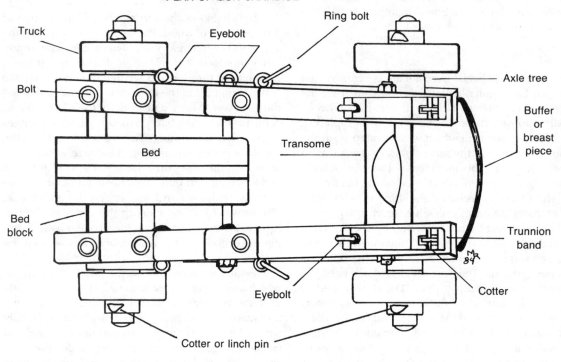

PLAN OF GUN CARRIAGE

Fig. 16-6. Plan of a gun carriage, top view.

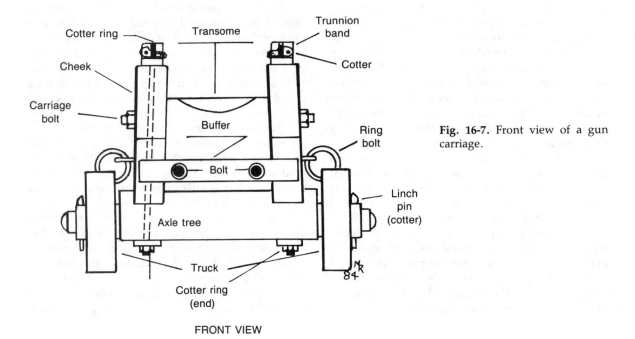

Fig. 16-7. Front view of a gun carriage.

FRONT VIEW

Fig. 16-8. Rear view of a gun carriage.

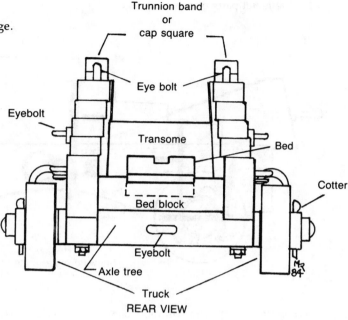

Trunnion band
or
cap square

Eye bolt

Eyebolt

Transome

Bed

Bed block

Cotter

Eyebolt

Axle tree

Truck

REAR VIEW

axletree was the *bed block*. Atop the bed block rested the *bed*. A mortised joint fitted the bed to the bed block. A carefully carved groove was cut the entire length of the bed at its centerline. This groove fitted the tongue of the *quoin*, as noted in FIG. 16-9. The groove was referred to as the *slide*, and is shown as a part of the top view of the bed in FIG. 16-6. A bolt passed through the forward edge of the bed binding it to the cheeks. The bed did not extend from cheek

to cheek, completely filling the rear area of the carriage, but was a part of the bed block (FIG. 16-6).

Ironwork

Ironwork had to be added (FIG. 16-10). When a gun and carriage were shifted into position at another location or moved about the ship, the cannon was *unshipped*. This was not a difficult task. The cotter was removed from the eye of the *trunnion band* (British),

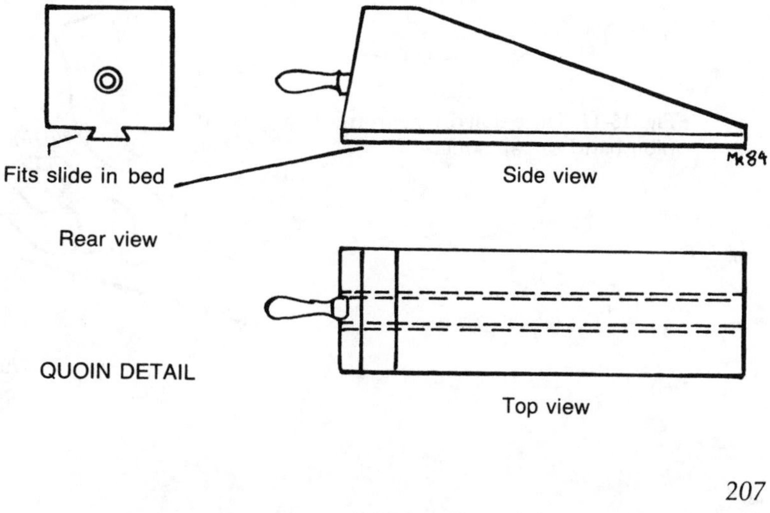

Fig. 16-9. The details of the quoin.

Fits slide in bed

Side view

Rear view

QUOIN DETAIL

Top view

Fig. 16-10. The metal parts of a gun carriage.

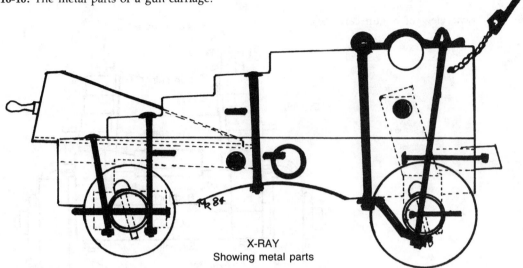

X-RAY
Showing metal parts

or *cap square* (FIG. 16-11). The trunnion band was lifted, freeing the trunnion of the gun, and the unit was removed. This was done aboard ship with a sling arrangement under the gun, usually rigged to a yard. Block, tackle, and sweat did the rest. Cannons were transported from, to, and around a ship slung beneath the ship's boats.

The metal part of the carriage somewhat resembled a hasp on a barn door. The rear hinge was the eyebolt that passed through the cheeks of the carriage

and into the axletree and axletree brace iron. To prevent loss of the cotter, it was fastened to the carriage with a short piece of chain.

Eye and ring bolts were fastened at the sides of the cheeks and at the center of the rear axletree to assist in securing and operating the gun. The training and "operating" tackle was hooked here. With the exception of the ring bolt at the rear axletree, the eye and ring bolts were placed on opposite sides of the carriage through the cheeks. The rear eyebolt

Fig. 16-11. The details of the trunnion band or cap square.

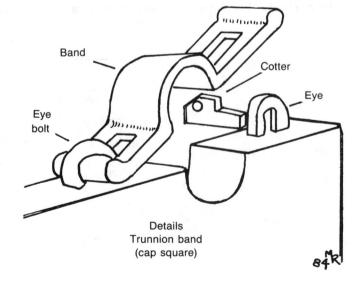

Band

Cotter

Eye

Eye bolt

Details
Trunnion band
(cap square)

passed through the axletree and was used to secure the preventer or train tackle.

Train tackle was also secured in the two eyebolts located in the sides. One was located at the first step below the base ring. The other eyebolt was in the upper part of the cheek at the area midway between the base and first reinforce rings. Consider this location as the edge of the third step. Two heavy ring bolts were placed in the bottom segment of the cheek, at the area just behind the first reinforce ring of the gun, below the rear edge of the top step of the cheek and just ahead of the edge of the bed. The breeching ropes were fastened to these ring bolts and *seized* (or wrapped), not knotted. Train and preventer tackle were fitted with hooks for removal and storage.

Positioning the Gun

Training and elevating a gun aboard ship was a matter of sweat and handspikes. Maximum elevation and depression both were limited to about 15 degrees. Elevation changes were accomplished with the handspike and quoin. Applying leverage with the handspike, fulcrum at the step and pressure at the breech, the gun was lifted from the quoin. The gun captain or the gunner's mate then would force the quoin forward or rearward to the new elevation. Sometimes there were marks on the bed and quoin to mark positions of range and elevation. These marks were not accurate, however.

Guns were heavy. TABLE 16-1 includes contemporary information taken from British naval sources. The figures used are from mid-eighteenth century, about the time of the American Revolutionary War. Not all classes are listed. TABLE 16-2 lists nomenclature of guns of the seventeenth century. There were, for example, six classes of 24-pounders, three of 18-pounders, three of 12-pounders, five of 9-pounders, and six of 6-pounders. Changes in windage and charges are not indicated.

No range is indicated. Range could vary with the windage, wear of the bore, charge, and quality of the powder. Permit a few random samplings of range at this point. The extreme range of a 32-pounder was, with a 10-degree elevation, about 2,900 yards. A 12-pounder could reach a maximum range of a mile. Point-blank range was about 300 yards. The ranges that could be reached, and the elevations, guns, and powder to reach them, is a study unto itself. One-half mile was considered a good fighting range.

CLASS (inches)	LENGTH (feet)	WEIGHT (lbs)	CALIBER (inches)	CHARGE (lbs)	WINDAGE
42 PDR	10	6500	7.03	17	.35
32 PDR (long)	9.5	5500	6.43	14	.33
32 PDR (short)	8	4900	6.43	11	.33
24 PDR (long)	9.5	5000	5.84	11	.30
24 PDR (short)	7.5	4000	5.84	8.5	.30
18 PDR (long)	9	4200	5.30	9	.27
18 PDR (short)	6	2700	5.30	6.25	.27
12 PDR (long)	9	3200	4.64	6	.24
12 PDR (short)	7.5	2900	4.64	6	.24
9 PDR (long)	9	2850	4.22	4.50	.22
9 PDR (short)	7.5	2600	4.22	4	.22
6 PDR (long)	9	2450	3.67	3	.19
6 PDR (short)	7	1900	3.67	3	.19
4 PDR	6	1200	3.22	2	.18
3 PDR	4.5	700	2.91	1.50	.14
1/2 PND (swivel)	3.5	150	1.69	.25	—

Table 16-1. Naval Guns.

Table 16-2. Seventeenth Century Gun Types.			
Type of Gun	Length	Caliber	Shot Weight Lbs
Cannon	11'0"	7"	42 Plus
Cannon drake*	8'10"	7"	42 Plus
Demi-cannon	11'	6"	32
Demi-cannon drake	8'6"	6"	32
Culverin	8'13"	5"	18
Culverin drake	6'-7'6"	5"	18
Demi-culverin	8'-11"	4"	9
drake	6'	4"	9
Saker	6'9"	3"	5
Saker drake	5'-6'6"	3"	5
Minion	9'	3"	4
Falcon	—	—	2 or 3
Falconet	—	—	1 or 2

*A drake is a shorter and lighter version of a standard gun. Drakes also were characterized by a tapered bore.

The facts listed in TABLE 16-1 should assist you greatly in building guns for your scale ship models. For the most part, you will find that the guns supplied in kits are grossly out of scale.

THE TOOLS AND THE CREW IN ACTION

A gun, as it would be mounted aboard a ship, is useless weight without a gun crew to work it. With a crew, it becomes a weapon.

In the early days of the gun aboard ship, it was not the ship's crew that worked the gun. Weapons of this sort were the property of the army. Soldiers came aboard to fire guns and board enemy ships. Sailors were needed to sail. By about the fourteenth century, ship's company were in charge of guns. The entire crew was a fighting unit. Marines were now the soldiers of the sea. They guarded the ship's officers and ship's property. During combat they engaged the enemy with small arms from the tops, and hand-to-hand combat on the decks. Sailors fired the guns and assisted in the boarding when needed.

Gun crews, depending on the size of the ship, varied in number. The average gun crew of the mid-1700s numbered nine. With the increase of fire power and training, and the availability of better equipment, the crew could be as small as five men. This was the size of the crew during and after the American Civil War. Each had a specific position. Every man had a job. Working together was the key to success. The time needed to load, aim, and fire had to be as short as possible. Training and discipline often determined the outcome of a battle.

Tools

Each man of the gun crew had his position and function. He also had his special tools. The gun captain could be identified at once. Slung over one shoulder on a chord hung his powder horn (FIG. 16-12).

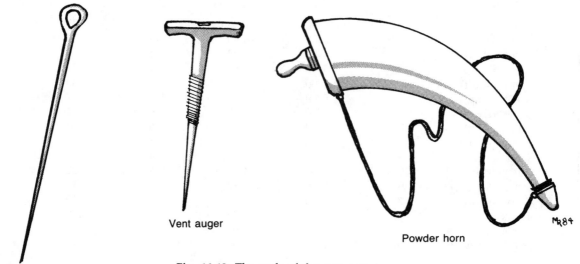

Vent pricker

Vent auger

Powder horn

Fig. 16-12. The tools of the gun captain.

Sticking out of his belt was his *priming iron*, or *vent pricker*.

Not far from the gun captain's position of command would be a tub filled with sand or water. Leaning out over the edges was the *lintstock* (FIG. 16-13). It might be made of fancy metal and wood items or simple sticks wound with sputtering slow matches. Extra coils of spare, slow-burning matches were placed in notches along the rim of the tub, their fired ends over the wet sand or water for safety. They were ready to be fitted to the linstock. During the heat of battle, no one had time to light a slow match with flint and steel or from a burning lantern. They look a lot like the medical caduceus without the wings. The snakes would be spitting sparks from a red glowing tongue. Leaning against the gunwales would be long poles with metal tools attached.

The *worm* looked like its name (FIG. 16-14). Two counter-faced corkscrew like prongs were attached to the ferrel on the end of the pole. The worm was used to pick out and remove cartridge pieces that remained after firing.

The *sponge* was easily identified (FIG. 16-14). The sheepskin cover over a 1-foot-long wooden core or a brushlike affair attached to one end of the pole was inserted wet to extinguish any sparks or smoldering cartridge pieces. In the interest of conservation of equipment and ease of handling, sometimes the sponge would be combined with the *rammer* on one staff (FIG. 16-14).

The rammer was a round-shaped device made of wood with a hollowed out center. Its function was to ram home the cartridge, wadding, and shot. Rammer and sponge were sometimes affixed to a stout rope with bindings to stiffen the ends. This "flexible" tool could be used to sponge and ram without the need to have a man lean out and expose himself to enemy fire.

The *hand ladle* (FIG. 16-14), a device for placing loose powder in the firing chamber of the bore, was soon discarded with the invention and use of the cartridge. Hand powder measures, or *gunner's ladles* (FIG. 16-14), were needed in certain instances. They, too, were discontinued in later years.

Gunner's quadrants and *gunner's levels* were carryovers from the artillery days. These tools, invented by Tartaglia in 1545, didn't change in style or use until after the Civil War. They will not be discussed at this time.

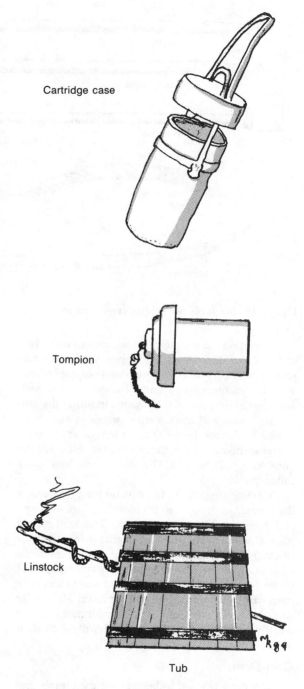

Cartridge case

Tompion

Linstock

Tub

Fig. 16-13. A few more items involved in the gun's operation.

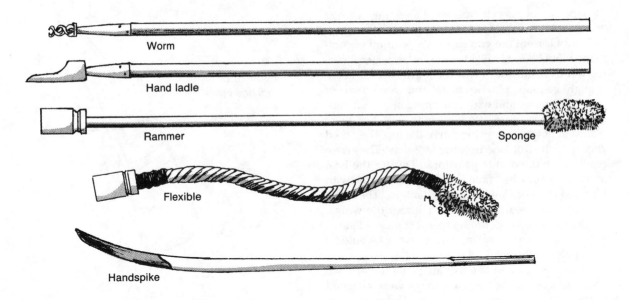

Fig. 16-14. The tools of the gun crew's trade.

Rounding out the gunner's equipment was a pair of *handspikes* (FIG. 16-14). These heavy wooden bars with slightly curved ends were usually capped (shod) with iron on the working ends. The curve at the business end of the handspike assisted in lifting the gun off the quoin and in making changes in elevation. Placed under the horns of the carriage at the rear, the handspikes enabled the crew to lift and move the guns from side to side. The side-to-side location is called the *azimuth*.

The *tompion* (FIG. 16-13), a wood plug inserted in the muzzle of the gun to protect it against weather, could be considered equipment. The lead shield placed over the vent hole also might fall into the classification of protection equipment. The leather *cartridge case* (FIG. 16-13) was the property and equipment of the powder monkey. His function was to serve the guns with powder from the powder room. He usually served two or more guns. The powder monkey was usually a ship's boy. Many were hardly into their teens.

Gun Drills

The crew needed to become a functioning unit with this equipment. Gun drills were part of ship's routine and, if the captain was a good commander, were held often. Assuming that the crew is now trained, let's go into battle.

The call to quarters, the rapid tattoo of a drum, or the blasting call of a bugle, and the crew sprang into action.

While some broke out the tools, others cast off the lashings. Heavy guns were a danger to the ship, the crew, life, and limb if not secured against weather. The training tackle was used to secure each gun in the position for sea (FIG. 16-15). The muzzle of the gun had been snuggled against the gunwale above the closed, and often caulked, gunport. The gun was lashed by the muzzle and held by the training tackle. A rope passed over and around the end of the gun to secure it and snug up the breeching rope. *Chocks,* wooden wedges, were sometimes forced under the rear trucks to lock the carriage in position. At the call to "battle stations," the sea lashings were cast loose and the gun was made ready.

The tompion was removed. "Load," would be the cry from the gun captain. All was ready.

The cartridge, premeasured powder in a flannel bag, would be inserted in the muzzle and rammed home. A shot was taken from the racks which lined the bulwarks and hatchways. It went down the bore and was rammed home. Next came the wad. The sequence was the same as "ramming home" the ball.

The *apron*, a piece of lead shield over the touch hole, was removed by the assistant gun captain (gun-

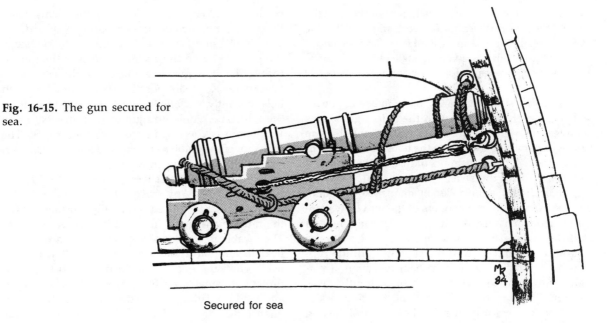

Fig. 16-15. The gun secured for sea.

Secured for sea

ner's mate). All was ready to prime for firing. At this point, depending on the gunnery officer's commands, the gun was either primed or "run out" (FIG. 16-16).

Priming was done by the captain of the gun crew. First he would insert the priming iron into the vent hole and pierce the flannel of the cartridge. From a box at his belt, he took a priming tube, usually a quill filled with a fine grade of powder mixed with spirits of wine (alcohol). In earlier times, or if no priming tube was used, he would fill the vent hole with powder from his horn. In later times his gun would have been fitted with a lanyard, priming pan, and flint.

Now the captain made sure his gun was "well and truly laid."

Sights didn't exist. The gunner had to know his gun. First he found the "line of metal" (FIG. 16-17). This elevation factor was that slight difference between the angle formed by the sighting over the gun, from base ring to muzzle, and the centerline of the bore.

The line of metal was determined by the gun captain when he was introduced to his new gun. Inserting his pick to the bottom of the bore through the vent hole, he would make a mark on the pick. The pick was taken to the muzzle and stood up in the

Fig. 16-16. The gun ready for action.

24 - Pounder ready for action

213

bore. A mark was made at the height of the muzzle. The difference between these two marks was the line of the metal. The Spanish called it "killing the *vivo*." In some guns this would be an angle of 1 1/2 degrees, corresponding in range for a 24-pounder of about 900 yards.

A *dispart sight* (FIG. 16-17), more in use by the artillery man than a sailor with the ship's guns, was a metal foresight on the muzzle. It provided a line of sight parallel to the axis of the bore. It was not reliable at sea. Artillery gunners didn't need to contend with the roll of the swells.

Elevation was controlled by handspike and manpower. One or more members of the gun crew were assigned to "handspike the piece," raising the gun off the quoin. The second captain would move the quoin under direction of the captain until the captain was satisfied with the proper elevation. *Training* the gun, or changing its azimuth, was accomplished with handspikes and training tackle. Such assignment was given by the captain of the gun crew in countless drills. When all action in laying in the piece was finished, according to the eye of the gun captain, the crew waited for the gunnery officer's command.

The Gun in Battle

Depending on battle conditions, the command could vary. In most cases it was, "Fire as your guns bear." Broadsides were seldom loosed all at once. Consider the impact of 30 to 40 guns of all caliber going off at the same time. It would tear the ship apart. Also, the weapons of the day were not accurate or effective at long range. An exception was when the ship's captain felt it would be an effective move. An example would be to attempt to sink the enemy when he is almost alongside and preparing to board.

"Fire!" shouts the gun captain and he sidesteps the piece to avoid the backward rush of the gun in recoil. The slow match is touched to the vent hole. First there is a small "poof" of flame from the touch hole. Instantly it is followed by a flash and a roar from the gun. The whole unit jumps back in recoil. The movement is checked by the breeching ropes. The first shot of the battle has been fired and is on its way, a sure hit for a good crew.

No time to rest or cheer on this job. The gun is ready to reload. Any pieces of the cartridge left in the bore must be picked out by the wormer. Down the muzzle she goes, followed by the wet sponge. The swabbers and loaders go at it with a will. The flexible rammer and sponge (FIG. 16-14) would be used when the enemy was near enough to pose a threat with small arms fire. The bore is now cleaned and ready. Loading is repeated in the order and sequence just described. In no time the captain was shouting his order to have the gun run out and standing by to fire after laying his piece.

There were times when the round ball of iron shot was replaced by other forms of projectiles (FIG. 16-18). The command might come down the line of guns to load with chain or bar shot. Chain, bar, expanding bar, and crossbar were all used to aiming for and destroying the masts, yards, and rigging of the enemy ship. A helpless target is soon destroyed. Some captains favored *grapeshot*, which was nine iron balls packed in a cylindrical canvas bag. Musket balls were sometimes used against ship and personnel. The musket balls were loaded into round metal cylinders or canisters. Antipersonnel shot was for close range, under 200 yards. *Lanrage, langridge* (FIG.

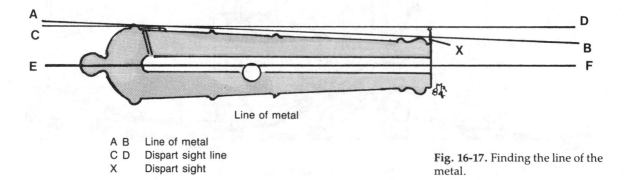

A B   Line of metal
C D   Dispart sight line
X   Dispart sight

Fig. 16-17. Finding the line of the metal.

16-18), or ''bitty-bites'' as some navy wag called them, were canvas bags filled with scrap metal to inflict damage to the rigging or tear the flesh from the crew.

Fire was the most feared happening at sea. Sometimes, but not often, *carcasses* were loaded into the bore. These hollow projectiles were loaded with combustibles and used against forts and suitable targets.

Hot shot, which presented a greater danger when made ready aboard ship than to the enemy when fired, was primarily a ship-to-shore weapon.

As the action grew hotter and the firing intensified, firing became ragged. Some crews were not as fast as others. Casualties resulted in slower action. Often guns were out of action because a well-placed ball had unseated the gun from the carriage.

Gunnery was not an accurate science, not was it effective. The wooden hulls could take punishment. It was an unusual occurrence that the ship went down as a result of the direct *hulling* (holes) produced below the waterline by shot.

Most captains attempted to place their ships alongside the enemy. Vessels fought yardarm to yardarm, more than once so close that the gunports on lower decks could not be opened. They were blown open at the first discharge. There was no need to aim. Every shot was a hit at this range.

Speed in loading was what counted. Brawny arms, cool heads, and training won battles. Three broadsides in 3 1/2 minutes was set by the *Dreadnaught* of the Royal Navy in the Napoleonic Wars. Three in 6 minutes was the usual time.

When it was all over—the average gun duels at sea did not last long—the surviving members of the crew patched things up. They attended each other and secured their weapon. If they could be spared, or if enough of them remained, their watch was ''sent below'' for much needed rest. If not relieved, then on to repairing the ship.

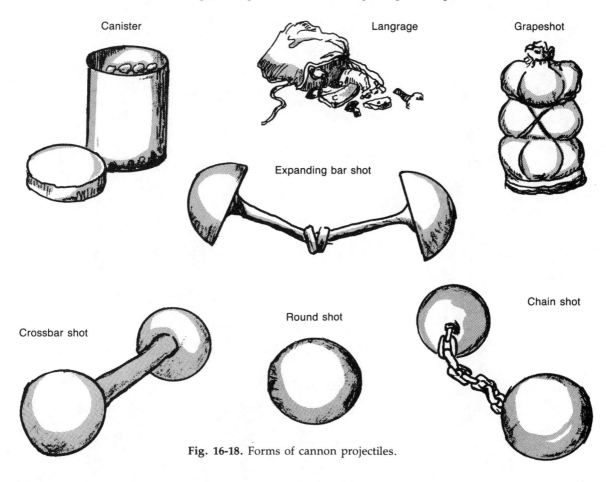

Canister

Langrage

Grapeshot

Expanding bar shot

Crossbar shot

Round shot

Chain shot

Fig. 16-18. Forms of cannon projectiles.

SEVENTEEN

Fittings

All good things which exist are the fruit of originality.

—JOHN STUART MILL

MANY BUYERS OF SHIP-MODEL KITS ARE NOT CONtent with just what ''came in the box.'' Maybe the first time, but then discontent sets in. They begin to customize. Upgrading a kit and aiming for near museum quality is more the rule than the exception.

The scratch builder, on the other hand, builds his ship model, making most of the parts himself. He buys commercial parts only if they suit his needs. The pure scratch builder, one who builds all the parts himself, is rare indeed. He buys only the raw materials.

The greatest problem is securing fittings in proper scale and period. Not every part or fitting meets all the criteria of proper scale and accuracy. Keeping within the limits is difficult without a little planning.

Selection of material for the fittings is another factor to consider. Wooden blocks look good on a wooden model. A painted metal block, properly roved and strapped, and correctly painted, looks just as good.

An all-brass winch, cleat, bit, steering wheel, or porthole polished to perfection aboard a yacht might seem fine, but it would look out of place on a tramp steamer or navy destroyer. Wire rigging is fine on a latter-day sailing ship or a sleek clipper. Would it be acceptable on a model of the *Mayflower*? Yes. Wire rigging on a model in a scale that is so small that the rigging is almost like a spider's web is correct. It is the material of choice and should be used.

Let's take a quick look at the types of ready-made fittings and materials that are available. Remember, your desires, as well as pocketbook, will determine what the purchase should be.

Wooden sailing ships can be outfitted with parts exclusively in metal or wood, or in a combination of both. Don't overlook linen line for rigging. A complete discussion of the subject of line and rigging is given in Chapter 13.

The modeler of a modern sailing vessel, a steel-hulled vessel, or a navy ship will find almost all of the fittings made of metal. They will, in most instances, be painted.

Simulation of fittings in plastic, especially when painted, is becoming commonplace. The day is not too far distant when most types of fittings will be manufactured from various forms of petrochemicals. Greater detail can be shown and all materials, like wood blocks, simulated. Not only will you find blocks with wood colors, but with wood grain. The grooves for rope stropping will be almost perfect. Metal stropping can be added by the modeler in the later-period blocks.

This demand for plastic comes not only from the radio-controlled ship modeler, but from the static builder as well. Both are seeking detail and accuracy with less weight. Traditional materials—wood and brass—are going by the board.

Companies that manufacture ship-model kits limit their fittings to be scales of their kits. Most of their fittings are stock items found in their kits. This limitation is undoubtedly the greatest problem for both distributors and hobby shop owners alike. Not only must there be a variety to satisfy the demand, but the variety must be available in assorted scales.

BILLINGS, DENMARK

Assorted brass, wood (deadeyes and blocks), and plastic fittings for both period and modern ships are available from Billings, of Denmark. Parts and fittings are in metric scales of 1:100 to 1:20. An interesting line of brass winches, ladders, and stanchions is offered.

For the name of the nearest dealer or source of supply, write:

ALTECH MARKETING, INC.
P.O. Box 286
Fords, NJ 08863

AMERANG LIMITED
Commerce Way Lancing
West Sussex BN15 8TE

METAL AND PLASTIC FITTINGS

The fittings that are primarily offered by makers of radio-control kits featuring fiberglass, styrene, and vacu-formed hulls are manufactured by other companies. American companies tend to purchase the fittings for their kits from other manufacturers. A few have an assortment of fittings and parts that are sold separately.

If you need fittings for a modern ship model, especially for a radio-controlled model, contact:

ROBBE
180 Township Line Rd.
Belle Mead, NJ 08502
(201) 359-2115

DUMAS PRODUCTS
Dumas Boats
909 East 17th St.
Tucson, AZ 85719

DYNAMIC MODELS
P.O. Drawer "C"
Port Jefferson Station
NY, 11776

NORCO MARINECRAFT MODELS
P.O. Box 2192
13556 Chase St.
Arleta, CA 91331

Other companies also offer fittings for modern vessels. They often are cottage industries and come and go. Keeping tabs on them is difficult.

Dumas and Robbe also offer a full line of running hardware. Propellers and other power needs are sold by most modern fittings sources.

PERIOD MODEL FITTINGS

Scaled wood and brass fittings, including decorative items simulating ship's decorations and carvings, are often required by modelers. If you are content to use the same fittings that are furnished in kits, you can get them from the makers of several lines of kits. Many are suitable for period ships. Some, with a little modification, can be used on modern ships. Scales offered are mostly 1:50 and 1:75. The companies are all European: Dikar, Artesania Latina, Euro, Mantua, Sergal, Pan/Art, Aeropiccola, Amati, and Steingraeber.

There are no American manufacturers of elaborate brass fittings for period models. Continental manufacturers, many with standard scales, duplicate the fittings from vessels they have chosen to offer as kits. Period ships have many fittings that are interchangeable among the kits offered.

It is common knowledge that many of the fittings offered by different companies, even in different countries, come from the same manufacturer. In truth, original manufacture of fittings is a rarity in the world of ship-model kits.

The world-famous makers of ship model fittings are:

THE WEB MODEL FITTING CO.
63 Uppleby Rd., Parkstone
Poole, Dorset 8H12 3DB England

STAB S.A.
35, rue des Petits-Champs
75001 Paris, France

These two companies are establishing themselves in the United States as ship modelers seek new sources of fittings. Stab fittings, as indicated in the catalog, can be secured from:

STAB USA
P.O. Box 143
West Lebanon, NY 12195

Selected scale fittings come in the range of their respective kits. Not all fittings shown in the manufacturers' catalogs are stocked by American sources. You will need to shop around. In some instances, direct purchase from the European manufacturer might be an advantage. You can contact the overseas manufacturers and sales outlets that sell fittings. Their advertisements are seen in periodicals and publications in all languages.

METAL AND BRASS FITTINGS

A wide variety of scale ship-model fittings are offered by American manufacturers. Britannia is the metal used by Bluejacket (FIG. 17-1). White metal mixture, almost all lead, is produced by Model Shipways and A.J. Fisher. Most hobby shops and mail-order houses feature their products.

Fig. 17-1. Metal fittings cast in Britannia (Courtesy of Bluejacket Shipcrafters, Inc., Castine, ME).

Fittings are offered in a wide range and will accommodate several scales. Refer to the respective catalogs. The fittings are available at very low costs. Distribution is by direct sales to public and through special arrangement with retailers and selected quality mail-order houses.

BLUEJACKET SHIPCRAFTERS
Castine, ME

A.J. FISHER, INC.
1002 Etowah Ave.
Royal Oak, MI 48067

MODEL SHIPWAYS
39 W. Ft Lee Rd.
Bogata, NJ 07603

The fittings of European manufacturer Aeronaut Modellbau have been sold by many American outlets. Although the fittings are not primarily identified as such, the variety and quality cannot be denied. The company, which does not sell directly to the public, will provide the names of their dealers. Write them at:

AERONAUT MODELLBRAU
Stuttgarter Strabe 18
Postfach/P.O. Box 384
D-7410 Reutligen 1
West Germany

NAVAL SHIP FITTINGS

Fittings for naval vessels from World War II and 1955 to date are now available. They are made of styrene, G.R.P., polyester, white metal with many materials in combinations. While predominantly produced for the British ships, many are designed and used on American and other navy ships. All are in one-eighth scale (1:96).

Sirmar fittings are found in several British kit offerings. The production has been expanded, and "shop sales" are expected to expand by the maker in England, Paul Beckley. English and European ship modelers are becoming familiar with these fittings. Most items are reported to be ideal for use in scratch-building radio-controlled and static warship models. This constantly enlarging lightweight selection of accurately scaled fittings, including aircraft, for British and American naval warships is now being offered

to ship modelers and shops in America and Great Britain.

The fittings are available from:

SIRMAR SHIP MODEL FITTINGS, LTD.
7 Old Barn Rd., Wordsley
Stourbridge, West Midlands
DY8 5XW England

THE DROMEDARY
6324 Belton Dr.
El Paso, TX 79912

PHOTOETCHED FITTINGS

The wonders of accomplishment boggle the mind when it comes to the inventiveness of ship modelers. Constantly searching for newer and better materials, more expressive of detail and adhering to scale, they have come upon the photoetched (brass) method.

While the actual production of fittings is not their forte, the preparation of the fittings can be. All that is required is a steady hand, a few fine-pointed pens, black ink, sprays, paper, and knowledge. For the last item on this list, read the article "The Black Art of Photoetching," by Loren Perry, as it appeared in the *Scale Ship Modeler* (Vol. 8, No. 6, Nov. 1985).

Another reference, should you not find a copy of the magazine, is to contact a manufacturer of photoetched brass items. There are several sources. Begin in the classified listings of your telephone directory under "Photoetching" or "Chemical Milling." Your local library also has several interesting books on the subject. Some are quite detailed and complete.

Mr. Perry suggests that, after you have accomplished the drawing and layouts, you contact a company that does photoetching. Several are mail-order companies. One such, the one Mr. Perry uses, is:

FOTOCUT
P.O. Box 120
Erieville, NY 13061

If you are not interested in making your own photoetched fittings, you can obtain ready-made photoetched fittings for your scale model ship model from commercial sources. The companies in the following sections began with a modeler making a sheet of fittings for his own use. The commercial possibilities became clear, and the modeler added a new faction to his lifestyle. He became a cottage industry.

Brass (Naval) Ship Fittings

The process is the same. To my knowledge, the seller is not the manufacturer. The fittings are formed in sheets and are sold as kits containing either loose parts for assembly or parts mounted on adhesive sheets. All are in accurate detail and scales of 1:350, 1:400, 1:600, and 1:700.

Some companies are introducing 1:96 scale warship fittings. Fine workmanship of such items as a radar reflector and railings are captured in perfection.

Several commercial manufacturers produce photoetched fittings. They can be found throughout the ship modeling world. Corel, Panart, and increasing numbers of wooden kits contain photoetched fittings and intricate decorative fittings. Sheets of photoetched, deep-cut, thicker-type fittings for period ships are now available directly from the manufacturers.

The outlets of brass photoetched fittings for modern vessels in the United States include Bluejacket Shipcrafters and:

LOREN PERRY'S
Gold Medal Models
12332 Chapman Ave. #81
Garden Grove, CA 92640

MASTERPIECES IN MINIATURE
P.O. Box 2485
Saugatuck, CT 06880

Fittings for Period Ships

For the modeler of period sailing ships, a new line of brass fittings, produced by the photoetching process, became available in 1986-87. The "stamped" brass chainplates, mast bands, backing links, and fittings of this nature are not detailed enough to represent the actual part. Eyebolts, jackstays, and ringbolts, formed from round brass wire, are not small enough or accurate in their rendition. The parts of a period vessel that were handmade on a forge, mostly from flattened metal, are now available (FIG. 17-2).

The "purist" scratch modeler can find these items, which involve such time-consuming, eye-straining work, in the commercial world. He could, if he desired, draw the parts and either etch them himself or contract a manufacturer to do the etching.

The small parts will be affixed to a flat adhesive backing (FIG. 17-3). Scales will be the popular 1:48,

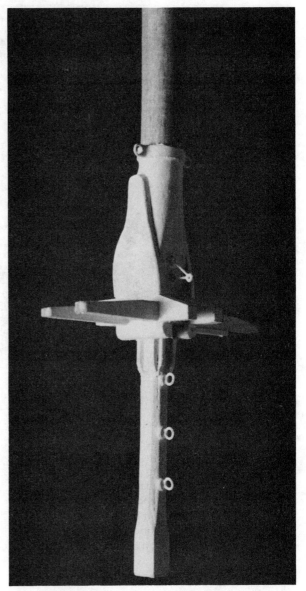

Fig. 17-2. Flat metal fittings of photoetched brass installed on a mast (Photo courtesy of Coldsprings Iron Works).

1:64, and 1:96. Several scales can be used on the same model, varying the sizes of rings, bolts, backing links, etc.

The company that will be offering the newest combinations and collections is Coldsprings Iron Works (development and production by Roger Teagarden). The fittings are distributed by The Dromedary.

Fig. 17-3. A sheet of photoetched brass fittings and the model they are being installed on (Photo courtesy of Coldsprings Iron Works).

While it would be an enormous undertaking, both physically and financially, to stock all the scaled sizes and varied fittings needed to build ship models, a few shops and mail-order outlets attempt the task. The demand created by modelers such as you, coupled by your demands for a reliable source, force the stocking by other outlets.

You will soon settle into your personal source of "ship's parts." Keep a notebook containing examples and illustrations of where you might secure the fittings for your model. It will be your personal portfolio.

EIGHTEEN

Metal on Ship Models

Ideas are like beards, Men do not have them
until they grow up.

—VOLTAIRE

A SCALE SHIP MODEL IS NOT ALL WOOD. NOR FOR that matter, unless so constructed, is it all metal, plastic, or fiberglass. Some parts can be made of metal. The lines of rigging on board will be some type of fiber. Metal lines (cable) and chain are reserved for the ultraminiature model of latter-day clippers and barks. In the construction of a ''plastic'' ship-model kit, however, might be no metal at all.

CASTING METAL PARTS

Some metal will be used in the incidental parts, referred to as *fittings*. That term covers a vast array of items. If you want to use parts and pieces made of metal, then you must meet two criteria. Workability is one; color is the other.

The most important physical characteristic of the metal part is workability. The metal used must be hard enough to accept fine details. It must be soft enough to be worked with hand tools or homebound equipment. The material (metal or alloy) should not be so soft as to be damaged or dented by rough handling, nor so hard as to require industrial tools to shape. If the part is to be cast, then the metal should have a workable melting point. Homemade castings are not difficult to accomplish. A modeler might resort to one of the many methods of small-scale foundry work in creating fittings that are not available commercially.

You must make a master model. It can be a carved wood, shaped plastic, metal, or plaster model that will be duplicated in metal. You also need an investment material, such as plaster of paris, dental plaster, or any molding plaster that will withstand the heat of the molten metal. Consider sand casting for larger pieces. A little foundry work completes as many fittings as are required.

Several texts are available to assist you in making special parts. The public library has a collection of volumes on the topic of casting. A recommended book is *Foundry Work For the Amateur* by B. Terry Aspen (Model and Allied Publications, Argus Books). This relatively inexpensive booklet will get you started on the work of casting your own fittings, guns, decorations, and figureheads in metal.

Commercially manufactured cast fittings are made of combinations of metals that have low melting points. The metals in formulation might not all have low melting points. They must combine to give the strength and workability of the combined metals. The physical properties of the weakest metal then are no longer a problem.

These metals are known by such names as pewter, Britannia, white metal, bronze, and brass. Such "casting" metals should not require the heat of a blast furnace. Electric furnaces are available should you desire to do your own casting. It is an art that is too lengthy to discuss at this time.

Metal used as a fitting aboard a ship model should not deteriorate or discolor with time unless that is your desire. In some instances, "aging" gives an added effect to a ship model. For example, a bit of rust here and there gives character to a model. It becomes lifelike.

There should be no flaking or peeling of paint from exposure to the elements or lack of air. You can prevent the so-called "white metal disease" by applying a primer coat to the fitting before the final coat of the desired color of paint. The primer prevents the reaction between the lead content of the metal and the chemicals in the paint.

If air circulation is restricted, not only does the paint flake off, but a white powder sometimes appears on the surface. This phenomenon occurs when the model is placed in a display case where there is not adequate ventilation. The white powder is the formation of lead oxide.

METAL ON SHIPS

In only a few exceptions should untreated metal be used on a ship model. The most objectionable feature of using "raw" fittings, so to speak, is that they are the wrong color or that their shine distracts. However, you do want a shine on the parts of the ship that represent polished brass, gold-leaf decorations, brass hand rails, or other ship's deckwear known to be made of brass.

Cannon, until the days when they were made of milled steel, were cast of bronze or iron (FIG. 18-1). They were deep brown in color with a hint of green due to the patina effect of the sea air. Some were painted black. The turret and deck guns of modern navies are painted.

Fig. 18-1. Shiny brass cannon installed on a model of the *Albatross* kit by Mantua (Model and photo by Dimitrios Economides).

The same subject of shine in the wrong places might be said of belaying pins, bitts, and cleats. In the early days, they were made of wood, and were brown in color. Later, in the days of the steel-hulled sailing ships, they were made of cast iron or steel. You could logically assume that they would be of a wood color if wood, or perhaps a silver hue if cast in metal.

In real life however, the iron belaying pins, as well as the other tie-off locations, were painted to prevent rusting. White or black was the usual color of the belaying pin, not brass.

Ironwork on early-period wooden ships was forged, hammered metal from the blacksmith's shop. In later years, it was manufactured. Metalwork aboard a ship became an item to be mass-produced. All metalwork was painted black since it rusted in the sea air and constant immersion in water.

Metalwork was painted black even if the ship was painted other colors. All Royal Navy ships until the Crimean War had the ironwork painted black. The paint was a varnish mixed with lots of tar. As time progressed and the wooden hulls became steel, the paints became better formulated and more dependable. Then more reliable paints were manufactured, which did not need to be hand-blended on the job. The black color of the ironwork was replaced. Aboard most merchant ships, without regard to construction or location, everything was painted the same color, including hull and ironwork.

There is an exception. What were allowed to remain in their natural state were the bright, polished brass decor fittings aboard yachts, liners, and some latter-day warships (1900s). During wartime, however, all the shine and show would disappear under coats of paint.

The blocks of the working rigging were made of wood in the early days of sail. They ranged from a light wood (new) color to a deep brown, almost black. The older the block, the darker its color. The coats of preservative accounted for the variance of color.

Metal strops appeared about the mid to late 1800s. These strops and hooks were iron and usually painted black. Don't leave them brass colored—steel (wire) maybe, but not brass. Metal blocks could be considered a recent innovation, considering the time man has been using blocks at sea. They were painted to prevent rust. Modern sailboats now boast shiny blocks of rustless materials. Some are chrome-plated. Deadeyes and other parts of the standing rigging were all coated with tar, and should be black in color on your model.

Metal deck furniture and fixtures were painted, as would be expected. Their color depends on their place in history and the type of ship. Winches, cranes, capstans, etc., bear a distinct color arrangement. You would not find a completely painted wooden capstan aboard an early sailing ship. The metal bands were painted black, but not the main body. You must paint the capstan or winch on a freighter of the 1900s.

Consider the color of the ships themselves. Wooden ships were varnished, and paint was used sparingly in the early days. Battleship gray would be as out of place on the *Constitution* as blood-red gun carriages on a World War I destroyer. If you wish to build museum-quality ship models, proper colors are a must. Research is time consuming, but mandatory, for good modelers.

PREPARATION OF METAL

Proper preparation of metal that is to be painted is as important as a fine painted finish. Cleaning and priming is as much a part of painting as the application of the paint. If paint is carefully applied, it still can peel and flake over an improper base. The slightest scratch not only shows the metal color underneath, but begins the destructive process.

Remove all greases and oils using solvents, such as benzine, acetone, or other volatile cleaning agents. A detergent solution, such as dishwashing liquid, also works well. Air-dry the parts cleaned in solvents. Use clear water to rinse parts cleaned in detergents in clear water and allow them to dry completely before painting. It is sometimes advisable to combine the two methods. Clean with the solvents and then wash in detergent. Use a soft-bristled brush to clean the areas containing fine details.

If at all possible, paint the parts before you place them on board or assemble them. It makes a neater job and there is less frustration. Avoid painting the surfaces where the parts will adhere to another structure, especially for wood-to-wood contacts. Water-soluble wood glues can't penetrate. Even the super glues have trouble holding components together on painted surfaces.

Prime cast-metal fittings after cleaning. Most paint manufacturers make a priming paint. It is usually a gray color. The primer prevents the surface color from contacting the metal. It seals the metal beneath the color. The special primer for white metal fittings uses an amyl nitrate solvent. Floquil, Testors, Humbrol, and others have their recommended mixtures of paints and solvents. (See Chapter 8.) Some modelers use the primer solvent to clean the parts they intend to paint. Primers are strongly recommended when the final finish will be a gloss color. Enamels are not a flexible surface covering, and will peel and flake if the undercoating is not primed.

You should not paint ''pure'' metal fittings such as brass or copper unless absolutely necessary. You can, however, use chemicals to change the color of metal fittings. The surface is literally etched in color. You can darken brass from a light brown to jet black. You can discolor copper with heat or chemicals. With a little care, you can hue copper from multicolored variations to greens and blacks. There is a particular color copper hull plates take when they have been exposed to sea water or air.

Both brass and copper will change in time all by themselves because of the exposure of the surfaces to the chemicals in the air. If you wish to keep the color of brass or copper clean and shiny, then you must exclude contact with the air. A coating of shellac, varnish, or lacquer will do the trick. There is, however, something to be said in favor of the natural patina imparted to brass, bronze, and copper by air contamination. You choose.

USING CHEMICALS TO COAT METAL

Coloring and etching of metals have been done over the years by various ''experts'' expounding their favorite methods. Some of them have been difficult and dangerous to use.

Older Methods

One method of older times used 1/2 ounce of white arsenic mixed with 1/4 ounce of antimony sulfide in 1 gallon of hot water. The fitting had to be heated before immersion into the solution. Another method of blacking brass consisted of heating the fitting and placing it in a hot solution of copper acetate and ammonia carbonate.

Yet another method involved blue vitrol in ''very hot'' water with a little strong salt. The soda solution was allowed to cool, then was filtered and the precipitate saved. Liquid ammonia was added to the precipitate to form ''a clear blue-colored solution.'' This, so says the instructions, gives the metal a deep violet hue.

The most complicated idea was using an electrical plating method. The color from the black nickel solution prepared in distilled water is achieved by the length of time the current is on. It sometimes took hours. The fitting was cleaned in acid solutions before blackening. It had to be dipped quickly and then neutralized the part dissolved.

Modern Solutions

Today, safer and better solutions are available to blacken brass and color copper or bronze. The chemical formulations, protected by patent, contain selenium, alcohol, and nitric acid. They will blacken brass, steel, iron, nickel silver, pewter, Britannia, copper, solder, and some parts made of Zamac.

These preparations do not work on aluminum or stainless steel. They work poorly on metals compounded with lead such as white metal. Special formulas are available to stain these metals if you so desire.

The longer the solution is allowed to remain, the darker the hue or color. Exercise care with these solutions. Since they are formulated with acid, they might dissolve some of the fine details of the surface if the part is left soaking too long. When the color is achieved, stop the process with a clear-water rinse. Buff lightly to remove any surface grains. Test the color and lacquer if desired.

There is some danger in using these products. They do contain an acid. Contact with the skin or eye is harmful. Follow the manufacturer's instructions. If they are not included with your purchase, ask for them.

Metal toners, as they are called by another maker of metal coloring solutions, are available from Bluejacket Shipcrafters. The names of the products are grouped as Brass Brown, Pewter Black, Brass Black, Ferro Black, etc. Pre Kleen is the detergent solution offered by Bluejacket Shipcrafters. Note that the solutions are all various shades of blue in color and the instructions state to dilute 1:1. Each metal toner is sold in a separate 2-ounce plastic bottle.

Blacken-It, a product of A-West of Colton, California, is well-known in the hobby world and used by most modelers for darkening metal parts and fittings. It is an all-purpose solution that produces all the same conditions as the Bluejacket products by adjusting the timing of immersion, rather than the strength of solution. It comes ready to use in 1- and 4-ounce bottles. Local hobby shops might carry other toners under different brand names.

Patina solution is available from Anchor Tool Company of Chatham, New Jersey, and other jewelry supply houses. This solution is primarily used by jewelers and metalsmith manufacturers. It is used by ship modelers to achieve the green color of copper that has been acted on by sea water. To achieve the tone, repeatedly brush the solution on the surface to be colored by patina. Then allow the solution to air-dry. Stop the reaction completely when the desired color is achieved by rinsing in clear water. Lightly buff the surface to remove the powder and some of the excess color. Lacquering is recommended to achieve a lasting color. The chemicals in the air will continue the process of patina over a period of time.

Diluted solutions of sulphuric acid will also impart the desired color to copper. Copper sulfate is the green color resulting from the chemical action of salt water and air pollution.

Wood can be aged as well as metal. Water spots allowed to form before the finish coat of flat varnish is a tribute to the modeler's skills. A-West makes a product that works on the wood itself. ''Instantly ages the wood,'' says Terry West, owner. The product, also available in 1-ounce samples or 4-ounce bottles is called Weather-It, as you should have expected.

REFERENCES

Reviews of the methods of staining, etching, or coloring metals on models can be found in most publications devoted to this hobby. These methods have been varied and around for a long time. There have been many writings on the subject. Suggested readings would be, in the case of ship models, *Ship Modeler's Shop Notes*, (Nautical Research Guild) and *Building Ship Models*, (Calvin & Sons of England). Unfortunately the second book is out of print. *Ship Modelling Hints and Tips* by Crane, and *The Ship Model Builder's Assistant* and *The Built Up Ship Model* by Charles Davis contain references to the subject.

The back issues and current printings of the periodicals *Model Ship Builder* (Phoenix Publications), *Scale Ship Modeler* (Challange Publications), *Ships in Scale* (Model Expo Publishers), *Model Boats* (Model and Allied Publishers), and *Model Shipwright* (Conway Maritime Press) are all good sources of hints on metal darkening and painting. The last two publications are published in England. The periodical *Model Ships and Boats*, now defunct, featured many references to coloring metals.

Lastly, but not leastly, check with your local druggist or chemistry teacher. Since most of the staining, blacking, and coloring of metal as proposed on these pages is a chemical process, why not go to the most knowledgeable source?

Aging a ship model is an art. The right amount of ''discoloring'' is as important as the proper historical colors of the ship itself. A ship model that shows the ravages of the life of a ship at sea has a charm all its own.

NINETEEN

Dandyfunk

Men love . . . newfangledness
—GEOFFREY CHAUCER

THE TERM *DANDYFUNK*, COMES FROM THE DAYS OF the windjammers. It was the meal often served on a Friday, which was composed of all the leftovers of the week. Pickles, crushed ship's biscuits, fats, jam, or molasses were all mixed together. Often it was quite good.

This is a gathering of ideas that have worked for others. They have been gathered over the years from written and verbal sources to be tried, used, discarded, and reused. It is not suggested or implied that all of the ideas presented are, or can be attributed to, me. Wherever possible, the source is given.

RUDDER HUGGER

After the hull is assembled and the deck sealed, a new problem might arise. The rudder keeps jumping its pintles out of its gudgeons. Herewith is reproduced *Roos' Rudder Hugger* (FIG. 19-1).

TREENAILS

Treenails are those very small wooden pegs used to hold planking to the hull and decking to the beams. They were the fasteners of the past and are not hard to make.

A drawplate is not hard to find or make. You can make your own by drilling a series of holes with decreasing diameters in sheet metal (FIG. 19-2). A flattened tin can will do. Remove, but don't smooth the burr. It's the cutter.

Materials: Any straight-grained hard or semihard wood. Bamboo makes the finest. Try barbeque supply areas of supermarkets or gift shops. Toothpicks, birch in most cases, are sharpened and prerounded. Use them.

Method: Square the wood by splitting lengthwise. Sharpen the end of your split stock. Push the pointed end through your drawplate. Draw through by pulling the sharpened end through successively smaller and smaller holes. A little piece of sandpaper increases your grip. Pliers crush.

DEVICE FOR SPLITTING STOCK TO MAKE TREENAILS

A wood block is prepared to be held in a vise. Add another block below the top segment and not only glue it but ensure the union with screws.

Force two scalpel or other disposable blades, keeping the edges parallel into the top block (FIG. 19-3). A touch of super glue will prevent loosening or movement. The distance between the blades will determine the size of the stock. To square it up, run through twice, turning 90 degrees on the second pass.

COILING LINE

Not all line was coiled on the deck the same way in every ship. Not all coils were circular. Pictures speak louder than words. See FIG. 19-4 from the *Ashley Book of Knots* by Clifford W. Ashley (Doubleday,

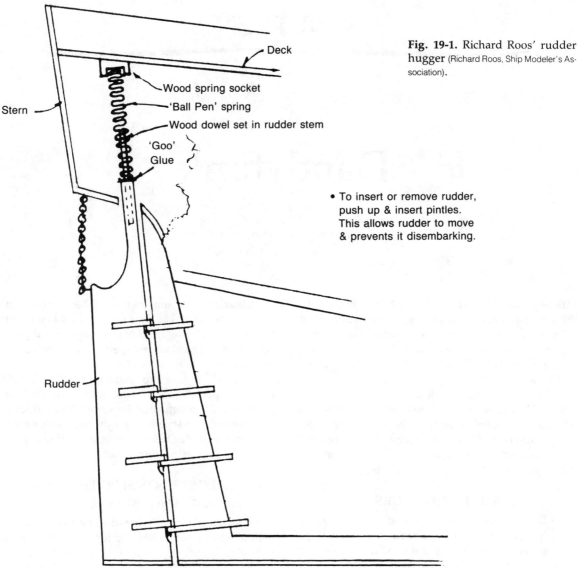

Deck

Wood spring socket

'Ball Pen' spring

Wood dowel set in rudder stem

'Goo' Glue

Stern

Rudder

Fig. 19-1. Richard Roos' rudder hugger (Richard Roos, Ship Modeler's Association).

• To insert or remove rudder, push up & insert pintles. This allows rudder to move & prevents it disembarking.

Dorant Co. New York, 1944).

To arrange the coil, place the line on the sticky surface of a piece of waterproof tape. Saturate the completed coil with white glue thinned with water. When dry, fix the coil to the deck with glue applied to the coil and peel away the tape.

You can use wax paper to arrange the coil. Again, use the white glue solution.

MAKING SMALL CASTINGS

There comes a time when you need several items of identical construction. I give as examples, the wreaths around the gunports, decorations of old-time ships, cannon barrels, even aircraft for modern carriers. To construct each in perfect form takes time. Why not cast them?

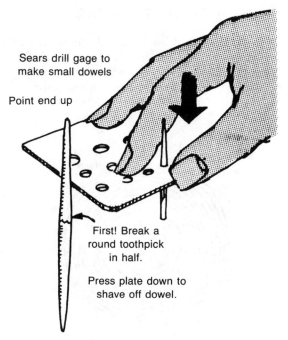

Sears drill gage to make small dowels

Point end up

First! Break a round toothpick in half.

Press plate down to shave off dowel.

Fig. 19-2. Making treenails from toothpicks (Courtesy of Northshore Deadeyes, Ltd.).

William Greg of Columbus, Ohio, has a method involving the use of silicone rubber molds and casting resin. FIGURE 19-5 shows his method.

Supplies, including dyes to make the casting gold, bronze, or the color of your choice, are availa-

ble. In fact, the art of resin-casting is a challenge in itself. Check out your local craft store and ask about this casting method.

SEIZING DEADEYES: A THIRD HAND

This method of seizing deadeyes is from Marlin Quick.

Materials: Spring clothespin, shroud line of choice, and seizing line of proper proportion.

Method: Cut the working end of (tip) clothespin flush. Hold the clothespin in a vise or other steady device. Place the deadeye in the shroud line and pinch the ends in the clothespin. Allow room for seizing below the deadeye.

Tie the seizing with an overhand knot. Tighten at the top of the clothespin. Lock the seizing by tying another overhand knot.

Wrap the line in the seizing of your choice. Tie off and secure with a drop of glue.

MORE METHODS FOR SEIZING DEADEYES

Materials: Plastic straw, or tube, brass, copper, or aluminum tube 1/8-inch diameter or smaller; annealed or brass wire, at least three times as long as the tube. If a brass or plastic tube is used, crimp or flatten one end slight (FIG. 19-6).

Method: See FIG. 19-7. 1 Double the wire and insert it through the tube, forming a loop at the top, or crimped end. 2 Place the line around the dead-

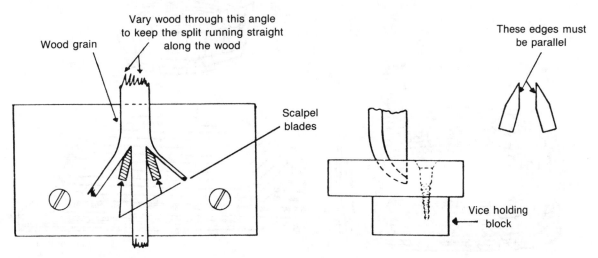

Fig. 19-3 A device to split wood in preparation of making treenails.

eye. Do not tie. 3 Draw the loop snugly. 4 Seize the deadeye.

Choose the method of seizing. (A) Wrap the line completely around as in *round* seizing, or (B) use the double or triple *crossed* seizing, as shown in FIG. 19-8.

This method, and the method preceding, can be done after the shroud line is placed on the model.

DEADEYE SPACING

Now that we have seized the deadeyes in a proper fashion, let's discuss how to get some even spacing. First, a method to make a deadeye spacer for both upper and lower mast locations is shown in FIG. 19-9.

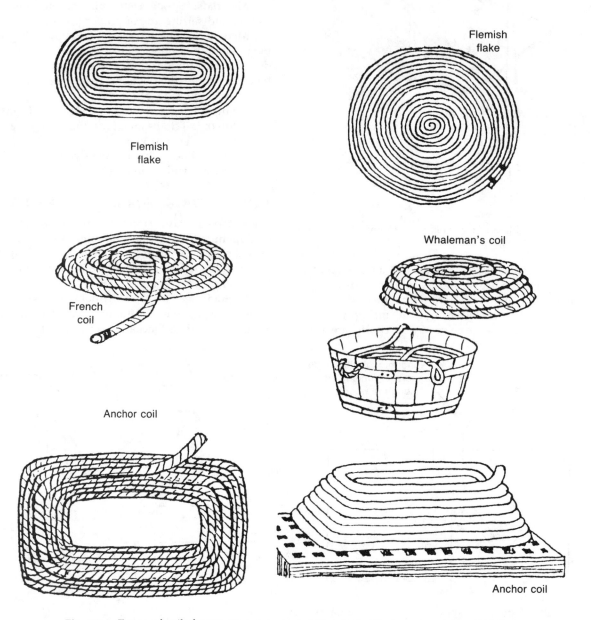

Flemish
flake

Flemish
flake

French
coil

Whaleman's coil

Anchor coil

Anchor coil

Fig. 19-4. Types of coiled rope (Original drawing in *Ashley's Book of Knots*, courtesy of Argus Books).

232

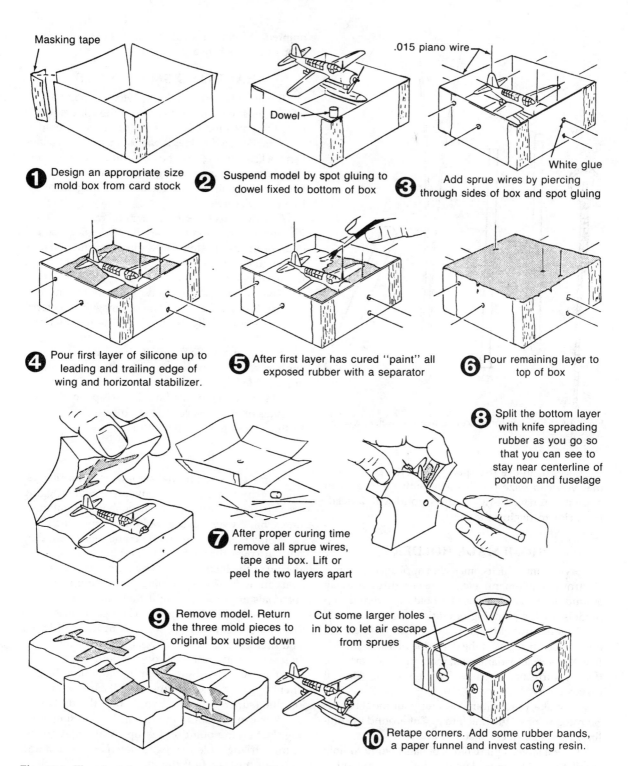

1 Design an appropriate size mold box from card stock

Masking tape

2 Suspend model by spot gluing to dowel fixed to bottom of box

Dowel

3 Add sprue wires by piercing through sides of box and spot gluing

.015 piano wire

White glue

4 Pour first layer of silicone up to leading and trailing edge of wing and horizontal stabilizer.

5 After first layer has cured "paint" all exposed rubber with a separator

6 Pour remaining layer to top of box

7 After proper curing time remove all sprue wires, tape and box. Lift or peel the two layers apart

8 Split the bottom layer with knife spreading rubber as you go so that you can see to stay near centerline of pontoon and fuselage

9 Remove model. Return the three mold pieces to original box upside down

Cut some larger holes in box to let air escape from sprues

10 Retape corners. Add some rubber bands, a paper funnel and invest casting resin.

Fig. 19-5. The steps in preparing a silicone mold.

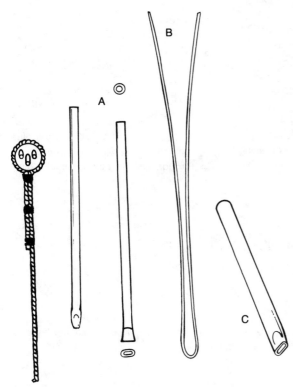

Fig. 19-6. Materials for making a deadeye seizer (Courtesy of V. Lusci).

pointed objects, in a readily accessible position. It keeps the bench neat.

HANDLING SMALL NAILS

Small nails, brads, lill pins, etc., used in modeling are most difficult to handle. If the start is incorrect, the part might split. They are hard to hold.

A magnetized holder is easy to make. From a broken hacksaw blade, use the two ends with the holes. Grind down the cutting edge to slightly less than the length of the nail. Square the end and magnetize the two end pieces.

Cut two pieces of nonmagnetic material (fiber, Plexiglas) slightly longer than the blade pieces so the ends protrude. Fasten these pieces to the ends, as shown in FIG. 19-11. Use a small nut and bolt to hold the unit together.

The magnetized hacksaw blade holds the nail against the squared edge. The nonmagnetic material keeps it erect. A slightly tap with the hammer and the nail is ''set.''

For nonmagnetic material—brass lill pins, nails, copper, etc.—use tweezers, either straight or offset at an angle.

Make a small incline board of scrap wood. Place the nails on the surface. Tap slightly and all will roll to the same direction (FIG. 19-11).

Second, to use the spacer, see FIG. 19-10. Note that you can seize the deadeye with the spacer in place if you haven't rigged the shroud with a deadeye prior to rigging the mast.

HOMEMADE HOLDERS

Styrofoam, which comes with appliances, radios, electronic equipment, etc., is never thrown away around our house. It is ideal for holding inverted ship models for the planking operation.

This lightweight, soft material will not damage the exposed portions of the deck side of a ship model. It will not mar or damage stanchions, bulwarks, or deck protrusions (houses, hatches etc.). Also, it carves easily.

To make a snug-fitting nest for your model in the Styrofoam, press the hull into it. Cut around the outline, then cut excess material away.

I use a large, square block of balsa wood to hold small tools, like pins, knives, dividers, and other

RIGGING AIDS

Some areas of a model are too small for fingers. That's why tweezers were invented. Some rigging areas require reaching in and pushing or pulling a line. That's why rigging tools were invented.

Some modelers buy ready-made sets. Often they later discover that there is something lacking in the design of the instrument. Why bother buying when you can, with a little planning, make your own. The materials are probably right there in your home.

Consider crochet hooks. They come in several sizes so the opportunity for making a set of larger and smaller tools exists. Check out the sewing or notions center in your local department store.

You can extend the reach by mounting the crochet hook on a piece of dowel. Drill a hole and force or glue (super glue) the handle into the dowel.

You can customize the needle by grinding or filing. Flatten the point on the tip. Add variations by using a triangle file. An extra notch on the end and you can push or pull the line.

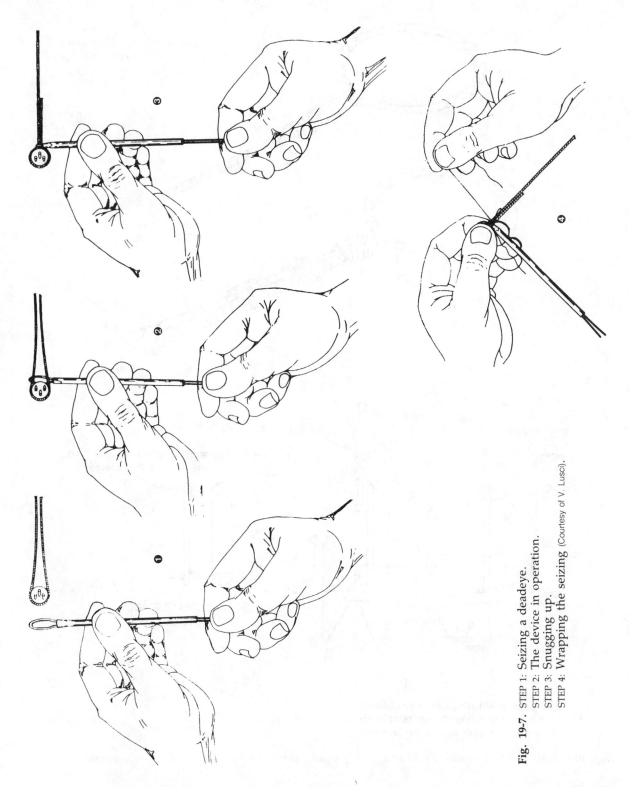

Fig. 19-7. STEP 1: Seizing a deadeye.
STEP 2: The device in operation.
STEP 3: Snugging up.
STEP 4: Wrapping the seizing (Courtesy of V. Lusci).

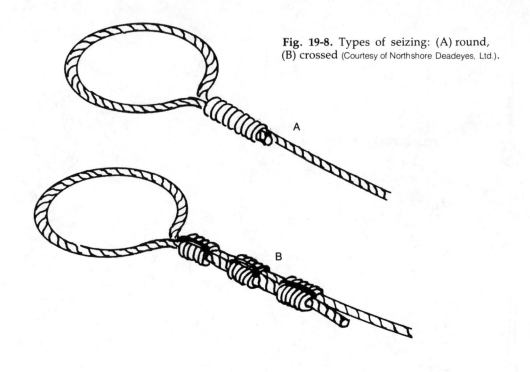

Fig. 19-8. Types of seizing: (A) round, (B) crossed (Courtesy of Northshore Deadeyes, Ltd.).

A

B

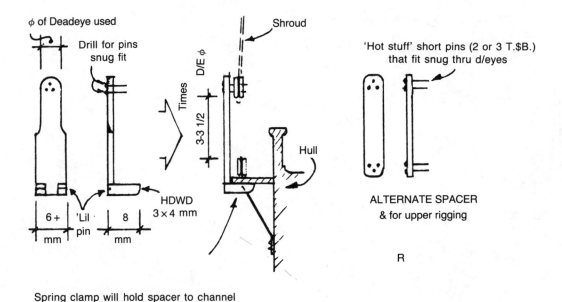

φ of Deadeye used

Drill for pins snug fit

Shroud

Times

D/E φ

3-3 1/2

Hull

6 + mm 'Lil pin 8 mm

HDWD 3 × 4 mm

'Hot stuff' short pins (2 or 3 T.$B.) that fit snug thru d/eyes

ALTERNATE SPACER & for upper rigging

R

Spring clamp will hold spacer to channel while temp'y securing shroud, remove spacer & seize. Make for your basic φ for future use.

Fig. 19-9. Roos' deadeye spacer and instructions to build (Courtesy of Richard Roos, Ship Modeler's Association).

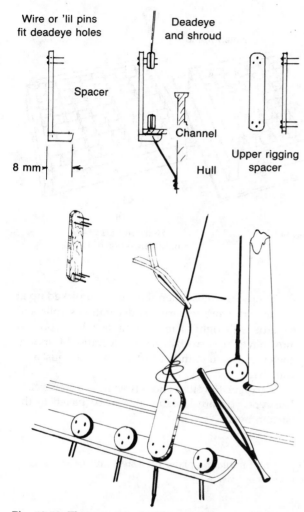

Wire or 'lil pins
fit deadeye holes

Deadeye
and shroud

Spacer

Channel

8 mm

Hull

Upper rigging
spacer

Fig. 19-10. The spacer in Action (Courtesy of A. Richard Mansir).

BUILDING A HATCH

One of the most frustrating problems for ship modelers is the construction of hatches. The grating, either commercially purchased or scratch-built, must be fitted into a frame. Following is a method to assist you in solving this dilemma.

The material (grating) should be at least 1/4 inch larger in width and length than the intended hatch. Secure a piece of 1/32-inch-thick soft balsa. If you intend to show a closed hatch, paint the balsa black before using. Glue the grating to the balsa (FIG. 19-12).

After the wood has dried completely, you can cut it to the required size. Then construct, stain, and/or paint the hatch. Add the hardware. If you wish to "open" the grating, simply sand off the unpainted balsa. The hatch is ready to install on the ship.

RIVETED STEEL HULLS

Construction of a static model of a steel-hulled ship calls for a little simulation. Even the smallest model should give an indication of the ship's construction under a coat of paint.

Materials: Manila folder or cardstock material, even business cards (unprinted side) make excellent riveted plates. Thickness can vary. Do not use material over 1/64 inch.

Glue is preferred and recommended. Use the white glues sparingly to avoid wrinkling (FIG. 19-13).

Method: Cut the plates to final size. Paper cutters ensure straight ends. If plates are to overlap, allow ample material to simulate riveted plates.

Glue the plates to the hull. After the plates are positioned on the hull, indicate the location of the rivets with a sharp-pointed pencil. Then simulate the rivets by placing a drop of glue (Sobo) on the plate. Use a fine toothpick or needle. If the drop is out of place or too large, take it off and replace it.

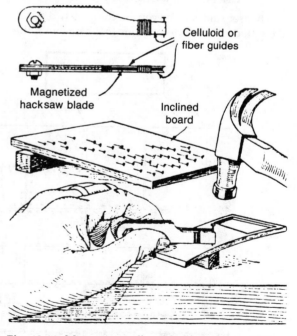

Celluloid or
fiber guides

Magnetized
hacksaw blade

Inclined
board

Fig. 19-11. Magnetic small nail holder (Courtesy of Norman V. Davidson).

237

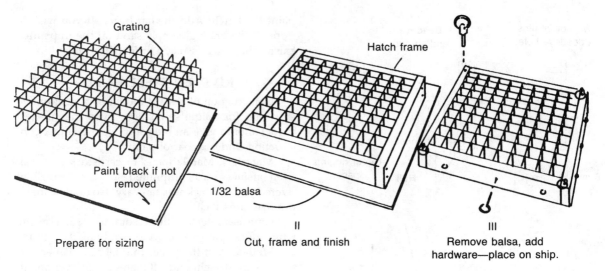

Grating

Hatch frame

Paint black if not
removed

1/32 balsa

I

Prepare for sizing

II

Cut, frame and finish

III

Remove balsa, add
hardware—place on ship.

Fig. 19-12. Framing a grate (Courtesy of Northshore Deadeyes, Ltd.).

When the rivets have dried, paint the hull with two coats of shellac. Apply the finish colors and add weathering colors for effect above and below the waterline.

CARVING DECORATIONS

There are times when you are completely dissatisfied with the "cast" decorations that came with the kit. There are times when the stuff you picked up at the jewelry store to serve as decorative scrolls and wreaths isn't right. There are times when you just must have the correctly carved decoration. Carving, however, as you found out after many tries, just ain't your bag.

Go to the toy store and buy some children's clay. The type you are looking for can be baked in the kitchen oven.

Fig. 19-13. Simulating plates on a steel hull (Courtesy of Northshore Deadeyes, Ltd.).

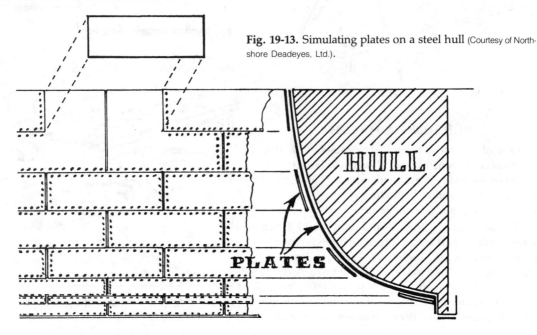

HULL

PLATES

Sculpture your decorations in clay using small tools, such as discarded blades and dental picks. You can make a slew of special sculpting tools from wood dowels of different diameters. See your local art store for ideas, or better yet, buy some of their offerings.

Bake the finished product in your oven following directions. You can apply them directly to the ship after gilding with paints. One farsighted and "proper purist" used gold leaf over his carvings.

As a bonus, the sculpture carving can be a master model for reproduction if you need more than one (FIG. 19-5). You can make a mold using plaster of paris. Build a form. Coat the master model with a separating media. A heavy soap solution works fairly well; light oil works even better. Do not use detergents. Pour the plaster into the form over the model. After the plaster has set, carefully remove the master carving.

To reproduce several carvings, use the mold after it has dried thoroughly. All traces of moisture must be removed, or steam might build up within the mold and cause an explosion.

Coat the inside of the mold with a separating media that will not dissolve the clay. Force small bits of clay into the mold. Press each particle firmly into the area to eliminate air pockets. Smooth off flush

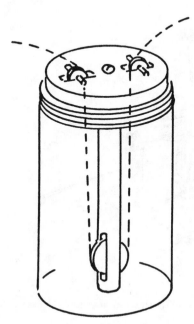

Fig. 19-14. Line staining or waxing jar.

with the top of the mold. Bake in the oven as before. Remove the decoration.

Repeat this procedure as long as the mold retains the crisp reproduction of the master. If you still need more, make another mold from the original.

MAKING A GRAPNEL ANCHOR

Materials: Fishing hooks of the size for proper scaled anchors; a metal file to shape the hooks; a soldering iron and solder to position.

Method: File off the sharp points and barbs. Remove eyes as required from hooks before soldering. A hook with the lower portion removed can serve as the central core of the anchor. Using a larger size can save you the trouble of making the top ring of the anchor.

Remember the scale and keep the ring to it. Solder the hooks together, allowing surplus solder to form a solid shaft. Shape the shaft by removing excess solder. Color the anchor with blackening agent. Add wood stock if needed.

STAINING LINEN LINE

The linen line that is just the right size is the wrong color. It will be a shroud. Shrouds are black or deep brown because they were part of the standing rigging and were heavy with tar.

Waxing line should be done with as deep a penetration of wax as possible. Make a solution of beeswax by dissolving in turpentine or benzine. It can be as fluid as you require. The solvent will evaporate, leaving wax deep in the fibers of the line. The job can be accomplished with the little gadget shown in FIG. 19-14.

Materials: A glass jar of appropriate size; two small shelves and one larger size, brass; a wood dowel; a screw, brass rod, and solder.

Method: Cut slits in the jar top for the entrance and exit of the line. Solder the brass rod as an axle for the shelves.

Through a hole drilled in the center of the jar top, fix the dowel with the larger sheave at the lower end. Fill with solutions and draw the line through.

BELAYED LINES

The authentic look of lines hanging off a belay pin can add to any sailing ship model. If you want to make them off the model, try this method.

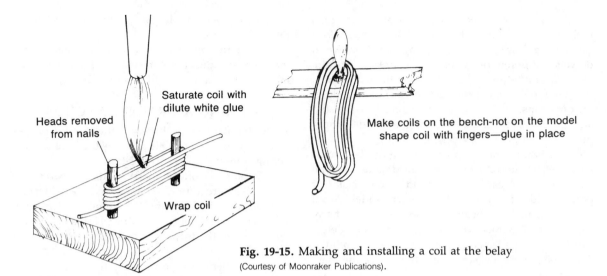

Heads removed
from nails

Saturate coil with
dilute white glue

Wrap coil

Make coils on the bench-not on the model
shape coil with fingers—glue in place

Fig. 19-15. Making and installing a coil at the belay
(Courtesy of Moonraker Publications).

After the line is properly belayed to the pin, snip it off.

Make your coils in the proper lengths with white glue off the model. While it is still damp, drape the coil over the belay pin. Press into shape and allow to dry.

Two methods of shaping are offered, see FIGS. 19-15 and 19-16.

MAKING
CHAIN AND RINGS

There might come a time when the commercial sizes of chain aren't right for your scale model. FIGURE 19-17 shows how to make your own chain.

FIGURE 19-18 shows a method for making your own rings.

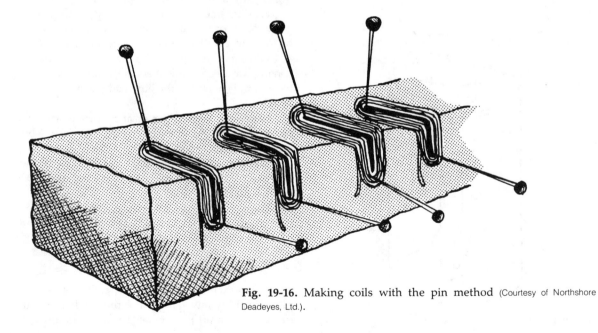

Fig. 19-16. Making coils with the pin method (Courtesy of Northshore Deadeyes, Ltd.).

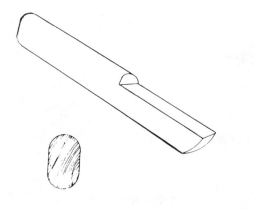

1. Shape a dowel like this
2. Wrap wire

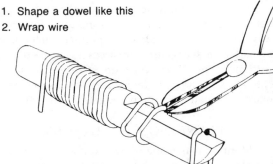

3. Move links down and snip

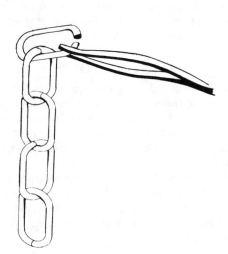

4. Connect and close links
   with tweezers—solder
   if necessary

Fig. 19-17. Making your own chain links (Courtesy of A. Richard Mansir).

FITTING PLANKS IN SPECIAL PLACES

Eyeballing as a way of shaping wood planks is costly. Shaping a plank without a pattern is wasteful. With a piece of plastic tape—the frosty-on-the-roll variety—a pencil, and a little thought, you can solve this problem.

Press the tape on the planks that will be next to the fitted unit. Run a soft pencil over the edge. Pull up the tape and stick it to your planking material. Cut to the outline. Remove the tape and fit the shaped unit to your model (FIG. 19-19).

This method works well on any area, except the sheer and garboard strake.

PAPER ON SHIP MODELS

Strathmore paper, available at your local art supply store, is excellent for some unusual applications. Thin molding along the wales, rings on guns, waterways, and other areas that offer a solid backing can have paper added as a building material. Saturate the paper with glue, and sand it after drying.

Whole models have been made of paper, and are masterpieces. FIGURE 19-20 shows a few additional suggestions.

PAINTING SMALL PARTS

There are hundreds of ways to hold a small object to apply paint. A small needle that you embed

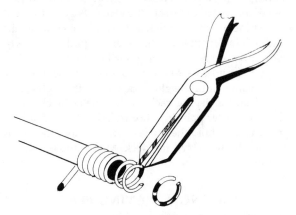

Make rings by wrapping wire around dowel or nail-slip coil off form and snip individual rings

Fig. 19-18. Making your own split rings (Courtesy of A. Richard Mansir).

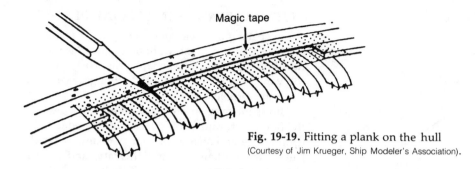

Fig. 19-19. Fitting a plank on the hull
(Courtesy of Jim Krueger, Ship Modeler's Association).

in a dowel, can be a holder. Push the point into the wood and paint the part. Allow it to dry on the needle.

You can work Plasticine (clay) to a pointed mound and place the part on the tip while you paint it. Two-way tape (sticky on both sides), available at photographic or drafting supply outlets, is very useful. It is great for hundreds of uses besides holding small pieces for painting.

DRESSMAKER'S PINS

If you have been modeling a while, then you know that dressmaker's pins are not always used to hold cloth together. Without these handy items, balsa airplanes would cease to be assembled. Rings, bolts, and block attachments would not be found small enough on ship models. Railroad models would never make it to the track. (See FIGS. 19-21 and 19-22.)

These handy little items come in brass and steel, and several lengths and diameters. A package or two would be of great help in your building.

Bend pins to a 90-degree angle and use them to hold planks until the glue dries. Push through cardboard and a drying rack to dry metal blocks and deadeyes after painting. Predrilled holes and a pin into the deck hold the carriage firm without the need to glue the wheels to the deck. Mount the gun over the pin in the carriage.

MAKING A WAVING FLAG

A flag rippling in the breeze on a sailing ship creates a sensation of movement even in a glass case. Cloth is great, but it must be stiffened. You can use starch, thinned white glue, shellac, even lacquer or aluminum foil. (See FIG. 19-23.)

COPPERING A HULL

There were a few tips on the application of copper plates in Chapter 10. Following are a few more ways to simulate the plates. A pounce wheel, used by pattern makers and seamstresses, has its uses in ship modeling. Wherever there is a need for a row of rivets, a pattern of fastenings or nails, use a pounce wheel or create your own gadget (FIG. 19-24).

PLANKING A SOLID HULL

Mention was made of the experience gained in the planking of a solid hull. Delay the placement of the deck until you have completed the planking. You can then hold the hull upright on a working stand. To do the bottom, try screwing in a wood block and clamping the assembly in a vise (FIG. 19-25).

MAKING EYEBOLTS

I never seem to have enough eyebolts the right size. Even the commercial sources don't have them in some of the sizes I need to keep in scale. Oversized eyebolts are an eyesore in scale ship modeling. The solution is to make your own with round-nosed pliers (FIG. 19-26).

Suffice it to say that there are several customized round-nosed pliers in my collection of tools. My optician uses a tool with a groove filed in one tip. I bought one to use for holding a fine pin, wire, or other material of choice.

CONSTRUCTING FIFE RAILS

All too often the builder of a scale ship model neglects to add strength in the fife rails. Although you might not see a need for rigid fixation or strength of construction in this piece of deck furniture, it

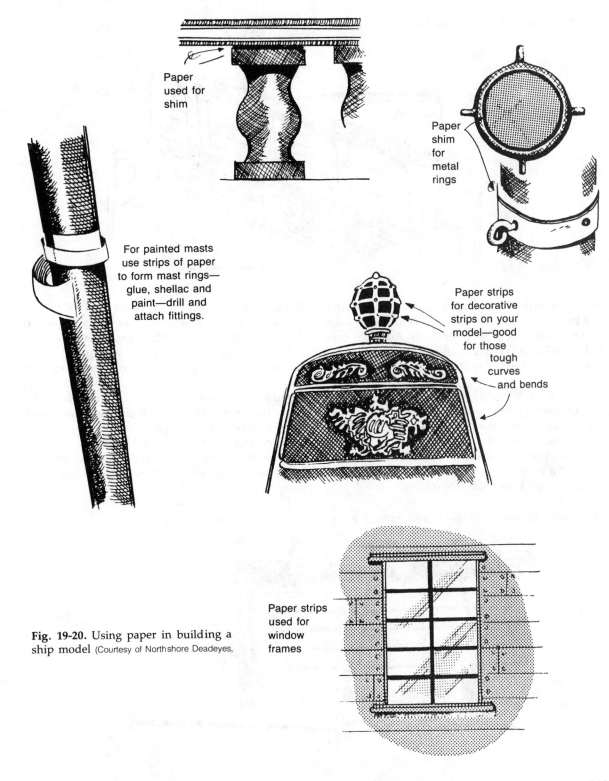

Paper used for shim

Paper shim for metal rings

For painted masts use strips of paper to form mast rings— glue, shellac and paint—drill and attach fittings.

Paper strips for decorative strips on your model—good for those tough curves and bends

Fig. 19-20. Using paper in building a ship model (Courtesy of Northshore Deadeyes,

Paper strips used for window frames

243

Fig. 19-21. Dressmaker's pins become eyebolts (Courtesy of Northshore Deadeyes, Ltd.).

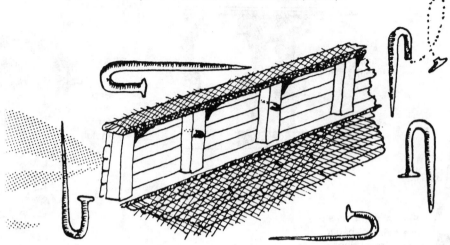

should be strong. Consider the number of lines that will belay there. Consider also the mounting tension as the pull of these lines accumulates. Avoid the frustration of having your fife rail pull loose. Follow the simple hints in FIGS. 19-27 and 19-28.

JOINING PIECES OF WOOD

Timbering a ship requires all the tricks you can find. In the construction of the real vessel, there were some that, even without the help of glue, such as modelers use, were stronger than a length of wood without a joint.

Three quick methods are offered;

✪ Butt end strengthened and held by a dowel.
✪ Use of a wood spline. Plywood is recommended for strength because of its cross-grained layers.
✪ The "scarfed" joint, just as it was in real ships.

There are several scarfing joints. They range from the simple angled bevel to the multitoothed unions found on the keels of ships of the line (FIG. 19-29). Accuracy demands that you familiarize yourself with these methods of joining wood.

I recommend good research. Pick the strongest joint, no matter what period if that's your thing. After all, this is your ship and you can build it any way you want.

Fig. 19-22. Dressmaker's pins used as lank holders (Courtesy of Northshore Deadeyes, Ltd.).

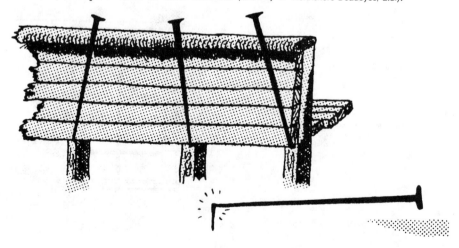

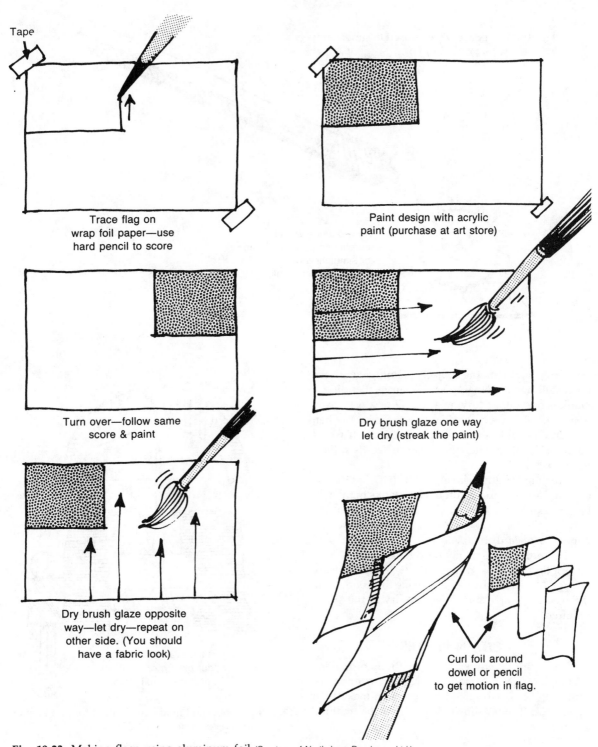

Tape

Trace flag on
wrap foil paper—use
hard pencil to score

Paint design with acrylic
paint (purchase at art store)

Turn over—follow same
score & paint

Dry brush glaze one way
let dry (streak the paint)

Dry brush glaze opposite
way—let dry—repeat on
other side. (You should
have a fabric look)

Curl foil around
dowel or pencil
to get motion in flag.

Fig. 19-23. Making flags using aluminum foil (Courtesy of Northshore Deadeyes, Ltd.).

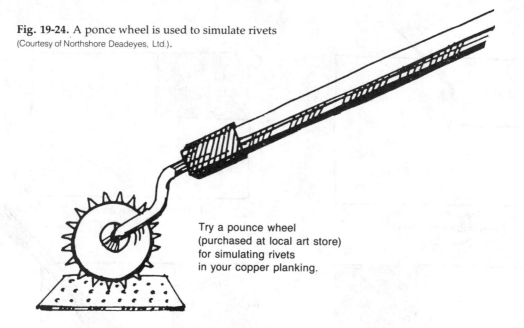

Fig. 19-24. A ponce wheel is used to simulate rivets (Courtesy of Northshore Deadeyes, Ltd.).

Try a pounce wheel
(purchased at local art store)
for simulating rivets
in your copper planking.

While we are on the subject of joining wood, we must talk about going around a curve. Bending a plank is one thing; curving a caprail or a waterway is another. The wood just doesn't want to bend when the piece is a thicker one of a larger scale. It won't bend hardly at all when the broad surface is subject to intense strain.

Scarfing a curve is in order (FIG. 19-30) for caprails. You can make cutouts for planks in the nibbing strake at this time (FIG. 19-31). You can cut the curve of the rail or the waterway with the use of a paper (cardboard) template.

Thinner caprails do not need to be scarfed. A little application of a razor (FIG. 19-32) can release enough tension in the wood to make the bend. Soak the wood in water and allow it to dry in the shape required.

CHAIN PLATES

There are several excellent methods of making chain plates. Many modelers rely on commercial sources. Others who build from scratch make their own. FIGURE 19-33 shows three ''scratch'' method chain plates.

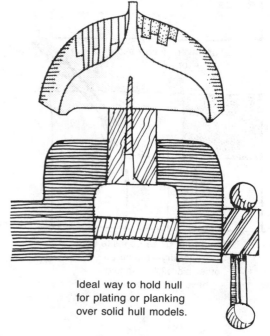

Ideal way to hold hull
for plating or planking
over solid hull models.

Fig. 19-25. Solid-hull model in position for planking or coppering (Courtesy of Northshore Deadeyes, Ltd.).

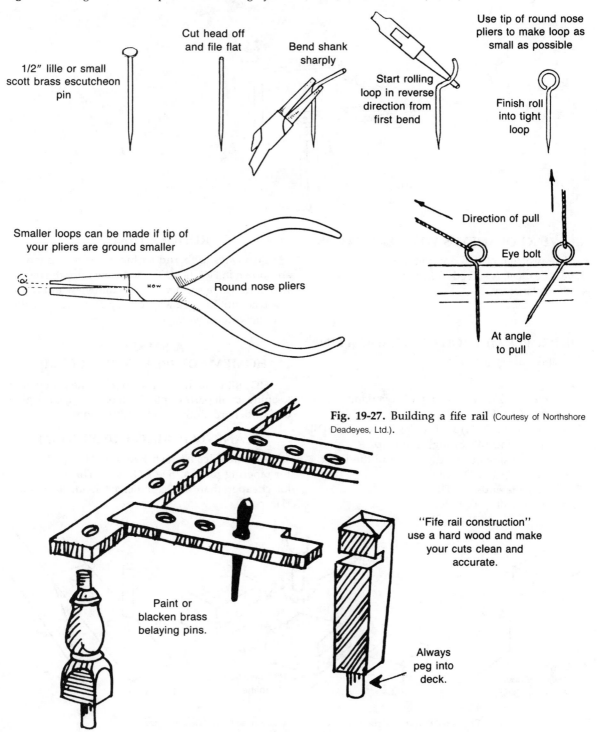

Fig. 19-26. Using round-nosed pliers and bending eyebolts (Courtesy of Northshore Deadeyes, Ltd.).

1/2″ lille or small scott brass escutcheon pin

Cut head off and file flat

Bend shank sharply

Start rolling loop in reverse direction from first bend

Use tip of round nose pliers to make loop as small as possible

Finish roll into tight loop

Smaller loops can be made if tip of your pliers are ground smaller

Round nose pliers

Direction of pull

Eye bolt

At angle to pull

Fig. 19-27. Building a fife rail (Courtesy of Northshore Deadeyes, Ltd.).

Paint or blacken brass belaying pins.

"Fife rail construction" use a hard wood and make your cuts clean and accurate.

Always peg into deck.

247

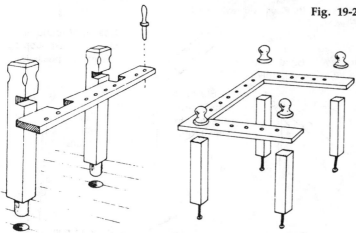

Fig. 19-28. Assembling and installing the fife rail.

REEVING DEADEYES WITH LANYARDS

The problem of determining the proper way to reeve a deadeye is solved. Refer to FIG. 19-34 which is self-explanatory.

THE PROPER METHOD OF SEIZING A LINE

Follow along in FIG. 19-35.

1. Start the seizing with a loop (A) overlapping the bottom end (D).
2. Cover the loop (A) with turns of the line (D). Place the end (B) through the loop.
3. You are just about ready to secure the work.
4. Pull lines C and D taut.
5. Cut off the ends (C, D).
6. Fix with a drop of glue.

RUDDER HINGES

Two ways to fix rudder hinges on a ship model are shown in FIG. 19-36. The top view is for the model with a movable rudder. The bottom view indicates, if you are not fussy, a way to hang your rudder without allowing movement.

A SMALL
HOMEMADE (PLANKING) CLAMP

FIGURE 19-37 shows how to solve the problem of keeping small parts or planks in place while the glue dries. Richard Roos developed the idea.

PLANK-TAPERING GUIDE FORM

Another idea from Dick Roos is a holding device for tapering planks. See FIG. 19-38. This device is a lot cheaper than the commercial item, a tabletop clamp.

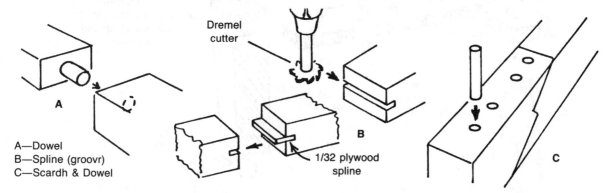

A—Dowel
B—Spline (groovr)
C—Scardh & Dowel

Dremel cutter

1/32 plywood spline

Fig. 19-29. Joining pieces of wood (Courtesy of Northshore Deadeyes, Ltd.).

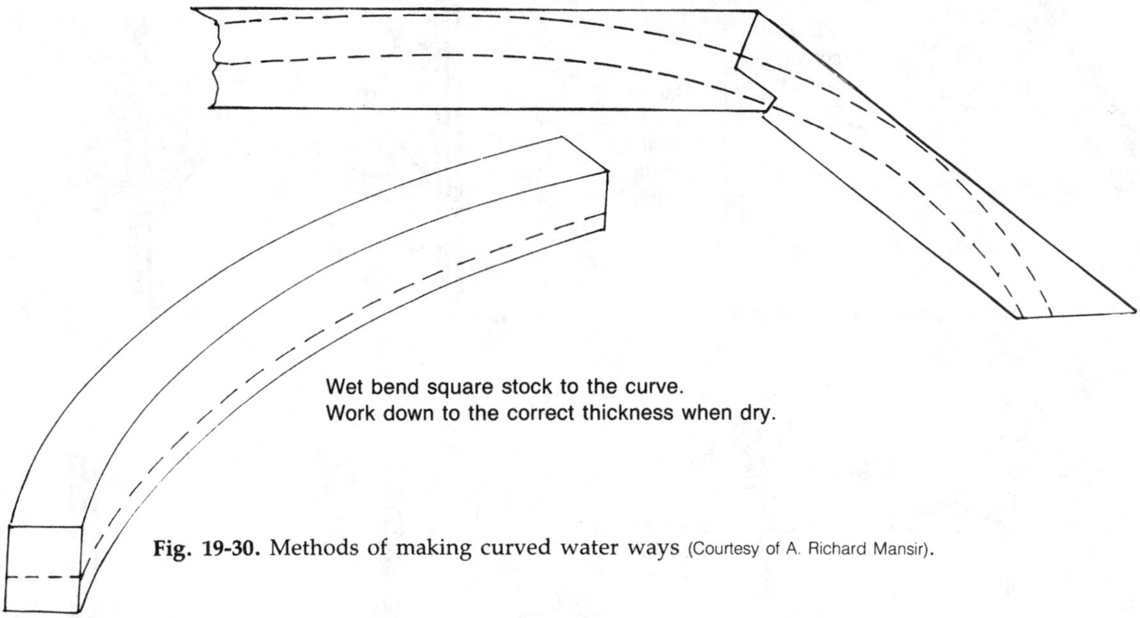

Scarf together pieces of wide stock saw to the curve

Wet bend square stock to the curve.
Work down to the correct thickness when dry.

Fig. 19-30. Methods of making curved water ways (Courtesy of A. Richard Mansir).

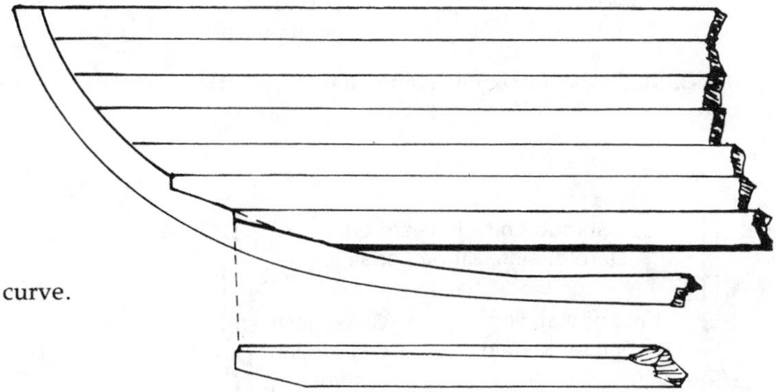

Fig. 19-31. Knibbing the plank at the curve.

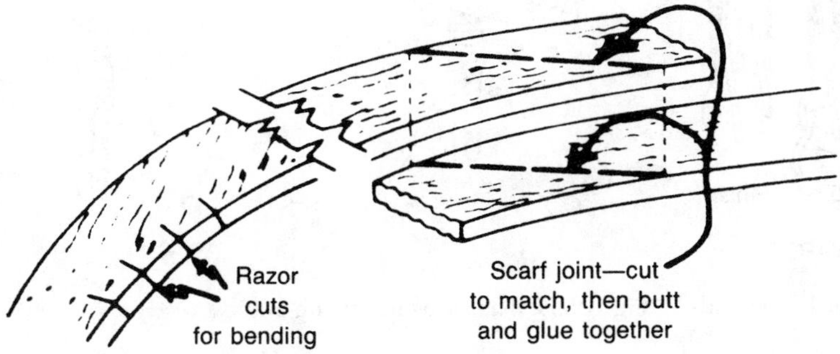

Fig. 19-32. Making a rail cap curve
(Courtesy of Marine Models).

Razor
cuts
for bending

Scarf joint—cut
to match, then butt
and glue together

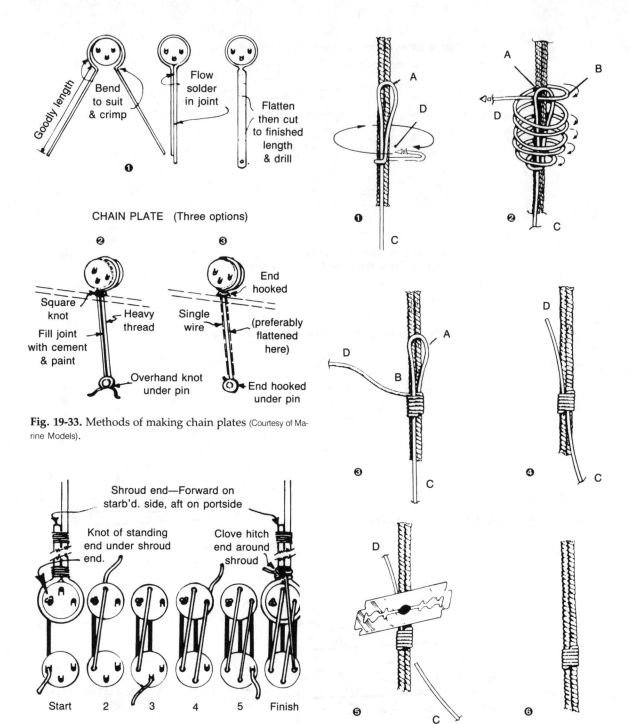

CHAIN PLATE (Three options)

Fig. 19-33. Methods of making chain plates (Courtesy of Marine Models).

Inboard view of DEADEYES & LANYARDS

Fig. 19-34. The proper way to rove a lanyard in a deadeye (Courtesy of Marine Models).

Fig. 19-35. The steps in seizing a line (Courtesy of V. Lusci).

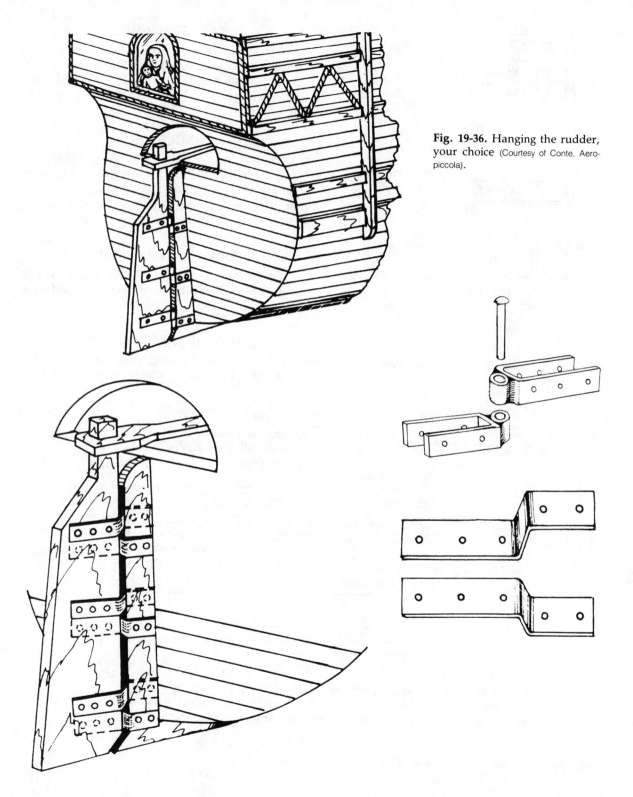

Fig. 19-36. Hanging the rudder, your choice (Courtesy of Conte, Aeropiccola).

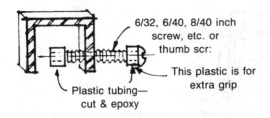

6/32, 6/40, 8/40 inch screw, etc. or thumb scr:

This plastic is for extra grip

Plastic tubing— cut & epoxy

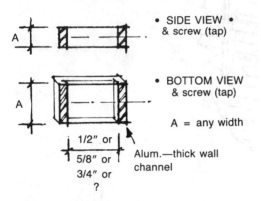

A

• SIDE VIEW •
& screw (tap)

A

• BOTTOM VIEW •
& screw (tap)

A = any width

1/2" or
5/8" or
3/4" or
?

Alum.—thick wall channel

Fig. 19-37. A homemade Mini-"C" clamp (Courtesy of Richard Roos).

RAIL STANCHIONS

Modern ship models in smaller scales demand smaller stanchions. If you can't find them commercially, you can make your own. It is not hard if you follow along with FIG. 19-39. All materials and tools are available.

BUCKETS

Buckets aboard a ship? Of course. There were many varieties of buckets. In the early days they were wood or canvas. FIGURE 19-40 shows a few to ponder. Sponge and lintstock tubs are not classed with buckets. Check them out in your research.

HOLDING A SMALL CARVING

Save the slashed fingers. Mount your carving on another piece of wood with rubber cement and carve in safety.

USEFUL INFORMATION

Measuring is one thing; converting is another. Included in this book is a table on converting from

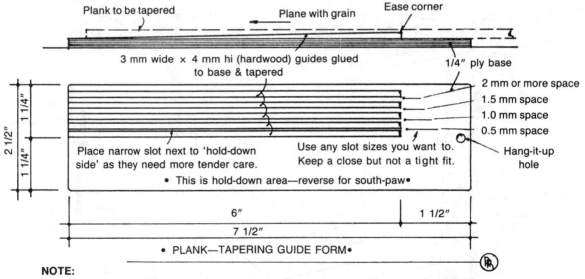

Plank to be tapered

Plane with grain

Ease corner

3 mm wide × 4 mm hi (hardwood) guides glued to base & tapered

1/4" ply base

2 mm or more space
1.5 mm space
1.0 mm space
0.5 mm space

Hang-it-up hole

Place narrow slot next to 'hold-down side' as they need more tender care.

Use any slot sizes you want to. Keep a close but not a tight fit.

• This is hold-down area—reverse for south-paw•

2 1/2"
1 1/4"
1 1/4"

6"

1 1/2"

7 1/2"

• PLANK—TAPERING GUIDE FORM•

NOTE:

Because the thin planks wiggle, I start planing holding the planks more to the higher end of the guide, moving it forward as I process. With practice, you can taper more than 1 plank at a time by using the wider slots you have made: P.S. watch the finger tips.

Fig. 19-38. The plank tapering guide form (Courtesy of Richard Roos).

RAIL STANCHIONS

Rail stanchions come in various sizes but the builder must make his own at certain times. A simple gig, silver solder, a microtorch, and cardboard template are all that is needed.

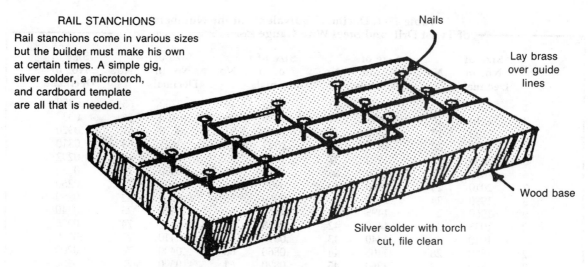

Nails

Lay brass over guide lines

Wood base

Silver solder with torch cut, file clean

Fig. 19-39. Making rail stanchions from brass wire (Courtesy of Northshore Deadeyes, Ltd.).

meters to inches and vice versa. TABLES 19-1 and 19-2 list more conversions from inches. You can copy the table with your favorite duplicating machine and mount them on the wall for each reference.

Although this section could go on forever, open-ended as it is, we must stop somewhere. I trust that there were included in this collection of hints, tips, and dodges a few you did not know and can use.

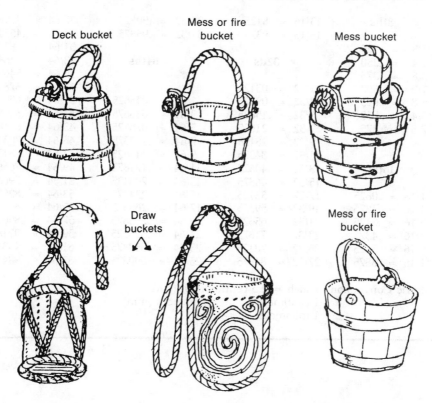

Deck bucket

Mess or fire bucket

Mess bucket

Draw buckets

Mess or fire bucket

Table 19-1. Decimal Equivalents of the Numbers of Twist Drill and Steel Wire Gauge (Courtesy of National Screw Co.).

No.	Size of No. in Decimals	No.	Size of No. in Decimals	No.	Size of No. in Decimals	No.	Size of No. in Decimals	No.	Size of No. in Decimals
1	.2280	17	.1730	33	.1130	49	.0730	65	.0350
2	.2210	18	.1695	34	.1110	50	.0700	66	.0330
3	.2130	19	.1660	35	.1100	51	.0670	67	.0320
4	.2090	20	.1610	36	.1065	52	.0635	68	.0310
5	.2055	21	.1590	37	.1040	53	.0595	69	.0292
6	.2040	22	.1570	38	.1015	54	.0550	70	.0280
7	.2010	23	.1540	39	.0995	55	.0520	71	.0260
8	.1990	24	.1520	40	.0980	56	.0465	72	.0250
9	.1960	25	.1495	41	.0960	57	.0430	73	.0240
10	.1935	26	.1470	42	.0935	58	.0420	74	.0225
11	.1910	27	.1440	43	.0890	59	.0410	75	.0210
12	.1890	28	.1405	44	.0860	60	.0400	76	.0200
13	.1850	29	.1360	45	.0820	61	.0390	77	.0180
14	.1820	30	.1285	46	.0810	62	.0380	78	.0160
15	.1800	31	.1200	47	.0785	63	.0370	79	.0145
16	.1770	32	.1160	48	.0760	64	.0360	80	.0135

Table 19-2. Decimal Equivalents (Courtesy of National Screw Co.).

8ths

1/8 = .125
1/4 = .250
3/8 = .375
1/2 = .500
5/8 = .625
3/4 = .750
7/8 = .875

16ths

1/16 = .0625
3/16 = .1875
5/16 = .3125
7/16 = .4375
9/16 = .5625
11/16 = .6875

13/16 = .8125
15/16 = .9375

32ds

1/32 = .03125
3/32 = .09375
5/32 = .15625
7/32 = .21875
9/32 = .28125
11/32 = .34375
13/32 = .40625
15/32 = .46875
17/32 = .53125
19/32 = .59375
21/32 = .65625
23/32 = .71875
25/32 = .78125
27/32 = .84375

29/32 = .90625
31/32 = .96875

64ths

1/64 = .015625
3/64 = .046875
5/64 = .078125
7/64 = .109375
9/64 = .140625
11/64 = .171875
13/64 = .203125
15/64 = .234375
17/64 = .265625
19/64 = .296875
21/64 = .328125
23/64 = .359375
25/64 = .390625
27/64 = .421875
29/64 = .453125
31/64 = .484375
33/64 = .515625
35/64 = .546875
37/64 = .578125
39/64 = .609375
41/64 = .640625
43/64 = .671875
45/64 = .703125
47/64 = .734375
49/64 = .765625
51/64 = .796875
53/64 = .828125
55/64 = .859375
57/64 = .890625
59/64 = .921875
61/64 = .953125
63/64 = .984375

Metric Conversion: 1 inch = 2.5 centimeters, (cm)
1 centimeter = 10 millimeters (mm)
1 millimeter = .04 inch

TWENTY

Essential Gadgets

No one knows what he can do till he tries.
—PUBLILIUS SYRUS

GREAT SHIP MODELS HAVE BEEN BUILT WITH nothing but a cutting blade, a saw, and sandpaper. Perhaps some modelers have used even less. I offer as an example the famous *Prisoner of War* ship models of the 1800s. These detailed models were made literally with a knife, a bone, and a hank of hair. It isn't the tools, power or hand, that make a great modeler, it's the experience.

Ship modelers, like any builders, are searchers, scroungers, savers, and buyers of gadgets. They are searching for ways to do it better, faster, and cheaper than the last time. The strongest influence about building anything is the creation of something out of nothing.

The disassembled parts are available with instructions. Gathered together and placed in a container, they become a kit. A modeler who refers to himself as a scratch builder might gather and create from raw material. Is he not assembling a kit? He has his own designs, finds his own plans, and gathers every material he thinks he needs.

Creation begins with the thinking process and finishes with the physical application of skill. The greatest challenge to accomplishment is innovation. Innovation is gadgetry.

The sad part is that most of the gadgets, labor-saving devices, and tools perfected by an individual will never find their way to a commercial source. They could have been a great benefit to fellow modelers. Alas, there will be no saving of time from the assistance of a dedicated builder who desires not a profit, but a simple saving of time.

Many who do not practice innovativeness have heard of a new item that will satisfy this need to "save time." They see something in a shop or catalog, read an article of recent or vintage date, or hear about it from a friend.

After a use or two, the item falls into disfavor. Through lack of use or plain forgetfulness it will begin to gather dust, and finally be thrown or given away. So much for that item. It was a useless gadget.

Just what is a *gadget* anyway? *Webster's New World Dictionary*, describes a gadget as "any small mechanical contrivance or device." Another definition given is "any small object, especially something relatively useless or superfluous." That about sums it up. Two opinions in one statement.

I must take issue with the second definition. Not all gadgets are useless. Without a doubt, everything that is created to accomplish a task could be considered a gadget. What some consider a gadget, is a most prized and useful tool to others.

From where do all the gadgets come? They are the products of laziness, invented by those who just didn't want to spend time doing things the way they have always been done. Gadgets are contrived and

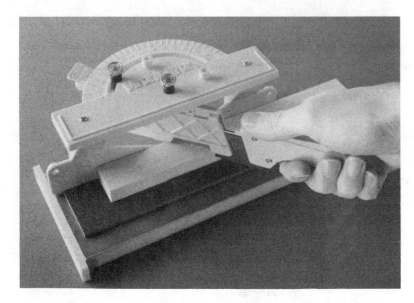

Fig. 20-1. The Miter-Rite (Photo by Ted Dobson).

perfected by individuals who saw an easier way to do it. As a case in point I give you the miter box.

A MITER BOX AND A SEIZING DEVICE

Theodore A. Dobson made the original model of his MITER-RITE out of presswood. This same material was incorporated in the earlier production models. Members of his ship model club, The Northshore Deadeyes, were impressed after a presentation of his ''gadget'' at a meeting.

The members noted that the device held the blade perfectly perpendicular at all times. It cut angles the same every time. It was their insistence at obtaining a unit for themselves that prompted Ted to go into manufacturing.

The units now offered for sale, after much experimentation, are made of high-impact plastic (FIG. 20-1). ''It can never wear out and it's the last one you'll ever have to buy,'' boasts the maker. The blade, which is included, is an X-ACTO Razor Saw No. 239. It is easily replaced, as is the cutting board. The entire mechanism is mounted on non-mar rubber feet.

The cut is adjustable in 1-degree increments to a range of 65 degrees on each side of the 90-degree center cut. A memory stop gauge, adjustable both left and right, can be set, then moved aside for a different cut. This, as Ted assures the buyer, will make every cut ''true to the setting'' and perpendicular because of the construction of the blade holder.

Fig. 20-2. The String-Along (Photo by Ted Dobson).

Cutting capacity is 9/16 inch thick. The widest recommended cut is for 2 inches. Plastic, as well as wood and soft metals, can be cut accurately.

A previous gadget invented by Mr. Dobson was his STRING-ALONG, a seizing, or wrapping, device. (FIG. 20-2). This is a device for twisting line around another line, such as to fasten a deadeye, with continual tension. Although it was invented by a ship modeler for his contemporaries, it has found other devotees. One friend of mine, not a ship modeler but a fisherman, bought one to tie flies.

Both gadgets are available from:

THEODORE A. DOBSON
1416 South Cortland
Park Ridge, IL 60068

MAKING ROPE

Particular ship modelers make their own rope. *Cable-laid*, as the name denotes, is a very heavy and strong rope usually used for anchors. It has a right-hand twist. *Rope-laid* has a left-hand twist (FIG. 20-3). There isn't much true cable-laid line available for ship modelers from commercial sources. Sizes needed for variations in scale, the limited amount needed by each purchaser, and the difficulty of making machinery designed for such production, are some of the reasons cable-laid line is not available. Also, it is not profitable. For the sake of accuracy and in an attempt to keep even the lines in scale, some modelers make their own rope.

The device used is known as a *ropewalk*. The name comes from the old method of working the material in long sheds and literally "walking" it into coils and skeins. The mechanical process contains three or more counter-rotating heads, a continuing source of material (linen, hemp, etc.), threads, a guiding bobbin, and a tension (weight) to work the twisting action.

A miniature ropewalk can be made from a fixed base of three hooks and three hooks mounted on a turning handle made from two bars of wood (FIG. 20-4). It is crude, but effective. The works from an old

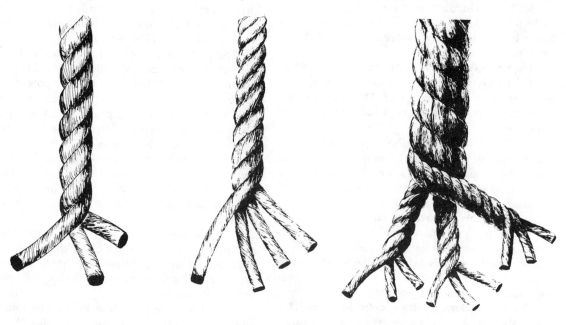

Three-stranded **Hawser Laid** rope ("z" laid) twists from right to left, counterclockwise.

Four-stranded **Shroud Laid** rope also twists from right to left, counterclockwise.

Nine-stranded **Cable Laid** rope, twists three hawser laid ropes together in a clockwise direction.

Fig. 20-3. The lay of the ropes aboard ship (Courtesy of Moonraker Publications).

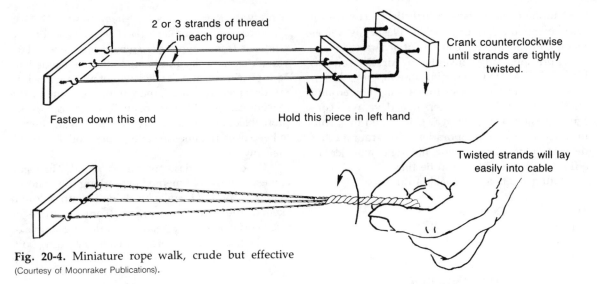

Fig. 20-4. Miniature rope walk, crude but effective (Courtesy of Moonraker Publications).

alarm clock, or progressively sophisticated metal, shopmade models with elaborate gears are variations on this theme.

Michael J. Heinrich, ship modeler, designed and perfected his device after much trial and error. The crude beginning slowly evolved into the finished product offered today.

The headstock contains three corotating spindles. The tailstock is geared for corotating operations, such as a serving and seizing device. This incorporates, in effect, two machines in one. Cranks are provided at both ends.

ROPEWORKS is molded in high-impact styrene. All the moving parts are in "derlin." Two swivels, four weights, eight screws, a length of nylon guide line, and complete instructions are provided. All necessary hardware is included.

No base plate is provided. The two units can be mounted on a portable wood base, on the workbench, or with one unit stationary and the other movable (clamped at the desired length). Any type of ship model "string" can be used, so you can make your rope as long as practical (FIG. 20-5).

The rope-making machine is offered through the hobby shop, mail-order houses, as well as direct sales by:

FLOGGING THE PUBLIC DOMAIN ENTERPRISES, LTD.
611 North Midland Ave.
Upper Nyack, NY 10960

CUTTING SMALL PIECES

Small pieces of wood or plastic are hard to cut in an accurate fashion. Holding on to them for the cut is frustrating. Setting up a miter box is time consuming. La Guillotine provides a practical way to make a quick clean cut (FIG. 20-6).

The principle is the same as the original invention during the French Revolution. Instead of gravity making the "cut," however, it is the power of the operator. A sharp downward pressure on the cutter bar, and the wood or soft plastic is neatly severed. The bar is quickly returned to the raised position by a spring. The unit is constructed of maple wood.

You can make angled cuts by adjusting the locking "fence." A protractor and the cutting length rule are marked on the base by a decal. The cutting line is clearly indicated. A Plexiglas safety guard prevents accidents.

Extra blades are available. The cutting action is not conducive to keeping a blade sharp. The force of the blow drives the cutting edge through the work, rather than slicing like the angled blade of the beheading French model.

Fred Nagel, ship modeler in need of a gadget, invented this one. His company was called the *Bowsprit*. He has since sold the manufacturing rights. La Guillotine is available from:

STAN GORDON ENTERPRISES
P.O. Box 5482
Sherman Oaks, CA 91413

MITERING TOOL

Getting the right angle is important in any modeling work. Since the work is miniature, the ''gadget'' should also be a miniature of the full-sized original. This makes it usable in smaller sizes.

The Universal Miter is offered by Jarmac, a maker of miniature power tools. The tool is 2 1/8 inches long. It has a brass handle and steel adjustment blade. Write to:

JARMAC
P.O. Box 2785
Springfield, IL 62708

CLAMPS

Another offering from Jarmac is the 4-inch clamp. The unit is constructed of rigid plastic and is light enough to be used for the most delicate work. It serves to hold parts as a vise clamp, and the large opening allows the entire part to be included for clamping.

Stan Gordon Enterprises also makes a miniature framing clamp. The material is brass. After the material is cut at 45 degrees, the adjustable clamp can be used to hold the frame (picture, deck grate, dollhouse windows, etc.) while the glue dries.

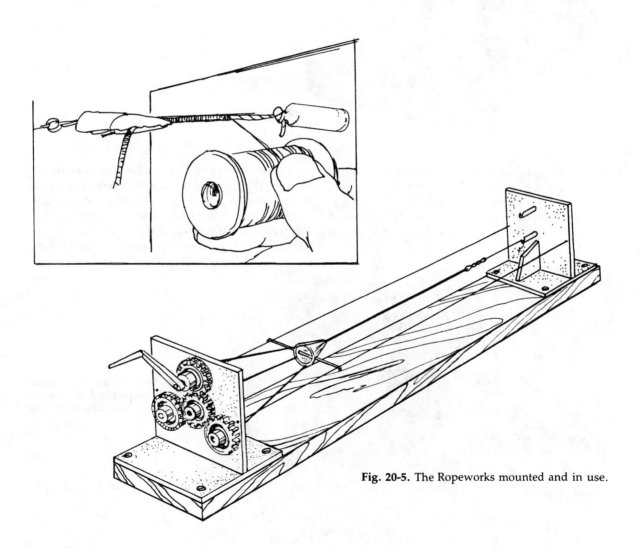

Fig. 20-5. The Ropeworks mounted and in use.

Fig. 20-6. La Guillotine, a device for rapid cutting (Photo by Fred Nagle).

THICKNESS SANDER

Too big to be called a small gadget, this next item is a precision instrument. It is a thickness sander. It will accurately dimension wood from .005 inch to .75 inch thick. The device will handle up to 3 inches in width (FIG. 20-7).

Power is supplied by a one-sixth horsepower electric (110 volts) motor. Construction is of metal. An innovative adjusting mechanism of specially machined parts is incorporated for changing the sanding depths. A flat milling table ensures a flat surface. An essential dust collector is designed into the unit.

Fig. 20-7. The thickness sander as developed by Gene Larson (Photo courtesy of Model Ship Marina, Alexandria, VA).

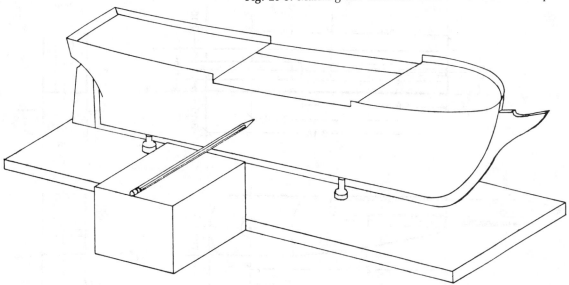

Fig. 20-8. Marking the waterline with a wood block and pencil.

The tool accepts commercially available sanding drums. It is available from:

GENE LARSON
Model Ship Marina
P.O. Box 15201
Alexandria, VA 22309

A MARKING GAUGE

A takeoff on a precision instrument used by a tool and die maker, a marking gauge, started as a pencil fixed to a block of wood (FIG. 20-8). That was fine for marking a waterline. There was no adjustment, however, and a different block was needed for each model. Dividers were unsteady tools to use in measuring a fixed point from a base, such as a tabletop, to a place (waterline) on a model. The end of the frustration came with a waterline gauge marker.

The variations are limitless. FIGURE 20-9 shows a product from the hand and mind of Tom Palen of Fullerton, California. His efforts resulted in a block that slid and could be held in a desired position. The center upright was slotted, and the block drilled to receive a machine screw. A couple of washers prevented the head of the screw from gouging into the wood on one side and the thumb (set screw) from biting on the other.

Perhaps you would like to try your hand at making your own gadget. A set of drawings and dimen-

sions are provided in FIG. 20-10. There is a little catch. While there is a plan, of sorts, no instructions will be given. Feel free to use the wood of your choice and finish it as you desire. Incidentally, the thumb screw fits a 1/4-inch national, coarse-treaded machine screw. Washers were placed between wood and turning metal parts.

ROOS' GADGETS

If you feel that making gadgets was (or could be) fun, or you are now on an "I can make it for my-

Fig. 20-9. Tom Palen's waterline marker. The construction is wood and easily made (Photo by Tom Palen).

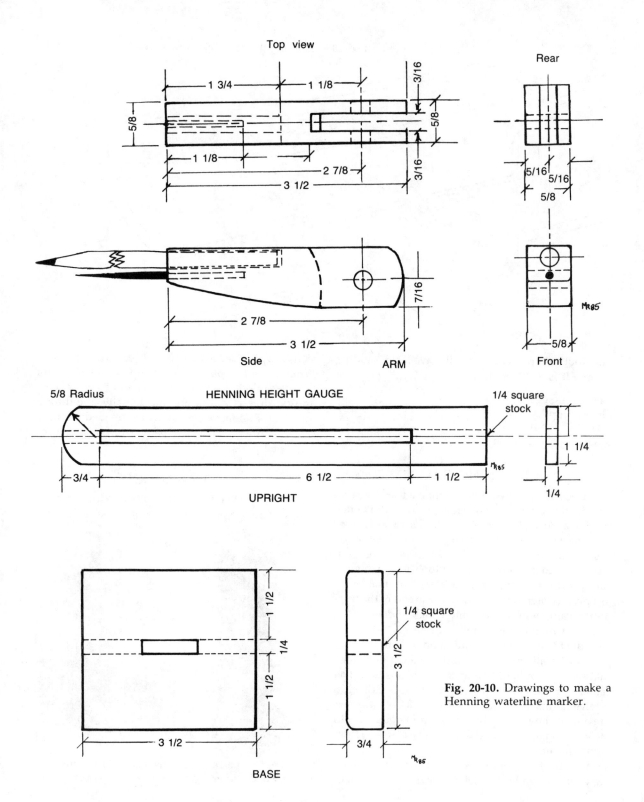

Top view

Rear

1 3/4

1 1/8

3/16

5/8

5/8

1 1/8

2 7/8

3/16

3 1/2

5/16 5/16

5/8

7/16

2 7/8

3 1/2

Side

ARM

Front

5/8 Radius

HENNING HEIGHT GAUGE

1/4 square
stock

3/4

6 1/2

1 1/2

1 1/4

UPRIGHT

1/4

1 1/2

1/4 square
stock

1/4

3 1/2

1 1/2

3/4

Fig. 20-10. Drawings to make a
Henning waterline marker.

BASE

self'' kick, I will throw in a couple from the mind of Richard Roos. The commercial product for the *Small Parts Sprung Holder* (FIG. 20-11) is manufactured in plastic by Mascot Tools and featured in that company's catalog. It is a gadget from the jewelry profession. You can secure a copy by writing to the address listed in Chapter 3.

Undoubtedly, you will have already noticed an abundance of drawings and submissions by Richard Roos. His gadgetry is boundless and there are times when its classification escapes me. Take a look at FIG. 20-12 and see if the similarity to the commercial product stirs in your mind.

GLUE GUN

Two items for your consideration do not belong under this heading or even in this chapter. They are commercial products pure and simple. They were made for other uses. However, since they have been given a rebirth as something beyond their intended use, let's call them gadgets.

The "glue gun" was originally a product for the dental profession. The new name is mine. It was used in the doctor's office as an irrigation syringe. Often it was dispensed to the patient to use in washing out particles from between the teeth or to irrigate a dry socket after an extraction. That's how I came by mine.

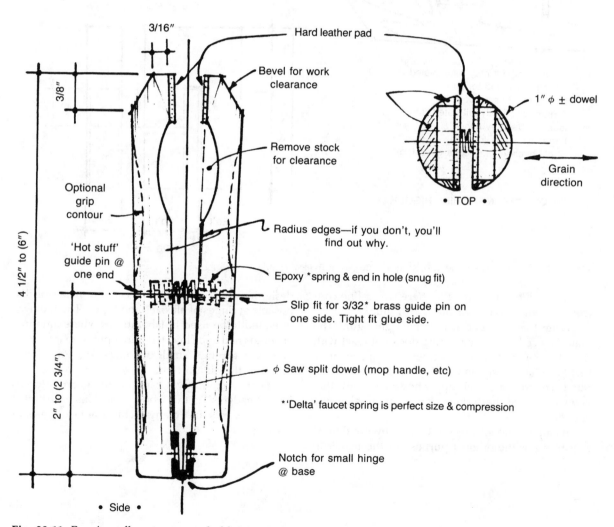

3/16"

3/8"

Hard leather pad

Bevel for work clearance

Remove stock for clearance

1" φ ± dowel

Grain direction

• TOP •

Optional grip contour

4 1/2" to (6")

'Hot stuff' guide pin @ one end

Radius edges—if you don't, you'll find out why.

Epoxy *spring & end in hole (snug fit)

Slip fit for 3/32* brass guide pin on one side. Tight fit glue side.

2" to (2 3/4")

φ Saw split dowel (mop handle, etc)

*'Delta' faucet spring is perfect size & compression

Notch for small hinge @ base

• Side •

Fig. 20-11. Roos' small parts sprung-holder (Courtesy of Richard Roos).

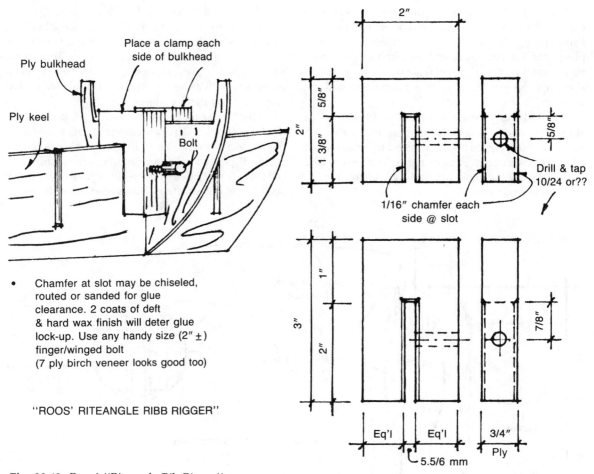

Place a clamp each
side of bulkhead

Ply bulkhead

Ply keel

Bolt

2"

5/8"

2"

1 3/8"

5/8"

Drill & tap
10/24 or??

1/16" chamfer each
side @ slot

3"

1"

2"

7/8"

Eq'l   Eq'l   3/4"
Ply

5.5/6 mm

- Chamfer at slot may be chiseled, routed or sanded for glue clearance. 2 coats of deft & hard wax finish will deter glue lock-up. Use any handy size (2" ±) finger/winged bolt (7 ply birch veneer looks good too)

"ROOS' RITEANGLE RIBB RIGGER"

Fig. 20-12. Roos' "Riteangle Rib Rigger" (Courtesy of Richard Roos).

The possibility struck me that here was a fine control for liquids. Why not fill it with glue?

From that moment, it became a glue gun. The material used in manufacturing does not react with the white glues. It did not react with the epoxy mixes that I used in an experiment. The relative cost, when purchased from a dental supply house, is so low that you can discard the syringe along with any leftover epoxy.

It came as no surprise to be told by my dentist that this was the original purpose of the maker in designing the syringe. Monoject is a maker of disposable syringes of all sizes and types. The tool was intended to be used in laboratories where amounts of liquids had to be injected under pressure into areas or molds through small openings or with a high-pressure flushing action.

There are, and will continue to be, an outpouring of "gadgets" in this world. What I have illustrated in a few words and many pictures are examples of gadgets.

TWENTY ONE

Research, Vocabulary, and Conversation

It is a capital mistake to theorize before one has data.
—A. CONAN DOYLE

THE PROGRESS MADE IN ANY UNDERTAKING IS based on your ability to know the facts. Without the security of fact, the entire project seems like a sham. Facts are, by far, one of the most important items in the building of an historic ship model. The facts must be verified. Once this is done, then the duty of every good ship modeler is complete. His model will be a statement of historical truth.

You should know, for example, that the vessel being modeled is of a specific length. This is an established fact. You then know that the scale to which the vessel is being built will result in a similar, but reduced, established length. The beam has been established as a specific width. The height and structure of the masts have been incorporated into the building of the scale model based on these figures. The model will be a representation of that particular ship. There is no need to question the measurements based on accurate information.

When doubt begins to creep into the project, then research is mandatory. Is this a true representation of the ship it is going to be? Have I assured myself that this model will be an exact historical rendition in miniature? Where do I begin?

Each ship, if she ever existed, had a name. Her name was registered somewhere. Someone took notice of her and she has left a record. Begin by looking for her name in the records.

Every ship, like every person who has ever lived, was relegated to a particular time of the past, present, or perhaps the future. First establish a time frame. Then search for her name in that specific time frame.

Names of ships have transcended time and existed in several periods. If, as an example, you are doing a model of the *Enterprise*, the period of time that she lived in would denote the vessel you wish to model. A steel-hulled vessel and turbine-powered engine is not the ship that served her nation in the 1700s. A ship with Warp-drive engines and speeds beyond that of light and operating on star time is not the ship of waterborne history, but of science fiction. All are vessels that bore and still bear the name of U.S.S. *Enterprise*. The distinction is the time of the ship's existence.

There were eight U.S.S. *Enterprises* listed in the *Dictionary of American Naval Fighting Ships,* Volume II (United States Government Printing Office, Washington, DC). They ranged from the first ship captured from the British in 1775, a sloop, all the way to CVN (N)-65, America's first nuclear-powered aircraft carrier launched in 1961. The range also included a motorboat, the sixth *Enterprise,* which served in a noncommissioned status in the 2nd Naval District during World War I.

Incidentally, there are eight volumes in the *Dictionary of American Naval Fighting Ships* just mentioned. Volume I was published in 1959 under the direction of the Navy Department, Office of the Chief of Naval Operations. This is the official listing of United States Navy ships. Correct histories of all ships, including the Confederate States Navy, are presented for your information in alphabetical order by the ship's name and designated number. Updated with corrections, the last of the series was published in 1981.

THE LIBRARY

Will you find the books and material you need in your library? Not always. The largest library located in the largest city in the world does not always boast of being complete on every subject. It is a place to start, though.

We live in a world of instant communication and instant information. Computers and cable networks link all peoples, literally. The telephone reaches into the most remote places in the nation. Radio and satellite contact reaches the rest.

With this contact and with the added membership of the library networks of the United States, your local library can secure a specific book for you. The length of time you must wait is based on rarity, availability, and value.

Over 3,000 libraries are hooked into a computer network. Some libraries are also linked to the libraries of universities. Many of these universities have exchange programs with libraries in other nations. If there is a computer terminal in your library, you have a key to unlock the libraries of the world.

After a quick search of the records, you can come up with a title, an author, or even a publisher. The computer can search for a clue in a fraction of a second. A scan can be made for a name, a number, even the ship's cat.

In case you don't know the exact title of the book, ask to see the standard reference books entitled *Subject Guide To Books In Print.* They will help. If the book is out of print, there are microfilmed or computerbanked titles of back issues of periodicals or out-of-print books.

If you wish to engage in a little hard-driving research of your own, I suggest a visit to your library. The first book you should ask for is *Knowing Where To Look: The Ultimate Guide To Research* by Lois Horowitz (Writer's Digest Books, Cincinnati, Ohio, 1984). There are others dealing with the subject of research, but this one opened my eyes.

OTHER SOURCES

If you can't find what you are looking for at the library, you must make a course change. It is time to head for a museum. Does it have to be a Maritime Museum? No. Museum personnel are dedicated individuals. History and the preservation of historical objects is their prime motivation. History is history and they will be most happy to assist you in the discovery of information.

Without a doubt a maritime museum is best when you are seeking information about ships. There are both public and private maritime museums. National museums, both here and abroad, are the great repositories of maritime history. They are not all located in places convenient to you, however.

If there is not a museum near you, correspondence is required. Where can you find the addresses of the world's great maritime museums? Your local library has them on file.

After you have selected the ones that you feel will best suit your purposes, compose your letters with care. Be as specific as you can. Don't ramble. Establish the facts that you require. Your answer might be a while in coming, so be patient.

The United States National Archives (7th and Pennsylvania Avenues, N.W., Washington DC 20408) is most cooperative in assisting modelers. The Army and Navy Division is responsible for the records concerning ships and maritime vessels. Plans and specifications of many such ships of the past are on file at this institution, and copies are available for a slight fee.

If you are planning to visit one of these facilities, secure, in advance, the papers and identification you will need to gain direct access to the material. You can accomplish this step with a letter or two.

While you are in the Washington area, don't forget a trip to the Washington Naval Yard. This vast complex contains a section devoted to the history of the United States Navy. Write to the Division of Naval History, Building 220, Washington, DC 20734, if you need help. The folks there will be very helpful in locating a ship, or the history of the naval ship under construction in your shop, to satisfy your building or historical desires. Having an opportunity to see, study, and perhaps photograph the models on display makes a trip there worthwhile.

Need I mention the Smithsonian? The Department of Transportation, in particular the Naval History Section, also will be most happy to receive you and assist you in your projects. Again, I urge you to make your preparations well in advance. Correspondence is in order before, after, and if you are unable to cross the threshold in person. Telephone calls are not remembered.

I speak from experience. There have been several occasions for me to be inside these institutions in the nation's capital. Advance preparations made the all-too-short visits memorable. When I am in need of help and can't "pop off to Washington," my letters are answered quickly and the desired copies of materials arrive in due time.

Ship models of contemporary ships also need to be researched. Kit manufacturers, in their haste to place a salable article on the market, are often negligent in their research. Popular ships are not reproduced in accurate scale models without continual research. If you want your model to look like the real thing, I know you will avail yourself of all the information you can gather.

Interest in ships of other lands, contemporary or otherwise, is gaining. Nostalgia about warships and merchant marine vessels is also of increasing interest. For these types of ship models, you will need to begin your search in other lands.

BRITISH SOURCES

The ships of long ago, many not even of British origin, are recorded in the great and world-famous National Maritime Museum of Greenwich, England. Sailing ships from the advent of recorded shipwright drawings, Admiralty models, paintings, and contemporary ships dating through both World Wars are among the vast sources of plans and information. Undoubtedly, this is the world's greatest collection of the history of man's great adventure on the waters.

While we are on the subject of British sources of information, if your interest tends toward modern

ship types of the Royal Navy, send a letter to:

MINISTRY OF DEFENCE
Navy Department DG Ships
Section 423b, Block B
Bath, Somerset BA1 5AB, England

EUROPEAN SOURCES

Has your interest turned to ships of France? In addition to their fine national museums and the famous Association des Amis des Musees de la Marine, located on Palals de Challiot, 75016, Paris, there is another address you might wish to use:

SERVICE HISTORIQUE DE LA MARINE
3, avenue Octave Greard
75007 Paris, France

The people at this institution are most helpful in securing updated information pertaining to French navy ships.

Another French source of ship model information is:

S.I.P.A. ANTENNE MARINE
2, rue Royal
7508 Paris, France

Now if you need to secure more ship's facts in Europe, and in particular Germany and German warships, contact the following:

OSTERREICHISCHES KRIEGSARCHIV
Hofrat Dr. Wagner
Siftgasse 2
A-1070 Wien, Austria

BUNDESARCHIV-MILITARACHIV
78 Freiburg/Br
Wiesenstalstr. 10 (Hochaus)
West Germany

A source of a more personal nature is:

PETER DEWITZ
89 Augsburg, Karwendelstr. 91
West Germany

It would be almost impossible to list all the sources of information concerning the ships of the world. Each nation has a repository of historical facts concerning its merchant and naval fleets. Each nation that has ships upon the seas also has, to some extent, a national museum.

Some of the newer nations, at least in name if not area, are not too busy struggling for survival that they won't help a modeler. They will, if you give them enough time, answer your requests. Most will be accurate. It is a question of national pride to see that one's ships are rendered in proper scale by modelers throughout the world.

VOCABULARY

I'll be a son of a gun if I haven't forgotten to mention a particular subject. Perhaps I had better steer a true course in giving some more advice. This isn't mere scuttlebutt. You would expect more of me than a simple fair-weather friend, and accuse me of being three sheets to the wind for slapdashing.

Each of the preceding sentences contains one or more terms of the sea that has crept into our everyday language. It was no fluke; I did this on purpose. (There I slipped in another.)

What I am showing, in a rather primitive manner, is that there is a special and personalized language spoken by every group, profession, and nation in the world. If you are going to build ship models and learn about ships, you should talk ship talk.

Should there be a statement that the ''binnacle was located abaft of the mizzenmast,'' would you know where to place it? Would you stable your ''flemish horse'' and what would you feed it? What is a pelorus, and what use is it anyway?

Don't, I beg you, think that the standard dictionary will also contain the special language of the sea. Webster, Funk and Wagnell, Random House, you name it, do not have complete lists of every word ever spoken or written. There are special collections. There are volumes that contain those special words known only to the mariner and the enthusiast of the sea. Many cannot be translated. So many have become a part of our everyday language that they have assumed a new meaning. They have lost their roots.

Undoubtedly there are sources of information, even a few in several of the books mentioned in previous chapters. For example, both *Encyclopedia of Nautical Terms Under Sail* and *Seamanship in the Age of Sail* by John Harland have good lists of terminology. The books that follow in this listing are devoted to the subject exclusively. They are but a few of the many.

The volume by John G. Rogers entitled *Origins of Sea Terms* (Mystic Seaport Museum, Mystic, CT, 1984) is a good place to begin. This is not a stuffy list or glossary. Written in a light-hearted manner, the 1,249 entries will draw you into the language of the mariner.

Sea Jargon, by Lew Lind (Patrick Stephens, Ltd., Cambridge, 1982) will further your knowledge of the colorful and coarse language of the British, Australian, and American navies, as well as the merchant service and the waterfront. You will be surprised to learn how many of the words contained therein have become standard conversation in our lives.

First published in 1920, the third edition of the small but power-packed book, *A Dictionary of Sea Terms*, by A. Ansted (Brown, Son and Ferguson, Glasgow) was published in 1985. Peter Clissold has revised the original text. This is the book of generations of ship modelers, historians, and sea buffs. Other books and listings that have followed owe their popularity to the continued interest of the landlubber in the terms and expressions of his cousin who went to sea. How many of us wish we had gone with him. If you must limit your library to one volume of sea terms, then this has to be it.

Not lastly, but with high recommendation, is *The Oxford Companion to Ships and The Sea*, edited by Peter Kemp (Oxford University Press, London, New York, Melbourne, 1976). My copy is getting dog-eared and the chances of your finding one are not too good. It has, after a long career and through a sense of demand and loss of profit, gone out of print. There are a few on the shelves of out-of-the-way bookstores. Ask at the library, seek one through the sources of a rare book dealer, but by all means look one over.

I refer to the *Oxford Companion* as my ''key to searching.'' The 37,700 items arranged in alphabetical order are a blend of the history of the sea, the terms of the mariner, and a short history of ships.

Foreign Texts

Conversation can take place without a spoken word. Once you have learned a language, it need not be vocal. Pictures talk. You will, if you are of such a nature, build many a ship model according to plans that do not have one word in your native language printed on them. You read pictures and understand drawing (construction) details.

You will browse through books in foreign tongues and understand what the author means. His illustrations, drawings, and photographs will all be a guide to his thoughts.

A long period of study of a text without illustrations will not be difficult as you select and identify familiar sea-faring terms. Parts of ships and the areas of their construction leap out at you from the jumble of strange language. You recognize standard terms. An anchor in English, becomes *anker* in German. It is not surprising that the similarity extends to French as *ancre,* to Spanish as *ancla,* and to Italian as *ancora.* The word *mast* is the same in English and German. The fun begins as it moves into other languages.

Originally published in German, *Historic Ship Models* by Wolfram zu Monfield (Sterling Publishing Co., USA; Argus Books, England, 1985) contains an unusual feature. There in black and white is the long-needed dictionary of words. Parts of ships are printed in the back just before the index. The five major languages of the ship modeling world are represented. Each word lays in a parallel vertical column next to its counterpart. There is no need for definitions. If you know the word in your language, there is no need for description or text.

Preceding this feature, a memorable book is found: a collection of parts, descriptions, locations, and the right and wrong way to represent these features on a ship model. This is the book ship modelers bent on accuracy dream about, all 342 pages of it.

Each page is resplendent with line drawings. The strength of this book is in its comparison, not only of the actual nautical words, but also the construction features each nation contributed. The differences in each country's style of construction are noted. No longer do you need to wonder what made the stem and beak of one nation different from another. How decorations and fittings differed are shown. Instant guidance and construction hints are available.

It was my luck to be able to compare the original *Historische Schiffsmodelle,* subtitled *Das Handbuch fur Modellbauer,* by the same author, with the English translation. I learned that you did not need to speak the language to learn from the text. My high-school German is at best poor. The pictures spoke to me. The words, which I learned from the dictionary at the back, seemed to pop off the page. This was way back in 1976 that I bought my copy. Here I am with the English text 10 years later, and the original version was just as clear then as the updated (native) words are today.

Encyclopedias

Encyclopedias exist, have been compiled, and are printed on every subject imaginable, including the sea. These are the type of volumes that are found in most public libraries. They can, and perhaps should be, in your library.

The Encyclopedia of Nautical Knowledge by W.A. McEwwn and A.H. Lewis (Cornell Maritime Press, Centerville, MD, 1953) is a good place to begin. The listings, in alphabetical order, are most complete in their description of nautical items, terms and phraseology. A word that stumps you should be a word that you want to learn.

Another publication from Cornell Maritime Press is the *Ocean and Marine Dictionary* by David F. Tver. This book, published in 1979, is as stated on the dust jacket, "An up-to-date AUTHORITATIVE READY REFERENCE to all aspects of marine and ocean environment. INDISPENSABLE for the professional or anyone studying the life of the sea." The capitalized words are the publisher's not mine. I can attest to the fact that the statement is true. Between the covers of this volume, I found definitions that enhanced by understanding of the world of ships and the seas on which they sailed.

First published in 1890 and republished in 1977 by Argus Books Ltd. (England) is the authoritative *Illustrated Marine Encyclopedia,* by Capt. H. Paasch of Belgium. He was a much decorated seafarer of his country, and also the author of *Keel to Truck.* This is a volume for the ship modeler who is fascinated by the era of transition from sail to steam.

A facsimile edition of the book by Lt. George S. Nares, of the Royal Navy, first published in 1862, has been published by Gresham Books of Surrey, England. This, like its updated American version, *Eagle Seamanship* for the U.S. Coast Guard sailing vessel of the same name, is referred to in Chapter 11. Both were produced as training manuals for cadets aboard the H.M.S *Britannia* or U.S.C.G. *Eagle,* respectively.

Strongly similar in content and drawings as the books by George Biddlecomb, *Art of Rigging,* and Darcy Lever, *Young Sea Officer's Sheet Anchor,* it is distinct in its approach to the new propulsion of steam-powered ships. The heavy concentration of writing is still directed toward sail, but new terminology such as "rudder and screw" is now being mentioned.

RESEARCH SOURCES

Should your interest be dedicated to naval ships—they make exciting models—I offer alternate measures of research. Mentioned previously are the sources of information to begin your research. They will do until, as it most assuredly will, a need for historical accuracy begins to manifest itself. American naval buffs, go for *A Bibliography of American Naval History*, compiled by Paolo C. Coletta (Naval Institute Press, Annapolis).

The volumes contained in the National Maritime Museum in Greenwich, England, also have been cataloged. There are several because of the complex classifications, nature of subjects, and sheer numbers. Fortunately, the books and reference material have been divided into eras. *Part One: The Middle Ages to 1815* has been published. The remaining periods are following rapidly. If your local library does not have a copy, you an purchase one for a reasonable cost from Her Majesty's Stationery Office or the museum itself. Just write for:

National Maritime Museum
Catalogue of the Library, Vol. 5
NAVAL HISTORY
Part 1: The Middle Ages to 1815

Like to look at pictures of models contained in the selected museum of your interest? Many, including the National Maritime Museum, have photographic catalogs of their collections. Why not ask for one?

It is impossible to list all the volumes and references devoted to our favorite subject. This is the duty of the libraries, lexicographers, and historians. What have been presented are a few examples of the types of texts needed to get you into the habit of accurate research and speech.

Lists of such books have been prepared by others. They have, as would be expected, omitted a few volumes that are considered by others as vital. They also have listed volumes that are rare and valuable. These volumes are out of the reach of the average modeler because of both price and availability. They are listed, however, and that in itself is a completed chore for your behalf. There will be lists that follow as new books appear and older ones become classics.

Where do you find such lists? Occasionally they are printed in periodicals. A good example is the two-part list by Charles O. McDonald. His writings, *Sailing Ship Technology: Some Bibliographical and Book Collecting Notes for Ship Modelers, Marine Artists, Historians and Others*, appeared in The Nautical Research Journal, 26-4 and a subsequent issue. You can obtain this list by writing the Nautical Research Guild.

Portia Takakjian has published two excellent lists of books for ship modelers in the periodical *Ships in Scale*. This list is most informative, although several volumes are unobtainable without great sacrifice on the part of the seeker.

Vocabularies of the sea and accumulated knowledge of nautical history, customs, and manners will find their way into your life. They, the people you will communicate with, and the pictures that will stimulate, are out there waiting for you.

TWENTY TWO

What Kind of Ship Modeler Are You?

I like work; it fascinates me.
I can sit and look at it for hours.
—JEROME K. JEROME

YOU BUILD SHIP MODELS, OR YOU PLAN TO—GOOD for you. This might not be your first attempt at model building. You have proven, at least to yourself, that you have the talent. Now you are ready to do ship models. How do you wish to classify yourself as a ship modeler?

There is no standard or system of classification for ship modelers, nor should there be. Standards have been established, however, in the classification systems set up for ship model exhibitions and contests. The classes do not denote skill.

CATEGORIES OF SHIP MODELS

CLASS A: Scratch-Built Model. Model built entirely from scratch materials by the builder with no commercially fabricated parts except cordage, chain, and belaying pins.

CLASS B: Modified Scratch-Built Model. Model built from scratch, but supplemented by the use of some commercially fabricated accessories.

CLASS C: Modified Kit Model. Model built from materials provided in a commercial kit, supplemented by commercially fabricated part or by scratch-built parts.

CLASS D: Kit Model. Model built entirely from materials provided in commercial kits.

SPECIAL: Subcategories. Model built and/or displayed in any of the following methods: Antiques,

Waterline, Cross Section, Sailing, Half Hull, Bone/Ivory, Diorama, Power.

The talent of a builder who has entered a ship model in a competition is a matter for the judges to decide. The methods of building and the materials used are discussed in detail as the rules for each show are laid down. The basic items of these discussions are given in the publication, *Ship Model Classification Guidelines* published by The Department of Ship Model Sales and Service (Mystic Seaport Museum Stores, Mystic, CT 06355). The categories provided by The Mariner's Museum Ship Craftsman Competition, and by Mystic Seaport Stores, Inc. were used to establish these guidelines.

There is, to my knowledge, a ship model club based on a single strength of purpose. They have no judged events. There is no classification or rating of models. The Baton Rouge Ship Modeler's Association has kept to this premise. Their annual *exhibitions* (shows) are just that, shows. No model is refused. No model is classified. No model is judged. Attending their meetings and viewing their annual exhibition is an experience in learning. It is a refreshing taste of independence.

These are ship modelers who, through these exhibitions and "show and tells," build better ship models with each attempt. Their skills and their club's expansion is based on mutual cooperation.

PROFESSIONAL MODELERS

Now is as good a time as any to bring up a crude subject: money. Fun is fun, but a buck is better along the way if you can earn it from what you did by having fun.

How much should you charge for building a ship model? Let me begin by saying that the following outline is not a hard and fast set of rules or conditions which determine what you should get for building a ship model. Based on what you consider your time is worth and the strength of your reputation, you should set a price. You are entitled to be paid a just fee for your labor of love.

An artist earns and can justify his fees by his reputation. A struggling art student cannot expect to be paid on the same scale as an established artist, even if his talent is beyond that of the most well-known in his field. In the world of creative talent, a name and a reputation outweigh any claim to a justifiable price. Newcomers must wait for their name to be established. Some never make it.

How do you get a reputation? The established battle cry of the cub scout is your answer. "DYB!" is the shout heard at almost every den and pack meeting. It means *do your best.*

After a while, of doing your best, things begin to happen. Your work is not only admired and praised in your presence, but talked about to others. You present a gift of a ship model to a friend or relative, one created by your own hand and presented out of love. It is something that will be admired and praised by the owner. He shows it off with great pride to every visitor to his home or office. Soon you are approached to build a ship model for a friend or another relative. Your admirer sent the individual to you because he is proud of your ability. You are flattered that you are thought of so highly.

As an act of appeasing their conscience, the person who asked you to build a model might offer to buy the kit or pay for the materials. Haven't your eyes been opened yet? They will pay for your model. How about paying for your time?

Calculating a Wage

Let's discuss that aspect of your modeling life—time. The minimum wage is $3.65 an hour. Suppose the ship model you built (kit or otherwise) took you 50 hours to build. Let's do a little figuring: $3.65 × 50 hours = $175. Not much at today's rapidly changing salary scales. It isn't the kind of money you could live on. Untrained labor makes that much for 50 hours of work. What about the price of the materials (kit or otherwise)?

Suppose the time it took to build a ship model to your standards, which we know are very high, was 1,000 hours. $3.65 × 1,000 hours = $3,650. Impressive figure. Yet many who sell their models, including all forms of other models not only ship models, sell themselves short. If they got minimum wage, that would be fine, but they don't.

If you have ever sold a model, take a moment to calculate just how much your time was worth and how much you actually sold your time for. Don't forget to add the cost of materials. It boggles the mind to think that that is all you got for your hours of labor, not to mention materials.

How much should you demand for your time? That, as the poets say, depends on the boldness of your heart and the glibness of your tongue. How much should you charge for the completed ship model, without the display case? A case should be an extra, or if included in the price, so stated. At least while you are establishing your name and reputation, use the following rule of thumb.

First, calculate the cost of the materials—all the materials. This might be tough if it is a scratch-built model, but make a stab at a figure. A kit has a price, true, but what about the things you buy to add to the price when you customize that kit? An accountant might even suggest that you amortize the equipment and tools that you use. For our discussion, however, you are not at this stage a true professional. You are just a guy trying to figure what to charge to build a ship model in your spare time. Now you have a figure. Multiply it by 100.

That's what I said, 100. The average price of a wooden ship model kit is $80. The average time to build such a kit, regardless of what you are led to believe, and based on the average time a modeler works, is 325 hours.

Back to the calculator, and we have 100 × $80 = $800. Now doesn't that sound great? What about the time it took you to build this beauty? I now offer this calculation: $800 ÷ 325 hours = $2.46. That's what you got paid for the ship model per hour.

Commissions and Contracts

Most haven't the courage to ask even that fee. It should be a lot more, and it will be as your eyes open to some other facts. Try the word *commission*. Somebody is actually going to pay you to build a ship model for them and they came to you and asked you to do it. Flattered? You should be. Beware the pitfalls of commissions and the guy who asks you to "build me a model, I'll pay you for it. How much?"

Understand that a commission is a contract. Contracts, even among friends or relatives, should be in writing, with as much spelled out as possible. Choose whatever form of writing you wish, making it as detailed as you require. Any lawyer will tell you contracts can be broken by the sharp-minded and are honored by the dull-witted. He makes his living by knowing which is which. Don't be afraid to ask for his advice.

Spell out the name(s) of the vessel, the size and scale of the vessel, how it will be built (type), and the approximate delivery date. Allow some leeway in the date. The world does not run on a timetable. Here's the strongest hook in your document. "You no take away till you pay!" Word it any way you select but get it in there. Should you feel that this is not proper for a beginning professional, at least have some understanding (in writing) how payment will be made.

There can be no hard and fast rule, or even a sample of a "legal" contract for a commission or sale of a ship model. Seek out the services of a good lawyer if you intend to get into this facet of ship modeling. My belief is that you are better off seeing a lawyer before you need one. Consignment without agreed consent is financial stupidity.

Once the agreement is in writing and an understanding is established, you can begin your construction. Don't forget you promised to build a ship model for a client. That building must be your best or I promise you that your career will be very short. There are "cheats" at both ends of a deal in ship modeling for commissions. Don't be the one. You made a promise to deliver your best work. Do so.

Reputation

Time passes. Your reputation grows and you find that you have a selection of ship models you have built. Some are still around the house. The collection is becoming a little large and you need the room to show off your "better" models. Much as you hate to do it, you decide to part with some of them. It's time to sell a child of your creation. How are you go-

ing to sell it? How do you advertise?

Begin with one of your friends who has admired your work and made an offer. You might not get what you think the model is worth, but who established the price? Then, again, your friend might get a real bargain. It all depends what happens from that first sale on your way to establishing yourself. You might, if all is ripe for your talents, find others coming to you for models. The word is spreading; your reputation is growing. Word of mouth and continued demand create the best reputations. It is a slow way to build a following.

Another way to create a reputation long before you sell your first (surplus) ship model is to become a proven winner. A wall full of blue ribbons, plaques, acknowledgments, or silver cups and trays is impressive to the potential buyer when he visits your abode. Where did all these honorariums come from? You won them in ship model contests and competitions.

Winning "best in the show" works wonders for a modeler's reputation. You must enter to win, however. The other entrants all have the same dream as you do.

Winning any recognition in ship modeling enhances your reputation. Talent will prevail; skill will triumph.

Advertising

Don't forget the media coverage that comes with these honors. You become a novelty. People who build ship models or are skilled with their hands are in great demand in news copy. Those who love ship models but don't build them will seek you out. They saw your face and remembered your name. Publicity is free; advertising is what you pay for.

Don't be afraid to advertise. A small ad in your local paper, shopper's news, and organizational publications will bring queries. It can work to your advantage. Most of your acquaintances know you build ship models. Now they will know that you offer them for sale or will build to order. Print up some business cards. Don't be ashamed to pass them out at every opportunity. If you are going to be a builder for profit, then let people know about it, without shame and with a great deal of pride.

There is a negative side to all this promotion. You will lose the fun part of this work. Now it is for a living. You might find that you are rushing through, or building several models at once to increase production, income, and meet deadlines. Greed might appear. You might take on more than you can handle in an attempt to increase income.

Galleries

The gallery entrepreneurs might now enter your life. Your prize-winning ship models can be a great source of income to you and the seller of your models. There are, for the most part, many reputable galleries and sales outlets for ship models. Perhaps you have visited one. Were you amazed at the asking price for ship models? That's only the price it is being sold for. It is not, repeat not, the price the artist gets for his labors.

Don't be misled by the advertisements of galleries, individuals, etc. to "buy your ship model regardless of degree of skill." There are ads in almost every ship modeling publication with offers to buy ship models. These are the slave markets of ship modelers. Your ego, the low price you get for your work, the resale to the unwary buyer, etc., hurts everyone. Homes are proudly displaying the trash of ship models built for a quick profit, sold at unbelievable prices, and cherished by unknowing individuals. People don't want quality; it costs too much. They buy novelty because it satisfies the need for something different at a low price. Ship models are a popular novelty.

If you sell your works outright, then the gallery can, and does, place its price on your work. Many respected gallery owners and their representatives will, if asked, establish a "fair" price as requested by the modeler. Call that if you will, a minimum price. Again, that is not the price that the modeler is getting. Whatever that price is, he gets it and gets out of the picture. The profit belongs to the gallery. If this is your choice, then that's it. You sold a little part of yourself. Your child is no longer yours.

Consignments

Sales on consignment is another method to move models. *On consignment* means that the item is your property and will be returned to you if it is not sold. The selling price is established either by you or the sales outlet. What you receive as your part of the selling price is a matter of wheeling and dealing. The gallery has to make a buck or two, you know. As in all dealings with a third party, get the agreement in writing.

Try to visit the gallery or sales outlet while your model is offered for sale. You might be surprised at the "asking" price. You were surprised when you visited a gallery and saw the prices on some of the inferior (to your) work. Did you ever think your work would fetch such a price?

Will your models ever sell in the four-, five-, or even six-figure range? Why not? Keep believing that they will. Your talents are not any less than the established names, and by comparison of workmanship alone demand as much, if not more, than the staggering sums you have heard about. All you need to remember is that it takes time, talent, and maybe a good agent to get to the top.

When you reach the stage of having an agent because you are so busy building you haven't time to "make deals," we will call you by the name you have earned: a professional modeler.

Record of Work

In the meantime, while you work your way toward an agent, keep a photographic record of your works. This is your portfolio and can make the difference between a sale at a profit and a give-away program. Take good, clear, color shots of your work and mount them in an album. Then you can show a prospective buyer what you have to offer from your collection. You can make copies to send to a client. A commission could result. Should the desired model not be available in your portfolio, at least the client can see what you are capable of producing.

Be prepared for visits by buyers to examine your ship models. Buyers are available and must be satisfied. You will be justified in the price you are asking. If you are a professional, act like one.

One last word on being a professional ship modeler. You are no longer the free spirit that you once were. Your time is spoken for and you are contract labor. Except for those rare moments of freedom to select what you want to build, someone else will tell you what you have to build. You are a professional, and what was once done for fun is now being done for a living (FIG. 22-1). After all, it was your choice. Good luck on your new career.

This career can come at any age or stage of your life. Perhaps, like many of the professional modelers of today, modeling wasn't what you wanted to do for a living. You sort of drifted into it. After the tide had run out under the bridge a few times, you began to see things in a new light. Enjoy.

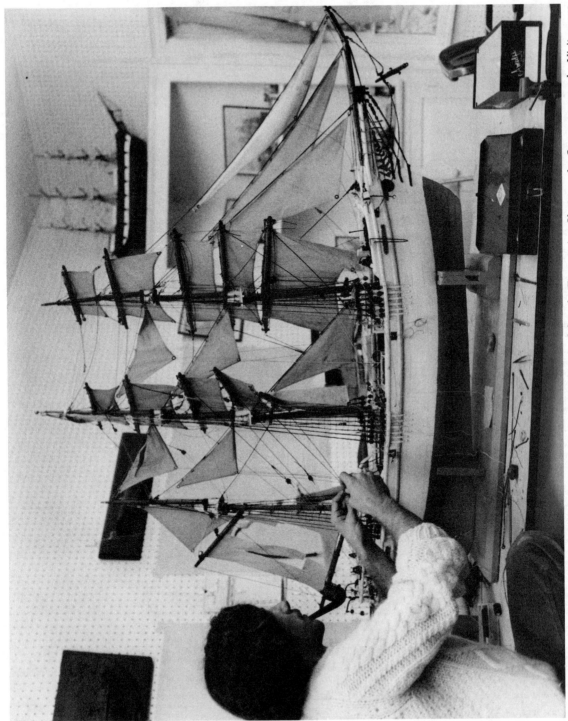

Fig. 22-1. A staff member at Mystic Seaport Museum restores a ship model in the Restoration Shop on the Seaport grounds. Visitors are welcome to watch the building and restoration of ship models (Photo by Lester D. Olin).

INDEX